BAROQUE PIETY

Baroque Piety

Religion, Society, and Music in Leipzig, 1650–1750

TANYA KEVORKIAN

ASHGATE

Published by
Ashgate Publishing Limited
Gower House
Croft Road
Aldershot
Hampshire GU11 3HR
England

Ashgate Publishing Company
Suite 420
101 Cherry Street
Burlington, VT 05401-4405
USA

Ashgate website: http://www.ashgate.com

British Library Cataloguing in Publication Data
Kevorkian, Tanya
Baroque piety: religious practices, society, and music in Leipzig, 1650–1750
1. Music – Social aspects – Germany – Leipzig – History – 17th century 2. Music – Social aspects – Germany – Leipzig – History – 18th century 3. Music – Germany – Leipzig – 17th century – History and criticism 4. Music – Germany – Leipzig – 18th century – History and criticism 5. Music – Religious aspects – Christianity 6. Pietism – Germany – Leipzig – History 7. Leipzig (Germany) – Social life and customs – 17th century 8. Leipzig (Germany) – Social life and customs – 18th century
I. Title
780.9′432122′09032

Library of Congress Cataloging-in-Publication Data
Kevorkian, Tanya.
Baroque piety: religion, society, and music in Leipzig, 1650–1750 / Tanya Kevorkian.
p. cm.
Includes bibliographical references.
ISBN-13: 978-0-7546-5490-2 (alk. paper) 1. Leipzig (Germany)—Church history—17th century. 2. Leipzig (Germany)—Church history—18th century. 3. Public worship—Germany—Leipzig—History—17th century. 4. Public worship—Germany—Leipzig—History—18th century. 5. Music—Germany—Leipzig—17th century—History and criticism. 6. Music—Germany—Leipzig—18th century—History and criticism. 7. Music—Social aspects. 8. Music—Religious aspects. 9. Piety. I. Title.

BR855 .K48 2006
274.3′212207–dc22

2006033066

ISBN 978-0-7546-5490-2

Typeset by GCS, Leighton Buzzard, Bedfordshire
Printed and bound in Great Britain by MPG Books Ltd, Bodmin, Cornwall.

Contents

Acknowledgements		*vii*
List of illustrations and table		*xi*
Abbreviations		*xiii*
Introduction		1
I.	**Congregants' everyday practices**	
1	Experiencing the service	29
2	Seating the religious public: church pews and society	53
II.	**The producers**	
3	The clergy, the city council, and Leipzig inhabitants	77
4	Elites in and beyond Leipzig: the Dresden court and the consistories	99
5	Leipzig's cantors: status, politics and the adiaphora	123
III.	**The Pietist alternative**	
6	Sociability and religious protest: the collegia pietatis of 1689–1690	147
7	The Pietist shadow network	169
IV.	**The construction boom and beyond**	
8	Social change and religious life	195
Conclusion		219
Bibliography		223
Index		245

Acknowledgements

This book has been in the making for many years, and the list of people and institutions I wish to thank is correspondingly long. Numerous institutions have provided generous financial support. The History Department of The Johns Hopkins University provided graduate assistantships from Fall 1990 to Spring 1993 and during Spring 1995. The German Research and Exchange Service awarded a research fellowship from Fall 1993 to early 1995. The Institut für Europäische Geschichte in Mainz awarded a writing fellowship from July 1995 to April 1996. I found some material while doing research on a grant from the American Bach Society in Fall 2004. Millersville University has provided research and travel-to-present funds, course releases, and a sabbatical leave in Fall 2004. Thanks also go out to staff members at the Stadtarchiv Leipzig, the Archiv der Nikolaikirche and Stadtbibliothek in Leipzig, the Sächsisches Hauptstaatsarchiv and the Sächsische Landesbibliothek in Dresden, the Archiv der Franckeschen Stiftungen in Halle, the libraries of the University of Geneva, the Lutheran Theological Seminary, and the University of Pennsylvania, the Widener and Law Libraries at Harvard University, the Library of Congress, and the Interlibrary Loan staff at Millersville University.

Many people have helped make this a truly interdisciplinary project. Francis Bremer, Peter A. Brown, Donald O. Franklin, David Gramit, Christine Johnson, Robin A. Leaver, Benjamin Marschke, Lucinda Martin, John McLarnon, Emmet McLaughlin, James Van Horn Melton, Margaret Menninger, Robert Sayre, Jeffrey Chipps Smith, Jonathan Strom, Erik Thomson, William Weber, and students in History 223 and History 505 at Millersville University have all read parts of the book. Their many insights have greatly improved arguments as well as specifics. Robert Beachy, Matthew Dirst, Jesko Graf zu Dohna, Andreas Glöckner, Katrin Keller, Terence McIntosh, and Carrie Lee Smith have given advice on specific points. Hillary Gates, Meaghan Shirk, and Mary Wallick have provided valuable editorial assistance. Heidi May and the team at Ashgate have likewise offered valuable comments and advice.

During my undergraduate studies Harold Garrett-Goodyear, Margaret Irwin-Brandon, Robert Schwartz, and others at Mount Holyoke College gave me a solid grounding in both history and music and encouraged my interdisciplinary interests. Jeffrey Brooks, Richard Goldthwaite, Vernon Lidtke, and Orest Ranum of the History Department at Johns Hopkins University, and fellow graduate students Dirk Bönker, Christine Johnson, and Daniel Rabuzzi were all an important part of my graduate training. In Leipzig and Halle, Herr Prof. Dr. Helmut Bräuer, Herr Prof. Dr. Detlef Döring, Frau Dr. Katrin Keller, Herr Prof. Dr. Udo Sträter and Herr Prof. Dr.

Hartmut Zwahr gave valuable advice. Other graduate students in Leipzig, Dresden, and Halle, especially Robert Beachy, Pall Bjornsen, Reimar Huber, Anne-Kristin Kupke, Margaret Menninger, Moira Roberts, and the late Carola Wessel provided camaraderie and a ready ear for archival discoveries. Marit Dvorak and Derek Shanahan, Margaret Eichler, John McLarnon, Darla Williams, and others have made Millersville University a congenial place. Emmet McLaughlin, Joy Wiltenburg, and others have made the Philadelphia Area Consortium of Early Modernists a supportive group for discussing trends in early modern history. Sarah Berrian, Dorothy Graaskamp and other friends have also offered encouragement. And Mittens the cat has always interrupted my writing at the right time.

It is an especial pleasure to thank Mack Walker for his encouragement, support, incisive comments on major and seemingly minor points, and for pushing me to question my assumptions about sources and arguments. He has read not only the dissertation but also the book. My thanks also go to Irma Walker for her warmth and hospitality.

Finally, it is with much gratitude for their love, support, and advice that I dedicate this book to my parents, David and Elisabeth Kevorkian, and to my sisters, Barbara and Jennifer Kevorkian.

Lancaster, Pennsylvania
July 2006

Earlier versions of portions of this work have previously appeared in the following articles: (2004) 'Changing Times, Changing Music: "New Church" Music and Musicians in Leipzig, 1699–1750,' in William Weber (2004), ed., *The Musician as Entrepreneur, 1700–1914: Managers, Charlatans, and Idealists*, Bloomington: Indiana University Press, 61–80; (2002), 'The Reception of the Cantata during Church Services in Leipzig, 1700–1750,' *Early Music*, 30, 26–45, reprinted (2006) in Carol Baron, ed., *Bach's Changing World. Voices in the Community*, Rochester: University of Rochester Press, 174–189; (2000), 'The Rise of the Poor, Weak, and Wicked: Poor Care, Punishment, Religion, and Patriarchy in Leipzig, 1700–1730,' *Journal of Social History*, 34, 163–181; (2000), 'Clerics and their Career Paths in Early Modern Leipzig,' *Zeitsprünge. Forschungen zur Frühen Neuzeit*, 4, 290–306; (1998), 'Piety Confronts Politics: Philipp Jacob Spener in Dresden, 1686–1691,' *German History*, 16, 145–164; (1996), 'Laien und die Leipziger religiöse Öffentlichkeit 1685–1725,' *Leipziger Kalender/Arbeitsbericht des Stadtarchivs Leipzig*, 86–97.

List of illustrations and table

Illustrations

Leipzig: view of the city from the southeast, engraving by I.G. Ringlin, *c.* 1720 17

'The New Marble Altar in the Church of St. Thomas in Leipzig,' print by J.C. Weigel, from J.S. Riemer, *Continuatio annalium Lipsiensium Vogelii*, ms., 1714–71 22

'The Former Organ in the Church of St. Nicholas in Leipzig,' watercolor by Carl Benjamin Schwartz, *c.* 1785 36

Pew chart, ground floor of St. Nicholas's Church, 1750 57

Leipzig, views of eight buildings, engraving, 'Scenographiae Lipsiacae,' 1749 196

Table

Pewholding by occupation 60

Abbreviations

AdN	Archiv der Nikolaikirche, Leipzig
AFS	Archiv der Franckeschen Stiftungen, Halle
BJ	*Bach-Jahrbuch*
BSK	*Beiträge zur Sächsischen Kirchengeschichte*
BzBf	*Beiträge zur Bachforschung*
GdP	Martin Brecht et al., eds (1993–2004), *Geschichte des Pietismus* (Göttingen: Vandenhoeck & Ruprecht), vol. I, ed. Martin Brecht (1993), *Der Pietismus vom siebzehnten bis zum frühen achtzehnten Jahrhundert*; vol. II, ed. Brecht and Klaus Deppermann (1995), *Der Pietismus im achtzehnten Jahrhundenrt*; vol. IV, ed. Hartmut Lehmann (2004), *Glaubenswelten und Lebenswelten*
NBR	Hans David and Arthur Mendel, eds (1998), *The New Bach Reader: A Life of Johann Sebastian Bach in Letters and Documents*, rev. Christoph Wolff (New York: Norton)
PuN	*Pietismus und Neuzeit*
SAL	Stadtarchiv Leipzig
SHStADD	Sächsisches Hauptstaatsarchiv Dresden

Introduction

In August 1730, in a lengthy and impassioned memo to the Leipzig town council, Johann Sebastian Bach complained bitterly about his working conditions. He depicted the musical skills of students at the St. Thomas's school, who sang during church services, in dire terms and indicated that stipends from the council to some University students would improve the level of music performed in the churches. Bach also complained of the high demands that the international style of modern music placed on German musicians, and lamented that the workload of musicians employed in cities, in contrast to those at court, kept the former from distinguishing themselves. In October of that year, Bach wrote to an old friend in Danzig asking for help in finding a job because of tense working conditions, authorities who were 'odd and little interested in music,' and the high cost of living in Leipzig. For their part, in meetings also held in August, city councilors complained that Bach 'shows little inclination to work,' was not performing his teaching duties at St. Thomas's school, and that he had left Leipzig without obtaining councilors' permission, as stipulated in his contract (Bach and his wife Anna Magdalena had gone to the nearby court of Weissenfels to perform for Duke Christian's birthday). Councilor Johann Job went as far as to claim that Bach was 'incorrigible.'[1]

These complaints and the ongoing tensions that stood behind them have often been read as showing that Bach was an unappreciated genius whose colleagues and authorities stifled his creativity. Bach is better understood, though, in the context of the sprawling social, cultural, and political system that was the urban public religious arena of the Baroque era. Three intertwined, basic facets of that religious culture offer the key to understanding Bach's conflicts and his work in Leipzig more generally. They are the focus of this book. While they have mostly been examined separately, they need to be examined in relationship to one another in order to be fully understood.

First, religion was the main public arena in which ordinary people and elites, women and men, debated and negotiated fundamental issues on a regular basis. General social, cultural, and political changes were reproduced and contested through the many routines of everyday religious life. Most studies of early modern European religious life have focused on the period prior to about 1650; but religious life remained important well after that. This book follows its development to the

---

[1] Bach, 'Short but most necessary draft for a well-appointed church music' (*Entwurff*), 23 August 1730, *NBR*, 145–151; Bach to Georg Erdmann, 28 October 1730, *NBR*, 151–152; quote, 152; City council minutes of 2 and 25 August: *NBR*, 144–145; quotes, 145.

mid-18th century. It discusses important practices that have hardly been examined for any era, including those associated with the centerpoint of religious life, the worship service, asking how congregants experienced and contributed to the service, and how their experience was rooted in status and gender relations.

Second, Baroque music was embedded in religious culture, and at the same time structured that culture in important ways. The cantors were key civic appointees and they operated in a typically urban political environment. In his petition of 1730, Bach was writing as a client of the council, making a request for increased funds in a manner typical of council appointees. And when the councilors met, they were exercising their powers as the official patrons of religious life. Further, music was a major part of the religious experience, with congregants participating extensively in the worship service through it; but historians have for the most part ignored it. Musicologists' exploration of the social context of music in Baroque towns has also remained limited.

Third, conflict between Pietists and non-Pietists shook the entire religious system; it was the most serious religious conflict since the Reformation era.[2] Pietists functioned as loud and influential critics of mainstream practices to a greater extent than has been appreciated by historians who do not focus on Pietism. They articulated a coherent protest against the reproduction of secular status hierarchies, norms, and materialism in the religious arena. The Pietists formed groups called collegia pietatis that were not unlike modern Bible study groups. They also organized local and international networks that included people from all walks of life and partially overcame the hierarchies of their day. Leipzig and Saxony were key sites in the development of Pietism from the 1680s onward. Councilor Johann Job, who complained during the August 1730 council meeting that Bach was 'incorrigible,' was a leader of an informal network of Leipzig Pietists. His complaint about Bach reflects his impatience with the influence that secular music and the secular world were having on the cantor. His presence on the council also shows how Pietists became increasingly integrated into mainstream power structures. This book pays especial attention to the Pietist movement in relation to the religious culture surrounding it. Doing so helps us to understand how, when and why Pietism emerged as it did: it was in part a rejection of Baroque culture, including music.

---

2 Pietist scholars often use the term 'Orthodox.' This theological term is appropriate in that mainstream clerics and political figures called themselves Orthodox, defended a specific Lutheran dogma and characterized dissenters, including Pietists, as heterodox. However, the term does not adequately describe the variety of beliefs, practices, and structures of the religious arena. For lack of a truly fitting term, 'mainstream,' 'non-Pietist,' and 'establishment' are used here; 'Orthodox' is used to refer to specific figures or debates. Note that 'mainstream' and 'establishment' do not always apply, since many Pietists can be considered mainstream in their beliefs and practices; by the same token, non-Pietists themselves were diverse. See also below, 10 ff.

The religious field

This book builds on three disciplinary areas: the social history of religion (with some sociology), musicology, and Pietist history. It is addressed to readers in each of these fields, who are asked to excuse the inclusion of some background that will seem obvious to them. Foremost are the approaches of social historians of religion, especially of the Reformation era, which can be fruitfully applied to the 17th and 18th centuries. These approaches also offer tools to integrate the other two themes of this book. In the 1960s and 1970s, historians such as Natalie Zemon Davis and Bob Scribner began to ask how social status and gender influenced participation in the religious arena, what the roles and agency of ordinary individuals were, and what form relationships between ordinary people and elites took.[3] Since the publication of their pioneering works, historians have continued to develop new avenues of inquiry and new ways of working with sources in order to answer these questions. The examination of everyday practices, confessionalization and social discipline, and cultural production, often linked in individual studies, is particularly relevant here. Scholars have investigated a broad spectrum of everyday practices of public and private religious life, ranging from Marian devotion in Protestant Nuremberg to the raiding of monasteries in Henrician England.[4] They have demonstrated that ordinary people played a major role in shaping religious life, and that actions in the religious sphere were inextricably intertwined with people's social and political interests. Also, changes in attitude, belief, and practice were incremental and piecemeal.[5]

An emphasis on confessional structures developed by Heinz Schilling and others became influential in the 1980s. Researchers have noted that when nobles, city councilors, and clerics attempted to impose order on their subjects, goals were often expressed through religious policies.[6] Discussions of confessionalization have been closely tied to rulers' social disciplinary agendas. Schilling's concept of religion as a 'building block' of society, and his examination of rulers' social disciplinary and modernizing goals, has been a productive approach to studying the relationships of ordinary people to the elites, and the intersections of politics and religion. In addition, the confessionalization paradigm has inspired new research on the social

3 See Davis, *Society and Culture in Early Modern France* (Stanford: Stanford University Press, 1975); Robert Scribner (1981), *For the Sake of Simple Folk: Popular Propaganda for the German Reformation* (New York: Cambridge University Press).

4 See Lee Palmer Wandel (1995), *Voracious Idols and Violent Hands: Iconoclasm in Reformation Zurich, Basel, and Strasbourg* (New York: Cambridge University Press); Helen Parish & William G. Naphy, eds (2002), introduction, in idem, *Religion and Superstition in Reformation Europe* (New York: Manchester University Press), 1–22.

5 Ethan Shagan (2003), *Popular Politics and the English Reformation* (New York: Cambridge University Press); Parish & Naphy, eds (2002).

6 Heinz Schilling (1981), *Konfessionskonflikt und Staatsbildung. Eine Fallstudie über das Verhältnis von religiosem und sozialem Wandel in der Frühneuzeit am Beispiel der Grafschaft Lippe* (Gütersloh: Mohn); R. Po-Chia Hsia (1989), *Social Discipline in the Reformation: Central Europe 1550–1750* (New York: Routledge).

and political roles of clerics, which in turn has provided a differentiated view of relations among elite groups.[7]

However, the top-down perspective of the paradigm, its assumption that rulers' strategies were implemented, and its neglect of the perspectives of ordinary people have rightly been criticized.[8] When actual practices and interactions between elites and ordinary people are examined, a more complex picture emerges: rulers and clerics were not a monolithic group; they often adjusted to popular practices; and major initiatives from above might fail. Clerics were sometimes at odds with rulers, aggressively pursuing agendas of their own. And while rulers aimed to control those they governed by manipulating religion, townspeople and peasants often evaded official policies or used them to their advantage. Also, the success of a given policy was usually contingent on some form of collaboration with the governed.

Historians have often discussed culture as part of religion during the Baroque era, but there has been no systematic study of cultural production, especially in the Lutheran context. As Hartmut Lehmann has noted, the use of confessionalization as an organizing principle has led to a good understanding of some aspects of religious life, whereas the arts and other aspects have been neglected.[9] Ronnie Hsia has argued that rulers and clerics used persuasive methods, especially culture. He has called for an examination of the production of culture in early modern religion, noting great gaps in knowledge. He has focused on Catholic theatre and worship, briefly discussing Luther hagiography, schools, and hymnals, but arguing that Lutheran worship services allowed for only limited cultural expression.[10] Marc Forster discusses forms of Catholic religious culture such as pilgrimages, and the active participation of the laity in them.[11] A two-volume collection of essays on Baroque religiosity published in 1995 discusses intersections between religion, literature, and the arts, but it includes little focus on social history.[12]

Keeping in mind these contributions, the theory of fields as developed by Pierre Bourdieu and others provides tools to reconceptualize approaches to 17th and 18th century religion, and to examine cultural production. A good starting definition of a field is as an arena 'of production, circulation, and appropriation of goods, services,

---

7 For a summary, see Luise Schorn-Schütte (2000), 'Priest, Preacher, Pastor: Research on Clerical Office in Early Modern Europe,' *Central European History*, 33, 1–37.

8 John Headley et al., eds (2004), *Confessionalization in Europe, 1555–1700. Essays in Honor and Memory of Bodo Nischan* (Aldershot: Ashgate); Marc Forster (2001), *Catholic Revival in the Age of the Baroque: Religious Identity in Southwest Germany, 1550–1750* (New York: Cambridge University Press), esp. 12–16.

9 Hartmut Lehmann (1995), 'Zur Bedeutung von Religion und Religiosität im Barockzeitalter,' in Dieter Breuer, ed., *Religion und Religiosität im Zeitalter des Barock* (Wiesbaden: Harrassowitz), 3–22; 13.

10 Hsia (1989), *Social Discipline in the Reformation: Central Europe 1550–1750* (New York: Routledge), esp. 1–9 and 89–121; Hsia (2005), *The World of Catholic Renewal, 1540–1770* (New York: Cambridge University Press), 159–171.

11 Forster (2001).

12 Breuer (1995) et al., eds.

knowledge, or status, and the competitive positions held by actors … [a] structured [space that is] organized around specific types of capital or combinations of capital.'[13] Bourdieu has discussed the religious field, building on Max Weber's sociology of religion; other fields include the legal, academic and artistic.[14] The theory of fields has been formulated and applied mostly for the 20th century, but can be applied to the 17th and 18th centuries as well. One major difference is that early modern religious fields were less autonomous from politics and society than modern cultural fields such as the academy.[15] Along these lines, it is difficult to discern a musical field in the Baroque era, since the appointment and regulation of musicians, and the performance and reception of music, were so thoroughly embedded in broader religious, urban and/or court structures.

Emphasizing relations among actors in a field allows for a more neutral assessment of the roles of various groups than does an emphasis on social discipline or confessionalization. This does not mean that all groups have equal power. Thus, Bourdieu argues that relations of domination and subordination are central to the functioning of fields, an argument that holds in many ways for early modern religion. The Leipzig and Saxon elites – city councilors, Electors, clerics, and consistory members – established frameworks and held considerable institutional, social, economic, and cultural power. They did not hesitate to use that power to suppress activities they considered threatening. Also, almost all contemporaries seem to have accepted major inequalities of status and gender as appropriate. One dynamic to add to those that Bourdieu discusses is competition among elite groups. While the Saxon Electors might claim superior status, in practice the varied power bases of the individual elite groups gave them considerable leverage against incursion by others. Such competition could also work to diminish the power of all elite groups relative to ordinary people.

Relations among groups are negotiated through concrete practices. Throughout this book, everyday practices of pewholding, education, appointment, and the exercise of power are considered. Locating practices in the context of specific groups yields important insights into Baroque religious culture. The most important groups were property-owning Leipzig inhabitants (burghers), non-property owners, city councilors, clerics, musicians, Saxon Electors, and consistory officials. This book also compares the practices of Pietists and mainstream Lutherans. Ordinary people and authorities alike, with the partial exception of Pietists, made little effort to avoid secular categories of status, gender, property, and other forms of hierarchy,

---

13 David Swartz (1997), *Culture and Power: The Sociology of Pierre Bourdieu* (Chicago: University of Chicago Press), 117.

14 Pierre Bourdieu (1991), *Language and Symbolic Power*, trans. G. Raymond & M. Adamson (Cambridge: Polity); idem, 'Legitimation and Structural Interests in Weber's Sociology of Religion,' in S. Lash & S. Whimster, eds (1987), *Max Weber, Rationality and Modernity* (Boston: Allen & Unwin), 119–136. See also Craig Calhoun, et al., eds (1993), *Bourdieu: Critical Perspectives* (Chicago: University of Chicago Press).

15 Bourdieu posited that 'cultural fields progressively [develop] and [gain] autonomy from the political and economic fields.' Swartz (1997), 127.

which were openly carried over into the religious arena. Ordinary people competed to participate in the public religious arena, pursuing a variety of secular as well as religious interests there. The authorities worked hard to accommodate the interests of burghers and their families, roughly half the town's inhabitants. Baroque culture was thus formed in interaction among social groups.

Cultural capital held by actors in a field has value because people share a belief in the importance of that field and its defined ideals and interests, even if they disagree on many specifics. Bourdieu's concept of capital has been criticized and overhauled, but is still useful.[16] Forms of capital in the early modern religious arena included concrete objects such as pews, a valued and scarce resource that was the basis for church attendance; and, more abstractly, being considered theologically legitimate. Concrete forms of capital held by individuals usually corresponded to their status in the religious arena, and that status corresponded to their social and economic status, as posited by Bourdieu.[17] Pewholding patterns are a good example of this: the wealthy and members of groups such as the city council held the best pews, while the unpropertied held very few. More abstract notions such as theological legitimacy and superiority, though, could successfully be claimed by people from any social group; Pietists made especial use of such claims. It is also important to bear in mind that, as Bourdieu argues, there is no absolute correlation between status outside the religious field and status within it. Processes of social reproduction can mediate those relations. For example, clerics' education, and even to a limited degree pewholding, could raise an individual's status.

Philip Benedict has noted that 'the history of church institutions has rarely excited historians of early modern religious life.'[18] However, Bourdieu and others have rightly emphasized the importance of institutions in attempting to maintain orthodoxy and social and political control.[19] Institutions such as the consistories established the rules of everyday religious life. Further, city councilors, Electoral officials, clerics, and consistory members constantly engaged in turf wars. Foundational documents of the Reformation era such as the 1580 Electoral Saxon Church Ordinance, as well as customary routines, served as frequent points of reference.

Bourdieu's emphasis on the importance of the opposition 'between orthodoxy and heterodoxy,' and the ways in which this struggle relates to the 'maintenance or subversion of the symbolic order' among social classes[20] is relevant in two ways to Baroque religion. Firstly, the consistories, which were courts as well as arbiters of theological dispute, minutely regulated and often pronounced on what was orthodox. Secondly, the concept of the orthodox-heterodox dynamic helps integrate the Pietist-

---

16 See Francie Ostrower (1998), 'The Arts as Cultural Capital Among Elites: Bourdieu's Theory Reconsidered,' *Poetics*, 26, 43–53.

17 Swartz (1997), 129 ff.

18 Benedict (2002), *Christ's Churches Purely Reformed. A Social History of Calvinism* (New Haven: Yale University Press), xx.

19 Swartz (1997), 120 and passim.

20 Swartz (1997), 132, citing Bourdieu and Loic Waquant (1992), *An Invitation to Reflexive Sociology* (Chicago: University of Chicago Press), 106.

Orthodox conflict into a social history of religion. This conflict was a classic case of struggle between an established set of institutions and a smaller group with young, charismatic leaders whose members interacted in ways that the establishment characterized as illegitimate. This conflict differs from the Bourdieuan model in that many Pietists were not social or political 'outsiders,' although they considered themselves a persecuted minority.

* * *

Explorations of 17th and 18th century music are a second important point of departure for this book. Musicologists' long-standing inquiry into individual composers has generated important insights. In the field of Bach studies, for example, a powerful tradition of research has established the chronology of composition, revision, and performance of Bach's monumental output, with an especial focus on his work in Leipzig. Scholars have painstakingly reconstructed the social and political context of Bach's appointment as cantor in 1723, his working conditions until his death in 1750, the course of the liturgy, the church buildings and their ongoing renovations, and other Leipzig churches and musicians.[21] Many of the insights of this book could not have been developed without this research.

Since the 1980s representatives of the 'new musicology,' as well as some historians and sociologists, have challenged some of the core assumptions of traditional musicology, and offer models for integrating music into a social history of religion. They have increasingly emphasized social context, and have become eclectic in their methodological inspiration. They are showing that what 20th century scholars and music lovers conceived as a 'high' culture that transcended the societies around it was actually bound in numerous ways to those societies, and that music was an important part of general public discourse.[22] Further, as Tia DeNora and other sociologists argue, music does not merely reflect social relations. It also 'comes

---

21 Günther Stiller (1984), *Johann Sebastian Bach and Liturgical Life in Leipzig* (St. Louis: Concordia; German original, 1970); Ulrich Siegele (1997), 'Bach and the Domestic Politics of Electoral Saxony,' in John Butt, ed., *Cambridge Companion to Bach* (New York: Cambridge University Press), 17–34; Ernst-Heinz Lemper (1954), *Die Thomaskirche zu Leipzig* (Leipzig: Koehler & Amelang); Andreas Glöckner (1990), *Die Musikpflege an der Leipziger Neukirche zur Zeit Johann Sebastian Bachs*, = *BzBf*, 8; Robin A. Leaver (1997), 'The Mature Vocal Works and Their Theological and Liturgical Context,' in Butt, ed., 86–122; Christoph Wolff (2000), *Johann Sebastian Bach: The Learned Musician* (New York: Norton).

22 Alexander Fisher (2004), *Music and Religious Identity in Counter-Reformation Augsburg, 1580–1630* (Aldershot: Ashgate); David Gramit (2002), *Cultivating Music: The Aspirations, Interests, and Limits of German Musical Culture, 1770–1848* (University of California Press); William Weber, ed. (2004), *The Musician as Entrepreneur, 1700–1914: Managers, Charlatans, and Idealists* (Bloomington: Indiana University Press); James Van Horn Melton (2004), 'School, Stage, Salon: Musical Cultures in Haydn's Vienna,' *Journal of Modern History*, 76, 251–279.

to serve (in ways that can be documented and specified spatially/temporally) as a constitutive medium of social life … music can be understood as a medium through which social relations are forged.'[23] In line with these arguments, historians have begun to explore the various social functions of musical events. James Johnson has shown that 18th century Parisian opera and theatre audiences' late arrival, wandering about, and conversing during performances helped make going to the opera an important social occasion.[24] William Weber has shown that in secular concerts and opera houses, different groups within the audience had different goals in attending, and that their etiquette during performances varied.[25]

Conceptualizing the Baroque worship service as a performance by congregants as well as clerics and musicians as they moved through a specifically structured time and space helps us better understand relations among those groups more generally. Since large portions of the service were sung or chanted, congregants were actually active throughout much of the service. Furthermore, the evidence indicates that congregants sang with the chorale movements of cantatas and Lenten passions, including those of Bach. In addition, some congregants' selective reception of the rest of the cantata, organ preludes and postludes, and the hymns, Kyrie, etc., and their socializing with other congregants, show that people pursued their own goals in the course of the service, rather than merely conforming to the goals of clerics, musicians, and councilors.

Shifts in music were also integral to broader cultural change in the Baroque era, as at other times. Cantata and passion style was innovative and somewhat contested throughout the Baroque period, especially to the 1720s, and it was closely linked to the expansion of secular life and luxury consumption. Performance and reception were thus 'about' more than musical style. Some Leipzig city councilors, for example, expended considerable energy in appointing and supporting Bach and his music, while others were less supportive.

The concept of the adiaphora structured much of the Baroque debate on cultural change. Adiaphora have mostly been discussed in a theological context,[26] but they had important social dimensions. They were defined as technically neutral, but potentially either beneficial or harmful cultural and/or liturgical activities, both secular and religious. Which activities came under this heading? At issue, for example, was playing cards, dancing, and wearing liturgical vestments. But music, and activities associated with it, such as dancing, were the most-discussed adiaphora. Music could play this role because it was the Baroque art form which most pervaded

---

[23] Tia DeNora (2002), 'Music into Action: Performing Gender on the Viennese Concert Stage, 1790–1810,' *Poetics*, 30, 19–33. See also DeNora (2004), 'Historical Perspectives in Music Sociology,' *Poetics*, 32, 211–221; Timothy Dowd (2002), 'Introduction: Explorations in the Sociology of Music,' *Poetics*, 30, 1–3.

[24] Johnson (1995), *Listening in Paris: A Cultural History* (Berkeley: University of California Press).

[25] Weber (1997), 'Did People Listen in the 18th Century?,' *Early Music*, 25, 678–691.

[26] See Joyce Irwin (1993), *Neither Voice nor Heart Alone. German Lutheran Theology of Music in the Age of the Baroque* (New York: Lang).

everyday life, and in which the broadest social range of people actively participated. The debate was carried out beginning in the 1690s. Pietists emphasized the potential of secular music and modern church music to morally corrupt listeners. Orthodox writers, including musicians, defended musical activities to varying degrees, while the music of some composers, including Bach, did not conform to any one position in thc debate.

A reconstruction of the structures and practices of urban Baroque musical culture at their height is needed. Many musicologists as well as historians remain uneasy with the performance contexts of Baroque music. The idea that audiences did not pay full attention to musicians such as J.S. Bach or G.P. Telemann continues to elicit a snicker or a sigh. The traditional view of 'occasional' as opposed to 'absolute' music, inculcated in countless music history courses and textbooks, continues to exercise its hold. In this view, the public subscription concerts that emerged in the late 18th century, and at which non-representational, 'abstract' music was the primary focus, are depicted as a distinct improvement over earlier contexts such as church services, banquets, or royal processions, where music was one activity among many.[27] Also, in their specific studies, musicologists, historians, and sociologists have continued in a traditional emphasis on the genesis and development of Classical and Romantic style and its patrons, critics, and audiences. The time up to about 1770 or even later still often serves as a negative backdrop, a time when more traditional patronage forms and other features of Baroque culture declined, and new secular genres, concert venues, and audiences began to arise.

Present-day codes of audience behavior in the classical music world, including arrival before the beginning of a concert, silence during a performance, and applause at the conclusion of a piece, have also contributed to the naturalization of expectations about performance contexts, although these codes, along with the classical canon itself, were only slowly established in the course of the 19th century.[28] In addition, while the early music movement and its musician-scholars have added greatly to an understanding of Baroque performance practices, a conundrum emerges from their work. Most modern-day early-music performances are polished, well-rehearsed interpretations of works that were composed well over two hundred years ago; performers have become expert on historical scores, instruments, and techniques. But when Telemann, Heinichen, Fasch, and others led performances of their works during the Baroque era itself, those works were often brand new, and scholars are also finding that performances were often relatively ad hoc and under-rehearsed.[29]

---

27 James Johnson (1995) characterizes the music of the French Baroque theatre, with its dance interludes and audiences which socialized and occasionally interrupted performances, as ripe for reform, and contrasts those audiences to the rapt ones of the Romantic era: 23, 26, 57, 69, 257 ff. See also John Walter Hill (2005), *Baroque Music: Music in Western Europe 1580–1750* (New York: Norton), 491; on social context, see 112 ff.; 297 ff.; 305 ff.

28 William Weber (1992), *The Rise of Musical Classics in Eighteenth-Century England: A Study in Canon, Ritual, and Ideology* (New York: Oxford).

29 See Ulrich Leisinger, ed. (2002), *Bach in Leipzig – Bach und Leipzig. Konferenzbericht Leipzig 2000* (Hildesheim: Olms).

Finally, this study shows that the sources and approaches of social historians, which may initially seem to have no bearing on music, can illuminate musical life in ways that traditional musicological sources cannot. For example, the sources on pewholding allow for a reconstruction of the audiences of church music; sources on the appointment of clerics provide a point of reference and comparison to the appointments of musicians; and councilors' roles as patrons of the non-musical aspects of religious life provide essential context for their patronage of musical life. In contrast, sources that are directly related to music or a particular musician, such as scores, music treatises and criticism, correspondence, diaries, and appointment and payment records, while essential, usually provide limited insight into the broader social context of music.

* * *

The third point of departure for this book, a major research tradition on Pietism, has expanded well beyond an earlier focus on theology.[30] The ideas, interests, and roles of ordinary Pietists are beginning to be explored in detail.[31] Scholars are emphasizing the importance to the movement of innovative forms of sociability such as correspondence networks and collegia. Lay people worked closely with Pietist theology students and clerics. The previous, caricatured depiction of mainstream religion as an out-of-touch and oppressive 'Orthodoxy' is also being revised.[32]

[30] For a summary, see Jonathan Strom (2002), 'Problems and Promises of Pietism Research,' *Church History*, 71, 536–554. A multi-volume update of Pietist historiography: Martin Brecht et al., eds (1993–2004), *GdP*. See also articles in the journal *Pietismus und Neuzeit*.

[31] Hartmut Lehmann (1995), 'Vorüberlegungen zu einer Sozialgeschichte des Pietismus im 17./18. Jahrhundert, *PuN*, 21, 69–83; idem (2001), 'Grenzüberschreitungen und Grenzziehungen im Pietismus,' *PuN*, 27, 11–18; idem (2004), introduction, in *GdP*, vol. IV, 1–18; Ryoko Mori (2004), *Begeisterung und Ernüchterung in christlicher Vollkommenheit. Pietistische Selbst- und Weltwahrnehmungen im ausgehenden 17. Jahrhundert* (Tübingen: Niemeyer); Lucinda Martin (2003), 'Female Reformers as the Gate Keepers of Pietism: The Example of Johanna Eleonora Merlau and William Penn,' *Monatshefte*, 95, 33–58 and (2003), 'Möglichkeiten und Grenzen geistlicher Rede von Frauen in Halle und Herrnhut,' *PuN*, 29, 80–90; Jonathan Strom (2001), 'Early Conventicles in Lübeck,' *PuN*, 27, 19–52; Ulrike Witt (1996), *Bekehrung, Bildung und Biographie: Frauen im Umkreis des Halleschen Pietismus* (Tübingen: Niemeyer); Johannes Wallmann (1992), 'Erfurt und der Pietismus im 17. Jahrhundert,' in Ulman Weiss, ed., *Erfurt 742–1992. Stadtgeschichte, Universitätsgeschichte* (Weimar: Böhlau), 403–422.

[32] Udo Sträter, ed. (2003), *Zur Rechtfertigungslehre in der Lutherischen Orthodoxie. Beiträge des sechsten Wittenberger Symposiums zur Lutherischen Orthodoxie* (Leipzig: Evangelische Verlagsanstalt); Jonathan Strom (1999), *Orthodoxy and Reform: The Clergy in Seventeenth Century Rostock* (Tübingen: Mohr); Monika Hagenmaier (1989), *Predigt und Policey. Der gesellschaftspolitische Diskurs zwischen Kirche und Obrigkeit in Ulm 1614–1639* (Baden-Baden: Nomos); Wolfgang Sommer (1988), *Gottesfurcht und Fürstenherrschaft. Studien zum Obrigkeitsverständnis Johann Arndts und lutherischer Hofprediger zur Zeit der*

However, as Hartmut Lehmann has recently noted, the exploration of the social dimensions of the Pietist movement is still in its infancy.[33] Pietists have also not been fully placed into the religious context from which they emerged and with which they continued to interact.

Historians to date have also not offered a convincing explanation for why Pietism arose as a social movement when it did. They have emphasized the difficult conditions following the Thirty Years' War, as well as ongoing epidemics and economic instability throughout the 17th century.[34] These crises were one root of Pietism, influencing individuals in the 1660s and 1670s. Even the plague epidemic of 1680 was a formative experience for some Leipzig Pietists. Further, some Pietists feared returning crises: their critique of contemporary cultural consumption was linked to citations of Old Testament prophecies of divine vengeance, and to New Testamentarian apocalyptic thought.

However, as we will see below, by the time Pietism became a broad social movement in the late 1680s, northern and central German trade centers such as Hamburg and Leipzig were experiencing an economic boom. Pietism was thus a complex response to social and cultural change. Any explanation for the rise of that movement should take into account the flourishing of Baroque culture from the 1680s onward in the context of increased prosperity for broad sections of the urban population. From the very beginning of the collegia movement (and even before), as noted by most historians of Pietism, a major theme for ordinary Pietists as well as student and clerical leaders was the condemnation of much secular culture and modern church music.[35] This critique actually attests to the fact that individuals had more disposable income to attend the opera, dances, and other festivities. Likewise, the authorities had more money to invest in church music. It should also be noted, though, that Pietists developed a strong and innovative culture of hymn composition, publication, and performance.[36] Further, they embraced some aspects of change, innovating in their communication networks and publication strategies.

This book also stresses the importance of the Saxon context of the Pietist movement.[37] Saxony has generally, and correctly, been regarded as a stronghold

---

altprotestantischen Orthodoxie (Göttingen: Vandenhoeck & Ruprecht); Sabine Holtz (1993), *Theologie und Alltag. Lehre und Leben in den Predigten der Tübinger Theologen 1550–1750* (Tübingen: Mohr).

33 Lehmann (2004), 13–14 and passim.

34 Mori (2004), 5–6, 92 ff.; Hartmut Lehmann (1980), *Das Zeitalter des Absolutismus. Gottesgnadentum und Kriegsnot* (Stuttgart: Kohlhammer), 61–93, 105–169; idem (2003), 'Engerer, weiterer und erweiterter Pietismusbegriff,' *PuN*, 29, 18–36: 23–24.

35 Mori (2004), 39, 59, 62 ff., 93, 256; Wallmann (1992), 415–416.

36 See Christian Bunners, 'Gesangbuch' and 'Musik,' in *GdP*, vol. IV, 122–142, 430–455; Irwin (1993); Gudrun Busch & Wolfgang Miersemann, eds (1997), *'Geist-Reicher' Gesang. Halle und das pietistische Lied* (Tübingen: Niemeyer); idem, eds (2002), *Pietismus und Liedkultur* (Tübingen: Niemeyer).

37 The present study combines elements of Johannes Wallmann's and other historians' 'narrower' definition of Pietism, and Hans Leube's 'narrowest' definition. Like the 'narrower'

of Orthodox Lutheran confessional structures and theology. However, it was also the site of dramatic breaks with the established system, and of the development of Pietism itself. Events in Saxony between 1686 and 1691 marked a crucial transition from a reform movement that was integrated into the mainstream, and that was welcomed by many later opponents of Pietism, to a movement in intense conflict with much of the mainstream. Those events also point to the importance of elite clerics and officials in leading to a broader Pietist movement. Philipp Jacob Spener, Senior Court Chaplain in Dresden from 1686 to 1691, was initially welcomed in Saxony. As senior cleric in Frankfurt, he had organized prayer meetings (collegia pietatis) from 1670, and published a widely read reform program, *Pia Desideria*, in 1675. These had generated some conflict, but many Orthodox theologians supported them.[38]

By 1688, though, Spener was feuding with the Elector on lifestyle issues and with Orthodox clerics on other matters. He was close to Leipzig student August Hermann Francke, who held collegia pietatis which came to include town inhabitants as well as students by 1689, a key shift. Both Spener and Francke were close to philosopher Christian Thomasius, who was attacking the Saxon consistories and ecclesiastical law. By 1690, Francke, Thomasius, and their fellows had been forced to leave Leipzig; by 1691, Spener had left Dresden for Berlin, all the departures following intense conflict with Orthodox Saxon clerics and political figures. Ryoko Mori has coined the term 'second wave' to describe the emergence of Pietism as a broad social movement after Pietist students dispersed from Leipzig to towns around central Germany in 1690.[39] Spener, Francke and Thomasius were part of a network of intellectuals and officials with ties to Saxony, including Samuel Pufendorf and Veit Ludwig von Seckendorff. It seems that these men initially thought Spener's position at the Dresden court provided a good opportunity to reform the Saxon ecclesiastical system from within. In the 1680s they did not anticipate that they would be able to develop a strong institutional base in Brandenburg-Prussia; they began to do this only after Spener's arrival in Berlin.

* * *

definition, it emphasizes the importance of sociability in collegia and the role of Spener; like the 'narrowest,' it considers intense conflict with non-Pietists, and events in Leipzig, to be key. The 'broad' definition argued especially by Martin Brecht, which considers Lutheran figures from the early 17th century onward such as Johann Arndt to be Pietists, is less useful for social history purposes. See Strom (2002), 538–542; Martin Brecht (1993), introduction, in *GdP*, vol. I, 1–10; Lehmann (2003); Johannes Wallmann (2002), 'Eine alternative Geschichte des Pietismus. Zur gegenwärtigen Diskussion um den Pietismusbegriff,' *PuN*, 28, 30–71; idem (2004), 'Pietismus – ein Epochenbegriff oder ein typologischer Begriff?,' *PuN*, 30, 191–224.

38 Martin Brecht (1993), 'Philipp Jakob Spener, sein Programm und dessen Auswirkungen,' in *GdP*, vol. I, 281–389; Wallmann (1992).

39 Mori (2004), 2 ff., 25 ff.

Some definition is in order here. This book uses the term 'Baroque' to refer to musical and other creative styles between about the 1580s and 1750. The religious practices and urban patronage structures that were associated with and helped to produce these styles are discussed as part of the Baroque era, but are not ascribed specifically 'Baroque' features. It seems that the term, originally Portuguese for an irregularly shaped pearl, was first applied to the arts in France in the 1730s in a discussion of music.[40] It thus became a descriptor toward the end of the era to which it refers, and it was a negative one. In France, Germany, and beyond, critics (although not all contemporaries) came to associate the dominant style of the day in music, art, architecture, theatre, and literature with heaviness, over-ornamentation, 'artifice,' and pedantry. By contrast, until the 1730s contemporaries had no one name for their artistic styles, although they did recognize specific, evolving characteristics of the arts, architecture, and literature that were shared (with regional variation) across Europe. Beginning in the late 16th century, for example, musicians referred to their style as the *stile moderno*, as opposed to the *stile antico* of the Renaissance, as a *stylus luxurians* in contrast to an earlier *stylus gravis*, and to a *seconda prattica* that followed a Renaissance *prima prattica*. From the 1720s, composers such as Telemann, Vivaldi, and Handel, who would now be labeled as Baroque, defined their musical style as 'galant;' implicit in this term was a rejection of what was perceived as an outdated style among many contemporaries.[41] Musicologists began to use the term 'Baroque' in the early 20th century. Currently, most art and music historians would agree that it can be used as a starting point for examining a variety of artistic developments.[42] Historians of early modern Germany have begun using the term to designate the post-Reformation era.[43] In addition, some historians of Spain, Italy, and France have argued that there was a more general Baroque culture, society, politics, and general sensibility.[44] These scholars have largely focused on the 17th century and its upheavals, and have not focused on music.

* * *

[40] Claude Palisca (2001), 'Baroque,' in *New Grove Dictionary of Music and Musicians*, 2nd edition, ed. Stanley Sadie, vol. II, 749–756 (New York: Macmillan), 749.

[41] Daniel Heartz (2003), *Music in European Capitals: The Galant Style 1720–1780* (New York: Norton), 16 ff.

[42] A thoughtful rejection of the term as indicative of any stylistic feature, on the grounds that styles were so diverse: George Buelow (2004), *A History of Baroque Music* (Bloomington: Indiana University Press), Introduction, 1 ff.

[43] Forster (2001); Lyndal Roper (2004), *Witch Craze: Terror and Fantasy in Baroque Germany* (New Haven: Yale University Press).

[44] See Rosario Villari (1995), Introduction, *Baroque Personae*, ed. Villari, 1–8 (Chicago: University of Chicago Press; trans. Lydia Cochrane), 1–8; Jose Antonio Maravall (1986), *Culture of the Baroque: Analysis of a Historical Structure* (Minneapolis: University of Minnesota Press, Spanish original, 1975; trans. Terry Cochran); Evonne Levy (2004), *Propaganda and the Jesuit Baroque* (Berkeley: University of California Press). See also Timothy Hampton, ed. (1991), *Baroque Topographies: Literature/History/Philosophy*, = *Yale French Studies*, 80.

In the chapters that follow, the three themes of public religious life, music and Pietism are interwoven, as they were for contemporaries. The first two chapters explore congregants' perspectives. Chapter One reconstructs the experience of the main Sunday morning worship service, focusing on the various roles of congregants, social uses of the service, participation in and reception of music, and the reception of the sermon. Chapter Two discusses the culture and practices surrounding pew-holding, which reached their high point during the Baroque era. Social relations were negotiated and reproduced in the religious arena most prominently through pewholding practices. Pews were a much sought-after commodity. Social status was reflected in where people sat in church, and in what type of pew they held.

The next three chapters examine the producers of public religious life. Chapter Three looks at city councilors, clerics, and their interactions with ordinary inhabitants. Councilors were the main patrons of urban religious life. That patronage was central to council governance in both theory and practice. Inhabitants claimed specific rights on the basis of the council's covenant theory of governance. Clerics were firmly embedded in urban society through their education, tutoring and living arrangements while they were students, through the appointment process by councilors, and through their pastoral duties once they were appointed.

Chapter Four examines the Saxon territorial dimensions of Leipzig's religious life: the Saxon Electoral court and the consistories. Councilors and clerics in Leipzig interacted often with the court at Dresden, which was at the height of its cultural and political influence in the 17th and 18th centuries. The roles of the Electors in religion shifted considerably during this time: Johann George III (ruled 1680–91) entered into major conflict with Philipp Jacob Spener, and Frederick August II, 'the Strong,' (ruled 1694–1733) converted to Catholicism. The consistories, although largely ignored by historians, were crucial to everyday religious life. They integrated local religion and territorial policies, and exemplified the blending of the religious and the secular in governance. Not least, they help to explain the longevity of the confessional regulation of religious life. This chapter also discusses Thomasius's attack on the consistories and ecclesiastical law.

Chapter Five examines Leipzig's cantors, especially J.S. Bach and his predecessor, Johann Kuhnau. The cantors' status illuminates some of the complexities of urban society. Cantors did not fit neatly into the major urban groupings of elite, burgher, and sub-burgher. Bach, for example, was internationally famed as a composer and performer, but his income and wealth placed him at the lower end of middling groups. City councilors appointed the cantors and closely regulated their teaching and compositional activities. This chapter also discusses the adiaphora debate and J.S. Bach's position relative to Pietism.

Chapters Six and Seven reconstruct the social history of Pietists in Leipzig. Chapter Six discusses the social dimensions of the collegia led by the young August Hermann Francke, especially the close cooperation among students and burghers. The Leipzig and Saxon authorities launched a major investigation and suppressed the meetings, demonstrating the limits on ordinary people's religious activities. Especially problematic to the authorities was the crossing of customary status, gender, and religious boundaries among participants. Chapter Seven reconstructs the shadowy Leipzig Pietist network that flourished from 1690 through at least the 1730s. It shows how Pietists responded to and themselves contributed to rapid social and cultural change. The Leipzig Pietists, mostly lay people, were close to Francke but were not limited to interactions with Halle Pietists.

One of the strengths of the Baroque religious arena was its ability to respond to social change. Chapter Eight examines how social and stylistic change influenced a wave of church construction and renovation beginning in 1699. A growing population placed pressure on church seating. City councilors and University professors organized the expansion, while burgher demand for pews largely funded it. Two styles were cultivated in the new spaces. One, influenced by and parallel to Pietism, emphasized simplicity, work with the poor, and inspirational preaching. The other was high Baroque style. Music was an important part of the latter: students including Telemann, Pisendel, Heinichen, Fasch, and possibly Handel, were active at two of the new churches, making Leipzig an incubator of galant style.

Leipzig during the Baroque era

In one sense, this book is a product of the fall of the Berlin Wall. While there was a robust tradition of Saxon social and cultural history within East Germany during the Cold War, Anglo-American and West German historians largely focused on towns in the North, South, and Southwest of the Holy Roman Empire, especially on Imperial towns such as Augsburg and Nuremberg.[45] Since 1990, easier access to sources has led to a dramatic resurgence of interest in Saxony by English-speaking historians and those from the former West Germany, although much of the research has focused on the 19th and 20th centuries.[46] Research on Pietism has also blossomed, with the archives of the Franckesche Stiftungen in Halle an important resource. Musicians and musicologists were able to bridge the East–West divide more effectively. Bach scholars in particular managed to communicate, with the Leipzig Bach-Archiv and the Neue Bach-Gesellschaft serving as important centers for research, publication, and meetings. But those interactions have been facilitated by the fall of the Wall, as access to libraries and archives has become easier. The extraordinarily rich sources in the archives and libraries of Leipzig, Dresden, and Halle illuminate everyday religious life from many angles. Sources include pew allotment records, letters by

[45] Important exceptions include Gerald Strauss (1978), *Luther's House of Learning. Indoctrination of the Young in Reformation Germany* (Baltimore: Johns Hopkins Press) and Susan Karant-Nunn (1987), *Zwickau in Transition, 1500–1547: The Reformation as an Agent of Change* (Columbus: Ohio State University Press). Anglo-American historians neglected Leipzig and Saxony even before the Cold War.

[46] James Retalleck, ed. (2000), *Saxony in German History: Culture, Society, and Politics, 1830–1933* (Ann Arbor: University of Michigan Press); Robert Beachy (2005), *The Soul of Commerce: Credit, Property, and Politics in Leipzig, 1750–1840* (Boston: Brill); Uwe Schirmer, ed. (1998), *Sachsen im 17. Jahrhundert. Krise, Krieg und Neubeginn* (Beucha: Sax).

ordinary Pietists, consistory correspondence, city council records, and the original protocols of interrogations of Pietists. Printed works such as ordinances, hymnals, sermons, cantata libretti, debate tracts, local chronicles, and autobiographies add further perspective.

Leipzig was a major early modern political, cultural, and economic center.[47] The city and its people shared many characteristics with other towns in the Holy Roman Empire. Leipzig's inhabitants had in common with other Saxons an accent (with variations), rulers, political celebrations and other observances, pressures of wartime, and a body of law. They shared a Lutheran identity and (also with variations) a worship style with people around Northern and Central Europe. Clerics fostered this identity by cultivating networks of correspondence, employment, and education. Leipzigers were also part of regional and more far-flung networks: many were born in, traded with, and visited other Saxon and Thuringian towns and villages, and to a lesser extent towns around the Holy Roman Empire. Leipzig merchants, artisans, councilors, and innkeepers were closely in touch with the inhabitants of other large Protestant north and central German trade centers, especially Imperial towns such as Hamburg and Frankfurt, as well as with those of towns like Dresden, Breslau, and Berlin; they also had contact with their peers in smaller central German towns like Jena, Grimma, and Eisenach, for whom Leipzig was a cosmopolitan center.

Leipzig had a magnified impact on the society and culture of early modern Germany due to its position as a university town, site of law courts, and trade center. Jurists, clerics, and musicians around Saxony, Thuringia, and beyond obtained degrees from the University (although many musicians, including J.S. Bach, did not attend university). The musicians, who included future cantors, organists, and court musicians, usually studied law, but were active in musical life during their studies. Merchants, printers and publishers, and nobles from around Europe converged on the city during the trade fairs. Individuals from around Saxony came to Leipzig for trials at the Saxon High Court and the Leipzig Consistory. And individuals from around the Empire submitted problems and read the opinions of professors in the four faculties of theology, law, philosophy, and medicine. Not least, figures whose activities were well known around Europe, including Francke and J.S. Bach, were active in the city.

Leipzig's location in a larger territory and its constant interactions with the court at Dresden distinguished it in some ways from the Imperial towns. For example, the Electors could take Leipzig into a war. However, in governance, religious practice, relations between councilors and ordinary inhabitants, the relative roles of trade and manufacture, and social structure, Leipzig was more similar to, say, Frankfurt than it was to smaller Saxon towns such as Gera or Zwickau. The wealth and status of Leipzig's merchant and jurist elites also provided considerable leverage against

---

[47] See Beachy (2005); George Stauffer (1993), 'Leipzig: A Cosmopolitan Trade Centre,' in George Buelow, ed., *The Late Baroque Era: From the 1680s to 1740* (Englewood Cliffs: Prentice Hall), 254–295; Wolfgang Martens, ed. (1990), *Leipzig: Aufklärung und Bürgerlichkeit* (Heidelberg: Schneider).

Leipzig: view of the city from the southeast, engraving by I.G. Ringlin, c. 1720 (Bach-Archiv Leipzig. Graph. Slg. 12/15, reproduced by permission).

incursions by the court, and relations between the city and court were symbiotic in many ways. By the same token, the Imperial towns were forced to deal constantly not only with the Emperors, but also with the large territories near them: Hamburg with Denmark, Augsburg with Bavaria.

* * *

The stories told here are bookended by several events. In 1650 Swedish occupying forces left Leipzig, returning local authority to the city council and marking the end of the Thirty Years' War era. This withdrawal marked the beginning of a prolonged period of relative peace in Saxony, the longest in the entire late medieval and early modern eras. Although the Electors participated in several financially draining wars, there was little military conflict in Saxony itself until 1756, when Prussia sparked the Seven Years' War by invading Saxony.[48] Much of the rest of the northern and central Holy Roman Empire was similarly at relative peace during this time, although the southwest, and by 1740 much of the Empire, faced turmoil. The Seven Years' War would inaugurate another era of more general turbulent political and military activity, as well as a dramatic shift in cultural tastes. J.S. Bach's death a few years earlier, in 1750, is often used as an end point in Baroque music chronologies.

The Baroque era is more often associated with Catholic than with Protestant areas. The movement crossed confessional boundaries, though, with Leipzig and other northern and central German towns emerging as centers of a late flourishing of Baroque culture from the 1680s onward. Nobles around Protestant Germany, notably the Saxon ruling house, the Wettins, also developed a sparkling Baroque culture. Political stability provided the framework for economic expansion and a steady accumulation of wealth, and for the eventual flourishing of high Baroque culture. The economic, political, and cultural parallels between German towns during the Baroque era, and Italian towns during the Renaissance as found by Richard Goldthwaite are striking.[49] In both cases, wealth was concentrated in large urban centers whose merchant elites were benefiting from an increase in trade. After periods of upheaval, urban and territorial political elites had consolidated power and achieved stability. Wealth was distributed relatively widely in the towns, and there was considerable social mobility. In this context, there was a major, renewable increase in demand for a wide range of goods, including art, both secular and sacred. Lay demand for liturgical services also led to an expansion of religious life.

---

48 Karl Czok, ed. (1989), *Geschichte Sachsens* (Weimar: Böhlau), 208–287. There was a brief Swedish occupation in 1706 during the Great Northern War, and a Prussian occupation in 1744 during the Second Silesian War.

49 Goldthwaite (1993), *Wealth and the Demand for Art in Italy, 1300–1600* (Baltimore: Johns Hopkins University Press). He argues (p. 45) that similar structural changes took place in England and France in the 18th century; these changes also took place in parts of Germany.

That is not to say that signs in 1650 indicated a prosperous future. On the contrary, Leipzig, like many other cities, had been hard hit during the Thirty Years' War.[50] Beginning in 1631, when Saxony entered the war, Leipzig was besieged five times; three major battles, including those of Lützen and Breitenfeld, were fought near the city; and the Swedish army occupied the city for eight years beginning in 1642. Severe financial pressure was placed on inhabitants by the Electors and by troops quartered in the city. Many buildings were damaged or destroyed by bombardments, and the 'suburbs' outside the town walls were completely destroyed. Thousands of refugees from the surrounding countryside streamed into the city when armies approached. The trade fairs barely functioned. Almost constant epidemics, high food prices, and periods of starvation accompanied all these phenomena.

In the aftermath of the war, recovery was slow. The population began to grow immediately after reaching a post-war low of 14,000, down from over 16,000 in the early 17th century. However, the population and birth and marriage rates reached their pre-war levels only in the 1670s.[51] The 1650s saw some rebuilding, but continuing subsistence crises. Recovery was probably slowed by unusually heavy flooding in 1651, 1655, and 1661, which destroyed crops and infrastructure around Saxony.[52] Epidemics of the plague hit the city, the last, in 1680, claiming over 2000 lives. Artisanal production remained very low; in 1656, for example, Leipzig tanners complained that their numbers had decreased from ninety to thirty since the beginning of the war, and that many of these were leaving the city for lack of a workshop or living space.[53] More money became available for construction projects in the 1660s. Whereas the best public works gestures the council had been able to make immediately after the war were to repair a bridge and a fountain, by 1663 the council was able to repair major damage from bombardments to the roof and walls of St. Nicholas's, one of the city's two main churches.[54] A replica of an Imperial 'fireball' that had fallen through the roof of the church in 1633 was suspended from the ceiling and remained as a memento of the war until at least 1750.[55] From 1668 to

[50] Detlef Döring (1984), 'Das Leben in Leipzig in der Zeit des Dreissigjährigen Krieges. Dargestellt anhand der Annalen des Zacharias Schneider,' *Leipzig: Aus Vergangenheit und Gegenwart. Beiträge zur Stadtgeschichte*, 3, 151–175.

[51] F.G. Leonhardi (1790), *Erdbeschreibung der Churfürstlich- und Herzoglich-Sächsischen Lande*, vol. II (Leipzig: Barth), 61–62.

[52] Stefan Miltitzer (1998), 'Sachsen – Klimatatsachen und Umriss von Klimawirkungen im 17. Jahrhundert,' in Schirmer, ed. (1998), 69–100.

[53] Karl Czok (1990), 'Leipzig nach dem "grossen Krieg" und im augusteischen Zeitalter (1648–1763),' in Klaus Sohl, ed., *Neues Leipzigisches Geschichts-Buch* (Leipzig: Fachbuchverlag Leipzig), 100–131; 102.

[54] Vogel (1714 & 1756), *Leipziger Geschicht-Buch oder Annales* (Leipzig: Lanckish), 649 and 714.

[55] Iccander (J.C. Crell) (1725), *Das in gantz Europa berühmte, galante und sehenswürdige Königliche Leipzig in Sachsen* ... (Leipzig: Martini), 36 ff.; pew chart of St. Nicholas's, fourth balcony level, 1750 (SAL, RRA, 250).

1671 the council built a combination orphanage, prison, and asylum, St. George's, to replace a building burned by the Swedish army in 1631.

Many southern German towns, including centers like Nuremberg and Augsburg, never fully recovered from the war; they also suffered from shifts within Europe of dominant trade routes and increasing rural production.[56] In contrast, numerous northern and central European trade centers prospered, including Hamburg, Frankfurt, Breslau, and Danzig as well as Leipzig, with the 1680s marking the beginning of a dramatic upswing in the economy. Merchants' and councilors' structural reforms and fiscal innovations combined with a world-wide expansion of trade to produce an economic boom in the city.[57] Building on the city's traditional position as an East–West crossroads, the Leipzig fairs, held three times a year for two or three weeks each, overtook Frankfurt's as the preeminent central European trade fairs. Increasingly integrated into the booming economy of the Atlantic world, Leipzig became the second leading German center for the distribution of colonial goods, after Hamburg.[58] Long-distance merchants like the Wincklers, Boses (godparents for the Bach family), and Richters specialized in gold and silver products, in silk, Dutch, English and Italian textiles, in luxury goods from the East Indies, and in commissions from merchants around Europe.[59]

Along with the economy, both secular and religious culture blossomed, modernized, and became more cosmopolitan. Architecture was one important element of that culture. A major wave of construction between 1690 and 1730 gave Leipzig a high-Baroque architectural profile. Several dozen leading merchants newly constructed or renovated imposing homes in the center of the city. A few built enormous formal gardens open to the public. These were located just beyond the former ramparts and moats surrounding the town wall, which were dried and filled in 1702–03 and turned into public promenades. The gardens and homes were admired by visitors from around Europe for their sheer size as well as their style. Councilors also presided over a number of public works projects: they updated the existing churches inside and out, newly built or reconstructed three additional ones between 1699 and 1713, and completed several major secular projects, including a bourse in 1678–79, street lighting in 1701, and a new and much larger house of St. George's between 1701 and 1704. Councilors modeled the Bourse directly on the Roman Capitol, or Senators' Palace, designed by Michelangelo: a fitting model of

---

56 Terence McIntosh (1997), *Urban Decline in Early Modern Germany: Schwäbisch Hall and its Region, 1650–1750* (Chapel Hill: University of North Carolina Press).

57 Robert Beachy (1999), 'Reforming Interregional Commerce: The Leipzig Trade Fairs and Saxony's Recovery from the Thirty Years' War,' *Central European History*, 32, 431–452; idem (2005), 22 ff. & 32 ff.

58 Karl Heinrich Kaufhold (1996), 'Messen und Wirtschaftsausstellungen von 1650 bis 1914' and Karlheinz Blashke (1996), 'Die Stadt Leipzig und ihre Messen,' both in P. Johanek & Heinz Stoob, eds, *Europäische Messen und Märktesysteme in Mittelalter und Neuzeit* (Cologne: Böhlau), 239–294 and 295–304.

59 Herbert Helbig (1980), *Die Vertrauten 1680-1980. Eine Vereinigung Leipziger Kaufleute* (Stuttgart: Hiersemann), esp. 27–31.

urban authority.[60] Leading individual councilors served as directors of the projects, in some cases even serving as architects.[61]

Architects, masons, sculptors, and painters from the Dresden court, Bohemia, Italy, Brandenburg, and elsewhere visited and were consulted and did some planning and building. Local professionals did the majority of the architectural design and construction, though, demonstrating superior design and workmanship early on and developing a distinctive local style.[62] These buildings dominated the city for decades. As late as 1811, Goethe wrote, 'Leipzig does not call the viewer back to a distant past; rather, these monuments attest to a recently passed era of trade, prosperity, and wealth.' [63]

Hamburg, Dresden, Frankfurt, and other large Protestant towns experienced a similar flourishing of Baroque architecture. Burghers built grandiose homes and gardens, councilors funded secular public buildings and new churches, and a combination of council and burgher contributions funded the Frauenkirche in Dresden, the Michaeliskirche in Hamburg, and St. Katherine's in Frankfurt.[64] On a lesser scale, Baroque burgher homes, town halls, and churches were also built in smaller towns around Saxony, Thuringia, and northern Germany, as well as in villages surrounding the major cities, where big-city councilors or minor nobles in touch with current styles served as patrons.[65]

From the 1680s onward, the culture of church-going attained a high point. The churches became steadily more crowded, with the council utilizing every possible space to add more pews, as well as adding churches. The interiors were not adorned nearly as abundantly with gilt, ceiling paintings, statues, multiple altars and chapels, and other details, as Catholic churches were. However, contemporaries could find visual plenty. Attention would be drawn to the occupants of special status pews such as those for brides and grooms, and to the truly ostentatious Electoral balcony or pew built in St. Thomas's in 1684, which the Electors and their families used on their occasional visits to Leipzig. Clerics' and altarists' green, white, red, and violet vestments, donated over the years by merchants and councilors, were made of precious silks, satins, and velvets, and trimmed and embroidered with gold and silver thread. Balconies were adorned with large statues and paintings on Biblical subjects, and painted representations of Scriptural passages. The shutters of the organs also

---

60 Kathrin Reeckmann (2000), *Anfänge der Barockarchitektur in Sachsen. Johann Georg Starcke und seine Zeit* (Cologne: Böhlau), 219 ff.

61 Nikolaus Pevsner (1928), *Leipziger Barock. Die Baukunst der Barockzeit in Leipzig* (Dresden: Jess, R [1990], Leipzig: Seemann), 34 ff.

62 Pevsner (1928), 34 ff., passim.

63 In *Dichtung und Wahrheit*; cited in Pevsner (1928), 4–5.

64 See Lutz Rosenpflanzer (2002), *Barocke Bürgerhäuser in Dresden* (Dresden: Verlag der Künste); Volker Plagemann, ed. (2001), *Die Kunst des protestantischen Barock in Hamburg* (Hamburg: Döllinger & Galitz); Reinhold Wex (1984), *Ordnung und Unfriede. Raumprobleme des protestantischen Kirchenbaus im 17. und 18. Jahrhundert in Deutschland* (Marburg: Jonas), 17 & 130.

65 Pevsner (1928), passim.

'The New Marble Altar in the Church of St. Thomas in Leipzig,' print by J.C. Weigel, from J.S. Riemer, Continuatio annalium Lipsiensium Vogelii, ms., 1714–71 (Stadtarchiv Leipzig, reproduced by permission).

had paintings on them, and these became most prominent when the shutters were closed during Lent. In 1720 a new, high Baroque altar replaced the late Renaissance altar in St. Thomas's. Made of black, red, and white marble donated by the Saxon Elector, with a large Gloria (sun) with gilded rays above it, the altar was designed and built by the Dresden court marble sculptor and silversmith. A family of Leipzig jurists and city councilors, the Borns, donated 3000 thaler, and the council donated 1000 thaler toward this showpiece.[66] Cantor Kuhnau composed a special cantata for the occasion.[67]

A rich and increasingly multifaceted Baroque culture developed not only in these churches, but also in pleasure gardens, coffee houses, and other locations. The expansion of trade was closely linked to the emergence of new forms of association like the coffee house, which are usually claimed by historians of the Enlightenment, but were equally sites of Baroque culture. The first Leipzig coffee house opened in 1694; by 1725, there were eight. A guide to the city written that year emphasized the activities and the mixing of people there: the coffee houses 'amuse those from Leipzig and elsewhere, those of high and low estate, and both men and women.' They were also

> famous on account of their elegance, view, and comfort, and the large assemblies that take place in them daily; and especially since all those who go there, whether to read periodicals or history books, or to play various witty and permissible chess, board, ladies' and billiard games, find very pleasant entertainment.[68]

Starting around 1700, the coffee houses and pleasure gardens also hosted performances of secular music by collegia musica, groups of amateurs consisting, in Leipzig, mostly of University students. By the 1710s two collegia were performing regularly. From 1729 one, led by J.S. Bach, performed Friday evenings from 8:00 to 10:00 pm; another, led by Johann Gottlieb Görner, played Thursdays at the same time. Bach's played to audiences of up to 150.[69] The collegia concerts were the first regular, public secular music performances in the city. The fairs generated other cultural activity. Merchants, book dealers, nobles, and many others, interested in the latest in culture as well as in trade goods, descended on the city, providing a large and cosmopolitan audience. The Leipzig Opera, which operated from 1693 to 1720, staged performances only during the fairs. The collegia added one performance a week during the fairs, and individual local performers, itinerant musicians, theatre troupes, and others added to the mix.

The consumption of new goods like coffee and tobacco also increased dramatically in Leipzig and other large German towns. Elites, members of intermediary groups

66 Herbert Stiehl (1984), 'Das Innere der Thomaskirche zur Amtszeit Johann Sebastian Bachs,' = *BzBf*, 3, 19–20.

67 SAL, J.S. Riemer, *Continuatio annalium Lipsiensium Vogelii*, ms., 1714–1771, 82–84.

68 Iccander (1725), 87–88.

69 Wolff (2000), 352–353.

like shopkeepers, and many artisans now studied and mastered a new repertoire of fashionable gestures to accompany that consumption. Women as well as men took and offered snuff, an elaborate and ritualized activity.[70] Men smoked a pipe of tobacco in groups after a meal, holding conversation appropriate to the occasion. Men and women drank tea and coffee from porcelain or stoneware sets, holding their fingers properly. Most middling and wealthy homes owned a set by mid-century for use in gatherings of family and friends. At home and in coffee houses, they followed protocol for maintaining polite conversation.[71] Servants and artisans as well as wealthier inhabitants stayed up-to-date in their wigs, hats, clothing, and shoes.[72]

In pursuing these new modes of consumption and socializing, Leipzigers, like townspeople elsewhere in Europe, were caught between the imperative of appearing galant in a newly cosmopolitan world, and an older, still vigorously preached view that luxury and many secular activities were sins that invited divine punishment. People in Leipzig had enjoyed luxury goods and secular entertainment before the high Baroque, and threats of divine vengeance as a consequence of high living had been a staple of religious rhetoric since antiquity. But the two worlds collided especially severely in the late 17th and early to mid-18th centuries. The rate at which new goods were introduced was fast, and followed hard times abruptly. Scholars have shown for England and France that intense debates (not necessarily religious) accompanied increased luxury consumption and secular sociability.[73] The same was true of the German towns. In Leipzig, Hamburg, Frankfurt, Breslau, and elsewhere, Pietists took the lead in criticizing consumption trends, and an extended debate on the adiaphora took place. Pietists were all the more critical since religious life moved in tandem with secular change. People wore their best clothes to attend church as well as secular festivities. In 1742, councilors discussed how to avoid injuries for women, wearing the popular *Reifrock*, who were falling off the baptismal font because their skirts were too wide.[74] In 1725, Enlightener Johann Christoph Gottsched's journal *The Reasonable Tatleresses* satirized a young woman who took snuff as well as offering it to her male admirers from her pew.[75] The inventory of the Bach household

---

70 Wolfgang Schivelbusch (1992), *Tastes of Paradise: A Social History of Spices, Stimulants, and Intoxicants* (New York: Pantheon; German original, 1980; trans. David Jacobson), 132.

71 Schivelbusch (1992), 167 ff.

72 Beachy (2005), 25 ff.

73 Maxine Berg & Elizabeth Eger (2003), 'The Rise and Fall of the Luxury Debates,' in Berg & Eger, eds, *Luxury in the Eighteenth Century: Debates, Desires and Delectable Goods* (Houndmills: Palgrave), 7–25; John Brewer (1997), *The Pleasures of the Imagination. English Culture in the 18th Century* (New York: Farrar Strauss Giroux).

74 *Kirche zu St. Nicolaus Verordnungen und Nachrichten ... 1740–1783*. SAL, Stift IX.B.4, report of 8 August 1742, 45–45a.

75 Gottsched, ed. (1725–26), *Die vernünfftigen Tadlerinnen* (R [1993], Hildesheim: Olms) vol. I, no. 33, 28 August 1725, 257–264; 264.

in 1750 included tea and coffee sets.[76] The same musicians played in both church and coffee house, and the style of the cantata was deeply influenced by secular styles.

Baroque religious as well as secular culture thus emerged in a context of dynamic social, economic, and cultural change. The new secular venues were soon to be associated with more far-reaching cultural change. For the time being, though, most cultural change developed and was contested in well-established public religious frameworks.

---

[76] *NBR*, 251.

PART I
Congregants' everyday practices

Chapter 1

Experiencing the service

Sunday morning services at Leipzig's two main churches, St. Thomas's and St. Nicholas's, were the central weekly services held in the city. Contemporaries considered these services the most important regular public meetings in the town, and most also thought of them as the core of an individual's religious life. How did congregants in the Baroque era experience these services? When they arrived in church, congregants did not merely listen to the service as it was produced by clerics, musicians, and secular authorities. Rather, they were a lively presence throughout the service, appropriating nearly every element of the liturgy, seating arrangements, and a range of expected behaviors to make the service a vehicle for social interaction and competition. This included attending and participating in the various parts of the service selectively. Examining their activities allows us to gain a more nuanced idea of individuals' religious experience and their relationship to the producers of the service.

Congregants' arrival, departure, seating and various other behaviors are examined first here, their reception of and participation in music second, and the reception of the sermon third. Bach scholars have laid the groundwork for considering congregants' activities by reconstructing the order of the liturgy in Leipzig, using church ordinances, hymnals, and other materials.[1] They have also examined performers and performance practices, instruments, and the layout of the churches. However, musicologists have only very recently taken an interest in the activities of congregants.[2] Historians have likewise neglected them, although they have studied the behavior of audiences of secular music, which in many regards was similar to that of congregants.[3] Finally, historians have recently established that mainstream

---

1 See Robin A. Leaver (1997), 'The mature vocal works and their theological and liturgical context,' in John Butt, ed., *The Cambridge Companion to Bach* (Cambridge: Cambridge University Press), 86–122; Günther Stiller (1984), *Johann Sebastian Bach and Liturgical Life in Leipzig* (St. Louis: Concordia; German original, 1970); Christoph Wolff (2000), *Johann Sebastian Bach: The Learned Musician* (New York: Norton), 255 ff. The 1540 *Agenda* of Duke Heinrich of Saxony, which was reprinted and used through the 1750s, established the basic order of service; see Stiller (1984), 34 ff. Hymns, other music, and the roles of congregants evolved considerably after that.

2 Joseph Herl (2004), *Worship Wars in Early Lutheranism. Choir, Congregation, and Three Centuries of Conflict* (NewYork: Oxford University Press).

3 William Weber (1997), 'Did People Listen in the 18th Century?,' *Early Music*, 25, 678–691; James Johnson (1995), *Listening in Paris. A Cultural History* (Berkeley: University of California Press), Chapter One. See Michel de Certeau (1984), *The Practices of Everyday*

Lutheran sermons were more accessible and relevant to congregants than was long supposed. [4] This study confirms that view, and elaborates on how congregants heard the sermon.

Services at St. Thomas's and St. Nicholas's were the most prominent of several Sunday morning services in Leipzig. By the 1710s around 9000 people of a total population of just under 30,000 headed toward church on Sunday mornings. Each of the main churches seated about 2500 people in pews allotted to individuals, and there were additional seats and standing room for about 500 more.[5] The New Church, opened in 1699, had over 1200 pews; St. Peter's, opened in 1712, about 460; and the University church, opened to the public in 1710, several hundred, with additional standing room in each.[6] Services there were similar to those at the main churches, although no cantatas were performed except on holidays. Most morning congregants at all five churches were burghers and their families. In addition, simpler services were held at the hospital church of St. John and in the chapel in the combined poor house, orphanage, mental asylum, and old age home, St. George's. Attending these were inmates of the houses, some burghers and, at St. John's, laborers and other poor people from the 'suburbs' just outside the city gates. The main churches were the only parish churches; the others did not baptize, marry, or offer funeral services. Finally, junior clerics conducted simple Sunday afternoon services at the main churches, and instrumental music was performed at them only on holidays. Attending these services were some burghers, laborers, and many servants and other non-family members of burgher households.[7] It is possible, although difficult, to

---

Life (Berkeley: University of California Press) on producers, consumers, and appropriation more generally.

4 Monika Hagenmaier (1989), *Predigt und Polizei. Der gesellschaftspolitische Diskurs zwischen Kirche und Obrigkeit in Ulm 1614–1639* (Baden-Baden: Nomos); Sabine Holtz (1993), *Theologie und Alltag. Lehre und Leben in den Predigten der Tübinger Theologen 1550–1750* (Tübingen: Mohr).

5 In 1708, city councilors listed the number of pews in St. Nicholas's: 769 men's *Stühle*, 343 men's *Bänklein*, 804 women's *Stühle* and 528 women's *Bänklein*, 2444 in all, noting additional places where people could sit and stand. These numbers correspond to those that emerge from the records on pew turnover. SAL, Stift VII.B.32, *Acta, Die Einführung des Klingelbeutels in hiesigen Stadt Kirchen und dessen Wiederabschaffung betr.*, 1708 (hereafter: *Klingelbeutel*), 5. St. Thomas's held about the same number of congregants: councilors noted that 'in the two churches of St. Thomas and St. Nicholas there are 6000 souls during the Sunday morning sermon.' Ibid., 16.

6 For the New Church, figures are derived from the church's account books (*Rechnungen*), 1698–1700 (SAL, no loc.). St. Peter's: *Rechnung*, 1712–13 (SAL, no loc.). The University Church: Wilhelm Stieda (no date, *c.* 1930), *Der Neubau der Paulinerkirche in den Jahren 1710–1712. Aktenmässige Forschungen über die Mitarbeit der Leipziger Gewerken* (Leipzig: no press), 80–82. Stieda's figures specify around 300 pews, but there were probably many more.

7 Christian Gerber (1732), *Historie der Kirchen-Ceremonien in Sachsen* (Dresden & Leipzig: Saueressig), 398; SAL, Tit.VIII.52., *Protocoll in Versammlung aller 3 Räthe*, 1682–1704, 25 August 1699, 296v.

reconstruct the practices of morning church-goers at the main churches; but there is very little information on other services.

Morning services and congregants' behaviors in St. Thomas's and St. Nicholas's were most like those in other large trade centers such as Frankfurt and Hamburg. In less wealthy towns church decoration, music, and congregants' attire were more modest. Further, there was great diversity in the specifics of the liturgy and in congregants' social composition and gestures from town to town, and even within one town.[8] Common hymns and prayers varied considerably, for example, and in places where there were Latin schools (such as Leipzig), Latin rather than German was used in chants. In villages, the liturgy and church décor were even simpler, and congregants' social composition less diverse. Contemporaries were aware of the local nature of liturgies. Noting that unfamiliarity with the Leipzig service bred unease among visitors, an anonymous author published a pocket-sized compendium of the order of services, important prayers, hymns, and chants in each Leipzig church in 1710 as an aid to visitors; an earlier one had been published in 1698.[9] In Frankfurt, such a guide had been published as early as 1599.

Congregants' roles in the worship service received little attention from contemporaries. While there are therefore few direct pronouncements on the subject, information can be gleaned from a variety of sources, including individuals' requests for pews, city council discussions regulating the elements of the liturgy, and church inventories and account books. Sermons and music include many indirect clues. Finally, some contemporary clerics discussed congregants' roles in the service in detail. Two stand out for their many references to specific practices. Christian Gerber, a Pietist pastor in a village near Dresden, published numerous works criticizing the lavishness of contemporary religious culture, as well as the inattentiveness of most people. His *History of Church Ceremonies in Saxony* is especially valuable.[10] And Adam Bernd, who was close to some of the Leipzig Pietists but did not fit neatly into any one group, was a highly charismatic preacher in his heyday at St. Peter's in Leipzig from 1712 to 1728. He was defrocked after suggesting in print that Catholics and Calvinists could attain salvation; remaining in Leipzig, he published an autobiography in 1738.[11] While both authors were highly opinionated, and Gerber had a heavy Pietist bias, their observations are corroborated by other sources.

Congregants and the course of the liturgy

Sunday morning services in the main churches started at 7:00 am, preceded by the ringing of bells, which both symbolized the public status of the service and reminded

8 Gerber (1732), 1 ff., 397 ff., passim.

9 (1710), *Leipziger Kirchen-Staat, das ist Deutlicher Unterricht vom Gottes-Dienst in Leipzig* (Leipzig: Groschuff).

10 Gerber (1732).

11 Adam Bernd (1738), *Eigene Lebens-Beschreibung* (Leipzig: Heinsius; R [1973], Munich: Winkler).

the population to congregate. As they did elsewhere in Europe, the wealthy arrived in carriages, which also picked them up after the service.[12] Most of the congregation, though, arrived on foot. In Leipzig, as in most other towns, this entailed a walk of no more than about ten minutes, and often less. References to full churches were frequent and demand for pews are constant throughout the Baroque era. Most seats were occupied during main Sunday services.

Members of a household sat separately during the service: pews were allotted to individuals, not families, and sections of pews were separated by gender. (Contemporaries usually used the term 'pew' to refer to one seat rather than a row of seats, so the term is used here to denote one individual's seat.)[13] Women somewhat outnumbered men: in St. Nicholas's, 56% of pewholders were women, a figure similar to that in St. Thomas's. While people from dozens of occupations were present in each church, they can be divided into three main groups: local elites (merchants, professionals, and city councilors), members of intermediary-status occupations such as notaries and scribes, and artisans (bakers, saddlers, smiths, etc.), each with their families. The elites were greatly over-represented among pewholders, members of intermediate groups somewhat over-represented, and artisans were present roughly in proportion to their percentage of the population.

Social hierarchies among burghers were reflected in the types and locations of pews. There were two main types of pews: regular seats, or *Stände*, and benches, or *Bänklein*, which were attached to the regular pews. The best pews, closest to and with the best view of the pulpit – where one could see and be seen – were occupied mostly by the Leipzig elites. The sections behind the pulpit, farther away from it, or behind pillars, were dominated by artisans. Additionally, starting in the 1660s the very wealthy began enclosing groups of ten to twelve pews around the edges of the churches. Most *Capellen*, or 'chapels,' as they were known, were built around 1700, two and three over another. They were socially and spatially parallel to opera house boxes, although whereas people in boxes were highly visible, those in *Capellen* were invisible if they chose: the windows could be curtained, and are shown with curtains drawn in contemporary illustrations. Many had separate entrances from the outside of the church, and many had libraries and braziers to keep them warm during the winter. Part of the power of holders of *Capellen* was thus to distance themselves from clerics and the liturgy, although occupants often did listen and participate.

Congregants attached an intense territoriality to attending the service. In a request for a pew in 1735, Anna Elisabeth Steinert, wife of a furrier, wrote, 'I have never been so fortunate as to have my own place to cultivate my devotions.'[14] The next year, the shopkeeper Johann Martin claimed that 'such a site and position [a pew]

---

[12] For Leipzig, see Bernd (1738), 209 & 279. For Rome, see Alexander Cowan (1998), *Urban Europe 1500–1700* (New York: Arnold), 134.

[13] *Stand* or *Stuhl* could refer generically to a *Bänklein* as well as to a larger pew.

[14] AdN, *Schriftwechsel Kirchenstühle betr. v. 1701*, ff. (hereafter: *Schriftwechsel*), III. 160./10., September 1735.

is almost indispensable to the comfortable practice of the worship service.'[15] Still, holding a pew remained an ideal for many people: despite ongoing construction of pews, there was always a shortage. The poor, visitors to town, and burghers who had no pew stood, forming a milling crowd at the rear of the church.[16]

* * *

The morning service was divided into three main parts. During the first hour chants, hymns, Scriptural readings, and the cantata were performed. This led to the second, central part of the service: the sermon, which also lasted an hour. Finally, communion was prepared and administered to the accompaniment of further hymns and/or a cantata, the pastor read announcements and prayers, and then said the final blessing. This part of the service lasted between one and two hours, depending on the number of communicants, which was highest on major holidays.[17]

In Leipzig, as around Lutheran Germany, people arrived gradually during the whole first hour of the service. [18] The goal of most congregants was to arrive by the beginning of the sermon, the central feature of the service in the eyes of ordinary inhabitants as well as in Lutheran theology and liturgical theory. Many people also left immediately after the sermon if they were not taking communion.[19] Leipzig's city councilors acknowledged widespread tardiness and early departure without comment in 1708, during discussions about introducing a collection bag: they decided to pass the bag during the sermon since the most people were present then.[20] Musicians also adapted. For example, in his *Complete Music Director* of 1739, Hamburg organist, composer, and music writer Johann Mattheson recommended to organists accompanying the congregation in singing hymns: 'As more arrive, the organ must swell as well; and as the congregation gradually disperses, the stops of the organ should diminish, too.'[21] There do not seem to have been any official efforts in Leipzig to force people to arrive promptly, although ministers such as Christian Gerber lamented the fact that so many people 'think that the service consists only of listening to a sermon.'[22]

Certainly the length of the service, and the fact that it began when it was still dark during the winter, helps explain why many people were not there for all of it. Moreover, the churches were unheated, making a long stay in church difficult to bear during the late fall, winter, and early spring. Bach himself apparently arrived

---

15 *Schriftwechsel*, III. 160./10. 1 January 1736.

16 Johann Michael Kuffs to St. Nicholas's Director, 15 April 1724. *Schriftwechsel*, III, 160./8.

17 Leaver (1997); Stiller (1984), 48 ff.

18 Herl (2004), 48 ff.

19 See Scheibel (1721), 79–80; Gerber (1732), 474.

20 *Klingelbeutel*, 26–29, 35, 38–39, 85.

21 Cited in Enrico Fubini, ed. (1994), *Music and Culture in 18th Century Europe* (Chicago: University of Chicago Press), 303.

22 Gerber (1732), 353.

late to the service sometimes.[23] However, the first hour of the service had a variety of social functions. For example, Gerber ascribed the lateness of the bourgeois to their unwillingness to rise an hour earlier, and to the fact that they spent too much time dressing, grooming themselves, and drinking coffee. All of this suggests that they could make a grander entrance when they did arrive. By contrast, 'common people,' Gerber wrote, insisted on working before going to church.[24]

Beyond the comings and goings of the congregation, the church was the arena for a variety of other activities. The layout of pews encouraged people to observe their fellow congregants and greet their neighbors as they arrived. Men, who occupied most of the balcony pews, could observe the women below. Typically insubordinate groups were responsible for some disturbances: students threw objects from their balcony onto women's pews,[25] and 'youth and other useless riffraff,' in the words of one councilor, retired to spaces behind *Capellen* to make noise.[26] Beginning in 1710, groups of people would leave nearby St. Nicholas's after the sermon in order to attend the University service, which started at 9:00 am. Communion, a time when music was often performed, was the occasion for another type of unrest. Contemporary illustrations show individuals proceeding in orderly rows to the front of the church, but the actual process may have been more disorderly. The Pietist Johann Christian Lange wrote in 1695: 'During services and especially during communion, a public disgrace and abomination is carried on through excessive opulence in dress, *alamodische* styles and manners, fleshly shoving for precedence, and the envy and jealousy awakened by all these.'[27]

Other activities were sanctioned by the city council and clergy themselves. For example, the collection bags passed during the sermon had bells attached and were carried with ceremonial pomp by four artisans dressed in uniform black frocks.[28] People were expected to stand for the reading of Scriptural texts and the final blessing, and to make other motions such as lifting their hands for prayer, which gave opportunity for subtle forms of non-conformity and social preening. Gerber claimed that ministers everywhere in his day had trouble getting all the members of the congregation, especially elites, to stand for the reading of the Epistle and Gospel.[29] Gerber argued that reverence, as shown by willingness to stand, had

---

23 Arnold Schering (1936), *J.S. Bachs Leipziger Kirchenmusik* (Leipzig: Breitkopf und Härtel, R [1968]: Wiesbaden: Breitkopf und Härtel), 149–150, note 3.

24 Gerber (1732), 352–353.

25 An Electoral decree of 1722 forbade this practice. AFS, D 57.

26 A.C. Platz to Leipzig city council, July 1720. SAL, Stift.X.39.a., *Kirchen-Stühle, Capellen und Begräbnis-Stellen betr.*, vol. II, 4^{v}. See also Julius Bernhard von Rohr (1723), *Vollständiges Ober-Sächsisches Kirchen-Recht, in welchem die Materien der geistlichen Rechts-Gelehrsamkeit ohne Einmischung der Päbstlichen Verordnungen, nach Anleitung des Göttlichen und natürlichen Recht ...* (Frankfurt & Leipzig: Martini), 907.

27 Lange to an unnamed 'father confessor,' 1 December 1695, copied into AFS, D 57: 42–77; 55.

28 *Klingelbeutel*, 26 ff.

29 Gerber (1732), 392–397; 396–397.

gradually declined since the early 17th century. In the late 18th century and perhaps earlier, there was another problem: in 1779, Superintendent Johann Gottfried Körner complained of the 'deafening noise caused by the clattering of pews when the women turn around before and after the reading of the Scriptural text for the sermon.'[30]

Numerous holidays and other occasions were marked by an intensification of ceremony and decoration. These included not only Easter, Christmas, and New Year, which were celebrated for three days each, but also the Marian festivals of Purification, Annunciation, and Visitation, which survived the Reformation in many Lutheran areas. Reformation Day and the investiture of a new governing city council were celebrated annually. Liturgically simple Days of Repentance and Prayer, held regularly on three Fridays during the year as well as when disasters such as war, epidemic, or flood threatened, were intended to avert divine wrath. Celebratory services were rung in more elaborately than others, one hour, a half-hour, and just before the service, using the full set of bells and with special bell changes. Colorful hangings, of which each church might have several sets, were brought out. One in St. Nicholas's was 'a decoration (*Schmuck*) in camel-colored atlas bordered on all sides with brightly colored fringes.'[31] Music at celebratory services was also more elaborate than usual, with brass and other instruments being added for festive effect. Adam Bernd wrote in the 1730s that people came to such services 'in masses' and were 'much more attentive than usual.'[32]

The congregants and music

Given such widespread tardiness and the variety of activities and distractions, how closely were people listening to and participating in the music of the service? Chants, hymns, and cantatas will be considered in turn, with a particular focus on the cantata. Each played different roles in the service, establishing specific relationships between musicians, clerics, and congregants, and they resonated in different ways with congregants.

Chants, performed in the first hour of the service, included collects, or sung prayers, and the litany. Through their performance, a relationship involving the pastor, the choir (which led and represented the congregation), and the congregation itself was established in a call-and-response pattern. Thus, after the pastor intoned the collect, the congregation and choir sang 'Amen' in response.[33] After several choir boys knelt before the altar to begin the litany with 'Kyrie,' the rest of the choir and the congregation responded 'Eleison;' the Greek was then followed by the

30 *Klingelbeutel*, 31 October 1779, 86v.

31 The *Schmuck* is described in the inventories at the end of church *Rechnungen*. Sexton Johann David Manitius mentions hanging it up for an investiture service: SAL, loose pages in St. Nicholas's *Rechnung* of 1699–1700: *Tit. Herrn D. Thomae Ittigs Superintendentes Investitur betreffend*, 21 November 1699.

32 Bernd (1738), 35.

33 Gerber (1732), 300.

'The Former Organ in the Church of St. Nicholas in Leipzig,' watercolor by Carl Benjamin Schwartz, c. 1785 (Stadtarchiv Leipzig, RRA 316, reproduced by permission).

German translation in the same pattern: 'Herr Lord Father in Heaven' answered by 'Have mercy on us.'[34] Gerber wrote that since singing was slower than speaking, one could better reflect on the words; also, 'the singing tone awakens the spirit and moves it more than if it were read.'[35]

While chants were relatively short and featured interaction among congregants, clerics, and choir, hymns were a more extended opportunity for the congregation to participate in the service. Hymns resonated with congregants in many ways. Beyond their use in church, they were probably the most pervasive music in early modern society. Beggars often sang them before town gates, on the street, or in front of people's homes in the hope of receiving alms.[36] Hymns were often sung during home worship, and were internalized through repeated singing. Hymnals were important possessions, often given at baptism and confirmation, and they saw much use, with individuals underlining passages and writing margin notes in theirs.[37] In some places, hymnals were kept in a special place above the window of the main room, or *Stube*.[38] Hymns occurred to individuals in moments of stress.[39] Many hymn tunes were also used for 'secular, even drinking and whoring songs,' as one contemporary wrote.[40] Conversely, many hymns used melodies taken from secular songs.

Hymn singing in church was associated with a variety of practices. In all areas, since men and women sat in different sections of pews, their experience of singing was that of singing in a block of other men or women. People sang the 16th century hymns written by Luther and other reformers by heart.[41] Some congregations would substitute one word for another, while in some rural areas only men sang certain hymns.[42] Commentators noted congregants' misunderstanding of some hymns.[43] With some Lutheran hymns two hundred years old by the early 18th century, some words had shifted in meaning, and were eventually changed in some hymnals. The use of hymnals, especially for the singing of more recent hymns, became more

---

34 Ibid., 265.

35 Ibid., 354.

36 Ibid., 259; Bernd (1738), 67.

37 See Patrice Veit (1998), '"Daheime seine Zeit mit singen, mit Beten und Lesen zugebracht:" Über den Umgang mit Kirchenliedern im aussergottesdienstlichen Kontext,' in Renate Steiger, ed., *Die Quellen Johann Sebastian Bachs: Bachs Musik im Gottesdienst* (Heidelberg: Manutius), 329–335.

38 Hans Medick (1996), *Weben und Überleben in Laichingen 1650–1900: Lokalgeschichte als allgemeine Geschichte* (Göttingen: Vandenhoeck & Ruprecht), 493 and passim.

39 Bernd (1738), passim.

40 Gottfried Tilgner (1717), preface to Erdmann Neumeister, *Fünff-Fache Kirchen-Andachten* (Leipzig: Gross), unpag.

41 Gerber (1732), 246.

42 Ibid., 247–249.

43 Ibid., 249; Gottfried Vopelius (1982), *Neu Leipziger Gesangbuch, von den schönsten und besten Liedern verfasset ...* (Leipzig: Klinger), Christoph Klinger, *Zuschrifft* and Georg Moebius, *Vorrede*; Rohr (1723), 806–808.

common after 1700, in Leipzig as in other towns,[44] part of a more general entry of the written word into the practice of the service. In villages, hymnals spread more slowly because of illiteracy.[45] By the 1710s it was common for individuals to bring their own hymnals to church in Leipzig.[46] From 1732 the numbers for hymns were posted on five boards around St. Thomas's; hymn boards were also introduced in other towns around this time.[47] By 1745, a beadle was noting that people with pews beneath the balconies complained that they could not read their 'books' in the winter.[48] Gerber recommended singing from hymnals because it reduced the social experience of (in his view, distractions from) the service: 'One's thoughts remain focused, the eyes do not wander here and there, and there is surely more devotion than when one sings the hymns one knows by heart without a book.'[49]

* * *

Like hymns, the cantata and passion had a long-established place in services.[50] They were performed by student and professional musicians under the cantor's leadership. In the second half of the 17th century, cantatas became more elaborate and longer, with more extensive instrumentation, and they were newly introduced in many smaller towns. The cantata and passion came to incorporate a variety of musical styles and genres: arias, recitatives, choruses, and/or chorales. Chorales were usually simple four-part settings of hymn verses. Many of the hymn harmonizations by Bach in modern hymnals, for example, originated as chorales. Choruses, by contrast, involved complex interplay among vocal parts. Cantata texts published by poet and minister Erdmann Neumeister, a vocal Orthodox opponent of Pietists, beginning in 1700 gave new importance to alternating madrigalian (free-verse) recitatives and da capo arias based on operatic song form. Arias had been used previously in cantatas, but Neumeister systematized their alternation with recitatives, and placed new emphasis on the da capo aria. Indeed, Neumeister specifically likened this type of cantata to the opera. These modern cantata texts were set by scores of composers, with the arias and recitatives featuring highly ornamented melodies and sometimes virtuosic instrumental solos. Some cantatas also included purely instrumental

44 Herl (2004), 104 ff.

45 Gerber (1732), 246. See also Karl Dienst (1996), '"Bringe Deine Bibel und Dein Gesangbuch mit zur Kirche …" Vom "Gesangbuch im Kopf" zum Gesangbuch in der Hand,' *Jahrbuch der Hessischen kirchengeschichtlichen Vereinigung*, 47, 67–74.

46 Bernd (1738), 302. Numerous hymnals were sold in Leipzig by the 1710s. SAL, Tit. VII.B.34.a., *Acta, das in der Peterskirche gebrauchte Gesangbuch betr.*, 1717–18.

47 Stiehl (1984), 35; Herl (2004), 162–163.

48 Stiehl (1984), 37.

49 Gerber (1732), 246.

50 See Friedhelm Krummacher (2001), 'The German Cantata to 1800' and Robin A. Leaver and Robert Marshall (2001), 'Chorale Settings,' both in Stanley Sadie, ed., *The New Grove Dictionary of Music and Musicians*, second edition, vol. 5 (New York: Macmillan), 21–32 and 747–763.

movements. Neumeister, Barthold Heinrich Brockes, and others pioneered a similar passion format in the 1710s which likewise soon became popular. Music that now seems archetypally traditional was therefore actually associated with innovation and secular music, in many eyes dubious qualities for the religious sphere.

In Leipzig, the cantors directed the cantata on alternating Sundays in the main churches. Passions were performed at Good Friday services. 17th century cantors such as Sebastian Knüpfer and Johann Schelle had stood at the forefront of central German cantata composition in an older style. Bach's predecessor Johann Kuhnau, cantor from 1701 to 1722, made significant strides in adopting the new cantata style, although somewhat reluctantly. This style was more fully embraced by Georg Philipp Telemann, then a law student at the University of Leipzig. In 1701 the council commissioned him to compose cantatas for performance every two weeks in St. Thomas's in order to impress visitors.[51] Telemann was appointed organist and music director at the New Church in 1704. He left Leipzig in 1705, but his successors continued to innovate at the New Church. For example, the first fully contrapuntal, instrumentally-accompanied, figural, Lenten Passion in Leipzig was performed there in 1717. This was probably Telemann's Brockes Passion.[52] Passion performances were introduced to the main churches in 1721; Bach's passions were thus composed for a newly established event. With Bach's arrival in Leipzig in 1723, Neumeister-influenced cantata and passion style made its way more fully into services at St. Thomas's and St. Nicholas's. Bach himself was a proponent of this style. His secular and sacred works were stylistically similar, and Bach often directly parodied his own work, arranging and adapting secular pieces for sacred use and vice versa. Another modern secular genre, French court dance, also influenced Bach and other composers, and Bach included numerous (untitled) dance movements in his cantatas.[53]

The innovative aspects of cantata style were familiar to congregants from their visits to the Leipzig Opera, which operated from 1693 until 1720, to coffee houses and gardens, dances, and other secular occasions. French dance was popular in Leipzig,[54] and some congregants would have recognized the rhythms upon which some cantata sections were based. It is possible that some congregants saw the cantata and, more generally, church services as a substitute for the opera after 1720.[55] This would have been especially likely during the fairs, when opera was performed. Without the opera as a meeting place and cultural venue, the churches became more important as places to mingle and hear music.

---

51 Ulrich Siegele (1997), 'Bach and the domestic politics of Electoral Saxony,' in Butt, ed. (1997), 17–34; 32–33.

52 Glöckner (1990), 79. It was performed in either 1717 or 1718.

53 Meredith Little & Natalie Jenne (2001), *Dance and the Music of J.S. Bach*, expanded edition (Bloomington: University of Indiana Press).

54 Ibid., 3 ff.

55 Thanks to Matthew Dirst for this suggestion.

Not all people approved of the carrying over of secular style into the church. Pietists were especially critical. For example, Gerber wrote that 'it often sounds so worldly and gay that such music would be more suitable on a dance floor or in an opera than in a church service.'[56] Others also had reservations. Thus, in his *Coincidental Thoughts on Church Music* of 1721, a defense of modern church music, which condemned Pietist and other 'enemies of music' and specifically championed Neumeister, Gottfried Ephraim Scheibel argued that dance rhythms had no place in church music, and that lengthy, purely instrumental preludes and other pieces, 'music of the instrumentalists,' should be limited.[57] Some clerics and parishioners complained their active participation was being reduced at important times of the service, since a cantata might replace congregational hymns.[58] And the anonymous author of the Leipzig liturgical and prayer compendium of 1710 recommended the reading of specific prayers 'while there is mere preambling on the organ, or lengthy music being performed (since some people do not particularly value figural and often operatic music).' Such reading of prayers, the author claimed, was a better use of time than 'useless chatter.'[59]

However, there are more indications that the 18th century style was welcomed by the public. Gerber himself wrote that 'people are so accustomed to such things that they think the service cannot exist without [organ and instrumental music], or that it would suffer greatly if they were left out.'[60] People flocked especially to hear the performances of passions. And the city council patronized music partly in order to impress visitors.

* * *

How attentively did congregants listen to Bach, Kuhnau, Telemann, and other composers? To what degree did they participate? How much of the often complex music and its theological meaning did they understand? In addressing these questions, it is important to consider the cantata's place in the order of the service, contemporary standards of polite listening, the use of librettos, and the overlap between cantatas and other genres.

Most cantatas were performed just before the sermon. In the case of relatively infrequent two-part cantatas, the second part was performed during communion. Thus, people were coming and going specifically while the cantata was being performed. Given this, and that some people were conversing with their neighbors, there was a substantial level of background noise throughout performances. Further, while it

---

56 Gerber (1732), 283.

57 Scheibel (1721), *Zufällige Gedancken von der Kirchen-Music, Wie Sie heutiges Tages beschaffen ist* (Frankfurt & Leipzig: self-published, R [2002] Stuttgart: Cornetto), 26, 74, 41, 50–51. See also Chapter Five.

58 Herl (2004), 107 ff.

59 (1710), *Leipziger Kirchen-Staat*, unpag. See also Chapter Five.

60 Gerber (1732), 279.

seems that sound projected well from the musicians' balconies, and the acoustics of the churches were well suited for music to be heard,[61] vocal and instrumental forces were quite small. The bulk of most cantatas for regular Sundays featured only one solo voice at a time. The number of instruments playing was also small, although vocal and instrumental forces were increased on holidays and other special occasions.[62]

Measured by present-day standards of punctuality and silence during Protestant services, and of regulated applause during classical-music concerts, Bach, his predecessors, and their musicians received less than perfect attention. However, these standards developed after 1750, and to judge Baroque audiences by modern classical music standards is to misunderstand them. In secular concerts and opera houses throughout Europe, careful listening was not equated with silence. It was common practice for audiences to arrive late, wander, and converse during performances. In secular performances during the 18th century, approval might be expressed by applauding individual arias or concert movements, and even by applause during a performance.[63] Finally, while many congregants listened to the hour-long sermon carefully, even that was accompanied by the passing of jingling collection bags. The environment would have allowed for those who wanted to listen closely to do so, while for others the music would have been peripheral. William Weber has suggested the term 'miscellany' to describe audiences' and producers' expectation that a given occasion would fill a variety of functions.[64] Also at work was a Baroque aesthetic which involved a layering of visual, aural, and social experiences. This layering was intended to intensify the effect of a given occasion on its audience.

Despite the presence of what we see as distractions, there are numerous signs that many congregants did pay attention to the music, and also that many of them were present for much of the service. In 1709–10, Johann Kuhnau introduced the practice of compiling and selling librettos for several Sundays' performances of cantatas to Leipzig. Librettos were available in bookstores and in some cases at the church door. They were also sold in other large cities such as Frankfurt and Hamburg, and in smaller towns like Delitzsch, a town of 4000 near Leipzig. Librettos were several pages long and included the text of a piece, specifying sections such as aria, recitative, and chorale and indicating any scriptural text. Unlike printed sermons of the day, cantata librettos in Leipzig did not name the composer or librettist, although those in Hamburg gave the composer's last name.[65] Some librettos for Bach's cantatas, and

---

61 See Armin Schneiderheinze (1987), 'Zu den aufführungspraktischen Bedingungen in der Thomaskirche zur Amtszeit Bachs,' *BzBf*, 6, 82–91.

62 Forces were small regardless of one's position on the debate about Bach's vocal forces.

63 Weber (1997); Johnson (1995), Chapter One; Stephen Wigler (1997), 'When the Moment is Right,' Baltimore *Sun*, 27 January, E1.

64 E-mail message of 22 March 2000.

65 See libretto reproductions for a passion by Telemann and a Magnificat by Mattheson, in Telemann (2001), 'Seliges Erwägen: Passionsoratorium in Neun Betrachtungen,' ed. Ute Poetzsch, *Musikalische Werke*, vol. 33, (Kassel: Bärenreiter), introduction, xlvii and Steffen

Telemann's in Hamburg, printed only the first line of chorales that were based on well-known hymns.[66] This indicates that the librettos were intended as a guide to new and unfamiliar lyrics, and not to texts known to congregants, or for which they had hymnals. As Delitzsch cantor and Leipzig University graduate Christoph Gottlieb Fröber wrote in the 1730s in the introduction to a libretto cycle, 'without reading, the musical texts can seldom be fully understood, because of the accompaniment of the intruments, and thus little fruitful and edifying effect is attained.'[67] Librettos sold well. Sales in Hamburg were lucrative enough to ignite a fight over printing rights between Telemann and a Hamburg printer that lasted from 1722 to the 1750s.[68]

While much of a cantata or passion text was new, the religious messages it expressed, its specific language, and its music overlapped in many ways with other parts of the service and with forms of music that people heard outside it. This overlapping made for a high degree of accessibility. The language of the text was the Scriptural language of shepherd and sheep, pasture, of salvation, death, heaven, the soul, trial, and faith. Specifically, cantatas were usually a direct commentary on the New Testament texts of the day; the epistle and gospel selections were read from the lectern shortly before the performance of the cantata. Passions retold the story of the last days of Christ. Parts of many texts shifted the third person and past tense of Scripture to the first person and present tense, bringing the subject into the listener's immediate frame of reference.[69]

The majority of Bach's Leipzig cantatas, and many of those of New Church composers, featured chorales that were popular hymns, often dating from the Reformation era.[70] Chorales would have brought the meaning of the whole cantata into focus for congregants. Indeed, they were especially suitable for a large town like Leipzig, with literate inhabitants who had recently started to bring their hymnals to church. Bach specifically developed a cantata format soon after his arrival in Leipzig that featured a concluding chorale, preceded by a series of arias and recitatives and

---

Voss (2005), 'Did Bach Perform Sacred Music by Johann Mattheson in Leipzig?,' *Bach Notes*, 3, 1–5; 2.

66 See Robin A. Leaver (1982), *Music as Preaching: Bach, Passions and Music in Worship* (Oxford: Latimer House); Martin Petzoldt (1993), *'Texte zur Leipziger Kirchen-Musik.' Zum Verständnis der Kantatentexte Johann Sebastian Bachs* (Wiesbaden: Breitkopf & Härtel); Martin Petzoldt (2000), ed. and intro, *Texthefte zur Kirchenmusik aus Bachs Leipziger Zeit. Die sieben erhaltenen Drucke der Jahre 1724–1749 in faksimilierter* Wiedergabe (Stuttgart: Carus); Hans Hörner (1933), *Gg Ph. Telemanns Passionsmusiken. Ein Beitrag zur Geschichte der Passionsmusik in Hamburg* (Borna & Leipzig: Noske), 112.

67 Winfried Hoffmann (1982), 'Leipzigs Wirkungen auf den Delitzscher Kantor Christoph Gottlieb Fröber,' *BzBf*, 1, 54–73.

68 Georg Philipp Telemann (1972), *Briefwechsel*, ed. Hans Grosse & Hans Rudolf Jung (Leipzig: VEB Deutscher Verlag für Musik), 28 ff.

69 Ulrich Meyer (1998), 'Bachs Kantatentexte im gottesdienstlichen Kontext,' in Steiger, ed. (1998), 371–388.

70 See Andreas Glöckner (1990), *Die Musikpflege an der Leipziger Neukirche zur Zeit Johann Sebastian Bachs*, = *BzBf*, 8. See also Chapter Eight.

sometimes an introductory chorale or chorus. In the case of the chorale cantatas composed mostly in 1724–25, the concluding chorale was the last verse of a hymn, and earlier movements were paraphrases of the earlier verses. Similarly, passion chorales by Bach and many of his contemporaries were settings of hymn verses which punctuated series of arias and recitatives.

Composers also made use of a variety of other techniques to intensify the audience's appreciation and understanding of the text. Brass instruments, especially the horn and trumpet, which symbolized divine and also earthly rulers, were usually reserved for festive occasions such as those celebrating the installation of a new sitting city council. The trumpet could also stand for the last judgement.[71] Such symbolism was easily accessible to listeners. The choice of major or minor key, ascending or descending melodic line, the return of a specific motive, and word painting could also be easily understood as underscoring a particular mood, fate, or word. Other, more esoteric, symbolism involving form, harmony and word-play, for which Bach is especially well known, would have been appreciated by only a few members of the congregation.

* * *

The question whether Bach's congregants sang cantata chorales has been raised from time to time, but is still considered an open one, with the majority of scholars thinking that congregants did not.[72] Much further study is needed to clarify the issue, and it is likely that a picture reflective of Baroque performance practices generally will emerge: practices varied from one area and time to another. Also, congregants may have sung some chorales but not others within one cantata or passion. Some preliminary observations are offered here.

Some evidence points to congregants singing with chorales, although it is to a degree ambiguous. Two Saxon contemporaries who were well aquainted with contemporary Saxon church music referred to the practice. In his *Coincidental Thoughts*, Gottfried Ephraim Scheibel, who had studied theology in Leipzig beginning in 1715 and referred to Leipzig several times in the text, wrote: 'Chorales are there so that the congregation can sing along, and correspondingly their melody is set without ornamentation.'[73] The context here was Scheibel's critique of cantata texts published by the Halle author Rambach. The chorales Rambach used, wrote Scheibel, were hymns that were not well known outside Halle, which kept congregants from fully participating. Here as elsewhere, Scheibel did not limit his

71 Ludwig Prautzsch (1998), 'Die Symbolische Bedeutung der Blechblasinstrumente in den Kantaten Johann Sebastian Bachs,' in Steiger, ed. (1998), 211–225.

72 Charles Terry (1933) posited that they did: *The Music of Bach: An Introduction* (London: Oxford University Press), 66. Robin A. Leaver (1982) argued that they did not, 15–17.

73 *Denn die Chorale sind desswegen da, dass die Gemeine mit singen kann, gestalltsam sie auch desswegen in ihrer Melodie ohne Zierath gemusiciret werden.* Scheibel (1721), 76.

observations to any one place or type of cantata. The implication is that people had the option of singing chorales. Scheibel also referred a passion performance that he had attended, apparently of a simpler type of 'chorale' passion than the style used by Bach. He noted: 'I was amazed at how attentively people listened and how devoutly they sang along.'[74] Gerber also referred to congregations singing passion chorales: 'Gradually [after the 1680s] the Passion story, which had formerly been sung simply and piously, began to be performed most elaborately with many instruments, with an occasional verse from a passion hymn, to which the entire congregation sings, after which all the instruments would again start in.' Gerber continued with a description of the first performance of this elaborate type of passion 'in an elegant city' where congregants in one *Capelle* 'sang the first passion hymn with great devotion from their books' [probably hymnals], only to be dismayed by an onslaught of 'theatrical music' immediately following the chorale.[75] Gerber too could have been referring to a variety of types of passion, but he may have been referring to the first performance of a figural passion in Leipzig, possibly Telemann's Brockes Passion, which includes five chorales.[76]

Some indirect evidence also points to the possibility of congregational singing of chorales in Leipzig. The placement of most of Bach's cantata chorales at the end of the cantata, just before the sermon, means that congregants were mostly seated, with hymnals in hand. They were therefore well positioned to follow along, and perhaps to sing. The fact that only the first line of a chorale was printed in many Leipzig and Hamburg librettos indicates that congregations at least opened their hymnals, unless they knew the entire hymn by heart. Given the pervasiveness of active hymn singing, many would have had difficulty remaining silent. The concluding chorale of the cantata Kuhnau composed and directed to celebrate the new altar in St. Thomas's on 25 December 1721, 'Alleluia, praise be to God we all sing from the bottom of our hearts,'[77] shows that concluding chorales were known in the main churches shortly before Bach's arrival, even if Kuhnau used them relatively little. And although there were ordinances and other sources that prohibited congregants singing with some parts of the liturgy, there do not seem to have been any prohibitions on congregational singing of the cantata chorale.[78]

---

74 Scheibel wrote that 'musical text was just the Suffering of Christ from a Gospel, with numerous chorales or verses from hymns and two or three arias interspersed.' Scheibel (1721), 30. See also Chapter Eight.

75 Gerber (1732), 283–284.

76 Glöckner (1990), 79; Carsten Lange (2000), 'Zur Aufführung von Telemanns Brockes-Passionsoratorium in Frankfurt am Main,' in Peter Cahn, ed., *Telemann in Frankfurt. Bericht über das Symposium Frankfurt am Main, 26./27. April 1996* (New York: Schott), 142–162; 161, note 58.

77 SAL, J.S. Riemer, *Continuatio annalium Lipsiensium Vogelii*, ms., 1714–1771, 84.

78 August Pfeiffer (1693), *Acht Catechismus-Predigten Von der Besserung des heutigen Christenthums …* (Lübeck: Krüger), 158–159; Paul Graff (1937), *Geschichte der Auflösung der alten gottesdienstlichen Formen in der evangelischen Kirche Deutschlands*, vol. I (Göttingen: Vandenhoeck & Ruprecht), 191. Thanks to Robin A. Leaver for these references.

Also, it is well established that congregations in Hamburg sang chorales in both passions and cantatas. Apart from references in librettos and other indications,[79] a dispute of 1764 demonstrates the practice. After 1750, Telemann altered some texts because the originals were perceived as too old-fashioned.[80] On one occasion cleric Melchior Goeze complained of the 'very unfortunate improvement of a new poet,' Klopstock, to an original hymn text by Luther that Telemann had incorporated in a cantata. He asserted that, when the altered verses had been used, 'the congregation became very confused when the first line and the melody were begun on the choir [balcony], and something completely different was sung from what it was used to. The congregation therefore, and very unwillingly, was forced to fall silent in the midst of singing.'[81] Telemann argued in return that he had already used this text five years previously, when the verses had been 'sung with edification by the congregations in all the main churches during the cantata.' Despite their different positions, both men assumed that congregants sang the chorale. It is also interesting to note that Goeze referred to the choir singing the first line of a chorale.

Some features of Bach's chorales might seem to a modern ear to have interfered with congregants' participation, but are less problematic when seen in context. Relatively few include brief instrumental interludes between phrases, which could potentially have thrown congregants off. But congregants were familiar with organ interludes, which were commonly inserted between phrases or lines of regular hymns.[82] The complex and varied harmonization of the chorales could also have been potentially confusing. But the melody, which congregants knew, was clearly audible in the soprano voice.[83]

Two other features, though, seem to indicate that congregations were not intended to sing all of Bach's chorales. In some cases different chorales within one passion use slightly different forms of the melody,[84] or the chorale melody is a variant of that in common hymnals. Also, while some of Bach's chorales rise only to a *d''* or *e''*, others are set quite high, rising to a *g''* or even an *a''*, beyond the range of most lay people. (Although it should be noted that Telemann's chorales in three of his best-known Hamburg passions, at least one of which was performed in Leipzig, also often rise to a *g''*, although rarely an *a''*.[85]) Most of Bach's Leipzig cantatas seem to have

---

79 Hörner (1933), 112, 115–116.

80 Ibid., 115.

81 Telemann to Hamburg council, 16 June 1764, and Goeze to Hamburg mayor, 14 June 1764, in Telemann (1972), 46 & 60–61.

82 Herl (2004), 138 ff.

83 Some scholars have argued that Bach shifted many chorales from an older (rhythmic) to a more modern (isometric) style. But hymnals in Leipzig and elsewhere published by the 1680s, including Vopelius's Leipzig hymnal, had already been making this shift. Leaver (1982), 16–17. See Johann Sebastian Bach (1954 ff.), *Neue Ausgabe sämtlicher Werke*, Serie I: Kantaten, Alfred Dürr, Werner Neumann et al., eds (Kassel: Bärenreiter).

84 Leaver (1982), 15–16.

85 Telemann (2001); Telemann (1964), performed in Leipzig (preface, Ute Poetzsch, xvi); 'Lukaspassion 1728,' ed. Hans Hörner & Martin Ruhnke, *Musikalische Werke*, vol.

been written so that the vocal parts were pitched a half tone lower than in modern usage (at A = 415 rather than A = 440),[86] so that his *g″*, for example, corresponds to a modern *f″* sharp. This is still higher than the *e″* at A = 440 (or *e′*, the octave lower, which men would sing) with which most modern lay people are comfortable.

Congregants and the sermon

The sermon was the focal point of the service in liturgical theory, placement in the service, and in the perception of congregants. Indeed, contemporaries often referred to the entire service as 'the sermon.' How attentively did congregants listen? Commonplace pronouncements suggest that the level of attentiveness was low. Complaints concerning people falling asleep are so numerous for all of Europe that they must reflect actual practice. Given the one-hour length of the sermon, it is not surprising that some people nodded off. Clerics also complained that their congregations did not absorb the meaning of sermons. However, a variety of evidence indicates that sermons were listened to, although often not as clerics intended them to be.

Pewholders, who made up most of the listeners to a given sermon, attached much importance to being able to see and hear the preacher. They, like the secular authorities, described and unofficially ranked sections of pews according to their position vis-à-vis the pulpit: opposite, in front of, or behind it. Pews were also described according to the view they gave of the preacher. The best pews offered clear sight and sound lines; pews far from the pulpit, behind a column, or at the rear of the church were considered much less desirable. Individuals regularly asked to exchange one pew for another because they could not see or hear the preacher. If people could not hear the sermon from a pew some, at least, did not think it worthwhile to hold it.[87]

The authorities recognized the importance of clear sight and hearing to pewholders. As part of a reform of Saxon pew laws in 1720, councilors of the Upper Consistory in Dresden noted critically that throughout Saxony, *Capellen* were built in such a way that 'many listeners are hindered in hearing the divine Word and in their *Prospect* of the pulpit and altar.' They called for construction which would not diminish pewholders' view or hearing.[88] The consistories even upheld the rights of

---

15, (Kassel: Bärenreiter); Telemann (1996), 'Johannespassion 1745 "Ein Lämmlein Geht und Trägt die Schuld",' ed. Wolfgang Hirschmann, *Musikalische Werke*, vol. 29 (Kassel: Bärenreiter). Of the ten chorales in 'Seliges Erwägen,' five rise to an *f″* and two to a *g″*. Of the nine chorales in the 'Lukaspassion,' four rise to a *g″* and one to an *a″*. Of the seven in the 'Johannespassion,' one rises to an *f″*, one to an *f♯″*, and two to a *g″*. The others rise to a *d″* or *e″*.

[86] Bruce Haynes (2002), *A History of Performing Pitch. The Story of 'A'* (Lanham, MD: Scarecrow), 239.

[87] Hans George Lampe to Director, *Schriftwechsel*, III.160.1., 5 December 1701; Maria Dorothea Salzer to Director, ibid., III.160.10., 16 June 1735.

[88] SHStADD, Loc. 4571, *Die vom Obern Consistorio projectirte neue Kirchenstuhlordnung*, Upper Consistory to August, 19 January 1720, 29^{v}–30.

students without their own pews. A dispute broke out in 1697 and 1698 when the Leipzig city council allowed six seats in the first row of the student balcony in St. Thomas's to be partitioned off and locked, and allotted to University professors and their sons. Students responded by breaking off the door, lock, and rear partition, which blocked their view, and threatening to disrupt the service if they were reinstalled. The Leipzig and Upper Consistories upheld the students' demands over the protests of the council.[89]

By contrast, music and musicians were not mentioned in requests for pews. This could simply mean that congregants did not think it was important to see the musicians, and that music projected reasonably well from the balconies. Also, while librettos made it easy to follow cantatas, there was no text for the sermon. Or perhaps it did not seem as important to follow music as it did to follow the sermon. Further, petitioners and the clerks who often wrote their requests were oriented to the interests of the addressees, the church directors, who were also city councilors. Pietist councilors in particular would have frowned on requests that emphasized the cantata.[90]

Some people described sermons and their impact in great detail. Many of them were associated in some way with Pietism, but were not necessarily Pietists themselves. For example, Maria Glafey wrote in 1724 that she had made Pietist leader August Hermann Francke's last Leipzig sermon of 1690 'the firm foundation of my heart.' The message of the sermon had been, 'God sees, God hears, God punishes.'[91] Aged fifty-two in 1724, Glafey would have been about eighteen at the time of the sermon. She was rooming with a Pietist city councilor in 1690, but she was not mentioned during the investigation into the collegia, or later in Pietists' letters. Adam Bernd described the strong impact of his sermons on numerous listeners, albeit likely with some exaggeration.[92] He also referred to himself and others discussing sermons during Sunday afternoon walks outside the town walls, apparently a common practice. Finally, not surprisingly, Leipzig Pietists often mentioned the powerful effect that sermons had on them when they wrote to Francke.

The Leipzig city council and other secular authorities around Germany tried to appoint clerics who were good public speakers. The ability to preach well, including having a pleasant voice and suitable regional accent, was a central criterion for appointment. In correspondence documenting appointment processes, councilors recommended pastoral candidates for being 'skilled in preaching,' of having 'handsome' or 'marvelous' skills in preaching.[93] Candidates who were criticized for poor

---

89 SAL, Stift. IX.A.1.a., *Akta, einige Bänke in der Thomaskirche, welche den Studenten gehören sollen ....*

90 Thanks to Christoph Wolff for this idea.

91 Glafey wrote from the old age section of St. George's. SAL, Stift III.A.17., *Acta, Die Untersuchung des Zucht-und Waysenhausses zu St. George alhier betr.*, 1724, 54–57^{v}.

92 Bernd (1738), 285 and passim.

93 SHStADD, Loc. 4687, *Ersetzung derer Ober- und Hoff-Prediger*, 1659–1696, 14 September 1664, 21–24; ibid., 30 November 1680, 74^{v}; ibid., 74; SHStADD, Loc. 7430, *Bestellung derer Superintendenten-Stellen* ... 1681–1704, 19 August 1692, 142. From searches for

delivery, as was one whose 'pronunciation while preaching [is not good], since, as one says, he is rumored to speak somewhat through his nose,'[94] were not appointed.

Sermons themselves had several properties that encouraged the listening public to pay attention. Their content and delivery made them accessible to audiences, their messages overlapped with and were relevant to parishioners' experiences outside the church, and in addition to their pastoral message, they often carried information about religious and political conflict. Clerics wanted to communicate their specific messages; they also wanted to suit popular taste and maintain their own power and popularity against that of the secular authorities and other clerics.

Traditional historical literature on Orthodox Lutheran sermons, which relied on harsh Pietist critique of mainstream practices, emphasized Orthodox preachers' excessive use of Latin, Greek, and Hebrew quotations, obscure references and allusions, and discussions of abstract theological isues.[95] Surely there were some inaccessible preachers. However, recent work has disputed the blanket criticism of the older view,[96] and an examination of sermons held in Leipzig supports the revision. Clerics inserted many of the learned references found in printed sermons when they published them. Sermons as delivered in church were made accessible to parishioners in several ways. They were structured according to a relatively simple scheme that parishioners heard each time they attended church. In separate sections, the week's Scriptural text was read, its meaning was explained, its theological significance and implications for daily life were detailed, means and impediments to fulfilling the dictates of the text were outlined, and finally the congregation was offered comfort on the subject addressed.[97] The liturgical year itself followed easily recognizable patterns. For example, the seasons of Advent and Lent led up to the major holidays of Christmas and Easter. Sermons were held to mark other occasions such as the fall harvest.

Further, a set number of dogmatic themes and Scriptural allegories common to all Christian denominations formed the basis of many sermons. These themes included grace and salvation, sin, repentance, and the sacraments.[98] Especially common among the positive allegories was that of the shepherd and his flock, which illustrated the roles of the preacher and his congregation and related the preacher's activities to those of Jesus. Also popular was the allegory of the vintner tending his vineyards. In an agrarian society, such allegories would have resonated with congregants. It was a rare Leipziger who had never travelled beyond the town walls, and vineyards as well as sheep were common sights in Saxony. As negative examples, the fates of Old

---

new Dresden court chaplains and Saxon Superintendents. For examples from Leipzig, see Chapter 3.

94 SHStADD, Loc. 4687, *Ersezung derer Ober- und Hof-Prediger-Stellen betr.*, 1706–37, 31 October 1707, 26–26^{v}.

95 See Hagenmaier (1989) and Holtz (1993), introductions and passim.

96 See Holtz (1993) and Hagenmaier (1989), passim.

97 In most printed sermons the beginnings of these sections were marked in the margins.

98 See Holtz (1993), 71 ff.

Testament cities such as Jerusalem and Babel were invoked to warn congregations of the consequences of sinful behavior. Clerics willingly took upon themselves the role of Jeremiah and other prophets and often compared Leipzig to these cities and others, including Jericho.

Preachers seem to have taken pains to explain the theological content of their sermons in simple terms, with everyday, commonsense illustrations. One example is a sermon which Orthodox Leipzig Superintendent Thomas Ittig held in May 1700 and was ordered to submit as delivered. In it, Ittig explained the Orthodox position on the complex but central issue of attaining salvation, then under debate, by applying the metaphor of the shepherd and his sheep: the good shepherd, Jesus, wants to care for all of his sheep, not only a few. To this end, he leads them all to green pastures and fresh water.[99]

Clerics' attempts to relate their sermons to everyday life could backfire: clerics complained that congregants often used the material in sermons as sources of secular anecdotes or even jokes. Johann Caspar Schade, a leader of the collegia pietatis in Leipzig and later pastor in Berlin, articulated concerns shared by non-Pietist as well as Pietist clerics. He claimed in 1694 that

> many people have the God-given ability to understand the sermon, but they try only to grasp its worldly meaning. When they remember enough of it afterwards to quote from it, they think it is enough to scold those who are not able to understand it. They do not allow the sermon to effect an inner change in them.[100]

However, Schade's statement itself, like similar complaints by Orthodox clerics, actually reveals that congregants did listen to sermons: people were able to 'quote from' them.

How an individual heard a sermon depended on his or her personality, social status, and gender. Clerics often did construct elegantly allusive sermons, not least in order to impress their elite congregants. They distinguished between elaborate oratorical form and a simpler style which aimed for comprehension by poorer congregants.[101] Most artisans and most women would not have completely appreciated a cleric in full oratorical flight. However, for educated male parishioners, who were about a quarter of morning worshippers in Leipzig's main churches,[102] sermons overlapped with familiar secular forms of oratory. Like other speeches, sermons were composed according to the rules of Latin rhetoric, and the preacher 'assumed the role of public orator par excellence.'[103] As elsewhere in Europe, members of the elites in Leipzig

---

99 SHStADD, Loc. 1791, *Acta, Die theologischen Streitigkeiten, des Termini peremptorii betr.*, 1700, 67 ff. See also Holtz (1993) and Hagenmeier (1989).

100 Schade (1694), *Wie die Predigten Göttliches Wortes anzuhören ... In dreyen darüber gehaltenen Predigten ...* (Berlin: Völcker), 19. See also Hagenmaier (1989), 67 ff.

101 Bernd (1738), 280.

102 31% of the pews in St. Nicholas's were men's *Stände*.

103 Peter Bayley (1980), *French Pulpit Oratory 1598–1650. A Study in Themes and Styles, with a Descriptive Catalogue of Printed Texts* (New York: Cambridge University Press), 38.

judged sermons much as they judged secular public speeches, rating them according to delivery and literary polish.[104] Every man with some Latin education, and some women, could analyse a sermon for its formal compositional qualities. Authorities who appointed clerics, good examples of elite male congregants, were able to offer detailed criticism of the trial sermons of candidates for pastoral office. For example, in 1722 jurist Johann Michael Wislau reported on a candidate for Dresden Senior Court Chaplain, court chaplain Meusch of Hanau in southwest Germany:

> His delivery is thorough and clear, the elocution pleasant, the meditations edifying ... his pronunciation is clear, his accent also pleasant, although in some words one notices a difference from the Upper Saxon dialect, for example in the letters S and St, which he hisses in the manner of the Swiss ...[105]

Wislau attached detailed outlines of the two sermons he had heard Meusch preach, with the sections *usus, applicatio, exordium* etc. neatly marked in the margins.[106]

Congregants were given further incentive to listen because sermons might include important information about political, ecclesiastical, and other issues. Clerics regularly used the pulpit to discuss epidemics, extreme weather, and other events. Using a system of Scripturally-based codes, they might also make thinly veiled attacks on the policies of the secular authorities. As elsewhere in Europe, clerics profiled themselves as the protectors of ordinary peoples' interests, which they sometimes claimed were endangered by the greed and corruption of secular government. Clerics might also admonish their listeners, and congregants were sensitive to this. In 1722 Adam Bernd was interrogated because a merchant's wife had been offended by his attack on women who were cruel to their servants, against the teachings of Paul.[107]

Clerics also used the pulpit to attack their clerical colleagues. Until the late 1680s, such attacks were usually aimed at Catholics and Calvinists. Beginning in 1688–89, the Pietist-Orthodox controversy was broadcast to the public from pulpits around Germany, and with great intensity in Leipzig. Clerics used Scriptural code to attack their opponents, with Pietists referring to the Orthodox as Pharisees, and Orthodox clerics expounding on the dangers of false prophets. The codes allowed clerics to make attacks that were clear to all listeners without using actual names or referring specifically to the debate, which was officially banned from the pulpit and press in 1690. By the early 18th century some clerics were attacking Enlightenment ideas.

Not least, the sermon resonated with congregants because it complemented or built on other parts of the service, a good example of how early modern printed and

---

[104] See Veit Ludwig von Seckendorff (1691), 'Discurs an statt einer Vorrede ...,' in idem, *Teutsche Reden ... 1660–1685* (Leipzig: Gleditsch), 29–68.

[105] SHStADD, Loc. 4687, *Ersezung derer Ober- und Hof-Prediger-Stellen betr. ab anno 1706–1737*, Wislau to August, 30 July 1722, 301–309; 303–304v.

[106] Ibid., Wislau to August, 310–315v.

[107] Bernd (1738), 296.

oral communication intersected.[108] A genre known as the 'hymn sermon' was based on specific hymns. Most sermons were based on the Scriptural passages read before the sermon, which were familiar to congregants. The cantata of the day had interpreted those passages just before the sermon. Furthermore, while the possession of Bibles was limited until the advent of the mass-produced Halle Bibles,[109] ownership was more common in large towns such as Leipzig than elsewhere, and many people owned copies of other religious literature as well.

* * *

Numerous factors account for the way Leipzig inhabitants experienced the Baroque worship service. When congregants came to church, in many respects they did not leave behind the activities of their everyday lives. Social and gender distinctions and concepts of property were carried over into church seating. There was no code dictating prompt arrival and silence, and the service had specific social functions. Hymns, the cantata, and the sermon resonated with music and lyrics that people knew from a variety of contexts. Such resonance, along with the use of hymnals and librettos, made the cantata accessible. Even if many congregants did not closely follow it, people who wanted to could listen more closely. Preaching was also more accessible than has often been thought, and the sermon included information that congregants could use in their everyday lives.

On another level, an important goal of the producers of services, one that was also pursued by many congregants, was to step out of everyday routine, to escape the pressures of 'the world,' and to attain a sense of wonder, awe, and devotion. Musical virtuosity, the emotional resonance of hymns, a variety of gestures, visual display, and clerical oratory were combined with Baroque intensity to work this effect in a way that people rarely encountered outside the service. Contemporaries were attuned to this layering, as their descriptions of services show. By contrast, the more mundane practices associated with churchgoing were taken for granted; this accounts for the paucity of descriptions of those practices. Things that we would classify as distractions seemed merely the norm.

If the service is regarded as an arena in which interactions among inhabitants, visitors, and urban authorities were negotiated and reproduced, a complex picture emerges. Congregants did their best to display a variety of social, occupational, and gender differences. Far from passively receiving the messages that the producers of the service meant to convey, congregants timed their arrival and departure and paid attention selectively, according to their varying social, musical, religious, and political interests. Neither congregants nor producers were uniform groups. And

---

108 See Elizabeth Eisenstein (1979), *The Printing Press as an Agent of Change. Communications and Cultural Transformations in Early-Modern Europe* (New York: Cambridge University Press).

109 Richard Gawthrop & Gerald Strauss (1984), 'Protestantism and Literacy in Early Modern Europe,' *Past and Present*, 104, 31–55.

there was no clear vision between producers and consumers. Finally, city councilors, clerics, and composers tailored the service to appeal to congregants' interests.

Chapter 2

Seating the religious public: church pews and society

At first glance, church pews would seem to be socially and politically neutral terrain. In 1737, for example, Zedler's encyclopedia defined a pew as 'a seat in church devoted to listening to the Word of God.'[1] Similarly, when individuals submitted written requests for pews, the reason they gave was that they wanted to 'hear the Word of God.' However, formalized statements such as these disguise the social dimensions of church seating. In Protestant towns around early modern Europe, including Germany, Scandinavia, England, and Scotland, as well as in Congregational, Anglican, and German Lutheran churches in colonial British America, people articulated a variety of gender and occupational distinctions and engaged in a broad range of sociable interactions from their pews. People often competed to be allotted a pew; there were even altercations during services over possession of a pew. The culture of pewholding was at its height during the Baroque era, which was also a time of dynamic change in pewholding patterns.

Gender and status distinctions among pewholders were reproduced through seating in a way that was clearly visible to churchgoers. The first part of this chapter examines how women's places in the church differed from those of men, and how members of different status groups held pews relative to their proportion of the urban population. This section also reconstructs the social profiles of people who did not hold pews. Non-propertied Leipzigers, who made up about half of the city's population, generally did not hold pews, and often attended afternoon services and those outside the main churches. The small number of non-Lutherans in Leipzig, who attended Catholic, Calvinist, and Jewish services, were thus excluded from the main public religious arena; they were also not allowed to own property.

The regulation and passing of pews from one holder to the next, examined second, was an important area for the negotiation of relations between the authorities and Leipzig. Those relations were not merely dictated from above. While secular and ecclesiastical law provided a framework for the construction and allotment of pews, regulation generally followed the taste and demands of propertied inhabitants. Families themselves generally arranged the transfer of pews, with the

---

1 Johann Heinrich Zedler, ed. (1737), *Grosses vollständiges Universal-Lexicon aller Wissenschafften und Künste*, vol. XV (Halle & Leipzig: Zedler, R [1961–1964] Graz: Akademische Druck- u. Verlagsanstalt), 753–754.

authorities brought in mostly to adjudicate disputes. A variety of informal practices complemented, ignored, or circumvented official rules.

Studying the culture surrounding pews also opens the way to new insights into the mingling of the social and the spiritual in post-Reformation Protestantism. Pews, the basis of churchgoing, were considered important material assets. They were allotted for a considerable fee, had the status of property, and were registered on official numbered diagrams. The third part of the chapter examines the contemporary conceptualization of pews as property (*Eigenthum*), associated with real estate or home-ownership.[2] Further, with increasing demand for pews beginning in the later 18th century, the unpropertied were increasingly driven from former free spaces and seats. And the construction of *Capellen* by the very wealthy represented a new form of property in the church. Shifts in pewholding thus both reflected social change in the city, and were a renegotiation of social and cultural relations in their own right.

Pewholding, a good example of everyday practices in the religious arena, had no direct theological significance. As a result, the dogmatic literature of the time largely ignored pews. There have been few historical studies of them, and no detailed reconstructions of seating.[3] However, the sources on pews, especially pew allotment registers, are rich.[4] They reveal the occupational structure of churchgoers, the reproduction of social hierarchy in the church, and how pews were passed on. This study analyzes the records on 5706 pew holders in St. Nicholas's, all those listed between 1686 and 1725 in the church's annual account books. Requests by individuals for pews, debates and regulations by the authorities, seating charts, and

---

2 Robert Beachy (2005), *The Soul of Commerce: Credit, Property, and Politics in Leipzig, 1750–1840* (Boston: Brill), esp. 13–17.

3 See Jan Peters (1985), 'Der Platz in der Kirche. Über soziales Rangdenken im Spätfeudalismus,' *Jahrbuch für Volkskunde und Kulturgeschichte*, 28, NF 13, 77–106; Reinhold Wex (1984), *Ordnung und Unfriede. Raumprobleme des protestantischen Kirchenbaus im 17. und 18. Jahrhundert in Deutschland* (Marburg: Jonas); Gabriela Signori (2002), 'Umstrittene Stühle. Spätmittelalterliches Kirchengestühl als soziales, politisches und religiöses Kommunikationsmedium,' *Zeitschrift für historische Forschung*, 29, 189–213; Claudia Ulbrich (1997), 'Zankapfel "Weiber-Gestühl,"' in Axel Lubinski et al., eds, *Historie und Eigensinn. Festschrift für Jan Peters zum 65. Geburtstag* (Weimar: Böhlau), 107–114. Pews are mentioned briefly in Friedrich Ostarhild (1961), *Die Nikolaikirche Leipzig* (Berlin: Evangelische Verlagsanstalt). See also Richard Gough (1981), *The History of Myddle* (ms., 1701–02, ed. David Hey, London: Penguin); Margo Todd (2002), *The Culture of Protestantism in Early Modern Scotland* (New Haven: Yale University Press), 318–327; Lars Edgren (1997), 'Craftsmen in the Political and Symbolic Order: The Case of 18th Century Malmö,' in Geoffrey Crossick, ed., *The Artisan and the European Town, 1500–1900* (Aldershot: Scolar), 131–150; Robert Dinkin (1970), 'Seating the Meeting House in Early Massachusetts,' *New England Quarterly*, 43, 450–464.

4 *Rechnungen*, (SAL, no loc.) and another register, *Einnahmen und Ausgaben* (AdN, Abt. III.532.). The records, made when a pew changed hands, specify the new and previous holder's name, location of the pew, and give the occupations of 65% of holders. Adult men were listed by their occupations; women and children were listed as the wives or children of their husbands or fathers.

other references provide additional information from the perspective of ordinary churchgoers as well as the authorities.

Church pews and Leipzig society

Church pews were first allotted in Saxony and other Lutheran territories during the Reformation era. While clerics and secular rulers had sat in ex-officio seats throughout the Middle Ages, and some merchants and guilds collectively held seats by the 15th century, it was with the Reformation that ordinary parishioners began to obtain their own pews. The 1520s and 1530s saw a boom in pew construction, with lay people staking out claims to particular areas and building immovable pews. The pews replaced altars that were removed in Leipzig[5] and elsewhere, and provided seating for the longer Lutheran service. Town councils and territorial rulers soon moved to regulate pew construction and allotment, as they did other aspects of religious life.[6]

In Saxony, allotment regulations and many practices were established by the late 16th century and were standardized and codified by the mid-17th century, evolving in step with other religious institutions and practices.[7] Developments in other Lutheran towns in the Holy Roman Empire were similar to those in Saxony, with Saxon law often being consulted for pew issues, as it was for other religious matters. Regulations in Lutheran Scandinavia and Anglican England followed similar patterns.

Pew construction, official debates on how to allot pews, and disputes over individual pews all peaked between 1670 and 1750. In Leipzig, as elsewhere, there was a constant shortage of pews despite ongoing construction and the availability of thousands of seats. The culture surrounding pews began to decline after the 1750s: there were fewer fights for pews, less official discussion and regulation of them, and even record-keeping on allotment became less thorough. Still, as late as 1790 a pocket-sized digest of Saxon laws on pews was published as a guide to clerics in resolving regular disputes over pews; this booklet was revised and expanded in 1830.[8]

While most of the rules governing the allotment of pews were general to Saxony, seating patterns in Leipzig reflected the part-open, part-closed nature of urban society. Seating was more inclusive and open than church seating in noble

---

5 David Peifer (1996), *Das religiöse Leipzig, oder Buch III des Leipziger Urprungs und seiner Geschichte* (ms, before 1602, ed. Erich von Reeken and Gerhard Löwe [Beucha: Sax], 50).

6 Wex (1984), preface.

7 Benedict Carpzov (1645 ff.), *Jurisprudentia ecclesiasticum seu consistorialis*, Lib. II, Tit. XXIII, *De Subselliis templorum eorumque jure*, 552–572 in the 1695 edition (Leipzig: Starck); Saxon Church Ordinance of 1580; Electoral decrees of 1624, 1674, and 1722.

8 Johann Christian Köhler (1790), *Abhandlung von Kirchenstühlen und deren Rechten in Chursächsischen Landen* (Dresden: Gerlach); rev. and ed. (1830) Ernst Moritz Schilling (Leipzig: Taubert).

residences, a reflection of the relative openness of urban society. In Leipzig and other towns without a court only a few occupations held specific pews or balconies. No specific rules dictated who sat in other pews. Representatives of many different occupations rubbed shoulders, and wealthy artisans moved in the social vicinity of the elites. In many court chapels and in churches shared by a town and court, by contrast, as well as separation by gender, every single row of pews was assigned to a specific group, and burghers were relegated to a few low-status pews, although court officials in Dresden, for example, had difficulty enforcing this order at their court.[9]

* * *

Social goals predominated in the construction and layout of pews. Town councils and congregants aimed to fit a maximum number of people into the church, and ordered seating in a way that clearly articulated differences in status and gender.[10] The comfortable reception of the service was not foremost in people's minds, and seating was actually uncomfortable for many pew holders. In part, contemporaries were hampered by the necessity of fitting pews into spaces that dated to the high and late Middle Ages. In addition, the liturgical focal points in most Lutheran churches, the altar, epistle pult, and pulpit, were separated, in a pattern dating to the late Middle Ages, with the altar in front, the pulpit placed partway up the central aisle, amidst sections of pews, and the epistle pult (lectern) often near the pulpit. Pewholders who sat between altar and pulpit had to turn in their seats as they followed different parts of the service.[11]

The positioning of pews encouraged people to interact with each other more than to follow the service. In most churches, many sections of pews actually faced other sections of pews rather than the altar or pulpit. Pews were arranged in numerous compact sections, not large blocks, in part because the authorities constantly squeezed new pews into remaining free spaces. People thus were likely to know their 'neighbors,' as adjacent pewholders were known. People also had a general grasp of who held other pews around the church. As Leipzig city councilors wrote in 1752, 'Leipzig is not large, nor is any of the churches here so big that everyone would not know within four weeks [after a pew became vacant] who is occupying a particular pew.'[12]

* * *

---

[9] Wex (1984), 94 ff., 120 ff., 135 ff.

[10] Ibid., passim.

[11] SAL, Stift VII.B.32, *Acta, Die Einführung des Klingelbeutels in hiesigen Stadt Kirchen und dessen Wiederabschaffung betr.*, 1708 ff. (hereafter: *Klingelbeutel*), 31 October 1779, 86–88; 86ᵛ. See also Chapter One, note 30, page 35.

[12] SAL, Stift X.41., *Generalia in Kirchen-Stuhl-Sachen betr.*, 1741, 11 November 1752, 20–22.

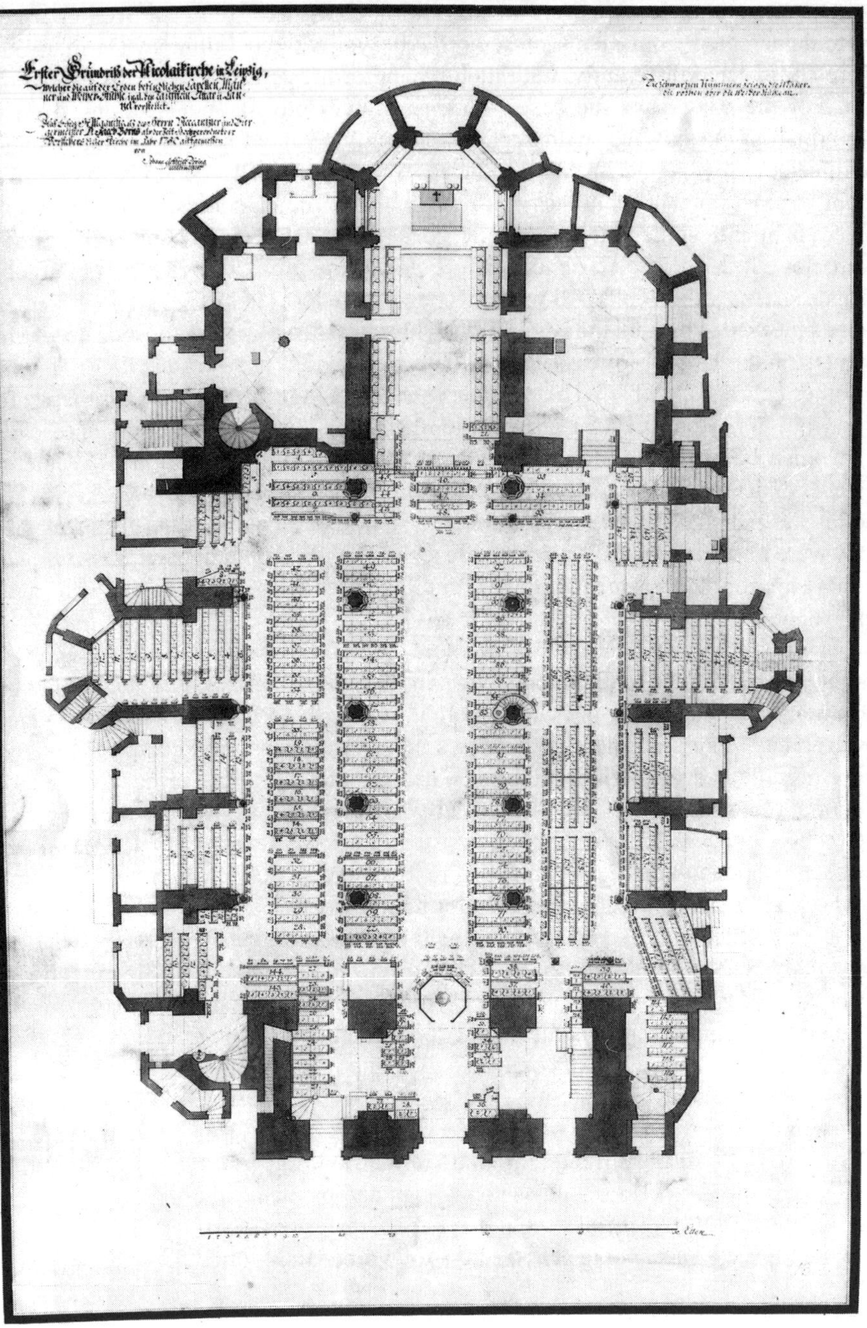

Pew chart, ground floor of St. Nicholas's Church, 1750 (Stadtarchiv Leipzig, RRA 246, reproduced by permission).

Distinctions in seating were most striking along gender lines. Women's pews were demarcated from men's in numerous ways. Around Lutheran Germany they were constructed differently, with men having armrests between seats and women not. For the most part, the sexes were separated into distinct sections from the Reformation era onward, with sections containing mixed seating gradually being removed. In towns and in many villages, women generally occupied most of the main, ground floors of churches, with most men in the balconies, although in some places men and women sat on opposite sides of the aisle, and in some villages pews were not allotted.[13] In St. Nicholas's in Leipzig, the ground floor became largely a female space by the 1680s. All women's pews were located there, and the few men's were squeezed in around the edges of the church, especially near the rear door. Most men sat in the largest, lower balcony; there were also two upper, smaller balconies. In other churches, including St. Thomas's in Leipzig, more men sat on the ground floor, but here, too, they sat around the rear and sides of the church. The seating of women below and men above reflected the common conception of women as listeners and recipients of religious wisdom: they sat below the preacher, whose pulpit was raised up from the floor. Men, by contrast, sat at a greater distance and, if they were in the balconies, above the preacher. Perhaps contemporaries also thought it more appropriate for men than women to navigate the often steep stairways up to the balconies.

In terms of seating, churches were more a female than a male space. There were slightly more women's than men's pews in the main churches, and the gender gap was more pronounced in the New Church, where 70% of the pews were financed by women.[14] The placement of women's pews at the front and center of the main floor accentuated their predominance. The church also seems to have been more important to women as a sociable venue than to men. Thus, most cases of contested pew allotment were for women's pews. One possible explanation for this is that whereas guilds and city government were available as public arenas in which men could be active, the church was the major public arena open to women.

Despite attemps to ban fleshly interactions, the prominence of the service as a sociable venue ensured that the boundaries between male and female churchgoers were not strict. Students threw objects from their balcony onto women's pews.[15] Church attendance as a basis for interactions among young, unmarried congregants was a running theme of a moral weekly edited and partly written by Leipzig Enlightener Johann Christoph Gottsched. This periodical, *The Reasonable Tatleresses* (a play on the English *Tatler*), was published in 1725–26, reprinted in 1738 and 1748, and distributed around Germany. In it, Gottsched and his fellow writers criticized practices such as young men and women gathering outside church during the service, women rising much earlier than usual in order to dress for the service, young men standing near the pews of women they admired, or finding places

---

[13] Wex (1984), 73 & 117; Ulbrich (1997), 108 ff.; Peters (1985), 78.

[14] Figures compiled from SAL (no loc.), New Church *Rechnungen*, 1698–1700.

[15] A Saxon Electoral edict of 1722 forbade students throwing objects. AFS, D 57.

in church from which they could stare at them.[16] In one issue of the journal, a fictive critic of these practices rhetorically asked: 'Is the church an opera house in which all kinds of romantic events may be played?' Men should 'distance themselves from our pews and take the places assigned to them.' The critic's conversational partner countered: 'Where else do [men] have as much opportunity to show us their social skills as in the church?'[17]

* * *

Next to distinctions along gender lines, those along status lines were most prominently displayed. The status of individual elite and artisan occupations was reflected with striking accuracy in a given group's presence among pewholders.[18] In St. Nicholas's, members of the elites, who made up no more than 10% of Leipzig's total population, held 43% of all pews. Members of intermediate groups, including shopkeepers as well as scribes, secretaries, protocol takers, and notaries, highly literate urbanites collectively referred to as *Schreiber* who made up no more than 5% of the population, held 14% of all pews. Artisans held 43%, which was roughly in proportion to their percentage of the population. Figures for St. Thomas's were similar.[19]

Among elite occupations, the dominant role of merchants in the city was reflected in their numbers among pewholders. More of the city's merchants and their family members held pews than did any other group. By contrast, the merchants' non-elite counterparts, shopkeepers, were far less well represented. Members of city councilors' families, while numerically fewer than merchants, were proportionally the best represented of any occupation. The councilors obtained their pews through their families and were allowed to retain them even though, as one official noted in 1697, 'many honorable men who are in public service and possess an official pew do

[16] Johann Christoph Gottsched, ed. (1725), *Die vernünfftigen Tadlerinnen* (Halle, R [1993] Hildesheim: Olms), no. 3, 17 January 1725, 17–24; no. 7, 14. February 1725, 55–56; no. 17, 25 April 1725, 134 ff.; no. 29, 18 July 1725, 230; no. 39, 26 September 1725, 308–309.

[17] Gottsched, ed. (1725), no. 3, 20–22.

[18] A point of comparison: a list of people active in all occupations in Leipzig in 1699. SHStADD, Loc. 10473, *Die von denen im Leipziger bzw. Meissnischen Kreis liegenden Städte gefertigten Tabellen*, 1699. Thanks to Katrin Keller for sharing this source.

[19] The allotment registers for St. Thomas's are not precise enough to allow for quantitative analysis. But pews there are often mentioned in other records as being of the same type and arrangement as in St. Nicholas's, and the social makeup of pewholders in both churches was similar. Many individuals actually held pews in both churches.

Table 1: Pewholding by occupation

Selected occupations:	Members in 1699:[20]	Pews held:[21]
City councilor	36	207
Merchant	141	576
Shopkeeper	156	179
Goldsmith, Jeweler	24	89
Wig maker	18	15
Baker	39	88
Printer	12	32
Bookbinder	17	26
Saddler, Harness maker	20	40
Tanner (*Lohgerber*)	52	140
Furrier (*Kürschner*)	45	58
Tailor	92	120
Shoemaker	73	83
Linen weaver	8	5

not set foot in their own pews for ten or twenty years.'[22] This allowed other family members to use those pews. Professionals such as doctors, lawyers, judges, men listed with the university degrees of licentiate and doctor, and their families were also well represented.

The prominent role of some elite groups, including city councilors, pastors, their wives, the judges of the Saxon Juror's Court, and men with a doctorate and a licentiate, was further reflected in their holding of *ex officio* pews and balconies. The colorful hangings put up on holidays also highlighted the position of the pews' occupants, associating them with the liturgy itself.[23] In towns where the guilds had more political and economic influence than in Leipzig, individual trades and groups of journeymen held their own balconies.[24]

In the world of artisans, members of at least fifty trades and their families held pews in St. Nicholas's: the majority of the roughly seventy trades that existed in the

[20] See above, note 18.

[21] Includes references to wives, sons, and daughters.

[22] SAL, Stift.IX.A.1.a., *Akta, einige Bänke in der Thomaskirche, welche den Studenten gehören sollen, betr.*, 1697–1708. Leipzig city council to Leipzig Consistory, 8 December 1697, 8^{v}.

[23] SAL, loose pages in the St. Nicholas's *Rechnung* of 1699–1700: *Tit. Herrn D. Thomae Ittigs Superintendentes Investitur betreffend,* 21 November 1699; *Klingelbeutel*, passim; in AdN, Abt. III.160., *Schriftwechsel Kirchenstühle betr. v. 1701*, ff. (hereafter: *Schriftwechsel*).

[24] See Peters (1985).

city.[25] Pew holding patterns accurately reflect different artisans' roles in the urban world outside the church. Members of prominent guilds, notably goldsmiths, bakers, and tanners, held proportionally more seats than their more humble colleagues. Goldsmiths, proportionally the best represented guild in St. Nicholas's, were an elite guild everywhere in Europe. They had an unusually long training period, worked with the most precious materials, and often designed their own products. Leipzig's goldsmiths drew their apprentices and journeymen from throughout Germany and beyond. Leipzig's bakers, who made a product of symbolic and political as well as nutritional importance, similarly held much power in Leipzig, as around Europe. Tanners in Leipzig, more prominent and cohesive than their peers in some other towns, and one of the few crafts to produce regular father-son dynasties extending over a century, produced leather of high quality which was shipped as far away as Italy. Trades for which contact and communication with large numbers of people was central were also well represented: pharmacists and barbers, innkeepers and tavernkeepers, book binders and printers. These trades benefited from the growth of the Leipzig trade fairs after 1680 and of the urban economy generally.

Less prosperous crafts whose members held proportionally very few pews included shoemakers and tailors; basketmakers do not appear at all.[26] Other little-represented trades include woodworkers (carpenters, turners, and coopers), fishers, and potters. While their products were essential, and some of their guilds were among the oldest and largest in Leipzig, as in other cities, the level of skill required for these trades was relatively low, production processes were simple and did not require much equipment, and the guilds were relatively weak. These artisans were also unable to fend off competition from peasant craftspeople, who produced cheaper versions of their products for sale in the city. There were also differences in status and pew holding within the branches of related trades. For example, ordinary smiths were much less well represented than the more specialized coppersmiths and tinsmiths, and book binders less well than printers.

In Leipzig as elsewhere, the two types of pews, regular 'seats' (*Stühle* or *Stände*) and simpler 'benches' (*Bänklein*), were constructed and positioned differently, in a way that reflected the status of their respective holders. *Stände* were arranged into regular square or rectangular sections made up of several rows. Rows of pews, and sometimes individual seats, were equipped with lock and key. By contrast, the benches were arranged around all four sides of sections of *Stände*. Benches could be

---

[25] See *Schriften des Vereins für Sozialpolitik*, 63 (1895), 66 (1896), and 67 (1897); entries for individual guilds in Zedler, ed. (1730 ff.); Elke Schlenkrich (1991), 'Der Alltag der Lehrlinge im sächsischen Zunfthandwerk des 15. bis 18. Jahrhunderts' (PhD thesis, University of Leipzig); Horst Thieme (1984), 'Quellen zur Wirtschafts- und Sozialgeschichte in den Handwerks- und Innungsbeständen des Stadtarchivs Leipzig (1182–1932),' *Leipzig: Aus Vergangenheit und Gegenwart. Beiträge zur Stadtgeschichte*, 3, 131–149; Jutta & Rainer Duclaud (1990), *Leipziger Zünfte* (Berlin: Verlag der Nation).

[26] Nicolaus Geissenberger (1895), 'Die Schuhmacherei in Leipzig und Umgegend,' *Schriften des Vereins für Sozialpolitik,* 63, 169–312; Max Hotop (1896), 'Das Korbmachergewerbe in Leipzig,' in ibid., 66, 141–172.

constructed in different ways. A drawing of St. Thomas's pews made in 1679 shows oval benches attached to the outsides of sections, and a diagram of St. Nicholas's pews of 1750 shows freestanding, narrow rectangular benches, also placed around sections of *Stände*.[27] In both diagrams, the benches were somewhat narrower than *Stände*. Many faced the rear or walls of the church, depending on which side of a section they were attached to. Holders of many benches therefore spent the service in a fairly uncomfortable position.

Elites held the majority (62%) of the 1573 *Stände*, and artisans 82% of the 871 *Bänklein*.[28] Members of intermediary groups held 16% of the *Stände*, and mostly occupied *Stände*. Church seating did partly transcend corporate boundaries, though, with people from different status groups being mixed to some degree. Thus, artisans and their family members occupied 23% of *Stände*. Most were members of high-status and luxury guilds: bakers, goldsmiths, wig makers, book printers and binders, and tanners. Indeed, the goldsmiths, wig makers, and book printers mostly sat in *Stände*. A few members of less well-off guilds also held *Stände*. For example, in pew #13 in St. Nicholas's, located in a back row on the ground floor opposite the pulpit, city councilor and mayor Johann Alexander Christ held a pew next to the smith's (*Hufschmied*) son Johann Gottfried Friedel. And pew #52, located in the second row in the first balcony behind the pulpit, was shared by a smith's son, a tanner, a jurist, and a merchant.

For the most part, though, sections of seats were mapped socially. In particular, the women's *Stände* that were closest to and had the best view of the pulpit were occupied mostly by elite women. The better the location of a section, the fewer artisans there were. The best sections of women's pews in St. Nicholas's were 'on the plaza' (*am Platz*), facing the pulpit and, not being enclosed by pillars, open to the view of much of the congregation. One section was completely dominated by elite women, with no artisans listed. By contrast, the sections of *Stände* behind the pulpit or farther away from it included far more artisans. There were even clear differences as one moved from the front to the back rows of individual sections of women's pews. The better sections of *Bänklein* also included more artisans from prominent and wealthy trades. Men's *Stände* on the ground floor followed the same pattern. On the first balcony, where the largest number of men's *Stände* was located, hierarchies were not as strict.

In general, members of the different elite occupations sat mixed together, as did artisans from different trades. There was no concentration of, say, merchants, tailors, or goldsmiths in any section. This was the case because there was a high rate of intermarriage among most of the artisanal trades. The elites were similarly connected by dense networks of intermarriage. Women's pews, both *Stände* and *Bänklein*, were generally more mixed than the men's, probably because the greater number of women's pews gave more women from artisanal backgrounds a chance

[27] SAL, *Grundrisse der Nikolaikirche*, 1750. RRA, 246–249; 1679 watercolor chart, St. Thomas's, parish house.

[28] Members of the elites held 7% of *Bänklein*, and intermediary-status groups held 11%.

at them than men. As a result, attending church implied more of a departure from corporate and family life for women than for men.

* * *

Just as Leipzig's social structure did not remain static, so pew seating evolved. Numerous changes over the decades were a precise barometer of shifts in the status of leading groups in the city. The construction of *Capellen* reflected the increasing wealth of leading merchants and city councilors, as well as the desire of the very wealthy to set themselves apart from ordinary churchgoers. Members of the book trade and a group of academics asserted themselves by occupying a new two-row, nineteen-seat balcony built in St. Nicholas's in the mid-1680s.[29] Not accidentally, the Leipzig book fair, and printing and dealing in general, were just entering a period of unprecedented growth. And book dealers and printers traditionally had close ties to the University of Leipzig. Prominent academics from the Mencke, Mylius, Kirch, and Feller families took seats in the first row. Several book dealers including, from 1701, Thomas Fritsch, shared the second row with two printers and the son of an engraver. This reflected close ties among members of the book trade: between artisans who were not individually prominent and their merchant colleagues, who were among the best-known figures in Leipzig.

Specific phases or moments in an individual's life might also be reflected in where he or she sat. The brides' and grooms' pews marked the transition from the unwed to the married state. In some areas, people who had been excommunicated might be required to sit in a special pew until they were readmitted to regular parishioner status.[30] In the 1650s and early 1660s, and possibly later, university students in their first weeks of study at Leipzig, Wittenberg, and elsewhere, known as 'foxes,' were forced by other students 'to take their place in the so-called fox corner in the churches' during a general hazing period, when they might also be forced to 'howl like a cat or dog' and crawl under tables during meals.[31] After they had endured this ritual, they could enjoy the student balconies.

* * *

While the range of occupations represented among pewholders in the main churches was broad, it was largely limited to property-owning Lutheran men and their families: about half of Leipzig's population. A broad spectrum of unpropertied Leipzigers, including day laborers and servants, as well as non-Lutherans, was all but missing

---

29 Rows 77 and 78. A professor of rhetoric and two notaries also held seats in the second row.

30 Jonathan Strom (1999) *Orthodoxy and Reform: The Clergy in Seventeenth Century Rostock* (Tübingen: Mohr), 1.

31 Johann Jacob Vogel (1714 & 1756), *Leipzigisches Geschicht-Buch oder Annales ...* (Leipzig: Lancke), 704–707.

from the lists of pewholders. The urban poor did, however, attend church. Because they did not sit in pews allotted to them, their presence is difficult to quantify, but it is possible to piece together a picture which extends our view of the relation between social structure and churchgoing.

Several factors contributed to the absence of poor and unpropertied Leipzig inhabitants among pewholders. They were less likely to have relatives from whom they inherited a pew than were artisans or members of the elites. Even if they did come into a family pew, they were sometimes not able to afford the allotment fee. The absence of sub-artisans was also the result of policy: as we will see below, the authorities considered home ownership a prerequisite to holding a pew. During Sunday morning services in the main churches, the poor were largely forced to occupy locations that reflected their social marginality: limited free seating, and standing room toward the rear of each church for 'common people' and 'common women.'[32] Some women sat on stairways that led to the balconies.

Many unpropertied Leipzigers attended other services. Numerous references indicate that servants sat in their employers' pews during Sunday afternoon services. The inmates of the combined prison, poor house, orphanage and home for the mentally ill, St. George's, numbering under 100 until 1704 and eventually several hundred in the new house completed in 1704, were forced to attend services in the house chapel. Of especial interest is the hospital church, St. John's, which like St. George's was located on the town wall in a marginal part of town. By the early 17th century and until at least the early 18th, many inhabitants of the 'suburbs' (*Vorstädte*) just outside the Leipzig walls made the church their own, confessing and taking communion as well as attending services.[33] At Easter and Pentecost of 1672, 635 people took communion, mostly day laborers, gardeners, journeymen, shepherds, people in similar occupations, and their families.[34]

The city clergy complained repeatedly about churchgoing at St. John's to the city council because of the loss of revenue that it entailed: clerics hearing confession received a small contribution, the 'confessional penny' (*Beichtpfennig*), which was considered a regular part of their income.[35] But the inhabitants of the *Vorstädte*, referring to themselves as 'we poor people' and as the 'loyal sheep' of a 'shepherd' who was beloved by his flock, continued attending regularly in spite of orders by the Electoral authorities and council to stop. They wrote that they had grown attached to the hospital pastor, regularly attended his services, and were too far away from

---

32 SAL, Tit.VIII.56., *Protocoll in die Enge*, 1694–1709 (hereafter: *Protocoll in die Enge*), 2 May 1698, 91. See also SAL, Stift X.39.b., *Kirchen-Stühle, Capellen und Begräbnis-Stellen betr.*, vol. II, no date (1708) (hereafter: *Kirchen-Stühle*, vol. II), 4–5v.

33 See Verena Kriese (1986), 'Die Leipziger Vorstädte – ihre ökonomische, soziale und verfassungsmäßige Entwicklung im 18. Jahrhundert' (PhD thesis, Karl Marx University, Leipzig).

34 SAL, Tit. VII. B. 61., *Das Beichte sizen und Communiciren in der St. Johannis Kirchen alhier betreffend,* 1670. Communion registers, 8 April 1672, 23–25v and 27 May 1672, 26–27.

35 Ibid., 1–1v, Leipzig ministry to city council, 14 August 1670.

the main churches.[36] The assertiveness of the *Vorstädter* is notable: they created a de facto congregation which was close to their homes and included their neighbors, and were under the care of a cleric who was familiar with their needs.

Very few members of religious minorities resided in Leipzig. In 1732, 200 Catholics and 280 Calvinists, most of them French Huguenots, lived in the city.[37] Members of both confessions had first been allowed to live in Leipzig around 1700. After a considerable struggle, the Huguenots were allowed to worship privately in French, and Catholics to worship in a chapel in the Electorally controlled Leipzig fortress, the Pleissenburg. A handful of Jews was informally allowed to live and worship in Leipzig from the early 18th century onward, but not officially allowed to reside there until the 1760s. Leipzig was unusual among German trading centers in having so little religious diversity. Augsburg and Breslau were shared by Lutherans and Catholics, and Frankfurt and Hamburg, both officially Lutheran, had significant communities of Calvinists, Catholics, and Jews. Berlin was open to minorities, especially after 1700. While the degree of mainstream tolerance for minorities in Hamburg and Berlin has often been exaggerated,[38] Leipzig's merchant and clerical elites, backed by a powerful centralized territorial government, were even less open than their brethren elsewhere.

By and large, the confessions remained separate until after mid-century. There was a limited amount of interaction, though. Some non-Lutheran apprentices and journeymen worked in Leipzig. Some Calvinist, Catholic, and perhaps Eastern Orthodox visitors to the fairs probably attended Lutheran services, just as curious Lutheran travelers attended Calvinist services or Catholic mass when they visited other areas, although clerics frowned on such experimentation. Some Lutheran Leipzigers also attended French Calvinist services in Leipzig. Indeed, clerics and the city council forbade German-language Calvinist services in an attempt to prevent their congregants from attending them.

---

36 Ibid., 10–12v, Sambtliche Nachbarschafft vor den Grimmischen u. Peters Thore ... to city council, 25 October 1671.

37 SAL, Tit.VII.B.126. *Specificatio der hier wohnhaften Catholischen und Reformirten*, 1732. See Ephraim Carlebach Stiftung, ed. (1994), *Judaica Lipsiensia. Zur Geschichte der Juden in Leipzig* (Leipzig: Edition Leipzig); M. Freudenthal (1928), *Leipziger Meßgäste. Die jüdischen Besucher der Leipziger Messen in den Jahren 1675–1764* (Frankfurt: Kauffmann); A. Kirchhoff (1874), *Geschichte der reformierten Gemeinde in Leipzig 1700–1725* (Leipzig: Kirchhoff & Wiegand); Paul Saft (1961), *Der Neuaufbau der katholischen Kirche in Sachsen im 18. Jahrhundert* (Leipzig: St. Benno); Siegfried Seifert (1964), *Niedergang und Wiederaufstieg der katholischen Kirche in Sachsen 1517–1773* (Leipzig: St. Benno).

38 See Joachim Whaley (1985), *Religious Toleration and Social Change in Hamburg 1529–1819* (New York: Cambridge University Press); Heinz Schilling (1993), *Die Stadt in der frühen Neuzeit* (Munich: Oldenbourg), 103.

Rules, regulations, and religious experience

Pew allotment was regulated by ecclesiastical law and administered by the Leipzig city council, the Leipzig and Dresden consistories, and clerics. Like their peers around Protestant Europe, these groups debated contentious questions and issued decrees and decisions beginning early in the Reformation era. Still, this official framework did not encompass nearly all of the details or broader cultural meanings of pewholding or church attendance. Families usually decided themselves who would receive a pew that had been vacated. A broad array of informally accepted practices, many pursued independently of the authorities, also existed.

Pews were passed on by the rules of secular inheritance: when one was vacated, the holder's nearest successors had the right to claim the pew. Individuals paid a one-time fee at the time of allotment. In Leipzig, this was three thaler for *Stände* and one thaler for *Bänklein*, a considerable sum. In return, people received a certificate which served as a deed of possession. St. Nicholas's certificates were about four inches by nine inches in size, printed on good quality paper, and were adorned with an engraving of St. Nicholas of Cusa. The church ordered them in large quantities from a Leipzig printer about once a year.[39]

A pew changed hands when its previous holder died or moved away from Leipzig. About three-quarters of pews in St. Nicholas's were transferred after their holders died. But the population of Leipzig was mobile, and many people moved from the city when they married or sought a job. Once they did, they lost their status as local parishioners, an ecclesiastical criterion that was a prerequisite for pewholding, and had to relinquish their pews. About one quarter of pews was passed on in this way.[40] The same rules of possession and transfer applied to men's and women's pews; the laws did not distinguish between the sexes. Women held their pews as individuals, and did not have to relinquish them when they were widowed or remarried, as they did many other forms of property. They passed them on to female relatives, and men passed theirs on to male relatives.[41] Older siblings had no right of precedence. Individuals could obtain a pew at any age. Most pews seem to have been allotted to adolescents or adults, but in some cases young children and even infants were ascribed pews.

Since pews were allotted to individuals, families sat scattered around the church, not together. Church attendance thus implied a transcendence of family boundaries for the duration of the service. The locations of the Weissmantel family's pews provide a good example. Andreas Weissmantel, the head of the carpenters' guild,

---

[39] Annual church *Rechnungen*.

[40] 18% of men's *Stände*, 28% of women's *Stände*, 27% of men's *Bänklein*, and 28% of women's *Bänklein*.

[41] One exception: the 1720/21 Saxon Church Pew Ordinance specified that widowers could retain their deceased wives' pews until their remarriage, while widows could not keep their deceased husbands' pews. SHStADD, Loc. 4571, *Die von dem Obern Consistorio projectirte neue Kirchen-Stuhl Ordnung betr.*, 1721, 10, 10^{v}–11.

who helped construct some of Leipzig's Baroque burgher homes,[42] held a *Bänklein* on the lower balcony facing the pulpit. He had held it since before 1686, and when he died in 1723 his son Johann Gottfried, then a carpenter's journeyman, took it over. Weissmantel's wife Sabina held a *Bänklein* in a section behind the pulpit and underneath the organ until 1696. Then she moved to a *Bänklein* in a better location, near the baptismal font at the rear of the church. Her daughter Regina Elisabeth took this pew over in 1702.[43]

The transfer of pews, however, followed family ties. Just as most property in early modern Europe was transferred within families, the majority of pewholders were allotted pews which had previously been held by their relatives. The average for all pews in St. Nicholas's from 1686 to 1725 was at least 61%.[44] Most frequently, children succeeded to pews left by their parents; siblings and cousins were also frequent successors. Less frequently, grandchildren, parents, and in-laws were allotted a pew. As a growing population made pews scarcer at the beginning of the 18th century, families increasingly kept pews for themselves.[45] In particular, there was a sharp rise in the number of 'cousins,' or *Vettern* and *Muhmen*, terms that could refer to more distant relatives as well as actual cousins,[46] among new pewholders.[47] Noticing the scarcity of pews available to non-relatives, in 1707–08 the authorities began to charge an extra fee or 'sweetener' of as much as several thaler to most new pewholders who were not related to the previous holders.[48] Those who paid it were among a fortunate few: many had to endure long waiting periods before obtaining a pew, and others never did. In particular, 'outsiders' who had settled in Leipzig often complained that they could not obtain a pew.

The actual passing on of pews was largely regulated by the families of holders. When more than one person was eligible for a pew, for example siblings or cousins, the family arranged for lots to be drawn. Most requests for pews in St. Nicholas's were therefore merely requests by one person for the pew of a relative. Cases in which two or more descendants fought over a pew and appealed to the authorities for a decision were small in proportion to total turnover, although numerous. Disputes usually arose when a pewholder had no direct descendants, and different relatives

---

42 Nikolaus Pevsner (1928), *Leipziger Barock. Die Baukunst der Barockzeit in Leipzig* (Leipzig; R [1990], Leipzig: Seemann), plates 6 and 34, unpaginated.

43 Men's *Bänklein* 267; women's *Bänklein* 498 and 249. Johann Gottfried's request for the pew: 12 June 1723. *Schriftwechsel,* III.160.8.

44 Since a relationship between new and old holders with different surnames was often not mentioned, the actual percentage was probably higher.

45 It was 46% in 1686–90, 53% in 1701–05, 63% in 1706–10, 70% in 1711–15, 74% in 1716–20, and 83% in 1721–25.

46 Zedler, ed. (1746), 'Vetter,' vol. XXXXVIII, 373–374) and (1739) 'Muhme,' vol. XXII, 30–31.

47 It was 2.5% through 1705, 11% in 1706–10, 18% in 1711–15, 25% in 1716–20, and 31% by 1721–25.

48 This fee was recorded in the allotment registers.

argued that they were the closest to the deceased.[49] Most concerned women's pews. In some cases, three or four parties petitioned the authorities, enclosing extensive family trees to support their argument that they were the closest relative. Other cases revolved around issues of residence. The Leipzig Consistory decided disputes. Usually the parties accepted the Consistory's decision, although a few cases were appealed all the way to the Saxon Elector.

Successors had to lay claim to a pew within four weeks of the death or move of the previous holder by writing or going in person to the church sexton or the city councilor who was the Director of the church.[50] The authorities strictly enforced the four-week deadline, demanding a fine when people missed it. They enforced the residency requirement even more strictly, and were especially unreceptive to claims to pews by individuals who had moved away from Leipzig.[51]

If people came into a pew that was better than one they already held, they were allowed to move to it. They had to give up their previous pew, but were allowed to designate a successor for it.[52] In their ongoing quest to sit in the best possible pew, people eagerly took advantage of this opportunity. They justified their requests to move by complaining about the pew they had, often calling it 'a poor, small pew' from which they could not hear or see the pastor well, even if it was a relatively good one.[53]

A vibrant set of informal practices also determined who sat in which pews. Many of these practices ignored or circumvented formal regulations. Some were frowned upon by the authorities, while others were regarded as acceptable. All point to the great value pews held in the eyes of Leipzigers. Many pews were not occupied by their regular holders for long periods of time. This occurred especially when the holder moved from Leipzig and did not transfer his or her pew to someone else. The authorities enforced the residency rule when they were informed, but in many cases they were not. Some abandoned or 'lordless' pews were eventually claimed by other family members.[54] In other cases, people frustrated by not having a pew of their own claimed a pew of a non-relative which they knew was unoccupied. For example, in 1701 the hatmaker Gabriel Hahn requested a pew whose 'former proper owner [*sic*] has married and settled in Zerbst.' As a result, for a long time 'various uncertain possessors have made use of it.'[55]

Further, many pewholders sublet their pews. The practice was referred to as 'renting' (*vermiethen*) and was repeatedly forbidden, as in an Upper Consistory

---

[49] See Leipzig Consistory decisions on contested cases between 1666 and 1715, SAL, Stift IX.A. no. 21, *Convolut mit 43 Consistorialabschieden* ... (hereafter: *Convolut*).

[50] This rule was made in the 1624 Saxon *Synodal-Decret.*

[51] See *Convolut*, case 33, 127–134^{v}.

[52] This was a principle in Leipzig Consistory decisions on five cases involving pews in St. Thomas's. *Convolut*, cases 4, 7, 8, 9, 18.

[53] 11% of men's *Stände* and 15% of women's turned over due to 'moving up,' as did 5% of men's *Bänklein* and 8% of women's.

[54] Valentin Leiche to the Director, 30 March 1701, *Schriftwechsel,* III.160./1.

[55] Hahn to the Director, 31 May 1701, ibid., III.160./1.

rescript of 1711 which forbade 'renting church pews for money.'[56] Individuals who rented pews mentioned this in their requests for their own pews, showing that the authorities did not object to the practice enough to prosecute it.[57] Even a Leipzig town employee engaged in this practice: in 1708 the Director of St. Thomas's complained that the town beadle was personally renting out pews that he stacked in an unsightly pile in a corner of the church and set up every Sunday.[58]

Although pews were technically allotted to one person, they were often used by other family members of the same sex. Many requests for pews in St. Nicholas's mention the desire for a pew not only for 'me' but also for 'mine' (*die Meinigen*), which included all members of the household: children, journeymen and apprentices, servants, and tutors. Likewise, claimants who had no pew in a church complained that neither they nor 'theirs' had the opportunity to attend the worship service. The practice of members of a household taking turns sitting in a pew increased the percentage of the Leipzig population that attended services at least occasionally. However, official sharing of pews was not allowed.[59]

Finally, pews were sometimes given to friends as a token of deep gratitude, usually for very generous ongoing support and care. The giver usually had no other means to repay the friend, who had taken on a role like that of a family member. Requests to make such gifts were highly emotional. For example, in 1720 Maria Dorothea Schwartzkopf wrote that after her husband Hans Jacob, a cutler, had died sixteen years previously and had left her and their two daughters 'in the greatest poverty and highest desperation, the dear Lord awoke a pious heart named Regina Rüdiger, who had mercy on me and my children and has provided bread and other food according to her ability, and generously continues to do so.' Schwartzkopf asked permission to transfer her pew to Rüdiger: 'I cannot repay her, since all I have in this world is a *Bänklein* in St. Nicholas'.[60] The authorities agreed to such requests reluctantly, since pews given to friends were no longer available to relatives. Some requests were approved only after being submitted several times, and recipients were required to pay a substantial fee of several thaler. Individuals who wanted to give their pews to a friend had to prove that they had no close relative, that their relatives already had pews, or that no relative wanted the pew in question.

Private property in the church

The conceptualization and treatment of church pews as property is perhaps the aspect of pewholding that seems most odd to modern sensibilities. But the investment

[56] Upper Consistory to Leipzig Consistory and city council, 23 September 1711, *Convolut*, 140, 142.

[57] Hans George Lampe to Director on behalf of his wife and daughter, 12 May 1701, *Schriftwechsel*, III.160./1.

[58] *Protocoll in die Enge*, 1694 to 1709, 20 June 1708, 507.

[59] Request of 31 March 1723, with director's note. *Schriftwechsel*, III.160.8.

[60] Request of April 1720. Ibid., III.160.6.

of church attendance with material significance is crucial to understanding early modern Leipzigers' religiosity: people did not see the religious arena as distinct from the material social world. There were two main connections between pews and property: pews themselves were treated as a form of property, and an individual's holding of a pew was closely associated with home-ownership. Beginning in the 1680s the propertied became more visible and the unpropertied less so, as a newly wealthy class of merchants and city councilors constructed *Capellen* and many of the unpropertied were ejected from previously open places.

Pews were technically the property of the church, and were considered allotted to individuals for the length of their residency in Leipzig. However, pews were routinely referred to as the 'property' (*Eigenthum*) of their holders. For example, in 1722 Anna Dorothea Raffel referred to her *Bänklein* as 'the pew owned and possessed by me.'[61] While pews technically reverted completely to the church with the death or relocation of their holders, and heirs had to request an allotment in writing, relatives were referred in law and common usage as 'inheriting' a pew.[62] In some cases, pews were even associated with the ownership of a particular building. They were transferred with the sale of that building rather than through the regular allotment process, and were not recorded in the pew registers. Although the practice was increasingly frowned upon after 1700 in Leipzig, it was still accepted.[63] Thus, in 1716 three adjacent men's *Stände* in St. Nicholas's which had long been associated with Auerbach's Hof (home of Auerbach's Keller) appeared in the register for the first time. The then owner of the building did not want to relinquish possession of the pews if he sold the building.[64]

The authorities respected pewholders' control of their pews. When maintenance, renovation, and construction work was done in the churches, councilors and clerics obtained the consent of pewholders in advance. Thus, when councilors discussed building a new group of pews in St. Thomas's in 1707, they noted that 'because there are privately owned pews there, and their owners (*Eigenthumsherren*) are not willing to give them up, opposition is to be feared.'[65] The authorities also warned construction workers not to damage or remove pews without the permission of their owners.

The Leipzig city council, like its peers in other Lutheran towns, took an interest in pews for several reasons. On a formal political level, the council was responsible for upholding Lutheran doctrine, and churchgoing was the means of communicating that doctrine to the population. On a more practical level, the council had authority over church property and responsibility to maintain the churches. It was this practical, fiscal responsibility that dominated almost all discussions of pews. Allotment fees were a major source of church revenue, and councilors discussed the financial

---

61 Raffel to the Director, 12 January 1722. Ibid., III.160.7.

62 *Kirchenstuhlordnung*, draft of June 1720; 7, 9–9^{v}.

63 Ibid., 8, 9^{v}–10^{v}.

64 Pew no. 136, seats 1–3.

65 *Protocoll in die Enge*, 2 May 1707, 478–479.

potential of pews openly. Throughout this period, in Frankfurt, Dresden, Leipzig, and elsewhere, entire church renovations and new constructions were largely financed by pew subscriptions. Councilors also discussed the financial potential of pews on other occasions, for example in 1702, when they debated dismantling the City Council Pew in St. Thomas's, 'to make to money' by selling the space it occupied to people to build *Capellen* and regular pews, and building a new City Council Pew from part of the proceeds.[66]

Notwithstanding the overall conception of pews as property, city councilors and consistory assessors attempted to maintain a distinction between pews as property and pews as objects of commerce, condemning the latter. Allotment fees were justified in terms of maintenance, and were not supposed to be excessive. The 'renting' of pews was forbidden. And the main reason that the authorities forbade the sale of pews along with a house, or bequeathing them in wills, was that in this way they entered the commercial market.

The city council, consistories, and many ordinary Leipzigers drew a strong connection between home ownership and the right to hold a pew. Men and women requesting the allotment of a pew frequently mentioned that they, or their wives or children, were burghers, a status that implied owning a home. Some petitioners specifically mentioned that they were homeowners as well as burghers.[67] By the same token, the authorities classified servants, soldiers, and other Leipzig residents without property as transients, not true parishioners, unqualified to hold a pew even when they were left one by a relative. Thus, in 1739 Anna Elisabeth Schmidt's request for a *Bänklein* in St. Nicholas's was refused because she did not clearly establish her relationship to the previous holder and because 'anyway she is presently only a roomer.'[68] By contrast, Leipzig burghers born elsewhere were not denied pews in principle, even if they did have difficulty obtaining them. This policy changed toward the end of the Baroque era, with the Dresden Consistory ordering in 1741 that permanent residents 'should also be considered true parishioners' even if they did not 'possess property or public office.'[69]

Some unpropertied Leipzigers fought for their right to a pew. In 1690, Regina Mölle asked to be allotted her deceased sister's pew. Her sister's daughters also claimed the pew, but Mölle claimed that she was, according to law, the closer relative.[70] The Leipzig Consistory denied her request on the grounds that she had lived outside Leipzig for years and, although she had returned, was married to a resident (*Zettelmann* or *Einwohner*). She was thus a 'temporary' but not 'permanent'

---

66 Ibid., 31 March 1702, 170–171.

67 For example, tavern keeper Niclaus Thondorff, request of 5 October 1735. *Schriftwechsel*, III.160.10.

68 Request of 22 August 1739 with note. *Schriftwechsel*, III.160.10.

69 To the Leipzig Consistory. SAL, Stift.X.41., *Generalia in Kirchen-Stuhl-Sachen*, 1741; 11 December 1741, 12–13^{v}. Confirmed in later rulings: Köhler (1790) and Schilling (1830), 39–40 & 43.

70 *Convolut*, case 21, 13–16; Leipzig Consistory to Upper Consistory, 27 February 1691 & Upper Consistory to Leipzig Consistory, 12 November 1691, 121–123.

parishioner. Her sister's daughters, on the other hand, were each married to Leipzig burghers. Mölle appealed her case to the Elector, but her appeal seems only to have reached the Dresden Consistory, which agreed with the Leipzig Consistory. Still, while Mölle lost her case, the fact that she appealed shows that at least some unpropertied people thought of themselves as having rights to pews, and that the identification of home-ownership with the right to hold a pew was not absolute.

* * *

Beginning at the end of the 17th century, changes in policy and pew construction brought about a reorganization of sitting and standing space. The presence of propertied Leipzigers increased, and many of the unpropertied were forced out. As we will see in Chapter Eight, the increasingly marginal status of the poor in the church was also reflected in plans to force them to attend catechism services starting in 1713 in St. Peter's and in the main churches.

In one form of change, the council built and allotted regular pews in spaces traditionally left to the poor in both of the main churches. In renovations begun in 1702, councilors replaced a broad staircase in St. Thomas's on which people who could not stand for the whole service had sat.[71] Councilors planned to do the same in St. Nicholas's.[72] In his complaint of 1708 about the beadle who rented out pews, the Director of St. Thomas's stated that those pews were set up 'in the open area in front of and behind the baptismal font ... which is used by common women who have neither *Stühle* nor *Bäncklein*,' and who now had 'no room in this area to attend the service.'[73] But rather than suggesting that the area be restored to these women, the Director recommended that regular pews be built in the area. The city council accepted his request, and decided to do the same in St. Nicholas's. Developments in other towns, such as Dresden, were similar.[74]

At the other end of the social spectrum, the council encouraged the construction of *Capellen* by newly-powerful city councilors, especially senior councilors, prominent merchants, and a handful of their widows. Some of these families had come to power relatively recently. Symbolizing the arrival of new prominent families, the construction of several *Capellen* required the relocation of epitaphs, a previous, more modest way of marking status, which commemorated members of formerly prominent, but now obscure families.[75]

---

71 Abraham Christoph Kase, memorial to council, 20 December 1713. SAL, Tit. VII. B.110., vol. 1, 1704 ff. *Acta, die Peterskirche betr.*, 129–133.

72 *Protocoll in die Enge*. Meeting of 31 March 1702, 170–171.

73 *Kirchen-Stühle*, vol. II, 4v.

74 Johann George II to Upper Consistory. SHStADD, *Kirchenstühle und Empor-Kirchen betr.*, 1690 ff., Loc. 4624. 30 December 1690; Upper Consistory report: 24 November 1690; 15–18, 19–20.

75 SAL, Stift.X.39.a., *Kirchen-Stühle, Capellen, und Begräbnis-Stellen*, vol. I, 121–122, 135.b., 137–140.

With *Capellen*, the concept of pews as property assumed a new dimension. Precursors first appeared in the 1660s, when several men obtained permission to enclose groups of already existing pews.[76] By the early 1680s the form and status of *Capellen* had assumed the shape they would retain for the next several decades. Styles were similar in the different churches. *Capellen* came to number over thirty each in the main churches, twenty-four in the New Church, and nineteen in St. Peter's. Possessors received the right to buy and own them outright, to bequeath them to their heirs, and to sell them to non-relatives as well as relatives. *Capellen* also differed in other ways from regular pews. Both male and female members of a family used them, along with guests. Many *Capellen* had their own entrances from the exterior of the church. Holders of *Capellen* thus did not have to interact at all with ordinary parishioners or even set foot in the church proper. One figure in Gottsched's *Reasonable Tatleresses* sarcastically commented about another, 'I doubt whether she would even go to church if she did not have her own *Capelle* in which she could take shelter from the vulgar odors of the common people by closing the windows.'[77] Many contained libraries and stoves, and had one or more burial places directly beneath them. *Capellen* continued to be sold and distributed among heirs for considerable sums of money through the 1760s. For example, in 1727 an heir of city councilor Georg Winckler bought the title to a *Capelle* in St. Nicholas's from his fellow heirs for 800 thaler, and to another in the New Church for 1000 thaler.[78]

In building *Capellen*, the most powerful Leipzigers changed the very structure of the churches. Construction was a large-scale undertaking, with prospective builders required to present detailed sketches and descriptions, and to persuade senior councilors (the *Enge*), who had to approve the projects, that construction would not adversely affect the church. This could be a difficult argument to make, especially as space grew scarcer with successive waves of construction. Many proposals involved adding interior or exterior stairways, breaking through walls, and building up to three levels of *Capellen* on top of another. Proposed sites were surveyed by a city councilor and a sworn guild master and then in most cases approved, although sometimes in modified form. The city council seems to have sensed that it was on uncertain ground in taking ownership in the church to these lengths: in several cases that involved extensive structural changes, the building contract stipulated that the owner would be responsible for any legal and building costs that might arise from complaints from individuals or other authorities. In any case, the finished *Capellen*, removed only in the late 19th century, were lasting monuments to their builders.

* * *

In conclusion, how people 'listened to the Word of God' depended on their social status and gender. They did not perceive the importation of social categories and

---

76 Ibid, Jäger to city council, 21 August 1682, 63–64^{v}.

77 Gottsched, ed. (1725), no. 9, February 1725, 65–72; 68.

78 *Kirchen-Stühle*, vol. II, 31 March 1727, 57–66.

the concept of property to be in contradiction, or as a hindrance, to the religious experience; rather, it was an integral part of it. Roughly the wealthier half of society, members of property owning families, formed the most visible part of the religious public. Elites experienced the service in relative comfort and, if they owned *Capellen*, even in spendid isolation. Artisans were more likely to have uncomfortable seats and to have to crane their necks to follow the liturgy. Still, they experienced the service along with the elites. By contrast, most of the unpropertied attended a different, simpler afternoon service in the main churches, or they attended other churches. As time went on, they were less likely to be able to occupy free spaces during main services.

The picture was more complex with regard to gender than to status. Women held more pews than did men, and occupied most of the best seats in the house, those with the best sight lines and sound. Their position beneath the preacher and below male congregants in the balconies, though, symbolically placed them in a subordinate position, objects of the gaze of men sitting in the balconies and of the preacher in his pulpit.

In constructing and allotting pews, city councilors responded to demand by burghers, while increasingly marginalizing the unpropertied. Councilors also pursued a profit. For their part, individuals largely organized the passing on of pews in consultation with their families, involving the authorities only to confirm possession and to settle a small percentage of contested cases. They also sublet, shared, and gave pews as presents: practices that might be frowned upon by the authorities, but were rarely prosecuted.

Despite status and gender differences, people of all social groups shared some basic attitudes. In particular, they highly valued pews and, by extension, church attendance, and they did their best to gain and hold on to pews. The elites were best able to realize their goals; but artisans were also active. Unpropertied individuals challenged the status quo when they could. Members of all groups also circumvented official regulations. And although there were objections to practices such as subletting that were seen as greedy or commercial, not a single voice is heard in this period objecting to the practice of pew allotment itself: to the investment of churchgoing with material and social significance.

PART II
The producers

Chapter Three

The clergy, the city council, and Leipzig inhabitants

Clerics and city councilors were the main local authorities in the religious arena. They were actors in a complex world of urban and territorial institutions, each with specific, minutely regulated, and intersecting rights and duties.[1] They were also important producers of religious culture. The goal of this chapter is to understand their places in urban society and their relationships to other inhabitants. Both clerics and councilors held a great deal of power in the religious arena. They and their families were highly visible, the focus of popular scrutiny and emulation as well as formal ceremony. In a variety of ways, though, they were accountable to burghers and non-burghers.

City councilors, examined first, played a role in every area of urban society and culture. In the trade metropole of Leipzig, the regulation of the fairs and of commerce generally was particularly important. Religion was another important field of activity. Religious norms, expectations, and duties structured councilors' theoretical mission, as well as many of their interactions with inhabitants. Historians have emphasized how councilors gained power during the Reformation through their assumption of new religious roles.[2] Less attention has been paid to how these roles made councilors reliant on and accountable to burghers. While ordinary inhabitants in Leipzig, as in many other towns, had lost direct participation in governance by the 1500s, they did have a voice in the religious arena. The theory of the covenant, which undergirded councilors' authority, emphasized reciprocal obligations on the part of the authorities as well as the governed. Matters that were defined in religious terms, including councilors' personal conduct, were subjects of urban gossip networks that helped to hold councilors to their proclaimed norms. Further, as Robert Beachy has emphasized, burgher status, property ownership, and burghers' rights were closely

1 See Christopher Friedrichs (2000), *Urban Politics in Early Modern Europe* (New York: Routledge); Alexander Cowan (1998), *Urban Europe 1500–1700* (New York: Oxford University Press); Heinz Schilling (1993), *Die Stadt in der frühen Neuzeit* (Munich: Oldenbourg); Mack Walker (1971), *German Home Towns. Community, State, and General Estate 1648–1871* (Ithaca: Cornell University Press).

2 See the above and Lyndal Roper (1989), *The Holy Household. Women and Morals in Reformation Augsburg* (Oxford: Clarendon).

associated,[3] giving burghers not only, as we saw in the previous chapter, a claim on pews, but also a broader claim on participation in the religious arena.

Clerics, examined next, emerged as a distinct, powerful occupational group by the early 17th century.[4] Historians have recently developed a detailed picture of this profession and its location in urban society. This chapter places especial emphasis on the social processes by which individuals became clerics. Historians have reconstructed where students studied and what they learned. Much less attention has been paid to theology students' everyday lives,[5] important especially in a town such as Leipzig where almost all clerics were graduates of the University of Leipzig. The majority of students roomed and boarded with burghers, and many served as tutors. Through those arrangements, future clerics became an integral part of the social and cultural fabric of Leipzig. Once they were ordained, clerics came in contact with a broader range of inhabitants – more so than city councilors – through their pastoral duties. Here relations shifted, with the pastor providing essential services and becoming more socially aloof. Patronage by individual councilors and other prominent Leipzigers before and after ordination was also important.

---

3 Beachy (2005), *The Soul of Commerce: Credit, Property, and Politics in Leipzig, 1750–1840* (Boston: Brill), esp. 13–17.

4 For a summary, see Schorn-Schütte (2000), 'Priest, Preacher, Pastor: Research on Clerical Office in Early Modern Europe,' *Central European History*, 33, 1–37 & C. Scott Dixon and Schorn-Schütte, eds (2003), *The Protestant Clergy of Early Modern Europe* (Houndmills: Palgrave Macmillan). See also Monika Hagenmaier (1989), *Predigt und Policey. Der gesellschaftspolitische Diskurs zwischen Kirche und Obrigkeit in Ulm 1614–1639* (Baden-Baden: Nomos); Sabine Holtz (1993), *Theologie und Alltag. Lehre und Leben in den Predigten der Tübinger Theologen 1550–1750* (Tübingen: Mohr); Anthony LaVopa (1988), *Grace, Talent, and Merit. Poor Students, Clerical Careers, and Professional Ideology in Eighteenth-Century Germany* (New York: Cambridge University Press); Wolfgang Reinhard (1988), 'Kirche als Mobilitätskanal der frühneuzeitlichen Gesellschaft,' in Winfried Schulze, ed., *Ständische Gesellschaft und soziale Mobilität* (Munich: Oldenbourg), 333–351; Luise Schorn-Schütte (1996), *Evangelische Geistlichkeit in der Frühneuzeit. Deren Anteil an der Entfaltung frühmoderner Staatlichkeit und Gesellschaft. Dargestellt am Beispiel des Fürstentums Braunschweig-Wolfenbüttel, der Landgrafschaft Hessen-Kassel und der Stadt Braunschweig* (Gütersloh: Gütersloher Verlagshaus); Wolfgang Sommer (1988), *Gottesfurcht und Fürstenherrschaft. Studien zum Obrigkeitsverständnis Johann Arndts und lutherischer Hofprediger zur Zeit der altprotestantischen Orthodoxie* (Göttingen: Vandenhoeck & Ruprecht); Jonathan Strom (1999), *Orthodoxy and Reform: The Clergy in Seventeenth Century Rostock* (Tübingen: Mohr); Bernard Vogler (1994), 'Rekrutierung, Ausbildung und soziale Verflechtung: Karrieremuster evangelischer Geistlichkeit,' *Archive for Reformation History,* 85, 225–233; John Michael Stroup (1984), *The Struggle for Identity in the Clerical Estate. Northwest German Protestant Opposition to Absolutist Policy in the 18th Century* (Leiden: Brill); Joachim Whaley (1992), 'Obedient Servants? Lutheran Attitudes to Authority and Society in the First Half of the 17th Century: The Case of Johann Balthasar Schupp,' *Historical Journal*, 35, 27–42.

5 One exception: LaVopa (1988).

The extent and quality of pastoral care for the city's population, generally considered inadequate in the literature on Pietism, are considered here. In giving background for the collegia pietatis, a recent account claims that 'With only two parish churches ... with five clerics each, the nearly 20,000 inhabitants of Leipzig were insufficiently cared for. One result was a massive movement away from the church (*unübersehbare Entkirchlichung*); further, pious individuals lacked pastoral care, and withdrew to individual religious practice.'[6] We will see that this characterization misses the mark. Pastors were overburdened, but they had a strong commitment to their positions and their congregants. They and councilors struggled to accommodate and regulate inhabitants' interests. For their part, inhabitants were assertive in seeking out not only, as we have seen, church pews, but also services such as communion.

Recent research has emphasized how clerics worked actively with secular authorities, while also criticizing rulers' policies from the pulpit. Here too, the situation in Leipzig was similar to that elsewhere. Members of the two groups interacted constantly. Many dealings were collegial, but there were also some tensions. Most importantly, councilors appointed and promoted clerics, thus fundamentally shaping the clerical estate. This process, which has not been sufficiently emphasized, is one focus here.

Councilors and inhabitants

Leipzig's city councilors shared much with their peers around Western and Central Europe. They were part of a close-knit network of merchants, jurists, high clerics, and academics, the urban 'social elite.'[7] They and their families were commonly referred to as *die Vornehmen* ('the elite'), while ordinary burghers and sub-burghers were known as *gemeine Leute* ('common people'). As in many other towns, a group of senior councilors, known in Leipzig as the *Enge*, made many of the council's decisions. Confirmation of their decisions in plenary meetings was largely formal. The specific form of the Leipzig council was more unusual: it was divided into three groups of ten to twelve each, with each group having one mayor. The groups rotated as the annual governing, or 'sitting' council. Councilors elected their own peers, and election was for life. From the mid-17th century onward, the ratio of lawyers, or *literati* to merchants was about 4:3.[8] Jurists held offices on the council requiring legal expertise, and increasingly dominated the *Enge*.[9] Merchants had experience with the details of trade and banking that made up much of the council's business,

---

6 Martin Brecht (1993), 'Philipp Jakob Spener, sein Programm und dessen Auswirkungen,' *GdP*, vol. I, 281–389; 335.

7 'Social elite:' Cowan (1998), 52.

8 See Gustav Wustmann (1895), *Quellen zur Geschichte Leipzigs. Veröffentlichungen aus dem Archiv und der Bibliothek der Stadt Leipzig*, vol. II (Leipzig: Duncker & Humblot), Introduction, 59–128; Beachy (2005), 1 ff.; 45.

9 Beachy (2005), 45–46.

and were also expected to contribute money from their own pockets in times of need.[10] Guilds, which played at least some role on many other town councils, were not represented at all in Leipzig after the 1540s.[11]

Just as the Leipzig elites were generally, the city council was more open to newcomers than councils in many other towns. This probably correlated to the city's steady economic expansion, which provided opportunities for new fortunes to be made and for new legal talent.[12] Almost half of the merchant councilors elected from 1680, and almost one third of the jurist councilors, were born outside Leipzig.[13] In towns with stagnant economies, by contrast, existing elite families clung to their power. Upward mobility into the council was made easier in Leipzig because there were no rules or organizations governing eligibility for council membership, as there were in Nuremberg, Augsburg, and Frankfurt.

The council's power, and the clout of individual members, varied with the city's fortunes. During most of the 17th century the council faced major challenges to its authority. Not only had Swedish occupying forces exacted huge payments and supervised the council's activities, but a burgher committee of sixty artisans had risen up in 1642. Like similar committees that arose around Germany,[14] 'the sixty' protested councilors' self-exemption from quartering soldiers and financial contributions. The Swedes authorized the group to administer quartering and contributions. The burgher committee's challenge left sufficiently deep scars that the council suppressed the publication of a chronicle discussing it as late as 1685. As councilor Michael Thoma wrote, such accounts might give rise to 'uncomfortable questions' from burghers.[15] Further, in 1628 an electoral commission had taken over the regulation of the city's finances because the city had fallen four million thaler into debt. The city was able to bribe its way to autonomy with a 70,000 thaler payment only in 1688.[16]

Coming on the heels of these challenges, the period from the 1680s to the 1750s saw the council's greatest display of power. Individual councilors and the council as a whole administered ever more cash. The pomp, ceremony, and oratory of council elections and investitures of new governing councils reached a high point. In contrast to times of crisis, there was intense lobbying for election to the council.[17] The council issued major legislation on numerous occasions, including its own constitution of 1688 and the begging ordinance of 1704.

The Leipzig city council's many roles in the religious arena, which were like those of its peers around Protestant Germany, were central to its theory and practice

---

10 Wustmann (1895), 63 ff., 88–89 ff.

11 Beachy (2005), 47.

12 Cowan (1998), 58–59.

13 Beachy (2005), 48–49.

14 Friedrichs (2000), 35 ff.

15 Detlef Döring (1984), 'Das Leben in Leipzig in der Zeit des Dreissigjährigen Kriges,' *Leipzig: Aus Vergangenheit und Gegenwart*, 3, 151–175; 157.

16 Wustmann (1895), 89 ff.

17 Wustmann (1895), 68–69; 94 ff.

of governance. During the Reformation, councilors had taken over many duties and responsibilities from the Catholic Church.[18] The administration of those areas, and the council's general mission, were formulated with an emphasis on the language of covenant and reciprocal corporate relations with burghers.[19] The covenant was a theme at the annual installation of a new governing council, held in the city hall. Heads of Leipzig guilds and neighborhoods were present as guests. The installation opened with readings of the first chapter of the Book of Joshua, Psalm 20, and a prayer by a contemporary author.[20] The reading from Joshua is of particular interest here: Joshua assumed the Mosaic Covenant as a ruler and conqueror of cities. The passage dwells on Joshua's pact with the population as well as God's pact with Joshua. God commands Joshua to succeed Moses as leader of the Israelites; there is a distinct parallel between Joshua and the city council. The heart of God's instructions is in verse 7: 'observe to do according to all the law, which Moses my servant commanded thee ... that thou mayest prosper whithersoever thou goest.' Joshua in turn speaks to 'the officers of the people,' who represent the burghers of Leipzig. The officers then swear fealty to Joshua as the successor of Moses and representative of God.[21]

The covenant concept informed many of the city council's practical rights and duties. It was the council's duty to ensure the spiritual welfare of all inhabitants, which encompassed not only the worship service but also education, poor care, and charity. As Francis Conrad Romanus said in his inaugural speech as governing mayor in August 1703, the council was to uphold 'inner peace' by cultivating churches and schools, and 'external peace' by sumptuary laws, jails, and *Polizey* in general. The good were to be rewarded, and the bad punished; justice and 'quiet obedience' were to be upheld 'not only by instilling fear, but also through good words.' Councilors themselves were to set a good example by their modest conduct.[22] They were viewed as being personally subject to the wrath of God if His commandments were not observed.

This mission translated into extensive oversight and administration of urban religious affairs. The council appointed all clerics, teachers, and other church and school employees. Just as importantly, the city council administered church property and finances. Each church was assigned a Director (*Vorsteher*), a senior councilor, usually a merchant, who also occupied a powerful position as one of four 'construction masters' (*Baumeister*), to administer its financial affairs. The Directors supervised

---

18 The council's *jus patronatus* was formalized in a Saxon decree of 1 May 1543. Reprinted in Erdmann Hannibal Albrecht (1799), *Sächsisch-luther'sche Kirchen- und Predigergeschichte*, vol. I (Leipzig: self-published), 12–17.

19 See Roper (1989); Gerhard Oestreich (1982), 'The Religious Covenant and the Social Contract,' in idem, *Neostoicism and the Early Modern State* (New York: Cambridge University Press), 135–154.

20 Wustmann (1895), 67.

21 The Bible, King James Version.

22 SAL, Tit. VIII.41., *Protocoll in den 3 Räthen* ... 1687–1709 (hereafter: *Protocoll* ... 1687–1709), 27 August 1703, 734–737.

the compilation of the annual financial records (*Rechnungen*) of each church and, working with sextons, directed day-to-day matters like maintaining churches and allotting church pews, as well as large-scale projects such as renovations. The council also administered the city's legacies and charitable institutions: the alms commission, two hospitals, and the house of St. George. In early modern Leipzig, as in other towns, the churches were major lending institutions, each turning over thousands of thaler in most years (and generating hundreds of thaler in interest). Most loans were made to individuals, often to build or buy a house; the Saxon crown and its bureaucracies were also frequent borrowers of thousands of thaler.[23]

The language of covenant and reciprocity masked the loss of most of Leipzig inhabitants' formal rights in government. Burghers did have the right to petition the council on specific issues. But their official roles were largely limited to symbolic support and approval. For example, they attended special, annual 'council election services' held in St. Nicholas's, the main public forum, where elections were marked and the political principles underlying them communicated. Sub-burghers had no formal political voice at all. Further, the council held fearsome powers over fellow inhabitants who were under its jurisdiction (as opposed to the University's or Consistory's jurisdictions): it could summon and interrogate them, fine and sentence them to jail, and it made laws that governed their work, housing, morals, and other dimensions of their lives.

However, in the course of administering their religious duties, councilors relied heavily on financial contributions by burghers. Pew allotment payments were a major source of income for church maintenance, and alms contributed during the service were the basis of poor relief. Charitable bequests made by individuals as early as the 13th century also accumulated to stately proportions.[24] Until the collapse of the German Empire in 1918, the interest on them was used for alms, scholarships, to supplement clerics' and other employees' pay, and for other purposes. And as we will see in Chapter Eight, the council financed the renovation and new construction of St. George's, the New Church, and St. Peter's largely by pew allotment fees and contributions attached to those fees.

In return for their contributions, burghers made a claim on active participation in religious life. Burghers also complained in some petitions for pews that they had been burghers for many years, paying taxes and supporting churches, schools, and the poor, but had not been able to get a pew.[25] We will also see in Chapter Eight that burghers' formal and informal demand for more religious services gave the impetus to the expansion of religious life from 1699. Even sub-burghers who received care

---

23 Loans, interest, and repayments were itemized in each year's *Rechnung*.

24 See H. Geffcken & H. Tykocinski (1905), *Stiftungsbuch der Stadt Leipzig, im Auftrage des Rates auf Grund der Urkunden und Akten des Ratsarchivs* (Leipzig: Bär & Hermann).

25 AdN, *Schriftwechsel Kirchenstühle betr. v. 1701* ff. (hereafter: *Schriftwechsel*), III.160.10., Johann Friedrich and Johanna Rosina Semmel to Director, 31 August 1735 and Niclaus Thondorff to Director, 5 October 1735; III.160.14., Stephen Richter to Director, 15 June 1753.

made claims. Widows, one of the least powerful social groups in urban society, claimed they were inhabitants worthy of the council's protection, which they could do on the basis of injunctions in Scripture. For example, in her petition for a pew in 1739, Christina Sophia Löschner highlighted her status as an eighty-year-old 'very poor widow' who received alms weekly from the council.[26] And Maria Glafey, an inmate of St. George's, also emphasized her poor widow status when she wrote letters protesting her ill treatment to councilor Bose in 1724. She went as far as to threaten him with divine punishment if he 'did too much to the widow.'[27]

Inhabitants also had access to less formal means of holding councilors, and clerics, to their proclaimed norms, or at least making them cautious about violating them. Networks of gossip were among the most effective. News spread rapidly, and it was nearly impossible to keep a secret. The types of gossip that were of most interest included extramarital sexual activity and socializing across social lines. These could easily take on political significance in a society where sexuality was tightly regulated and people were expected to conform to behavior appropriate to their status.

The relatively small population of Leipzig and the town's compact layout helped news to spread. Although Leipzig was a large city by German standards of the time, people had a good overview of their fellow urban dwellers.[28] Keeping track was made easier because Leipzigers, like other Europeans, organized themselves socially and spatially into households that were usually headed by a burgher couple. There were just under 1100 households in 1699 and no more than about 1400 by 1750.[29] Other people living in a household, including children, tutors, servants, apprentices, journeymen, and roomers were often named with reference to the burgher owners: 'Frau Gerber's maid,' 'the merchant Bose's clerk,' 'the widow Henschel's tutor.'

Councilors acted when they feared that a particular situation would become known to inhabitants. For example, in 1718–19 the council ordered a teacher at the house of St. George who was rumored to have a relationship with the house mother to resign after Maria Magdalena Wagenhold, a former inmate, spread gossip

---

26 *Schriftwechsel,* 160.10.10. 25 September 1739. A similar claim in ibid., 14 April 1735.

27 Tanya Kevorkian (2000), 'The Rise of the Poor, Weak, and Wicked: Poor Care, Punishment, Religion, and Patriarchy in Leipzig, 1700–1730,' *Journal of Social History*, 34, 163–181; 173 ff.

28 Council to Frederick August III, 3 November 1752, SAL, Stift X.41, *Generalia in Kirchenstuhlsachen betr.*, 1741 ff., 20–22.

29 F.G. Leonhardi (1790), *Erdbeschreibung der Churfurstlich- und Herzoglich-Sachsischen Lande*, vol. I (Leipzig: Barth) 47. The earlier number is identical to that of SHStADD, Loc. 10473, *Die von denen im Leipziger bzw Meissnischen Kreis liegenden Städte ... gefertigten und eingeschickten Designationes*. This number, low for a large town, making for about twenty people per household, can be perhaps explained by the fact that Leipzig developed largely within the former boundaries of the town wall, upward rather than outward, with many houses reaching up to eight storeys. See Heinz Füssler (1955), 'Leipzig im Zeitalter des Barocks und Rokokos,' in Heinz Füssler, ed., *Leipziger Bautraditionen* (Leipzig: VEB Bibliographisches Institut), 103–124.

of this relationship. Fear of bad publicity concerning corrupt administration of the house, along with conscientious individual councilors, also prompted extensive investigations of the house in 1721 and 1724.[30] More generally, councilors might mention with concern the impact that a given policy or, for example, the appointment of a given person as councilor, would have on the council's standing with 'the community' (*gemeine*) or 'the public' (*dem publico*).[31]

Gossip could be spread in many different ways. Carriers of gossip included lower officials such as sextons,[32] notaries, pub owners, bookstore owners, and other public figures. Servants seem to have been major conduits in practice as well as literature. Adam Bernd repeatedly mentioned his fears that all-knowing servants would gossip to their friends in other households, who would then tell their employers. In Leipzig student Christian Reuter's satirical plays of the 1690s, bourgeois characters spent significant amounts of time worrying about the transmission of embarassing events. Entire scenes are devoted to relatives and servants doing the actual transmitting.[33] Both Bernd and Reuter referred to salacious news, often embroidered and distorted, as becoming known to every person in the city. Even councilors talked. Upon taking office, they had to swear an oath to hold matters discussed in council meetings secret. They often broke this oath, however, despite repeated admonitions to observe it. In 1714, mayor Schacher claimed that the details of council discussions were commonly 'gossiped out' (*ausgeschwatzt*) within two hours of a meeting.[34]

Clerics and inhabitants

On first glance clerics, the first estate in early modern society, commanded even more respect than city councilors. If one pictures a Leipzig cleric in his distinctive garb of black robe and white lace collar, he conveys an impression of unquestioned authority, of standing apart from the rest of society as a member of a unique occupation. Clerics' duties, rights, and institutional organization distinguished them from other individuals and groups. But in their backgrounds, the processes by which they became clerics, and in their everyday lives as clerics they were an integral part of the social fabric of Leipzig, as they were in other towns.

The Leipzig clergy had its own organization, the City Ministry (*Stadtministerium*), which met regularly and usually acted as a unified group. At the head of the local hierarchy was the Superintendent. The Hamburg Senate and Rostock council had done away with this powerful position,[35] but in Leipzig and other Saxon towns this

30 See Kevorkian (2000).

31 Wustmann (1895), 66 (case of 1563) & 110 (case of 1739).

32 Johanna Reinhard to St. Nicholas's Director A.C. Platz, 6 March 1723, and Johann Carl Reinhardt to same, 15 July 1723, *Schriftwechsel*, III.160.8.

33 Reuter (1980), ed. Günter Jäckel, *Christian Reuters Werke* (Berlin & Weimar: Aufbau), 8–9, 23–24 & passim.

34 Wustmann (1895), 78.

35 Strom (1999), 61–62.

had not occurred. Until 1699, the Leipzig Superintendent presided over a ministry composed of a dozen clerics. Leipzig's two main churches were each headed by a main pastor, who was assisted by an archdeacon, a deacon, two subdeacons, and a junior, unordained 'Saturday preacher' (*Sonnabendprediger*). The Superintendent himself was head pastor of St. Nicholas's. Additionally, pastors served at the two hospital churches, St. John's and St. Jacob's. Beginning in 1699, the clergy expanded by four clerics, with a deacon and subdeacon being appointed to the New Church, a pastor (and eight unordained catechists) to St. Peter's, and a pastor to the house of St. George.

Clerics held a near monopoly on crucial services: they preached the Word of God, heard confession, and baptized, married, and buried people. On the side, many published their sermons and other works, through which people edified themselves at home. Clerics' day-to-day duties varied according to their seniority.[36] The head pastors at the main churches preached at the main Sunday morning and holiday services, and at one other service during the week. Archdeacons and deacons preached at weekday and vesper services. The main pastoral workload was carried by the deacons: at each of the main churches, one deacon served a week-long 'tour of duty' during which he performed all weddings, baptisms, and funerals.

The ultimate source of clerics' authority and cohesiveness was their office, or *Amt*. Clergymen placed great emphasis on the foundation of their office on both divine and official vocation.[37] The central mandate of the cleric's office was to speak the Word of God freely from the pulpit: to admonish all members of the congregation, including secular authorities, to obey Scriptural Commandments, and verbally to 'punish' those who did not.[38] Clerics cast this right in the language of responsibility, calling on the common metaphor of the shepherd entrusted with the welfare of his flock. Lax or 'mercenary' shepherds who allowed their flocks to stray would answer to God after their deaths.

The Leipzig Ministry was at the pinnacle of a local system that included church employees such as teachers and sextons, and clerics and other employees from Leipzig and surrounding villages. The formal relations among these groups and the secular authorities were displayed for all to see during the investiture ceremonies of new Superintendents. When Thomas Ittig was installed in 1699, a procession that went through the center of the city, from mayor Steger's house to the church of St. Nicholas, preceded the ceremony.[39] Walking in order were the Leipzig Consistory protonotary, the governing city council, the Leipzig Ministry, country pastors, city

36 See Günther Stiller (1984), *Johann Sebastian Bach and Liturgical Life in Leipzig* (St. Louis: Concordia; German original, 1970), 66–74.

37 See Martin Honecker (1968), *Cura religionis Magistratus Christiani. Studien zum Kirchenrecht im Luthertum des 17. Jahrhunderts, insbesondere bei Joh. Gerhard* (Munich: Claudius), 83–105.

38 See Sommer (1988), throughout.

39 Recorded by St. Nicholas's Sexton David Manitius. *Tit. Herrn D. Thomae Ittigs Superintendentes Investitur betreffend*, 21 November 1699. 2 loose fol. in SAL (no loc.), 1699–1700 St. Nicholas *Rechnung*.

schoolteachers, organists, and sextons, and finally country schoolmasters. The procession was brought to the public's attention by the ringing of the full set of St. Nicholas's bells. Ittig was installed during the worship service that followed. The highest Saxon cleric, the Electoral Senior Court Chaplain, presided. He brought Ittig's contract, signed by the Elector, which emphasized his duties and responsibilities to his flock. Clerics and school employees personally promised to obey the new Superintendent. Hierarchies were also reflected at the post-investiture feast at the Steger home, which was planned by the mayor's wife and cost 372 thaler (just over the council's annual salary for the Superintendent).[40] The Leipzig city clergy and other employees were treated to the meal, while country pastors had to contribute one thaler each from their churches. Lowest of all in status, 'the poor country schoolmasters had to go home hungry and thirsty.'[41]

A ritual such as an installation of a new Superintendent shows the Leipzig clergy and its relation to other groups at one moment in time. By contrast, the integration of individuals into the Ministry was a lengthy process.[42] Even after their educations, clerics spent a long time in junior positions as Saturday preacher or as catechist before they attained regular position as subdeacon in Leipzig, or deacon or pastor in a smaller town or village. From there, they might be successively promoted as deacon, archdeacon, and pastor at St. Thomas's or St. Nicholas's. [43] They were promoted as positions were freed up by the deaths or promotions of those above them. Constant turnover as well as shuffling among churches within Leipzig ensued. One benefit of this system was that by the time he attained senior status, a cleric was well acquainted with his colleagues and with a good portion of Leipzig's population.

Individuals from diverse backgrounds entered the Leipzig Ministry.[44] Leipzig clerics were the sons of artisans and of urban elites; they came from Leipzig, from smaller towns in Saxony like Wurzen, Zwickau, Leissnig, or from obscure villages like Liemehna, Pol-Ilma, or Wetteritzsch. They can be divided into two main groups, members of clerical and other elite/professional dynasties ('insiders'), and men who came from outside the system and worked their way up through it ('outsiders').[45]

---

40 Superintendent Deyling's (1720–1755) income was 350 Thaler. Reinhard Szeskus (2003), 'Johann Sebastian Bachs soziale Stellung in Leipzig,' in idem, *Bach in Leipzig. Beiträge zu Leben und Werk von Johann Sebastian Bach* (Wilhelmshaven: Noetzel), 1–63; 47.

41 See above, note 39.

42 See also Vogler (1994).

43 Catechists were generally first promoted to Saturday preacher, and from there to a regular position. Twenty-nine of the sixty-four catechists at St. Peter's appointed to 1750 were soon promoted, most to Saturday preacher, others to elsewhere in Saxony.

44 This study draws on Erdmann Hannibal Albrecht (1799), *Sächsische evangelisch-luther'sche Kirchen- und Predigergeschichte von ihrem Ursprunge an bis auf gegenwärtige Zeiten*, Bd. I, *Dióces Leipzig* (Leipzig, Selbstverlag), Christian Gottlieb Jöcher, ed. (1750), *Allgemeines Gelehrten-Lexicon*, (Leipzig: Gleditsch), Anon. (1777), and other sources. It does not reconstruct the social backgrounds of all clerics.

45 LaVopa (1988), esp. 28–46.

The sons of country pastors fall somewhere in between. These polarities remained constant throughout the 17th and 18th centuries.

There were limits to the openness of the system in Leipzig: for example, few men from sub-artisanal backgrounds were represented among the clergy, although there were a few who rose to the top of the hierarchy. However, it seems that there was no shift to excluding sons of artisans, as there was even by the end of thc 16th century in some areas.[46] Numerous sons of artisans became clerics, and Leipzig's elites encouraged social mobility through the clerical education and appointment processes. In addition, more positions actually opened up in Leipzig starting in 1699.

The Leipzig clerical system included individuals from around Germany, although the majority came from Saxony or Thuringia. At the entry level, 120 men were appointed to unordained junior positions as Saturday preacher or catechist between 1650 and 1750. Just over half (sixty-six) of them were later promoted to coveted regular positions in Leipzig. Some of those who were promoted outside Leipzig received positions in their home towns, perhaps at their request. The percentage of all clerics appointed at the main churches who were born outside Leipzig actually rose from 50% between 1650 and 1700 to 70% between 1700 and 1750. In all, 62% of the seventy-nine clerics who were appointed to regular positions between 1650 and 1750 (including some who had entered the system before 1650) were born outside Leipzig, and 38% were from Leipzig.[47] Natives of Leipzig had a somewhat better chance of being advanced from Saturday preacher to a regular position. But many non-Leipzigers were also advanced or newly appointed, including all four Superintendents and six of nine pastors at St. Thomas's.

While professional dynasties did not control the Leipzig clergy, they did play a prominent role in it. Clerics in Leipzig, as in the rest of Saxony and Protestant Europe, had begun to intermarry and form dynasties in the early years of the Reformation.[48] Members of these dynasties intermarried with other urban elites. For example, Christian Wagner, the son of Leipzig mayor Paul Wagner, married Dorothea Sophia Thomasius, the seventeen-year-old daughter of deceased Leipzig law professor Jacob Thomasius and sister of Christian Thomasius.[49] In Saxony, the influence of such families reached its height with the Carpzovs. At any time throughout the 17th century, two or more Carpzov relatives usually held positions as law professors,

---

46 Schorn-Schütte (1996), 85 ff.

47 Figures compiled from Albrecht (1799) & Anon (1777).

48 See Sommer (1988), 74 ff., 111 ff.

49 SAL, Tit.VII.52., *Protocoll in Versammlung aller 3 Räthe ...* 1682–1704 (hereafter: *Protocoll ...* 1682–1704), 6 November 1685, 60–61; Johann Benedict Carpzov (1694), *Doppelte Wittwen-Krone, an der WohlErbarn, Viel Ehr-u. Tugendreichen Frauen Dorotheen Sophien, geb. Thomasien, ... Hn. M. Chrn. Wagners ... sel. hinterlassener Frau Wittwen ... Leichbestattung 9.9.1694 in Pauliner-Kirchen* (Leipzig: Tietze).

political councilors, judges, or in the clergy, as high clerics or theology professors, in Leipzig, Dresden, and Wittenberg.[50]

* * *

Regardless of background, individuals entered the clerical estate through an extensive system of education and patronage. Common to almost all Leipzig clerics was their graduation with a degree of master of theology from the University of Leipzig. They thus shared a group of professors, learned similar material, and became familiar with the city and its ecclesiastical system. In this regard, they differed from their peers in towns such as Rostock, many of whom attended a variety of universities.[51] A second common thread running through clerical careers was personal acquaintance with established clerics or other urban elites, which often involved a stay at their houses. In a process Anthony LaVopa terms 'sponsored induction,'[52] prominent Leipzigers actively recruited and provided patronage for talented students. Many students and recent graduates lived with and worked as tutors of the children of Leipzig theologians, merchants, or city councilors. This patronage provided subsistence before a regular appointment, and also personally acquainted students with the people who might later appoint them, as well as with other influential Leipzigers. A tutoring job with a prominent family was thus the first step on the career ladder of many clerics. A stay with senior clerics was also common for the sons of well-to-do parents, even if it did not involve tutoring.[53]

In many cases, inequalities between the sons of artisans and elites endured. The time put in as a tutor could be long and difficult, and artisans' sons may have served longer in junior positions than the sons of elites. Still, the patronage system provided for more social mobility than was the norm in early modern society. The biography of Christoph Wolle (1700–61), the son of a tailor born in Leipzig and J.S. Bach's confessor from 1741, shows how local patronage and support by family members worked.[54] Wolle first attended school in Borna, near Leipzig, living with an uncle who was a haberdasher. He matriculated at the school of St. Thomas's, where he earned money singing at funerals, in 1715, and at the University in 1718. Different councilors gave him board, allowed him to borrow books from the city council's library, and employed him at the journal *Acta Eruditorum*. For ten years, Wolle lived in the home and tutored the children of city councilor Polycarp Gottlieb Schacher. In 1725 he began his clerical career, holding positions as catechist, Saturday preacher, and substitute before at last being promoted to a regular position, as subdeacon at

---

50 See Jöcher, ed. (1750), vol. I, 1691–96 on Johann Benedict Carpzov II (1639–99), later pastor at St. Thomas's and University professor.

51 Strom (1999), passim.

52 LaVopa (1988), 40; 28 ff. On the day-to-day life of poor students in Leipzig, see ibid., esp. 19 ff.

53 Albrecht (1799), 227 ff.

54 Ibid., 212 ff.

St. Thomas's, in 1739. He became deacon in 1740, archdeacon in 1741, Doctor of Theology in 1746, and extraordinary professor of theology in 1748. Other clerics from artisanal and small-town backgrounds included Abraham Teller, born in 1609 in the small town of Wurzen as the son of a furrier (a prosperous trade), appointed pastor at St. Thomas's in 1657,[55] and Jeremias Friderici, born in 1691, was the son of the head of the Leipzig fisher's guild, a minor guild, and became pastor of a hospital church in 1733.[56] Both Teller and Friderici were encouraged by prominent clerics and councilors.

For a handful of clerics, a poor background was actually featured prominently in contemporary biographical accounts. Salomon Deyling, appointed as Superintendent in 1720, and Bach's superior throughout his tenure in Leipzig, was the son of a dyer in the town of Weyda in the Vogtland.[57] Jöcher's biographical dictionary recounts that he 'was born to poor parents, whose only son he was,' that his father worked temporarily as a beer brewer in a town near Deyling's native village, and that for a time Deyling 'walked daily in all kinds of weather' to be instructed by the pastor in the village of Irsersgrün.[58] Jöcher reports that Adam Bernd was born in the outskirts of Breslau, where 'his father was a vegetable or cabbage gardner.'[59]

Clerics, like men in many other occupations, often married near the time that they were installed in their first regular positions and ordained. The backgrounds of Leipzig clerics' wives often reflected the clerics' original social backgrounds. As we saw, Christian Wagner, the son of a jurist and city councilor, married Dorothea Sophia Thomasius. By contrast, Johann Adam Gehr, long-time pastor at St. George's, who was born in the town of Freyburg in Thuringia as the son of a cantor, married Justina Schmetz, the eldest daughter of a Leipzig wine tavern owner.[60] However, status divisions do not seem to have been absolute: Bernd claimed that he was offered marriages to several women who later married very prominent men.

* * *

Clerics interacted with burghers, servants, and other inhabitants in numerous capacities. They did most extensively while they were students. The University-owned Pauline Collegium and Red Collegium accommodated only a small number of students. Therefore most students roomed and boarded with burghers, both artisans and elites, and often tutored those burghers' children. In 1741, a total of 1072 students, located in all four quarters of the town, resided in burghers' homes. In 1762, 911 students lived with burghers, and an additional 145 in the collegia

---

55 Ibid., 145.

56 Ibid., 247 ff.

57 Ibid., 93.

58 Jöcher/Adelung (1787), *Allgemeines Gelehrten-Lexicon, Fortsetzung*, vol. II, 684–685.

59 Jöcher (1750), vol. I, 1019–1020.

60 She was Gehr's second wife; they married in 1724. Albrecht (1799), 618 ff.

and professors' lodgings, for a total of 1056 students.[61] This made for an average of about two students per three burgher houses in the city. These numbers did not include *Magistri*, graduates of the University who often stayed in the city for years before finding regular employment and housing. Bernd and other tutors taught the girls, boys, and servants of a family, and talked with the servants in their spare time. They also provided informal pastoral advice. Arrangements were similar in other university towns. In cities with no universities, such as Hamburg and Breslau, gymnasium students played similar roles.[62]

Rooming experiences ran the gamut. Some students shared a room, either with a friend or with someone they did not know, which sometimes led to difficulties. Some rooms were heated and others were not.[63] Some students developed close relations with the families they boarded with, while others feuded with their landlords. Christian Reuter attained fame while he was still a student for lampooning his landlady, Anna Rosina Moller, and her children in his 1695 play '"L'Honnete Femme," or the Honorable Woman of Plissine' and its sequels.[64]

Theology students may have been more decorous than their fellows in the medical, philosophical, and legal faculties,[65] but they still socialized with other students and town inhabitants. Bernd, like most other students, often ate in pubs or gathered in them to 'smoke a pipe of tobacco,' drink beer, and talk. He earned some money playing card games with burghers in pubs. Bookstores were another venue for the exchange of gossip as well as for meeting people.[66]

Once they were appointed to a position, clerics' relations with town inhabitants became more formalized. They and their families lived in parsonages attached to their churches. Legally they, like other church and school employees, were under the jurisdiction of the Leipzig Consistory rather than the city council, and were not burghers unless they owned homes. Bernd emphasized the importance of staying socially aloof from congregants in order to maintain one's standing: 'It is better that people believe and know that ministers are human than that they actually see this.'[67]

However, clerics' pastoral duties brought them into constant contact with Leipzig inhabitants. Clerics' workload was heavy, and it grew in the course of the Baroque era. With eighteen clerics serving a city of 30,000 by the 1710s, or one cleric serving almost 1700 people, there would have been no expectation that every inhabitant would develop a close relationship with a cleric. During an average week-long tour in 1687, a deacon would have baptized about six babies, married one or two couples,

---

61 SAL, Stift.VII.C.151. *Acta Die Verzeichnisse der in Bürger-Häusern wohnenden Herren Studiosorum betr.*, 1731 ff.

62 Bernd (1738) on Breslau, 48 and passim.

63 Andreas Glöckner (1990), *Die Musikpflege an der Leipziger Neukirche zur Zeit Johann Sebastian Bachs*, = *BzBf*, 8, 71–72; Bernd (1738), 110 ff. & 154.

64 Reuter (1980).

65 Bernd (1738), 72–73.

66 Ibid. on pubs, 105 ff., passim; on bookstores, 110 ff., 226–227, 303.

67 Ibid., 57, 332–333.

and delivered funeral sermons for five or six people, also seeing the families of these individuals at the ceremonies. By 1727, this number would have risen to two or three weddings, eight or nine baptisms, and nine or ten funerals.[68] Senior clerics officiated at ceremonies for members of the elites.

Despite this workload, though, clerics managed to connect with inhabitants. As we saw in the previous chapter, the poor who congregated around the pastor at St. John's felt an attachment to him. We will see below that congregations could even become attached to substitutes. Already as students, future clerics counseled the people in whose homes they roomed and, along with ordained clerics, visited people at home when they were ill.[69] People who desired some level of pastoral care could thus seek it out. It is also important to remember that many people may not have desired a close pastoral relationship.

Inhabitants could develop a regular relationship with a cleric through confession. As a rule, they confessed around three or four times a year and had one 'father confessor,' often for years at a time. From the 1670s onward, clerics and councilors struggled to accommodate and regulate demand for confession. Many clerics heard confessions all day Saturday, but could not hear everyone on this day. In 1694 the council, noting the growing population, added times during the week for people to confess.[70] People could confess and take communion at the churches that were opened beginning in 1699. It also appears that people could get a cleric to hear confession upon demand: clerics and councilors tried repeatedly and unsuccessfully to keep people from confessing Sunday morning before and during the worship service (unless they were ill or pregnant), as well as in small groups in churches outside the town walls and at St. John's Church.[71]

Clerics exercised their duties even when these put them at mortal risk. For example, no fewer than six pastors at the hospital church of St. Jacob were installed and died in succession during the outbreak of plague in Leipzig in September 1680. Two clerics in other churches also died. In contrast, many burghers fled the city. Four other St. Jacob's pastors died between 1650 and 1750 after two years or less of service.[72] Pastors seem to have been aware of the dangers of infection. Thus, in 1691 a pastor from the Saxon town of Schmiedeberg wrote that he had caught a serious

---

68 Derived from Leonhardi (1790), 62.

69 See Chapter Six and Bernd (1738), passim.

70 SHStADD, Loc. 2061, *Rescripte, Consistorium Leipzig*, 1693–1702, Upper Consistory to Leipzig Consistory, 5 February 1694, 56–56^{v}; Alexander Wieckowski (2005), *Evangelische Beichtstühle in Sachsen* (Beucha: Sax), 26 ff.

71 SAL, Tit.VII.B.35., *Acta, Die Privat-Communion in denen Kirchen vor denen Thoren alhier betr.*, 1736; SAL, Tit.VII.B.18., *Acta Das Frühbeichten in hiesigen Kirchen betr.*, 1672–1776.

72 Anon. (1777), *Vollständiges Verzeichniß der Prediger in Leipzig, welche seit der Reformation des sel. Lutheri, nämlich von dem 1539 bis zu dem jetzigen 1777 Jahre zum Predigtamte berufen worden ...*, 3rd. ed. (Leipzig: Dürr), 65–70.

illness by sharing the communion cup with thirty sick Swedes 'who were hurrying from Hungary to Bremen.'[73]

Clerics and Leipzig inhabitants had more informal contacts as well. These could have a significant impact on a cleric's career. Bernd, who always specified the social status of the lay people whom he encountered, ascribed elite men and women much influence. They showered him with gifts or simply visited him, giving feedback on his sermons, requesting spiritual guidance or giving him career advice. Bernd also described prominent individuals on and off the council working hard, to the point of intrigue, in order to get one *Magister* or another appointed to a position. Members of the elites could also cause trouble for clerics. From their secluded positions in *Capellen* they could disrupt a sermon, intentionally or not, by talking loudly or even laughing.[74] They also complained to the authorities. Once, an older merchant's wife took personal offense at a sermon in which Bernd criticized the frequent hiring and firing of servants by women. She complained to one of his 'most distinguished patrons,' who had him summoned and questioned.[75] Bernd claimed to actually be relieved when some people did not attend his sermons, because he had to watch every word he said when they were there.[76]

The elites also held considerable power collectively, as pacesetters. Bernd measured his initial success as a preacher at St. Peter's in part by the large numbers of elites who attended his services, with forty carriages lined up to pick them up afterward.[77] By the same token, he noted that from 1721 onward, his popularity and *applaus* (approval) declined because the elites were going to hear the oratorically gifted Salomon Deyling.[78] Elsewhere he noted that all too often, a preacher fell out of favor with city councilors, who then 'seldom or never visited his church, as a result of which a large portion of the common people, who so often follow the example of the high, also leave.'[79]

In Bernd's narrative, as in the rhetoric of the city council and other official groups, the 'common people' figured prominently. However, Bernd did not ascribe them nearly as much power to help or hurt him as he did the elites. Most often, for him as for the secular authorities, they appeared as objects of pastoral care, with Bernd visiting the homes of numerous artisans throughout the city over the years. He described the gifts of ordinary people as modest, and never mentioned non-elite support as having much impact on his status.

Finally, clerics' relations with the laity depended on their backgrounds and positions in the Leipzig clerical hierarchy. All clerics seem to have kept some social

---

73 Johann George Meissner to Johann George III/Upper Consistory, 14 February 1691. SHStADD, Loc. 7430, *Bestellung derer Superintendenten- Stellen oder Inspectionen in denen Churf. Sächß. Landen.*, vol. II, 1681–1704, 120–120[v].

74 Bernd (1738), 96–97, 336; Gerber (1732), 396–397.

75 Bernd (1738), 296.

76 Ibid., 300.

77 Ibid., 209.

78 Ibid., 367–368.

79 Ibid., 293.

distance from the 'common people.' For Bernd and others such as St. George's pastor Gehr the elites figured as glamorous patrons or benefactors (or potential threats); in contrast, some other pastors were themselves elites, either by birth into a prominent Leipzig family like the Carpzovs, or by virtue of attaining a doctorate or prominent position, as Salomon Deyling did. Their status and family ties probably gave them more leverage in disputes with congregants and the authorities than lowlier clerics had.

Clerics and councilors

Relations between clerics and councilors were often collegial. The two groups had to work together daily, and some councilors had relatives who were clerics. Councilors often considered the interests of the Ministry when they appointed and promoted clerics, appointed sextons, renovated churches, or distributed stipends and legacies.[80] However, there were also areas of tension. As they did elsewhere, clerics considered it their duty to criticize unjust council policies, invoking the divine nature of their vocation and office as an unassailable foundation of authority. In 1641, during the Thirty Years' War, a junior cleric who evidently supported burghers delivered sermons calling for major reforms in city government, on pain of divine wrath. The Superintendent defended the sermon in the face of an attack by the council.[81] In less turbulent times, clerics were more likely to be summoned for pronouncements that offended some prominent individual.

Some conflict derived from the two groups' overlapping jurisdictions, which ostensibly complemented those of the clergy: the clergy was responsible for spiritual matters, and the city council for matters 'external' to religion such as church finances and property. Clerics held authority over individuals' souls; the council governed their bodies. But the daily activities and missions of each group could not be so neatly divided. Thus, clerics around Saxony repeatedly demanded insight into the churches' annual account books and over legacies, claiming that the money was used for religious matters, while town councils claimed that they alone had this right.[82] Even if their requests were not honored, clerics probably had a good idea of income and expenditures because sextons working in the churches, under the official direction of the church directors, performed many day-to-day duties such as paying bills, receiving materials, and giving receipts.

Councilors had an enormous impact on clerics through the appointment and promotion processes. The selection of clerics was time-consuming, and was a major

---

80 Clerics: *Protocoll* ... 1682–1704, 251^{v}–252^{v}, 253–254^{v}; SAL, Tit. VII.B.11., *Consistorialia,* vol. X, Varia, 1619–1767 (the Superintendents' service diary from 1640 to 1681) (hereafter: *Consistorialia*), 220^{v}–221. Sextons: *Protocoll* ... 1682–1704, 80^{v}–82; 153^{v}–155. The 1663 renovation of St. Nicholas, stipends, and legacies: *Protocoll* ... 1682–1704, 80^{v}–82; 153^{v}–155.

81 *Consistorialia*, vol. X, 213–213^{v}. See also Schorn-Schütte (2000), 34–35.

82 See Geffcken & Tykocinski (1905); *Consistorialia*, vol. X, 354–355^{v}.

area of influence through patronage. Other ecclesiastical employees, including cantors, organists and teachers, were appointed in a similar process. Councilors spent the most time and effort in appointing candidates to their initial positions. They decided promotions primarily on the basis of seniority, although for the high positions of archdeacon and pastor the voice, talent, and health of the candidates were also considered. The search process for new Superintendents differed from others: a broad search for the best candidate from Saxony or beyond was conducted for this prominent position.

Rules governing the appointment process were laid down in Saxon ordinances, and were the same in Leipzig as in other Saxon towns.[83] The process began when a position opened and candidates, usually between six and twelve, sent written letters of application to the city council. In a plenary meeting of the council, the presiding mayor read the list of candidates. Then, following council procedure for all matters, each councilor, in order of seniority, could give his opinion on the candidates and vote for three. The three candidates who received the most votes were invited to give trial sermons in the church where one would later serve. In a second session, councilors gave their opinions on the sermons and on other qualities of the candidates, and voted for one. The candidate with the most votes won; if the vote was tied, the mayor cast the deciding vote.

Candidates were selected according to many of the same principles that governed secular appointments. The 'links of patronage, familiarity, and informal influences' that Mack Walker has pointed out as central in smaller towns were equally important in Leipzig.[84] It was important for councilors to know candidates or to consult people who did: 'he has good testimony (*Zeugnis*),' 'is praised,' 'has a good reputation.'[85] More generally, they commented that a candidate was 'known' (*bekannt*) or 'unknown.' Individual councilors often encouraged a protégé to apply in the first place, and then convinced other councilors to vote for him.

In the same category as being known was being from Leipzig (a *Stadtkind)* or not (a *Frembder)*. Being from Leipzig was an advantage: 'He is a Leipziger, and should not be passed over if there is nobody better.'[86] Some candidates were sons of burghers who were known to city councilors. If the 'merits' of the father were mentioned, these candidates were uniformly appointed.[87] Two candidates who were the sons of councilors were elected without even having to deliver a trial sermon.[88]

Other factors also influenced appointments. One was power relations within the council: sometimes senior councilors, the *Enge*, decided on a candidate and the

---

83 Early rules: Emil Sehling, ed. (1902), *Die evangelischen Kirchenordnungen des 16. Jahrhunderts*, vol. I (Leipzig: Reisland), 375 ff. These were elaborated in later ordinances.

84 Walker (1971), 62.

85 *Protocoll* ... 1682–1704. 19 October 1691, 164^{v}–165^{v}.

86 Ibid., 25 August 1699, 296^{v}–298. This was similar in Rostock: Strom (1999), 56.

87 *Protocoll* ... 1682–1704. 30 December 1701, 324^{v}–325, 4 August 1702, 675–677; quote from the latter.

88 Christian Wagner and Friedrich Wilhelm Schütz. *Protocoll* ... 1682–1704, 6 November 1685, 60–61; 8 November 1699, 304–305.

larger council voted to approve the choice.[89] Another was the Electoral authorities, who occasionally 'suggested' candidates. For positions in villages, one consideration was sometimes that the candidate marry the previous minister's widow or daughter. In a discussion preceding the 1682 appointment of Justinus Töllner in the village of Panitzsch, one councilor mentioned that Töllner might marry the daughter of his deceased predecessor, so that the daughter and widow would be provided for. Another councilor argued that this should not be a consideration.[90] Similarly, Adam Bernd wrote that a potential position in the village of Krossen fell through partly because he did not want to marry the pastor's widow or daughter, as the noble patron desired.[91]

Along with secular criteria, ecclesiastical standards also shaped the selection process. Councilors discussed candidates' merits as future pastors in detail. Most discussed was preaching ability. Several councilors attended trial sermons, sometimes of all three candidates. Candidates were praised for good preaching style: 'I especially liked Hassert, who preached today, except his voice was somewhat weak; Werner was also good; and Pipping's sermon was not to be improved upon. His elocution, elaboration, and declamation were all good.'[92] And they were criticized for bad style: 'In his sermon yesterday it was noticed that he will not be well suited because his speech is not easy (*gelind*);'[93] or, 'he has no gift for preaching.'[94] No candidate who was thus criticized was appointed. Candidates were also judged on their general 'erudition' and on their character, especially whether they were pious, 'peaceable' as opposed to argumentative, and had a 'quiet' lifestyle. These general and character qualities were mentioned for every successful candidate; to a certain extent they were tropes, repeating requirements for clerics that were laid down in ordinances and clerics' contracts.

The congregation's preference, a criterion in territorial ordinances, was mentioned infrequently but was a decisive factor in several cases. (In contrast to places such as Rostock and the territory of Hesse-Kassel,[95] parishioners in Saxony had no formal right to participate.) Each time, the congregation was already familiar with the candidate. Justinus Töllner, ironically considering his later relations, was appointed partly because 'the subjects have a great affection for him.'[96] Töllner had lived with and tutored the children of the previous pastor since 1680,[97] and possibly taken over some of his duties. In 1693, a councilor expressed general satisfaction that the city of

---

89 Cases of 1692 and 1702. Ibid., 178^{v}–180^{v}, 329–330.

90 Ibid., 26 June & 16 August 1682, 2–4.

91 Bernd (1738), 208.

92 *Protocoll* ... 1682–1704. 15 August 1699, 294–295^{v}. On weak voices, see also Strom (1999), 51–52.

93 *Protocoll* ... 1682–1704, 6 July 1683, 24–25.

94 Ibid., 12 May 1699, 127–130.

95 Strom (1999), 47 ff.; Schorn-Schütte (1996), 60.

96 *Protocoll* ... 1682–1704, 26 June & 16 August 1682, 2–4. See also Chapter Seven.

97 Jens Bulisch (1997/1998), 'Justinus Töllners Weggang aus Panitzsch. Ein Beitrag zur Frühgeschichte des Pietismus in Sachsen,' *Herbergen der Christenheit*, 21/22, 69–86; 70.

Leipzig was able to produce so many candidates who were 'accepted by the church as well as the public.'[98] And in 1702, when Wilhelm Hassert was appointed as pastor at St. John's, councilors agreed that although the other candidates were also well qualified, Hassert 'has the good fortune to be ardently desired by the parishioners, who even yesterday tearfully requested his appointment.'[99]

Theological debates also determined the choice of clerics. Some councilors, most of them jurists, took an active part in the Pietist-Orthodox disputes. The most active Pietist was syndic Johann Job (1664/65–1736, councilor from 1711). In 1700 Job initiated a correspondence with August Hermann Francke, whom he had met six months earlier. He maintained intensive contact with him until Francke's death in 1727, serving as a main contact between Leipzig Pietists and Halle.[100] Another Pietist was Abraham Christoph Platz (1658–1728, councilor from 1683), a highly influential councilor and Saxon official. He was the son of a Leipzig merchant, was orphaned at the age of eight, and studied theology for ten years before studying law.[101] The many-sided merchant councilor Friedrich Benedict Carpzov (1639–99), who also attained a senior position and became a prominent contributor to the journal *Acta Eruditorum*, rebelled against his family's Orthodoxy. He corresponded with Francke, suggesting literary projects and complaining about his Orthodox relatives, and sent his daughter to Francke's school for girls in Halle.[102] Other senior councilors and their families, such as city judge Götze and his wife, also met with Francke and distributed Halle literature among likeminded friends.[103]

Supporters of the Orthodox clerical establishment were also active in the city council. In fact, the membership of the council and the Leipzig Consistory, which often defended the Orthodox clergy, overlapped: four Orthodox *literati*, Jacob Born (1638–1709, councilor from 1661), his son Johann Franz Born (?–1732), Gottfried Lange (1672–1748, councilor from 1710), and Johann Jacob Mascov were at some point between 1690 and 1730 also jurist assessors of the Consistory; Johann Franz Born and Lange eventually became its directors. Unlike their Pietist counterparts, the Orthodox councilors did not leave tracts and letters behind, but they were active nonetheless. Lange, Bach's main supporter on the council, was the son of a village pastor and studied theology before studying law.[104] He initially made his career at the Dresden court and was forced on the city council by Elector August the Strong.

---

[98] *Protocoll* ... 1682–1704, 25 September 1693, 204^{v}–206^{v}.

[99] Ibid., 27 March 1702, 329–330. Also ibid., 13 March 1702, 327^{v}–329 and *Protocoll in die Enge*, 10 March 1702, 158–160.

[100] Job to Francke, May 1700 & 14 July 1702. AFS, C 232: 1 & 12. Job wrote over 80 letters in all. E-mail of 5 March 1996 from Robert Beachy; Jöcher/Adelung (1787), vol. II, 2288–2289. See also Chapter Seven.

[101] Jöcher (1751), vol. III, 1627–1628.

[102] F.B. Carpzov to Francke, 1698–99. AFS, A 112: 257–345. Carpzov wrote a letter of support as early as 1690 for Francke (6 May 1690, D 84: 47–47^{v}).

[103] Johann Jacob Preusse to Francke, 9 December 1720. (AFS, A 174: 198).

[104] Jöcher (1750), vol. II, 2248; Siegele (1986), 54–57; Georg Christoph Wintzer (1718, with ms. additions), *Summarische Nachricht von dem Raths-Collegio in der… Stadt Leipzig*

Jacob Born supported the Orthodox clergy against the Pietists during the dispute over the collegia pietatis in 1689–90.[105]

Councilors worked to gain the appointments of clerics on their side of the debate, calling on informal networks of fellow councilors and clerics. Theological alignments rarely surfaced in official protocols, partly because all debate on Pietism was forbidden in 1690. A rare reference was Abraham Christoph Platz's defense of a candidate suspected of Pietism. Platz produced a letter of recommendation and noted that 'accusations of "Pietism" hinder many good things.'[106] Also, Johann Job, attempting to have a Pietist candidate appointed, wrote several letters to August Hermann Francke in 1720 during the search for a Superintendent to replace Johannes Dornfeld, and visited one candidate whom Francke recommended.[107] However, the council eventually elected Salomon Deyling, the choice of a competing council faction.

* * *

The councilors' mission, and many of their everyday activities, had a religious basis. Councilors gained much power through that mission and those activities, but were also tied by them to a set of responsibilities. Burghers expected to be able to participate in the religious arena, and to have councilors administer their duties and live their lives in accordance with specific religious norms.

Clerics constantly negotiated relations with people of every social group. Through rooming and boarding arrangements, students and inhabitants got to know each other well, with familiarity extending to whether someone snored, how much they ate, and temperament. Once they were ordained, relations shifted. While students were generally more dependent on burghers than the burghers on them, clerics belonged to a different estate and maintained some degree of aloofness. They baptized, married, and buried other inhabitants, and might be entrusted with the details of transgressions during confession. Stories about the former students likely continued to circulate, though, supplemented by stories of their personal lives as clerics.

Inhabitants sought out and received, often on their own terms, clerical services such as communion. Their voice was greatly magnified if they were a member of the elites, whether male or female. Servants, widows, and other non-propertied urbanites had a less powerful voice. Still, they could exercise some control by holding councilors and clerics to their proclaimed norms, however inegalitarian those norms were.

(Leipzig). Lange was also familiar with Pietism: he studied for a time in Halle and married Rahel Feller, the daughter of professor Joachim Feller, an early Pietist supporter.

[105] Jacob Born and Johann George Börner to Johann George III, 10 November 1690, SHStADD, Loc. 10330, *Den so gen.* Pietismum *betr. 1690 sqq.*, 68–104.

[106] *Protocoll* ... 1682–1704, 25 August 1699, 296v–297v; SAL, Tit.VIII.41., *Protocoll in den 3 Räthen* ... 1687–1709, 27 June 1708, 884–887.

[107] Job to Francke, 8 and 13 October and 27 November, 1720. AFS, C 232: 60–62.

Chapter Four

Elites in and beyond Leipzig: the Dresden court and the consistories

Everyday religious life in Leipzig had a territorial as well as a local context. The Saxon Electors' interest in religion was probably greatest during the Reformation era; but even Frederick August II, or 'August the Strong' (ruled 1694–1733), who converted to Catholicism in 1697, continued to take an interest and to use religious issues as an opportunity to further absolutist goals. As historians have found for early modern Europe generally, relations between Leipzig's elites and the court were often symbiotic.[1] Leipzig had legal and other talent that the court was eager to recruit, and money that the constantly cash-strapped Electors needed. Further, Leipzig councilors were regularly appointed to positions at the court. A town like Leipzig, with its trade, fairs, university, and entrenched elites who wielded well-practiced evasive strategies, was in a particularly good position to blunt the absolutist strivings of territorial courts. More generally in Saxony, as in other territories such as Württemberg, the towns, clerics, and consistories held on to their autonomy to a greater extent than in Brandenburg-Prussia. However, there were disputes on many issues.

While relations between courts and towns have been well explored, the lynchpins of the sprawling system of public religious culture, the consistories and the ecclesiastical law they administered, have been all but ignored in research since World War II on Lutheran areas.[2] This neglect is in part due to a lack of interest in institutional history, and in part to an overemphasis on shifts to secular governance

---

1 Christopher Friedrichs (2000), *Urban Politics in Early Modern Europe* (New York: Routledge), 65 ff.; Alexander Cowan (1998), *Urban Europe 1500–1700* (New York: Arnold), 43 ff.; Robert Beachy (2005), *The Soul of Commerce: Credit, Property, and Politics in Leipzig, 1750–1830* (Boston: Brill), esp. 56–61; Richard Dietrich (1983), 'Merkantilismus und Städtewesen in Kursachsen,' in Volker Press, ed., *Städtewesen und Merkantilismus in Mitteleuropa* (Cologne: Böhlau), 222–285; Heinz Schilling (1993), *Die Stadt in der frühen Neuzeit* (Munich: Oldenbourg), 35 ff.; Karlheinz Blaschke (1990), 'Die Kursächsische Politik und Leipzig im 18. Jahrhundert,' in Wolfgang Martens, ed., *Leipzig: Aufklärung und Bürgerlichkeit* (Heidelberg: Schneider), 23–38.

2 Luise Schorn-Schütte (1996), *Evangelische Geistlichkeit in der Frühneuzeit. Deren Anteil an der Entfaltung frühmoderner Staatlichkeit und Gesellschaft. Dargestellt am Beispiel des Fürstentums Braunschweig-Wolfenbüttel, der Landgrafschaft Hessen-Kassel und der Stadt Braunschweig* (Gütersloh: Gütersloher Verlagshaus), outlines the jurisdictions of consistories, 68–72; 344 ff.; David Sabean (1990), *Property, Production, and Family in Neckarhausen,*

in the Reformation era. Calvinist areas have been better researched.[3] The consistories typify the legal intersection of the secular with the sacred: the broad spectrum of cases brought before them ranged from property disputes to theological debates. They contributed to the durability of confessional structures and regulations into the second half of the 18th century in the face of growing resentment and change. Staffed by leading jurists and theologians, the consistories weathered August the Strong's absolutist inroads and decades of Pietist and Enlightenment critique. They connected the local and territorial levels of religious governance. They were Saxon institutions, but the members of the Leipzig Consistory, two jurists and two clerics, also held positions as city councilors, University professors, and Leipzig Superintendents.

The goal here is not to examine consistory rulings on specific issues such as premarital sex. Rather, it is to reconstruct the principles and mechanics that made ecclesiastical law and consistory governance central to everyday religious life. Underlying the authority and position of the consistories was the mostly unspoken assumption, shared by the majority of ordinary people as well as the authorities, that it was appropriate for religious life to be regulated through the law. The term 'social discipline' describes only part of the consistories' activities. Certainly, the consistories regularly disciplined clerics as well as ordinary people. However, the vast majority of cases was brought by individuals who were somehow competing in the religious arena. For example, people often petitioned the consistories about disputed pews. Johann Sebastian Bach brought and received complaints several times,[4] as did other musicians. Women who had become pregnant after having been promised marriage petitioned for monetary compensation, which they often received. Many cases involved jurisdictional disputes between institutions. Additionally, many cases, including individuals' petitions to receive legacies or stipends or village pastors' requests to enlarge their homes, involved no dispute at all.

Within a framework that remained stable from the late 16th to the mid-18th centuries, there was gradual evolution as well as some dramatic ruptures in Saxony, especially in the 1680s and 1690s. The ruptures provide important insights into the emergence of Pietism, and into the development of religious life generally. In Dresden, Elector Johann George III (ruled 1680–91) broke with Philipp Jacob Spener (1635–1705), Senior Court Chaplain from 1686 to 1691. Spener's assertiveness in carrying out

---

1700–1870 (New York: Cambridge University Press), 66–87, discusses a Neckarhausen *Kirchenkonvent* formed in the 1640s which apparently handled a narrow range of issues.

3 See Philip Benedict (2002), *Christ's Churches Purely Reformed* (New Haven: Yale University Press), 460 ff.; Margo Todd (2002), *The Culture of Protestantism in Early Modern Scotland* (New Haven: Yale University Press), 8–13 & 16–19; Paul Münch (1978), *Zucht und Ordnung. Reformierte Kirchenverfassungen im 16. und 17. Jahrhundert (Nassau-Dillenburg, Kurpfalz, Hessen-Kassel)* (Stuttgart: Klett-Cotta). On England, see Martin Ingram (1987), *Church Courts, Sex and Marriage in England, 1570–1640* (New York: Cambridge University Press); Jennifer McNabb (2006), 'Ceremony versus Consent: Courtship, Illegitimacy, and Reputation in Northwest England, 1560–1610,' *Sixteenth Century Journal*, 37, 59–81, esp. 63–65.

4 *NBR*, 109–110, 137–139, 143–144, 159–161, 189–193.

his traditional admonitory role, combined with his Pietist intensity, collided with Johann George's absolutist shift toward a more secular cultural style. Spener's institutional position as Upper Consistory assessor, and the support he received from Orthodox clerics and secular court councilors, were important dimensions of that conflict, but they have been neglected by other historians. Meanwhile, in Leipzig, the young jurist and philosopher Christian Thomasius launched a scathing and influential attack on the Saxon consistories and ecclesiastical law, which he was to continue throughout his career. Both Spener and Thomasius were close to August Hermann Francke, and the collegia pietatis formed a backdrop to their disputes. Another context was an informal network of elite clerics and jurists which came to include Samuel von Pufendorf, Spener, Thomasius, and Francke. These men initially saw opportunities to effect change in Saxony, but then shifted to neighboring Brandenburg-Prussia. While the Enlightenment per se is not a focus here, the controversy surrounding Thomasius demonstrates, as Eduard Winter and others have argued, that religious issues were at the center of the early Enlightenment.[5]

After briefly examining relations between Leipzig and Dresden, the first part of this chapter discusses the Electors' roles in religious life, including Spener's conflict with Johann George III, August's conversion, and the impact of these changes on territorial governance. The second discusses the consistories, their councilors or assessors, ecclesiastical law, and Thomasius's challenge to the system. The sources on these topics are rich. Archival materials include consistory records of various types, such as appointment records, rescript collections, and correspondence on specific cases. Published sources include Electoral ordinances, compilations, commentaries, and tracts.

The court, chaplains, and religion in Saxony

Dresden was a two-day trip by coach from Leipzig. It lay on the Elbe River in the southeastern corner of Saxony, not far from Bohemia and the Erzgebirge or 'Ore Mountains.' The city was a center of trade and manufacture in its own right, but the Electoral residence dominated it. Throngs of courtiers, artists, military people, and luxury suppliers gave the main impetus to the rise in the town's population, which overtook that of Leipzig by the 1730s. The Electors had played prominent roles on the stage of the Holy Roman Empire since the 15th century. They continued to pride themselves on their descent from their forebears who had supported Luther, and until August's conversion they were considered the leaders among the Protestant rulers

[5] Eduard Winter (1966), *Frühaufklärung. Der Kampf gegen den Konfessionalismus in Mittel- und Osteuropa und die deutsch-slawische Begegnung* (Berlin: Akademie), 47–106; Thomas Ahnert (2006), *Religion and the Origins of the German Enlightenment: Faith and Philosophy in the Thought of Christian Thomasius* (Rochester: University of Rochester Press).

of the Empire. By the 1660s, the Electors had developed Dresden into the major Northern German center of Italianate festive culture, music, and art collecting.[6]

People travelled frequently between Leipzig and Dresden, for a variety of reasons. Leipzig councilors visited the court, often for extended stays, to represent the city and fulfil their duties as Saxon councilors. Clerics visited as well. Musicians, including Bach, came to hear the opera and perform for various occasions. Travelling in the other direction, nobles from the court descended on Leipzig during the fairs to do business, socialize, and visit the Leipzig Opera. The Electors and members of their family visited too, making grand entries into the city and being royally hosted at the homes of leading burghers. On Sundays, they could attend morning services at St. Thomas's, using the Electoral balcony built in 1684. Some of the Electors' great accomplishments were showcased in Leipzig. For example, porcelain objects, the outcome of decades of intrigue and scientific development, were first publicly displayed at the 1710 Easter fair in Leipzig.[7]

While relations were often mutually beneficial, conflict frequently arose. The issues at stake, and the form that battles took, remained surprisingly constant from the later 16th to the mid-18th centuries, although the balance of power shifted back and forth. City councilors, electors, and courtiers fought most often over control of the city's financial resources and over the general autonomy and specific appointments to the city council and ministry. For example, the court periodically demanded oversight over fiscal information, but those demands were often not fulfilled. Thus, lists of legacies that had been demanded as early as 1712 had still not been sent in 1749.[8] From the later 17th century onward, the council's control over large amounts of money influenced political dynamics, as it had in the 16th century. This was in contrast to its time of fiscal crisis and oversight by Dresden from 1628 to 1688. Growing urban prosperity coincided with, and helped fund, the cultural and military pursuits of August the Strong. In an exchange of money for political rights that was common between towns and courts around Europe, August the Strong regularly extorted 100,000 to 200,000 thaler from the council in return for autonomy on specific appointment issues.[9] One key to understanding relations is that while the Electors had supreme, 'episcopal' authority, it was intermediate authorities (*Unterobrigkeiten*) such as the Leipzig city council and clerics that actually had specific and substantial rights, such as appointing clerics.

The court and council competed over appointments both to the clergy and the council itself. The court might hold up an appointment to remind the council of its subordinate position. On other occasions, such as when a courtier or member of the

---

6 See Helen Watanabe-O'Kelly (2002), *Court Culture in Dresden from Renaissance to Baroque* (Houndmills: Palgrave).

7 Watanabe-O'Kelly (2002), 225.

8 SAL, VII.B.33, *Generalia und Consistorial-Verordnungen wegen Administration derer Piarum causarum*, 1712 ff., 1, 3 ff., 16–21.

9 Gustav Wustmann (1895), *Quellen zur Geschichte Leipzigs. Veröffentlichungen aus dem Archiv und der Bibliothek der Stadt Leipzig*, vol. II (Leipzig: Duncker & Humblot), Introduction, 59–128; 90 & passim.

Electoral family 'recommended' a candidate, there was no open fighting. The electors also regularly pressured city councilors to elect clients of the court to the council. In most instances, those councilors did not generate open dispute, and remained on the council for decades.[10] One was Bach's supporter Gottfried Lange. A spectacular exception was Francis Conrad Romanus, who was made a councilor in 1700 at the age of thirty and mayor soon afterward. Romanus presided over major public works projects such as the installation of street lighting, as well as making urban money available for August, who was desperate to finance various projects. Soon, though, Romanus had exceeded his reach: in 1704, it became known that he had falsified city bonds and stolen money for his personal use. In 1705 he was removed from office, and he was imprisoned until his death in 1746. While this incident can be interpreted to emphasize the influence of absolutist policy on Leipzig, it is telling that Romanus was not in power long.

* * *

The theoretical basis of the Electors' powers in religious life was similar to that of the Leipzig city council. Reformation-era clerics, courtiers, and the Electors themselves conceptualized the Electors' role in covenant terms. Luther and later Saxon theologians likened the Electors to King David, calling on an exegesis of Psalm 101 for illustration.[11] In contrast to the interpretation of the covenant for the city council, the ruler here is a king; oblique references, missing in Joshua, are made to the 'wicked' nature of court life; and David makes no pact with the larger population. Otherwise, the message of both is similar. One part of Psalm 101 focuses on King David's promise to 'behave myself wisely in a perfect way ... set no wicked thing before mine eyes ... him that hath an high look and a proud heart will not I suffer.' Luther and others drew from this an emphasis on the Elector's role as 'father of the territory' (*Landesvater*), a good example of personal piety and probity for his subjects. Another part of the Psalm focuses on King David's promise that 'mine eyes shall be upon the faithful of the land ... I will early destroy all the wicked of the land ...' Here the Elector's duties as head of the territorial ecclesiastical system came to the fore: the obligation to ensure the teaching of Scripture and the security of clerics who preached the Word.

From the start, the Electors' relationship to religion, personified in their relationship to the highest Saxon cleric, the Senior Court Chaplain, contained tensions that were not present between the Leipzig city council and clergy. The ambition to exercise supreme authority in the territory collided with clerics' insistence on obedience to an even higher power. The ideal of reciprocal, corporate relations that underlay the

---

10 Ibid., 100 ff.

11 Wolfgang Sommer (1988), *Gottesfurcht und Fürstenherrschaft. Studien zum Obrigkeitsverständnis Johann Arndts und lutherischer Hofprediger zur Zeit der altprotestantischen Orthodoxie* (Göttingen: Vandenhoeck & Ruprecht), 23–73; passim. Bible, King James Version.

city council's rule, and provided a basis for the council to negotiate with clerics, was increasingly far removed from the Electors' goals. For their part, a series of high-profile Senior Court Chaplains, each well known and respected throughout the German Protestant world, publicly 'punished' bad behavior by the Electors and their courtiers from the pulpit of the court chapel.[12] Core aspects of absolutist court culture such as excessive drinking and lavish dining, hunting, and expansive festivities provided ample material for fire-and-brimstone sermons and for private conversations.

The Reformation-era Electors had been devout supporters of Luther, and conversion had initially brought considerable financial, political, and ideological gains. After the Thirty Years' War, though, the Electors began to perceive their traditional paternalistic role as a brake on their exercise of authority. To the chagrin of the Saxon estates, Johann George II (ruled 1656–80), Johann George III and Johann George IV (ruled 1691–94) followed a clear absolutist agenda. They increasingly exercised their cultural power through secular activities such as opera and other festivities modelled on the courts of Versailles and the Italian city-states. Johann George III built on the already impressive achievements of his father, personally recruiting Italian singers, instrumentalists, and composers for glittering performances at his court opera. Among them was Margherita Salicola, one of the first female opera singers to star in Germany, who was praised for her 'divine' voice 'as sweet and strong as a trumpet.'[13]

The Electors also pursued political and military glory in the Empire and farther afield. Within Saxony, they worked toward centralization and reducing the power of the estates.[14] Johann George III achieved fame as the 'Saxon Mars:' against the vehement opposition of the estates, he established the first Saxon standing army and personally commanded it in significant campaigns. This shift in the Electors' governing style was in marked contrast to the style of town councils and the territorial estates, which did not distance themselves from their traditional roles. In fact, conflicting views of the role of religion in governance became central to disputes between the Electors and estates. These developments were paralleled elsewhere in the Holy Roman Empire, notably in Württemberg, and to a lesser extent in the Palatinate and Hessen-Kassel.[15]

---

12 Sommer (1988), 23–73; 74–134.

13 Moritz Fürstenau (1861), *Zur Geschichte der Musik und des Theaters am Hofe zu Dresden*, vol. I (Dresden: Kuntze; R [1971], Hildesheim: Olms), 175 ff.; quote, 277 ff.

14 See Karl Czok and Reiner Gross (1989), 'Das Kurfürstentum, die sächsisch-polnische Union und die Staatsreform (1547–1789),' in Czok, ed., *Geschichte Sachsens* (Weimar: Böhlau), 208–287.

15 James Allen Vann (1984), *The Making of a State. Württemberg 1593–1793* (Ithaca: Cornell University Press), especially Chapters Four & Five; Günther Christ (1989), 'Fürst, Dynastie, Territorium und Konfession. Beobachtungen zu Fürstenkonversionen des ausgehenden 17. und beginnenden 18. Jahrhunderts,' idem, *Studien zur Reichskirche der Frühneuzeit* (Stuttgart: Steiner), 111–131; Dieter Stievermann (1991), 'Politik und Konfession im 18. Jahrhundert,' *Zeitschrift für historische Forschung*, 18, 177–199.

The renegotiation of confessional relations in Saxony peaked in the 1680s and 1690s. Confessional consensus at the court broke down when relations between Johann George III and Philipp Jacob Spener, who arrived as Senior Court Chaplain in July 1686, collapsed. Spener's office was considered the highest clerical position in the German Protestant world, and Spener's rank at the Dresden court was immediately below that of the top political figures at court. The office also carried with it two other functions: that of father confessor to the Elector and his family, and that of Upper Consistory member, a position that was the basis of his institutional power and contact with clerics in Saxony. The appointment of a new Senior Court Chaplain was treated as an affair of state, and was preceded by an elaborate courting ritual.[16]

Spener was received in Saxony with high expectations. It may be that Saxon clerics had hoped that Spener would be able to rescue a deteriorating confessional situation. They praised Spener's accomplishments to Johann George.[17] Earlier, they had responded favorably to his *Pia Desideria*, in which he had sharply criticized the moral shortcomings of rulers and courtiers.[18] In a letter to a former parishioner in Frankfurt, Spener wrote that he was warmly received in Dresden.[19]

But Spener's relations with the Elector soon became tense. His sermons were unusually sharp, focusing heavily on the sins associated with court life such as overly elaborate and revealing dress, hunting, carnival revelry, and lavish drinking and dining. Spener also offered specific if veiled criticism of projects close to Johann George, such as his importation of Italian musicians. Johann George showed his displeasure by attending a total of eight of Spener's sermons, and refusing Spener's requests for private audiences.[20] By October 1690 Johann George was claiming that he could not live in Dresden at the same time as Spener.[21] It seems that a struggle

---

16 The appointment records, which also include correspondence on the conflict: SHStADD, Loc. 4687, *Ersetzung derer Ober-und Hoff-Prediger-Stellen,* 1659–1696 (hereafter: *Ersetzung*). Franz Blanckmeister (1899) quoted these records without citation beyond 'Hauptstaatsarchiv Dresden,' *Sächsische Kirchengeschichte* (Dresden: Sturm), 209 ff. Paul Grünberg (1893), *Philipp Jakob Spener*, vol. I (Göttingen: Vandenhoeck & Ruprecht, R [1988], Hildesheim: Olms), 206–256, provides a good account based mostly on published works and letters, as well as an unspecified report in the 'Dresden archive' (251), but does not draw on the appointment records. See Tanya Kevorkian (1998), 'Piety Confronts Politics: Philipp Jacob Spener in Dresden (1686–1691),' *German History*, 16, 145–164.

17 Upper consistory councilors to Johann George, *Ersetzung*, 25 January 1686, 107–111.

18 See Johann Georg Walch (1739), *Historische und Theologische Einleitung in die Religions-Streitigkeiten der evangelisch-Lutherischen Kirche*, vol. IV, pt. 2 (Jena: Meyer, R [1985], Stuttgart: Frommann Holzboog), 1087 ff.

19 Spener to Anna Elisabeth Kissner, 13 July 1686, printed in August Nebe (1934–35), 'Aus Speners Dresdner Briefen an eine Freundin in Frankfurt a.M.,' *Theologische Studien und Kritiken*, 106, 253–300; 259–261.

20 See Sommer (1988), 206–218.

21 Grünberg (1893), 251.

over a specific lifestyle issue, as well as Spener's general critical attitude, were behind the fight. Perhaps tensions with his wife were an issue: Electress Anna Sophia was like many other noblewomen an ardent supporter of Spener and tried until the end to retain him in Dresden.[22] Whatever the reason, Spener and Johann George were equally unbending. The Elector was unwilling to pay the lip service to clerical demands that his predecessors had, despite their similar lifestyles.[23] And previous Senior Court Chaplains had been more tolerant of their charges' failings.

By February 1691, Johann George had decided to force Spener from his position. He wrote from the country estate of Dippoldiswalda to the privy councilors reminding them that he had moved from Dresden and chosen a new father confessor to avoid Spener. He continued with an order to use 'your prudence and dexterity, which are well known to me, and consider how best ... to attain [Spener's] satisfaction elsewhere' since he would no longer tolerate him.[24] The privy councilors responded with a horrified refusal to execute Johann George's order. In a memo sealed with each of their nine seals, they took recourse to 'our secular office, which we must not exceed.' They also argued that neither they nor any other humans were qualified to act in this matter, since Spener had been called to his position by divine vocation.[25] The councilors, like Spener and all clerics, emphasized the divine nature of a clerical vocation, which was merely executed by human hand. They stayed with this position in spite of two more, unusually harshly-phrased, orders from Johann George.[26] Spener's Orthodox Upper Consistory colleagues also supported Spener, even though they had been engaged in a full-fledged battle with him over the Leipzig collegia pietatis for over a year. As Samuel Benedict Carpzov wrote, 'it is unconscionable ... to *cassiren* any preacher, not to mention one who is in such a high position, without very serious cause.'[27]

The dispute between Spener and Johann George was resolved in a way that allowed both sides to keep face. During the standoff, arrangements were being made for Spener to be called as head pastor to Berlin. The call was officially sent in early April.[28] Spener was first called *to* Berlin and then allowed to resign from his position in Dresden, rather than being forced merely to depart from Dresden, as

---

22 *Ersetzung*, privy councilors to Johann George, 14 March 1691, 182–184^{v}: the privy councilors relay a request by the Electress to continue to have Spener as her father confessor and to have him preach in Dresden; Grünberg (1893), 254, citing letters from Spener to Rechenberg.

23 Sommer (1998), 104 ff.

24 *Ersetzung*, vol. I, Johann George to *Geh. Rats Directore und Räthe*, 21 February 1691, 171–171^{v}.

25 Ibid., 28 February 1691, 172–174.

26 Ibid., 3 March 1691, 177–177^{v} (cited here) and 18 March 1691, 198–200; councilors to Johann George, 14 March 1691, 182–184.

27 To the privy councilors. Ibid., 6 March 1691, 187–187^{v}.

28 Ibid., Frederick III to Johann George, 21 March 1691, 201–201^{v} and 1 April 1691, 208–208^{v}; Johann George to Frederick III, 29 March 1691, 207–207^{v}.

Johann George insisted on occasion.[29] Spener's partial victory and his support by privy councilors and consistory assessors show how religious constructs such as that of the call, and confessional institutions, could limit absolutism.

After Spener left, the Electoral house and government remained split between supporters of Orthodoxy and Pietism. With the death of Johann George III in November 1691 one party at the court, probably led by the dowager Electress, wanted Spener to be reappointed.[30] When Spener's replacement, the Orthodox Samuel Benedict Carpzov, until then the Dresden Superintendent, was appointed in March 1692, the standard phrase that he would serve as chaplain and father confessor to the dowager Electress and, interestingly, August and his fiancé, was crossed out of a draft of his contract.[31] August thus apparently sympathized with Pietists before he converted to Catholicism. His older brother Johann George IV was a Pietist who protected Pietist students and theologians at court and around Saxony.

August's conversion to Catholicism was certainly dramatic, and its effects far-reaching. But when one considers the backdrop of events that preceded it, it becomes clear that it was merely the last step in a longer process: August fully escaped the confines of 'punishing' clerics and pious estates. His conversion was not the result of religious fervor; August was a lukewarm Catholic. Rather, he converted in order to become eligible for election to the Polish throne. August received the title of King, and he became a player in politics and wars from Italy to Russia. Günther Christ's speculation that rulers who converted to Catholicism around 1700 were attracted by ritual at Catholic courts, which was well suited to absolutist style, also seems apt. August, like other rulers, was familiar with the style prevalent at Catholic courts and towns from his travels to Italy, France, and Vienna.[32] He continued his predecessors' importation of sophisticated culture, although with a shift to the French-inspired. Dresden consolidated its reputation as a first-rank European cultural capital.[33] Conversion to Catholicism also opened connections to courts throughout Europe. In 1719 August was able to arrange a marriage between his son Frederick August and Maria Josepha, daughter of the Holy Roman Emperor.

August's conversion did not, however, mean that religion ceased to play a role in Saxon politics. Rather, the role of religion was reinscribed in the context of ongoing competition between Electors and estates. Invoking Electoral Saxony's role as homeland of the Reformation and head of the Corpus Evangelicorum of the Holy Roman Empire, the Saxon estates demanded and received an extensive set of guarantees that Lutheranism would remain the one public confession in Saxony.[34]

---

29 Ibid., Johann George to privy councilors, 26 March 1691, 202–202^{v}; privy councilors to Johann George, 27 March 1691, 203–204.

30 Ibid., Upper Consistory to Johann George IV, 20 November 1691, 244–248^{v}.

31 *Ersetzung*, Carpzov's *Bestallung*, 10 March 1692, 276–279.

32 See Katrin Keller (1994), ed., *'Mein Herr befindet sich gottlob gesund und wohl.' Sächsische Prinzen auf Reisen* (Leipzig: Universitätsverlag).

33 See Watanabe-O'Kelly (2002), 193 ff.

34 See Czok & Gross (1989); Fritz Kaphahn (1922), 'Kurfürst und kursächsische Stände im 17. und beginnenden 18. Jahrhundert,' *Neues Archiv für sächsische Geschichte und*

August ceded his rights in religious issues to the Privy Council, which assumed leadership of the Corpus Evangelicorum. Religion emerged as one issue on which the estates could successfully demand rights. In areas such as taxation and the military, they lost influence under August as they had since the 1660s. By contrast, August and his government respected the religious 'rights' of the estates and of the larger Saxon population. As August or a high official wrote in the instructions to a councilor sent as Saxon representative to the Vatican in 1724 'the spirit of this people [the Saxons] ... is long accustomed to liberty ... Domestic affairs and the nature of the country demand that the people be governed gently ... most of the revenues of the Prince are provided by Commerce, which demands civil liberty and liberty of conscience.'[35]

August also continued to appreciate the political value of the religious arena. He kept track of clerical appointments,[36] and forced supernumeraries who were his protegés on the consistories, as he did on other institutions. Privy councilors consulted him frequently about individual appointments and theological issues. In the 1720s and 1730s, August contributed generously to the construction of the Frauenkirche, ironically intended partly as a rebuttal to his conversion, and lent court architects and artists to assist in its construction.[37] More generally, ties between the ruling house and subjects were reaffirmed in a religious context until well into the 19th century on occasions like the triannual 'Days of Repentance, Prayer, and Fasting' (*Buß, Bet, und Fast-Tage*). These Friday services continued to center on the well-being of the house and territory, and to include a prayer for the health of the house's members.[38]

The consistories and ecclesiastical law

It is well established that the Reformation was a legal as well as theological movement. As Gerald Strauss has shown, although there was much 'ambivalence' about the 'ties joining Christians to the law,' those ties were very strong.[39] And as John Witte has

---

Altertumskunde, 43, 62–79; Georg Wagner (1901/02), *Die Beziehungen Augusts des Starken zu seinen Ständen während der ersten Jahre seiner Regierung (1694–1700)* (Leipzig: Mutze). Johannes Ziekursch (1903), 'August der Starke und die katholische Kirche in den Jahren 1697–1720,' *Zeitschrift für Kirchengeschichte*, 24, 86–135, 232–280.

35 SHStADD, Loc. 3305, *Instruction pour le Comte de Lagnasco, Ministre du Cabinet et d'Etat General de Cavallerie ... 10. April 1724.* unfol., 21 fol. in *Instructions et Ordres du Roy pour le Comte de Lagnasco ... 1724. 1725.1726.*

36 Claus Petzoldt (1971), 'Studien zu einer Biographie Valentin Ernst Löschers. Löschers Berufung nach Dresden 1709. Konventikelwesen in Dresden zwischen 1690 und 1750. Katalog der Manuskripte Löschers 1688–1749' (PhD thesis, University of Leipzig), 53–54.

37 Watanabe-O'Kelly (2002), 201 ff.

38 SHStADD, Loc. 1887, *Die Ausschreibung der allgemeinen Buß- Bet- und Fasttage.* vol. I, 1603–1719 & II, 1720–50. *Kirchen-Gebete, 1700–1830*; SHStADD, Bibliothek, W 420.a.

39 Strauss (1986), *Law, Resistance, and the State* (Princeton: Princeton University Press), esp. 191–239; 208.

shown, beginning in the 1530s jurists and theologians collaborated in developing a legal system which carried many features of canon law into the areas of church and school personnel, marriage, and the administration of church property. Late 17th and 18th century Protestant jurists were to attack these 'vestiges' of Catholicism, but even they continued to incorporate canon law into their thinking.[40]

However, scholars over-emphasize the shift of power to secular authorities in the 16th century. They have emphasized the secular leadership of 'discipline masters' and marriage courts, often transitional institutions that preceded the establishment of consistories; of visitation commissions; and of shifts in legal philosophy.[41] Even when they discuss clerics' roles in developing the law, they do not discuss ecclesiastical law or the consistories. For the period after about 1600, there is a similar emphasis on the secular.[42] But the consistories, which also took shape in the course of the 16th century and administered many newly-formulated laws, did not represent a clear development toward secular control of religious life. Rather, they demonstrate an ongoing, strong and well organized presence by clerics in the administration of a wide range of legal matters, and a mutual influence of secular and religious legal categories in many areas.

The consistories were a presence in much of Protestant Europe. The Saxon consistories' activities and composition roughly resembled those in Brandenburg-Prussia, in Calvinist territories in the Holy Roman Empire and Switzerland, in England, and in many other Lutheran territories.[43] The consistories first emerged in the 1530s and 1540s, when the Saxon Electoral government and clerics began to organize permanent institutions to replace the defunct Catholic ecclesiastical system. These institutions succeeded the periodic visitations that had been initiated in the 1520s under the guidance of Luther.[44] The consistories' geographical and

---

40 Witte (2002), *Law and Protestantism. The Legal Teachings of the Lutheran Reformation* (New York: Cambridge University Press), esp. 53–85; Rudolf Schäfer (1915), 'Die Geltung des kanonischen Rechts in der evangelischen Kirche Deutschlands von Luther bis zur Gegenwart. Ein Beitrag zur Geschichte der Quellen, der Literatur und der Rechtssprechung des evangelischen Kirchenrechts,' *Zeitschrift der Savigny-Stiftung für Rechtsforschung, Kanonisches Abteil*, 5, 165–413.

41 See Harold Berman (2003), *Law and Revolution, II. The Impact of the Protestant Reformations on the Western Legal Tradition* (Cambridge, MA: Harvard University Press), 7 ff., 29 ff.; Witte (2002), passim; Roper (1989), *The Holy Household. Women and Morals in Reformation Augsburg* (Oxford: Clarendon), esp. Chapter One.

42 See Isabel Hull (1996), *Sexuality, State, and Civil Society in Germany, 1700–1815* (Ithaca: Cornell University Press), passim; Marc Raeff (1983), *The Well-Ordered Police State: Social and Institutional Change through Law in the Germanies and Russia, 1600–1800* (New Haven: Yale University Press), 19 ff., 44 ff., 82 ff., 147 ff.

43 See above, notes 2 & 3.

44 See Gerald Strauss (1978), *Luther's House of Learning. Indoctrination of the Young in Reformation Germany* (Baltimore: Johns Hopkins University Press); Emil Sehling, ed. (1902), *Die evangelischen Kirchenordnungen des 16. Jahrhunderts*, vol. I (Leipzig: Reisland), 33 ff. & 85 ff.; Hans-Walter Krumwiede (1967), *Zur Entstehung des landesherrlichen*

legal jurisdictions were based on the bishops' courts in Meissen and Merseburg, and were moved to Dresden and Leipzig respectively by 1580. The Dresden, or Upper Consistory was given supervisory powers over the Leipzig Consistory and a third consistory established in Wittenberg.[45] The Leipzig Consistory administered the area around Leipzig (the Leipzig *Kreis*), the Vogtland area bordering on Franconia, and all of Thuringia.

The consistories administered matters in three areas.[46] First were the secular affairs of clerics and school and church employees, including property and pensions. While such personnel matters seem trivial, they encompassed a huge administrative area in which financial and political stakes were high. In the 18th century there were around 2000 pastors in Saxony (of whom about 20% were in towns, and 80% in villages) and another 6000 church and school employees: sextons, organists, cantors, teachers, a vast skein of patronage.[47] The wives, widows, children, and servants of these men also fell under the consistories' purview. Second, the consistories handled sacred issues involving sacraments, liturgy, and dogma. This was the area of the three with the least activity in terms of cases brought, although cases did occasionally arise and were bitterly disputed. For example, many cases relating to the Pietist-Orthodox controversy were brought. Third were 'hybrid' (*mixti*) matters which had sacred as well as secular components. The most important of these was the vast area of marriage and sexuality, including betrothal, premarital pregnancy, divorce, and marriage dispensations.

Like lower courts throughout Germany, the consistories had the right to administer civil punishments: fines and jail, but not punishments that affected 'body and life.' Cases that could lead to corporal sentences were referred to the high secular courts. The Upper Consistory could also impose partial and full excommunication.[48] The jurisdiction of the consistories overlapped with that of secular courts, and in many

---

Kirchenregimentes in Kursachsen und Braunschweig-Wolfenbüttel (Göttingen: Vandenhoeck & Ruprecht).

[45] See Sehling, ed. (1902), 97 ff.; J.S. Göbel (1794), *Ursprung, Geschichte und Verfassung der Consistorien in den Chursächsischen Landen. Ein Beytrag zur Statistik von Chursachsen* (Freyberg: Crazische Buchhandlung); Helmar Junghans, ed. (1989), *Das Jahrhundert der Reformation in Sachsen* (Berlin: Evangelische Verlagsanstalt), esp. Ernst Koch, 'Ausbau, Gefährdung und Festigung der lutherischen Landeskirche von 1553 bis 1601,' 195–223 & Günther Wartenberg, 'Die Entstehung der sächsischen Landeskirche von 1539–1559,' 67–90; Günter Wartenberg (1988), *Landesherrschaft und Reformation. Moritz von Sachsen und die albertinische Kirchenpolitik bis 1546* (Gütersloh: Mohn); R. Merkel (1906), 'Zur Geschichte des Leipziger Konsistoriums,' *Neues Archiv für sächsische Geschichte und Altertumskunde*, 27, 279–310; Wilhelm Haan (1880), *Die Episkopal-, Consistorial- und Diöcesan-Verfassung im ehemaligen Kurfürstenthume und jetzigen Königreiche Sachsen vor und seit Einführung der Reformation bis ... 1878* (Dresden: Baensch). On the *Kirchen-Rat*, which existed in theory but not practice by the 17th century, see Göbel (1794), 10 ff.

[46] See 1580 *Kirchenordnung*, reprinted in Sehling, ed. (1902), 359 ff.

[47] Göbel (1794), 149.

[48] Sehling, ed. (1902), 1580 *Kirchenordnung*, 404–406.

cases no guidelines prescribed which authorities should hear a case. As Isabel Hull shows, the many levels of the early modern 'legal landscape' confused even contemporaries.[49] More specifically, this overlapping shows again the fluidity of boundaries between secular and ecclesiastical matters. Cases of adultery, rape, and impregnation and desertion of women were tried and sentenced in secular courts as well as in the consistories. In Leipzig, city council laws regulated many of the same areas that church ordinances did. Thus, in two of his disputes that involved the Leipzig Consistory, Bach addressed memos to the Leipzig city council as well.[50] Sometimes one case involved two courts; and institutions might compete for cases.

However disparate, all cases brought before the consistories were resolved by similar procedures. Many minor issues were decided through correspondence. Others involved personal appearances by the parties involved. Mighty theology professors as well as unruly villagers were obliged to submit petitions and appear. Commensurate with their status, the consistories occupied central, specific places in the urban topography. The Leipzig Consistory had a house in the Thomaskirchhof, the square across from St. Thomas's.[51] The Upper Consistory had chambers near the Electoral castle. People bringing cases or who had been summoned for interrogation were often able to pick up the decisions of their cases the same afternoon. They could confer with the consistories' secretaries, protonotaries, registrars, and copyists. They frequently travelled long distances from smaller towns and villages, and stayed in Leipzig or Dresden for one or more nights. According to the bylaws, the Leipzig Consistory met Wednesdays and Fridays from 9:00 am to 11:00 or noon. The Upper Consistory met Tuesdays, Wednesdays, and Fridays from 8:30 am to noon. Both also met, if necessary, from 3:00 pm to 5:00 or 6:00.[52] Important or controversial matters were referred by the Leipzig Consistory to the Upper Consistory, and from there to the Saxon privy council.

*   *   *

Two clerics and two jurists (*politici*) each sat as regular assessors on the Leipzig and Upper Consistories. Typifying the complex nature of early modern corporate identities as well as the position of ecclesiastical affairs in Saxon society, each assessor also served on at least one other institution. The Upper Consistory clerics were both *ex officio* members: one was the Senior Court Chaplain, and the other the Dresden Superintendent. One of the Leipzig Consistory clerics, the Leipzig Superintendent, was also an *ex officio* assessor. The other was often a University

49 Hull (1996), esp. 57 ff.

50 *NBR*, 137–139 & 159–161.

51 Göbel (1794), 67–70.

52 Upper Consistory: SHStADD, Loc. 7428, *Bestellung des Churfürstl. Sächsisch. Ober-Consistorii belangend*, 1587–1704 (hereafter: *Bestellung*), *Ober-Consistorial Instruction de ao. 1658*, 118–143. Leipzig: SHStADD, Loc. 1916, *Assessuren des Consistorii zu Leipzig betr.*, vol. I, 1618–1731 (hereafter: *Assessuren*), *Instruction vor das gemeinschafftliche Consistorium zu Leipzig*, 1658, 118–143; Göbel (1794), 47 ff., 73–74.

theology professor. The Upper Consistory was headed additionally by a president, who was required to be a nobleman and Electoral privy councilor. The director of the Leipzig Consistory was its senior *politicus*.

Jurists and clerics worked closely together in the consistories, although their collaboration was often marked by tension and competition. Formally, their duties were separate but complementary. Ordinances dictated that jurists and clerics were to decide matters that fell under their respective jurisdictions. But most cases were 'hybrid' which 'required joint knowledge.'[53] Jurists, and secular legal method, dominated everyday routine: *politici* headed each consistory, directed sessions and counted votes, and drafted all except purely theological decisions. As Zedler's encyclopedia noted in 1733, 'the trial process and mode of investigation have to be directed by jurists, who understand this handicraft.' Clerics insisted on their rights, but in a way that suggests that their opinion was often ignored, even in theological cases.

The assessors were tied to the secular state and service to the person of the Elector in several ways. At investiture ceremonies, power was conferred via a chain of oaths and handshakes that linked all members, in descending hierarchical order, to the person of the Elector.[54] Assessors swore an oath parallel to those sworn by jurists throughout Europe, a lengthy formula that included obedience to the Elector, obeying the Augsburg Confession, serving the Consistory and its clients well and without selfish, venal, or other dishonorable motives, and keeping the court's proceedings secret.[55] The jurist assessors also held secular offices. Most Upper Consistory *politici* were also Electoral court or appellate councilors. In Leipzig, consistory assessors often doubled as Supreme Electoral Court assessors; some were city councilors, and others were law professors. Their 'piling up of offices' (*Ämterhäufung*) was partly a result of assessors' long years of service as supernumeraries or substitutes, during which they could not make a living from their consistory practices. It also seems to have been an attempt by the Dresden court and the Leipzig city council to coordinate the exercise of power in different institutions. One person might be active in secular and ecclesiastical law and politics on the local, territorial, and Imperial levels. The phenomenon attained a high point with Jacob Born (1638–1709), who held positions as city councilor and later mayor, assessor and then head of the Juror's Court, Leipzig Consistory assessor, Supreme Electoral Court councilor, and law professor. Born also held positions as Appellate Councilor and Privy Councilor at the Dresden court. He served as the Leipzig city council's 'man in Dresden,' and was engaged

---

53 Johann Heinrich Zedler, ed. (1737), 'Consistorium Ecclesiasticum,' *Grosses vollständiges Universal-Lexicon aller Wissenschafften und Künste* (Leipzig: Zedler, R [1961–1964] Graz: Akademische Druck- u. Verlagsanstalt), vol. VI, 1035–1036.

54 For examples from 1661 and 1687, see *Bestellung*, 178–181 & 272–276ᵛ.

55 The basic oath was formulated by 1580. See Sehling, ed. (1902), 402–403. It was later elaboborated somewhat; see *Assessuren*, c. 1680, 44–44ᵛ, 47.

by the Electors in a number of sensitive and important issues.[56] Not surprisingly, the Leipzig Consistory complained repeatedly that Born was rarely in Leipzig.

Despite their ties to the Electors, consistory assessors successfully defended traditional corporate interests and confessional religious life during the Pietist-Orthodox and absolutist-estates battles. They were able to do this for several reasons. The right to appoint assessors was distributed among several institutions, limiting the influence of any one institution. The Dresden and Leipzig city councils named the Superintendents of their respective cities. The Dresden court selected the jurist assessors, but had to choose from a list of three candidates nominated by the consistories. Also, as the result of an agreement made in 1658 between Elector Johann George II and his three younger brothers, the Saxon cadet lines of Merseburg, Weissenfels, and Zeitz, received the right to alternate in filling every second open position. The appointment of assessors for life was also an important factor. This practice was accompanied by an elaborate system of appointing younger jurists as substitutes, supernumeraries, or adjuncts, since one or both of the *politici* on each consistory had usually reached an age when they were no longer able to perform their duties. Substitutes were ordinarily appointed with the formal expectation of eventually gaining a regular position. New *politici* thus already had considerable direct experience, often ten years or more, and had been integrated into the consistories' routine and interests.

During his reign, August the Strong instituted the absolutist policy of packing the Leipzig and Dresden consistories with legal expectants of his choosing.[57] He seems to have pursued this policy in part to provide patronage, and in part to challenge the traditional 'rights' of powerful institutions. The impact of the installations was minimal, since the new appointees did not become regular assessors until formal nomination by the consistories, many years later. Many moved on to other positions before they did.

August's attempts to force clerics on the consistories were more limited. The appointment processes for the theological assessors was more complex, clerics' qualifications more specialized, and the clerical hierarchy sufficiently powerful that opportunities for interfering with the traditional process were severely circumscribed. August installed only one cleric, the junior court chaplain Johann Andreas Gleich, as a supernumerary (without the expectation of ascending to a regular position) in the Upper Consistory in 1722, after three months of resistance. Gleich does not seem to have exercised much authority.[58]

The professional and social identities of individual assessors also contributed to the cohesion of the assessors, as James Allen Vann also found for secular

---

56 Christian Gottlieb Jöcher, ed. (1750), *Allgemeines Gelehrten-Lexicon* (Leipzig: Gleditsch), vol. I, 1255–1256.

57 For Leipzig, see SHStADD, Loc. 4709, *Advocaturen beym Consistorio zu Leipzig*, 1707–1765.

58 SHStADD, Loc. 1874, *Ersetzung der ordinar und extraordinar theol. u. polit. Raths-Stellen beym Ober-Consistorio*, 1625–1743, 150–150^{v}, 155–161.

Württemburg councilors.[59] Both the clerical and legal assessors had risen to the top of their professions. They had doctorates, making them the social peers of the lower nobility.[60] Having a background in both secular and ecclesiastical law, jurists did not necessarily perceive a conflict between the two areas of the law, which may have prompted them to defend clerical agendas and the autonomy of the consistories. Family connections were also important. Unlike the clerical profession, the top ranks of the legal profession were generally a preserve of established dynasties. Leipzig Consistory *politici* were recruited from the ranks of prominent Leipzig families such as the Borns and Carpzovs, and most Upper Consistory *politici* were the sons, sons-in-law, and/or grandsons of figures at the Electoral court.

* * *

In the course of the 17th century, Saxon ecclesiastical law grew into a vast but well-coordinated complex. As in other Lutheran territories, it was made up of three interrelated groups of texts. The first two, church ordinances and Lutheran dogmatic texts, were consolidated by 1580; the third, consistory decisions in individual cases, continued to evolve. The implementation of the Electoral Church Ordinance (*Kirchenordnung*), which standardized nearly sixty years of ordinance-issuing, and of the Book of Concord in 1580 was a landmark development.[61] The Book of Concord consisted of the 1577 Formula of Concord and several further texts: three early Christian creeds, the Augsburg Confession, and the original Saxon visitation ordinance.[62] The Formula, issued by leading Lutheran theologians who had been summoned by Elector August to codify dogma, laid down doctrine on issues disputed to then and became official doctrine in Saxony. The Book of Concord was commonly referred to as the 'Symbolical Books' (*Symbolische Bücher*) because all the texts had the status of 'symbols,' or creeds.

In the 17th and 18th centuries, the Book of Concord and the Church Ordinance had a huge influence on ecclesiastical practice and rhetoric, framing the terms of debate over issues large and small. Elector August had attempted to bring clerics more firmly under central control. But the Church Ordinance in particular was used by the ecclesiastical establishment as a weapon to defend its status and privileges

59 See Vann (1984).

60 See Strauss (1986), 165–190.

61 See Sommer (1988), 111 ff.; Ernst Koch (1986), 'Der kursächsische Philippismus und seine Krise in den 1560er und 1570er Jahren,' in Heinz Schilling, ed., *Die reformierte Konfessionalisierung in Deutschland – Das Problem der 'Zweiten Reformation'* (Gütersloh: Mohn), 60–77; idem, 'Ausbau, Gefährdung und Festigung der lutherischen Landeskirche von 1553 bis 1601,' in Junghans, ed. (1989), 195–223. The 'Second Reformation' from Lutheranism to Calvinism under Christian I (ruled 1586–91) was short-lived. See Karlheinz Blaschke, 'Religion und Politik in Kursachsen 1586–91,' in Schilling, ed. (1986), 79–97.

62 See J.T. Müller, ed. (1869), *Symbolische Bücher der evangelisch-Lutherischen Kirche* (Stuttgart: Liesching).

and, more generally, the confessional order, against incursions by the Electoral government. Consistory officials referred to the provisions of the Church Ordinance as their 'constitution' (*Verfassung*). They benefited particularly from the Ordinance's conservatism, the repeated injunction to prevent all 'innovation' (*Neuerung*) in religious matters. Any suggestion for change could thus be labelled as a dangerous departure from Luther's precepts, the intent of which had been best captured in 1580.

The embattled and generally pessimistic tone that pervaded the 1580 Church Ordinance also survived in many routine formulations, although often in new contexts. Originally, references to 'Satan's cunning and deceit' and of the difficult times facing the Saxon church were a response to the chaotic conditions of the Reformation era. Long after the Thirty Years' War, though, the language still gives the impression that all concerned perceived religious affairs as being in a constant state of crisis. Satan's instruments were variously interpreted to be a host of internal and external enemies: the other confessions, Islam, lax Lutheran clerics, secular rulers, and vain and prideful subjects.

In the third major area of ecclesiastical law, consistory decisions were issued in myriad cases on issues that were addressed briefly or not at all up to 1580. The 17th century codifications were more systematic, and paid more attention to intellectual underpinnings than the relatively ad hoc, pragmatic 16th century ordinances. The most important conceptual foundation, known as 'Christian' natural law, was elaborated extensively by jurists and clerics throughout 17th-century Protestant Germany. While the Christian natural law tradition became obscure after 1700, it was common currency throughout the 17th century; its proponents included Veit Ludwig von Seckendorff and Gottfried Wilhelm Leibniz.[63] The emphasis on the Ten Commandments in this natural law, and its connection to the Lutheran Aristotelian tradition, located it in marked opposition to the natural law of Grotius's secularist followers Pufendorf and Thomasius.

Importantly, jurists used this variant of natural law in both secular and ecclesiastical law. Parallels are exemplified in the work of Leipzig jurist Benedict Carpzov (1595–1666), author of two of the most important compendia of early modern German law: one on Saxon ecclesiastical law, and one on criminal law. Carpzov was a law professor as well as a judge on the 'Juror's Court' (*Schöppenstuhl*), a high Saxon court located in Leipzig. Although he apparently never served as a consistory assessor, he took a keen interest in theology and was a proponent of Christian natural law. Considering Scripture, in particular Mosaic law, to be the fount of all law, Carpzov famously read the Bible from cover to cover fifty-three times during his life; he also followed Scriptural models in structuring his compendia.[64] His *Jurisprudentia Ecclesiastica*

---

63 See Hans-Peter Schneider (1967), *Justitia Universalis. Quellenstudien zur Geschichte des 'Christlichen Naturrechts' bei Gottfried Wilhelm Leibniz* (Frankfurt: Klostermann).

64 Klaus Bollmann (1963), 'Die Stellung des Inquisiten bei Carpzov. Eine Untersuchung über den gemeinen deutschen Strafprozess des 17. Jahrhunderts' (PhD thesis, University of Marburg), 41.

seu Consistorialis (*Ecclesiastical or Consistory Law*) was published in 1649 and in seven later editions to 1721.[65] It became a reference work in Saxony and other territories, although Brandenburg-Prussian and other jurists produced similar works. It cited consistory decisions in innumerable individual cases, mostly from the first decades of the 17th century.

Benedict Carpzov's other major work, for which he is best known, was the criminal-law compendium *Practica Nova Imperialis Saxonica Rerum Criminalium*.[66] First published in 1635 and reprinted fourteen times to 1758, the *Practica Nova* became the standard work of criminal law in Saxony and throughout much of the Holy Roman Empire. It resembled the *Jurisprudentia Ecclesiastica* in its organization and empirical focus. Carpzov extensively applied the precepts of Christian natural law.[67] He organized the two main books of the *Practica Nova* thematically around the Ten Commandments and referred extensively to Scripture. Carpzov fit offenses that were not covered in the Decalogue into the Decalogic scheme: for example, he included crimes against the state under the Fourth Commandment on the grounds that the authorities were the equivalent of parents, and inserted personal insults under the rubric of theft by comparing an insult to the theft of honor.[68]

Many of the crimes discussed in the *Practica Nova* themselves had a religious dimension. They included witchcraft, which fell under the category of heresy and was not an abstract issue at the time. Contrary to legend, Carpzov did not sentence 20,000 or even 300 women to death as witches while he was a Juror's Court judge. From 1661 he actually worked against the implementation of death sentences in Saxony.[69] However, the trial and torture of suspects of witchcraft in Leipzig and elsewhere followed the guidelines of the *Practica Nova*. The torture was harsh: in the 1650s at least two women died under it, and another did as late as 1699.[70] In Leipzig

---

65 Carpzov (1645 ff.), *Jurisprudentia Ecclesiastica seu Consistorialis Rerum & Quaestionum in Serenissimi ac Potentissimi Principis Electoris Saxon ... Libr. III*. (Leipzig: Starck).

66 See Bollmann (1963), esp. 27–68; Sergio Moccia (1988), *Carpzov e Grozio. Dalla concezione teocratica alla concezione laica del diritto penale* (Naples: Editoriale Scientifica); Wolf Recktenwald (1956), 'Verbrechen gegen die öffentliche Ordnung in Kursachsen zur Zeit Benedict Carpzovs,' (PhD thesis, University of Bonn); Friedrich Schaffstein (1930), *Die allgemeinen Lehren vom Verbrechen in ihrer Entwicklung durch die Wissenschaft des gemeinen Strafrechts. Beiträge zur Strafrechtsentwicklung von der Carolina bis Carpzov* (Berlin: Springer; R [1986] Aalen: Scientia); Hellmuth von Weber (1949), 'Benedict Carpzov. Ein Bild der deutschen Rechtspflege im Barockzeitalter,' *Festschrift für Ernst Heinrich Rosenfeld* (Berlin: de Gruyter), 29–50.

67 Moccia (1988), 11–39.

68 Von Weber (1949), 34; Witte (2002), 10 and passim.

69 Manfred Wilde (2003), *Die Zauberei- und Hexenprozesse in Kursachsen* (Weimar: Böhlau), 68. Individual judges cannot be associated with sentences, and Carpzov did not serve on the court during the witch hunts of the mid-1650s.

70 Kurt Kuhne (1967), *Der Einfluß des Leipziger Schöppen Benedict Carpzov auf die Prozesse gegen die Hexen um Delitzsch* (Delitzsch: Kreismuseum Delitzsch).

and the area surrounding it, there were ten trials for witchcraft and related offenses between 1650 and 1750, including two charges of magic/quackery brought by a Leipzig physician (apparently against less educated competitors) in 1730. Of these cases, three women were released, one died under torture in 1699, one denunciator was imprisoned, and the outcomes of other cases are unknown.[71]

While the basic frameworks of ecclesiastical law and consistory practice did not change until late in the 18th century, there was considerable evolution on specific issues. For example, in 1723 jurist Julius Bernhard von Rohr noted that although an old decree mandated that no new hymns be introduced, 'this has gradually changed in practice.'[72] Reflecting changes such as these, in 1718 Upper Consistory *politicus* Andreas Beyer published his *Additiones* to Carpzov's text,[73] a substantial work that supplemented and revised many sections of the *Juisprudentia*, which had recently been reprinted unrevised. However, Beyer did not reconceptualize Carpzov's work as a whole. Rohr's nearly 1000-page *Complete Upper Saxon Ecclesiastical Law* incorporated more Enlightenment thinking, but also retained many features of traditional law. Rohr criticized Carpzov's *Jurisprudentia* for being written in Latin, which made it inaccessible to many people, for its 'popish principles,' and for its neglect of natural law.[74] However, he cited Carpzov and other 17th century jurists on numerous specifics. He retained the traditional criminal rubric 'witches and magicians,' calling for burning if they had harmed anyone, but was cautiously skeptical on the subject: 'if one does not want to indirectly mock territorial law, cast all historical faith into doubt, or even deny experience, one must maintain that there are witches.' Also, 'I firmly believe that in previous times, when the world was simpler and more naive, the judges burned some people as witches who never were.'[75]

* * *

The scathing attack on the Saxon ecclesiastical system by Christian Thomasius (1655–1728) gave a major impetus to broader questioning of the system. Thomasius grew up in Leipzig and began his career at the University of Leipzig, where his father Jacob Thomasius had also taught. He developed a multifaceted critique of the conjunction of the religious and the secular that was the hallmark of the confessional system.[76] In particular, he attacked the power of the clerical establishment, especially

71 Wilde (2003), 535 ff.

72 Rohr (1723), *Vollständiges Ober-Sächsisches Kirchen-Recht, in welchem die Materien der geistlichen Rechts-Gelehrsamkeit ohne Einmischung der Päbstlichen Verordnungen, nach Anleitung des Göttlichen und natürlichen Recht* ... (Frankfurt & Leipzig: Martini), 805.

73 Beyer (1718), *Additiones ad Benedicti Carpzovii, JCti, ... Jurisprudentiam Ecclesiasticam, vulgò Consistorialia* ... (Leipzig: Starck).

74 Rohr (1723), preface, unpaginated.

75 Rohr (1723), 902 ff.; quotes, 904–905.

76 Thomasius (1690), *Churbrandenburgischer Unterthanen Doppelte Glückseligkeit, so sie wegen des durch Churfürstliche scharffe Edicta verbesserten Geistlichen und Weltlichen*

in Saxony, in areas he claimed should either be open to interpretation by all laypeople, or administered by secular institutions that were under the control of secular rulers. Thomasius was in part religiously-motivated. He thought of himself as fighting, the better qualified for being a lay person, for the restoration of 'true' Protestantism.[77] Typically of early Enlighteners, he was well versed in Scripture, Luther's writings, and religious history; specific arguments for the reform of homiletic practice, church organization, and ecclesiastical law filled his writings.[78] Thomasius's writings had little effect on the day-to-day running of ecclesiastic affairs; most of the changes he proposed were not implemented until the late 18th century or even the 19th. But they were crucial in shaping contemporary debates, influenced jurists such as Rohr, and have influenced views of the proper relationship between secular society and religion to the present day. Thomasius's complaints have been taken at face value by most modern scholars, who have largely characterized the Saxon establishment much like the schematic 'other' delineated by Thomasius himself: intellectually exhausted, intolerant, and pedantic. While that critique certainly holds true in at least some regards, it obscures the social significance of that system.

The institutional focus of Thomasius's attack was the consistories: these were the channels through which clerics exercised power in areas he claimed to be inappropriate to them. Thomasius attached 'Christian' natural law and ecclesiastical law as a set of 'Popish relics.' Benedict Carpzov's *Jurisprudentia Ecclesiastica* came in for particularly harsh treatment for its 'many defects,' including its retention of canon law and for specifics such as Carpzov's assertion that it was appropriate to force people to take communion.[79] Thomasius protested that the consistories were dominated by the clergy, and called for the removal of a variety of offenses he defined as secular, such as adultery, usury, and stealing from a church, from their jurisdiction. He argued that since the consistories' power had been delegated to them by rulers, rulers had the right to make these changes. Secular rulers also had the

Standes zugeniessen haben in Außerlesene und in Deutsch noch nie Gedruckte Schrifften, in idem (1705), *Ausserlesene und in Deutsch noch nie Gedruckte Schriften*, vol. I (Halle: Renger), 22–23; (1722), *Historia Contentionis inter Imperium et Sacerdotium ... In usum Auditorii Thomasiani* (Halle: Renger), 342, 571; Thomasius & Enno Rudolph Brenneysen (1696), *Das Recht evangangelischer Fürsten in theologischen Streitigkeiten, gründlich ausgeführet, und wider die papistischen Lehr-Sätze eines Theologi zu Leipzig ... benebenst einer summarischen Anzeige und kurzen Apologie wegen der vielen Anschuldigungen und Verfolgungen, damit etliche Chur-Sächsische Theologen zu Dresden, Wittenberg und Leipzig nun etliche Jahre her besagten D. Thomasen beleget und diffamiret* (Halle: Salfeld), 125 ff., 172 ff.

77 See Winter (1966), esp. 47–106.

78 See Walther Bienert (1934), *Der Ausbruch der christlichen deutschen Neuzeit, dargestellt an Wissen und Glauben des Christian Thomasius* (Halle: Akademie), 422–474.

79 Thomasius (1722), 650–651; Thomasius & Brenneysen (1696), 49–50.

right to decide and demand the cessation of theological disputes, and to regulate the adiaphora.[80]

How did Thomasius's critique take shape? More research is needed to provide the full story. However, it appears that originally Thomasius and a network of powerful clerics and jurists who worked in or had other ties to Saxony intended to work toward the reform of the Saxon ecclesiastical system.[81] The men included Veit Ludwig von Seckendorff, Adam Tschirnhaus, Adam Rechenberg, Leibniz, Samuel von Pufendorf, and Spener himself. These men disagreed on some major theological and legal issues, but largely suspended disagreements among themselves for the duration of Thomasius's conflict in Saxony. They actively advised Thomasius. Thus, in several letters in 1688, Pufendorf encouraged him, attacked Orthodox figures, and discussed relations with Seckendorff and Spener.[82] In March, Pufendorf wrote: 'If the gentleman could penetrate the pedantry, he would be performing an immortal service to our fatherland.'[83] The men thought that Spener's presence in Dresden provided a good opportunity to challenge the Orthodox system. Connections among the men were extensive. Thomasius had corresponded with Spener since 1685, when Spener was still in Frankfurt; Spener had been a guest at the home of Thomasius's father. Spener was the father-in-law of Leipzig philosophy professor Rechenberg, who helped Francke and Thomasius during the investigation into the collegia pietatis.[84]

Thomasius began his attack in Spring 1688, with the publication of his *Monthly Conversations* (*Monatsgespräche*) in which he praised Spener's works while charging the Leipzig 'clerisy' with pedantry, preoccupation with entertaining rather than uplifting their congregations through their sermons, hypocrisy, and other sins.[85] In addition, Thomasius began holding collegia explaining Grotius's natural law. He thus entered a heated debate between two schools of interpretation of Grotius's major work, *De Jure Gentium Belli ac Pacis*. Orthodox scholars, led at the time by University theologian Valentin Alberti himself, claimed that Grotius's work was consistent with 'Christian' natural law.[86] A secularist tradition represented most prominently by Pufendorf, on the other hand, argued for a natural law founded on secular reason, from which revelation was excluded. Since 1678, Alberti and Pufendorf had been engaged in the most systematic exchange in the debate. Thomasius wrote that he

80 Thomasius & Brenneysen (1696), esp. 92 ff.; Thomasius (1695), *De jure Principis circa Adiaphora* (Halle: Salfeld).

81 See Winter (1966), esp. 63–86.

82 Emil Gigas, ed. (1897), *Briefe Samuel Pufendorfs an Christian Thomasius (1687–1693)* (Munich: Oldenbourg), letters of 31 March, 28 August, & 1 December 1688, 20, 26–27 & 30–33.

83 Gigas, ed. (1897), letter of 24 March 1688, 17–19; 17.

84 See Chapter Six and Grünberg (1893), 152 and passim.

85 Thomasius (1688–89), *Freimütige, lustige und ernsthafte, jedoch Vernunftmässige Gedancken oder Monatsgespräche über allerhand, fürnehmlich aber neue Bücher* (R [1972] Frankfurt: Athenäum); Bienert (1934), 152 ff.

86 See Schneider (1967), 247 ff.

had gradually merged from the 'darkness' of Orthodox interpretations of Grotius to become an adherent of Pufendorf's interpretation.[87] Personal animosity and a visceral dislike, by Thomasius and others of the Orthodox theologians, helped drive the dispute.[88] For example, Pufendorf wrote to Thomasius that Alberti's newly published *Epistola ad Seckendorfium* seemed 'to have come to the light of day either *per vomitum* or *per sedes*.'[89] Fuel was added to the fire when Thomasius supported August Hermann Francke beginning in 1689. The Saxon clerical establishment continued to be a target in Thomasius's writings after he left Saxony, in dedications and in the main body of his works, in both incidental and substantial pieces.[90] In contrast, Thomasius praised the Brandenburg-Prussian rulers and the intellectual and spiritual 'freedom' they provided.[91]

The Saxon establishment responded by reserving some of its harshest invective for this son of a Leipzig professor. In a 1690 report on the Leipzig collegia pietatis Samuel Benedict Carpzov, writing as Upper Consistory assessor, recommended that in order to restore order and the good reputation of the University of Leipzig, 'in particular, a prominent example should be made of the well-known wicked person (*böser Mensch*) Christian Thomasius ... who has always spoken for the Pietists.' The Leipzig Consistory argued that Thomasius 'has led astray the children of so many honorable people through his reckless principles.'[92] Eventually, Thomasius was forced to flee Saxony because a warrant for his arrest had been issued. He was the only anti-Orthodox figure to be thus charged; the rights of others, such as Francke, to publish, preach, or teach were revoked (as were those of Thomasius), but no warrants for their arrest were issued.

In the aftermath of Spener's conflict with Johann George, and of Thomasius's, Francke's, and others' departure from Leipzig, the territorial context of the debate

87 Thomasius (1709), *Drey Bücher der Göttlichen Rechtsgelahrheit, In welchen die Grundsätze des natürlichen Rechts nach denen dem Freyherrn von Pufendorf gezeigten Lehrsätzen deutlich bewiesen, weiter ausgearbeitet, Und von denen einwurffen der Gegner desselben, Sonderlich Herrn D. Valentin Albertyi, befreyet* (Halle: Renger, R [2001] Hildesheim: Olms), Introduction. See also Detlef Döring (1992), *Pufendorf-Studien. Beiträge zur Biographie Samuel von Pufendorfs und zu seiner Entwicklung als Historiker und theologischer Schriftsteller* (Berlin: Duncker & Humblot).

88 Gigas, ed. (1897), letter of 24 March 1688, 17–19.

89 Gigas, ed. (1897), letter of 28 August 1688, 26–27.

90 Thomasius & Brenneysen (1696), passim; Thomasius (1695); Thomasius (1717), *Institutionum Jurisprudentiae Divinae Libri Tres, in quibus Fundamenta Juris Naturalis secundum Hypotheses Illustris Pufendorffii perspicue demonstrantur, & ad objectionibus dissentientium potissimum D. Valentini Alberti, Professoris Lipsiensis, liberantur*, 6th ed. (Halle: Salfeld); Thomasius (1694), *Kurtze Abfertigung derer in der ausführlichen Beschreibung des Pietisten Unfugs enthaltenen Lästerungen* (Halle: Salfeld), a ten-page tract.

91 Thomasius (1690), 22–23; Thomasius (1722).

92 Cited by Carpzov to Johann George III, 6 May 1690. SHStADD, Loc. 10330, *Den so genannten* Pietismum *betr.*, 1690 ff., 21–23.

shifted. While the network continued to suggest and arrange appointments, mediate arguments, and correspond extensively,[93] the context became a newly-invigorated intellectual and political rivalry between Saxony and Brandenburg-Prussia, where Spener, Thomasius, Francke, and others found an institutional and intellectual home. Pufendorf, who had been in Berlin since 1686, helped mediate Spener's move there.[94] Spener in turn helped Francke as he founded the University of Halle in 1694.[95] And Seckendorff served as the first chancellor of the University. For his part, Elector Frederick III of Brandenburg-Prussia (King Frederick I in Prussia) was eager to offer these critics of the Saxon system a home. Halle, transferred from Saxony to Brandenburg-Prussia only in 1680 and just a day's trip from Leipzig, was a good place to establish competing institutions such as the University and Francke's institutions. Further, the attack on the Saxon ecclesiastical system complemented Frederick's attack on the ecclesiastical system within his territory.

* * *

What was the balance of continuity and change between 1650 and 1750? The consistories and ecclesiastical law remained the arbiters of myriad details of religious life. Within this framework, though, there was much evolution. While the laws concerning pews did not change much, for example, people in the mid-17th century would not have foreseen how coveted pews would become. The basics of the liturgy and many chants were unchanged, but many hymns, the cantata, and the music of the organ were different. In 1723, the year that Bach moved to Leipzig, witch-hunting laws were still on the books and a prominent jurist (like many other people) confined himself to cautious skepticism about their existence, although witch trials were largely a thing of the past.

Equally importantly, while there had been at least outward consensus on most major issues from the late 16th century to the 1680s, there was much greater heterogeneity of belief by 1750. Most clerics, philosophers, and jurists were influenced by some strand of Enlightenment thought. The Electors were Roman Catholic. Intense acrimony and attempts at suppression had accompanied the initial ruptures of the 1680s and 1690s. By 1750 people had to accept the existence of change and major differences of opinion even if they disapproved of these things.

The battles associated with Pietism – the break between Spener and Johann George III and Thomasius's dispute with Orthodox clerics – played crucial roles in the development toward greater heterogeneity of thought and belief. The first major public divisions among elites since the late 16th century, they were dramatic and enduring. Spener's break with the Elector was embedded in longer-range shifts in territorial governance, where rulers distanced themselves from their previous roles.

---

93 See Winter (1966), 63 ff.

94 Ibid., 70 ff.

95 See Martin Brecht (1993), 'August Hermann Francke und der Hallische Pietismus,' in *GdP*, vol. I, 440–539; 453 ff.

The controversy that Thomasius unleashed, with the tightly regulated ecclesiastical system at the center of his critique, stood at the beginning of Thomasius's career as an Enlightener.

Chapter Five

Leipzig's cantors: status, politics and the adiaphora

Musicians were among the most important producers of religious culture. Cantors were the leading musicians and directors of church music as well as, increasingly, of secular musical life in Leipzig and other large towns. This chapter explores how the two cantors of the first half of the 18th century, Johann Kuhnau (1660–1722; cantor from 1701) and Johann Sebastian Bach (1685–1750; cantor from 1723) negotiated a working environment rich in opportunity as well as conflict. Kuhnau and Bach operated in a confessional system that was bursting at the seams, but was capable of accommodating considerable change. Music historians have taken important steps toward placing the cantors in their social context. This chapter builds on and extends that work, examining the cantors' roles in urban society and their relations with the local and Saxon authorities. It shows again how religion was the arena where social and cultural change, relations among status groups, and interactions between the authorities and the governed were negotiated.

Cantors fulfilled a variety of duties as teachers, composers, and performers. Their office and their skills gave them an ambiguous status in Baroque urban society, a status that reflects that society's numerous criteria for ordering and ranking people, ongoing social and cultural change, and considerable opportunities for social mobility. The cantors' job description and status are examined first here. The cantors' many interactions with the Leipzig authorities are discussed second. Bach's conflicts with city councilors, clerics, and the Leipzig Consistory are the best known of these; but Bach, like Kuhnau before him, also had a range of routine interactions which were often neutral or positive. Councilors were important patrons of music, appointing and regulating the cantors; in fact, they set the stage for much music composition and performance in the city. In turn, patronage of musical life was a source of power and status for councilors. Councilors also played an active role in the schools, civic institutions where the cantors taught and had supervisory duties. In Leipzig, one councilor served as school director, and the council was ultimately responsible for student discipline, morals, and learning, the maintenance of the school buildings and the appointment, regulation, and payment of its school employees.

Musical patronage extended beyond the town walls to courts. Towns like Leipzig looked to residences at Dresden and elsewhere for inspiration, and councilors' musical policies were influenced by courtly pomp and circumstance. Some cantors were also active at courts. J.S. Bach had ties to several. At eighteen he was appointed to his first position, as 'lackey' at the court of Saxe-Weimar, where he performed as an instrumentalist as well as doing non-musical chores.[1] Later, as he steadily worked his way up in status, he was a valued organist, composer and Capellmeister at Weimar and Cöthen. He retained his ties there after his arrival in Leipzig, and also performed at Weissenfels and Potsdam.

Baroque-era ideas and debates about music, discussed third, were important to how cantors defined themselves, and to how they interacted with councilors and their audiences. Here the concept of the adiaphora was key. The adiaphora, or *Mittel-Dinge*, included liturgical vestments, secular and sacred music, dancing, and leisure pursuits such as playing cards.[2] 'Adiaphora' is a theological term, and the topic has generally been the preserve of church and music historians. However, the adiaphora straddled the religious and secular realms, and they were basic to everyday religion and secular life. The adiaphora were regulated in sumptuary ordinances, edicts about religious observance, and legal commentaries; ideas about them were articulated by councilors, territorial rulers, and consistory assessors when they appointed and regulated the activities of cantors and organists. All Lutheran writers, including Pietists, regarded music as something that had the potential to enhance religious devotion, political occasions, or secular pastimes, but also as something that might at any time threaten social order, piety, and morals. Pietists were harshest in their critique, but non-Pietist figures, including Enlighteners, also had many reservations: the 'use' of the adiaphora could very easily become a 'misuse.' Pietist pronouncements need to be seen in this broader context to be fully understood.

Pietism is a theme here beyond the adiaphora debate. Bach is usually brought into connection with Pietism through the texts of many of his sacred compositions, which emphasize the individual's spiritual journey and relationship with Christ, and which are often emotionally highly-charged. However, as Robin A. Leaver has pointed out, such lyrics had an older Lutheran as well as a more recent Pietist background, and were well within the mainstream of poetry, hymn, and cantata text.[3] Further, Bach was close to Orthodox rather than Pietist pastors and councilors throughout his life, although interactions he had with Pietists in Leipzig, especially city councilors, influenced his working environment.

---

1 Christoph Wolff (2000), *Johann Sebastian Bach: The Learned Musician* (New York: Norton), 68–69.

2 See Joyce Irwin (1993), *Neither Voice nor Heart Alone. German Lutheran Theology of Music in the Age of the Baroque* (New York: Lang). The 1580 Book of Concord affirmed the technically neutral status of the adiaphora.

3 Robin A. Leaver (1991), 'Bach and Pietism: Similarities Today,' *Concordia Theological Quarterly*, 55, 5–22. See also Leaver (1982), *Music as Preaching: Bach, Passions and Music in Worship* (Oxford: Latimer House). Christian Bunners, using a 'broad' definition of Pietism that includes earlier 17th century writers such as Arndt and Heinrich Müller, argues that Bach's use of texts based on Müller and others indicates a 'Pietist' influence. The present study, using a narrower definition of Pietism (see Introduction, note 37), disagrees. Bunners (2004), 'Musik,' in *GdP*, vol. IV, 430–455.

The cantors' status and job description

Like their peers around Lutheran Germany, the Leipzig cantors had two main sets of duties: teaching and directing music in the churches. They were also expected to direct music at weddings and funerals. In larger towns the cantors were installed as teachers in the Latin schools, and they were also musical figures in a broader sense, publishing their compositions and works of music theory, and directing music at civic events such as visits by a ruler.[4] The cantorate at the Latin school of St. Thomas in Leipzig was regarded as the premiere cantorate in Germany. Many highly-talented students there went on to become professional musicians. And a long line of St. Thomas's cantors, including Sethus Calvisius, Hermann Schein, and Johann Schelle was respected around Germany. Traditionally the cantors were true Renaissance men, university graduates who taught and often published in Latin as well as composing, performing, and conducting. Kuhnau, for example, not only practiced law until he became cantor, but was also known as a mathematician, music theorist, composer, and performer. His authorship of several novels and published volumes of music also made him well-known beyond Leipzig.

Since their office had been established during the Reformation, cantors' occupational duties around Lutheran Germany had gradually expanded. Throughout most of the 16th century, the job of cantor was regarded as a temporary one, often a stepping stone to a position as cleric. By the beginning of the 17th century, it had become a permanent post in many towns. In the course of the 17th century, instrumental music became increasingly common in the church service, and expectations rose that cantors would compose new music on a regular basis. Thus, whereas the 1580 Saxon Church Ordinance had actually forbidden the cantors to perform music they had composed, by 1688 Kuhnau wrote that this law was now obsolete.[5] The cantors also started to compose more secular music, and came to be regarded as city music directors as well as church and school employees. These shifts were gradual, and musicians remained defensive about their secular activities. For example, in the preface of his 1663 *Merry Madrigals and Canzonettas*, Leipzig cantor Sebastian Knüpfer wrote that '*ex officio*, it would be more proper for me to publish a sacred work,' and added that he had composed these pieces before he had been elected as cantor.[6] By the late 17th century, though, especially in larger towns, the expansion of the cantors' activities was well established. In addition, both secular and sacred music were rapidly becoming more elaborate, technically demanding, and cosmopolitan. Musicians were expected to be virtuosi and to compose more new music. New performance venues were opening up, including coffee houses,

---

4 See Dieter Krickeberg (1965), *Das Protestantische Kantorat im 17. Jahrhundert: Studien zum Amt des deutschen Kantors* (Berlin: Merseburger).

5 Stephen Rose (2004), 'Outlawed or Obligatory? Composing for the Church in Saxony 1580–1680,' paper delivered at the 11th International Baroque Music Conference, Manchester, England; Krickeberg (1965), 87–88.

6 Knüpfer (1999), *Lustige Madrigalen und Canzonetten*, ed. Bernd Baselt (Madison: A-R Editions), Introduction, Peter Wollny, x–xi.

opera houses, and pleasure gardens, creating more opportunities along with potential competition. At the same time, the cantors were expected to continue to fulfill their school duties.

* * *

Cantors did not fit neatly into the main urban groupings of the elites, burghers, and sub-burghers. Scholars have argued that cantors' cultural standing conveyed a higher social status than their income and some aspects of their job descriptions would indicate.[7] Leipzig's cantors lived in an apartment in the St. Thomas's school, as did the school rector. As they did elsewhere, they shared some features with clerics: unless they owned homes of their own in the city, they were not burghers; they, like clerics, lived in service apartments; and both occupations were exempt from military and watch duty.[8] However, a cantor's status was complicated by ties to the material conditions of schools and his duties there. Along with teaching, the cantor alternated with the rector and two teachers in a stint as 'inspector' at the school one week a month. He supervised meals and prayers and served as a night guard to make sure the boys returned to the building by their curfew, and to keep them from leaving the building during the night. The St. Thomas's school was overrun with rats and mice at least until the building's renovation in 1732.[9] Kuhnau wrote that all the school boys had scabies. One teacher during Kuhnau's time complained bitterly of spending all night during his weeks as inspector running around the building to keep track of the boys. Reinhard Szeskus argues that the unhygienic conditions in the building may have contributed to the deaths of five infant children of the Bachs between 1726 and 1732.[10]

Some scholars have emphasized the more positive aspects of Bach's position, while others emphasize his difficulties and low status.[11] Elements of both are justified; but the anomalousness of his position is most striking: his status and income did not match his fame as a musician. One factor was that Bach was the only early modern Leipzig cantor without a university degree. By contrast, as university graduates, his predecessors and successors were automatically much closer to the town's elites, if not members themselves. Furthermore, Bach would by no means have been considered wealthy. As Reinhard Szeskus argues, the value of Bach's

---

7 Krickeberg (1965), 100 ff.

8 Arnfried Edler (1983), 'The Social Status of Organists in Lutheran Germany from the 16th though the 19th century,' in Walter Salmen, ed., *The Social Status of the Professional Musician from the Middle Ages to the 19th Century* (New York: Pendragon; German original, Kassel 1971), 63–93; 73.

9 Reinhard Szeskus (2003), 'Johann Sebastian Bachs soziale Stellung in Leipzig,' in idem, *Bach in Leipzig. Beiträge zu Leben und Werk von Johann Sebastian Bach* (Wilhelmshaven: Noetzel), 1–63; 22 ff.

10 Ibid.

11 For a positive assessment, see Wolff (2000), 237 ff. A negative assessment: Szeskus (2003).

estate in 1750, 1122 thaler, placed him in the lower range of the town's middling groups. By contrast, the estate of St. Thomas's pastor Christian Weiss was valued at 37,749 thaler in 1736. That of Georg Heinrich Bose, one of the city's leading merchants, was a princely 79,941 thaler in 1731.[12] Bach's annual salary from the council was just over 100 thaler, lower than that of eleven secular council-appointed officials, including several *Schreiber* and accountants.[13] These officials probably did not have access to the many incidental fees that brought Bach's total income up to 700 thaler a year. But even that total was much less than the 1000 to 1200 thaler that he had been led to expect before he took the position.[14] Bach's official salary actually declined from the 400 thaler he had received annually in Cöthen. Additionally, his wife Anna Magdalena had received 300 thaler as a singer at the court,[15] whereas Leipzig, like other towns, had no positions for female singers. Bach's salary, like his rank, was fourth among school positions, not much lower than that of the conrector and rectors of St. Thomas's and St. Nicholas's. His salary was significantly below Superintendent Deyling's 350 thaler,[16] and Deyling had numerous other sources of income, including his position as consistory assessor and fees for hearing confession and for officiating at weddings and funerals.

But Bach was famous throughout the Holy Roman Empire. The Leipzig, Dresden, and Hamburg newspapers recorded his arrival in Leipzig, as well as performances at various towns and courts. He performed for August 'the Strong,' his son Frederick August III, and Frederick the Great of Brandenburg-Prussia. He also held titles as court composer at several courts. Many people praised him in exuberant terms, especially for his virtuosity on keyboard instruments. To give just a few examples, Minden school rector Constantin Bellermann wrote, 'Like Handel among the English, he deserves to be called the miracle of Leipzig.'[17] Music writer Andreas Sorge wrote of Bach as 'so great and world-renowned a virtuoso and Prince of Clavier [keyboard] players.'[18] And musician Georg Ludwig Heinrich Schwanenberger wrote to an acquaintance in Braunschweig, 'I could wish that you should once hear Mr. Bach on the organ … I never heard anything like it.'[19] Bach's skills, international renown, and office carried weight especially in a city like Leipzig which prided itself on its cultural activity. And as someone who had risen from small-town and relatively modest origins – his father was a town musician whose status and household organization resembled that of artisans[20] – Bach was in good company. Leipzig was full of prominent men who shared just such a background,

12 Szeskus (2003), 56–58.

13 Ibid., 43.

14 Wolff (2000), 244.

15 Wolff (2000), 205.

16 Szeskus (2003), 47.

17 Report of 1743. *NBR*, 334–335; 334.

18 Dedication of 1742. *NBR*, 335–336; 335.

19 Report of 1727. *NBR*, 325.

20 Ulrich Siegele (1991), '"Ich habe fleissig sein müssen ..." Zur Vermittlung von Bachs sozialem und musikalischem Charakter,' *BzBf*, 9/10, 13–19; 14–15.

including none other than some of the councilors who appointed him, such as Johann Job and Gottfried Lange. As we have seen, several of the clerics whom Bach knew well, including Christoph Wolle, Bach's father confessor from 1741 onward, and Superintendent Salomon Deyling, also had small-town, artisanal, or even village backgrounds.

Other indicators of Bach's social status are more difficult to interpret. Bach collaborated with librettists such as town governor Flemming, Enlightener and salonniere Mariane von Ziegler, and professor Johann Christoph Gottsched, which points to the fact that he moved in elite literary circles. Bach and his family also had social relations with members of the Leipzig elites.[21] For example, the Bachs and the merchant family Bose were friends, although the closeness of their friendship is up for debate.[22] In addition, University professors, councilors and their relatives served as godparents for the Bachs' children.[23] The godparents would have had ongoing relations with the children. In the pre-industrial era, though, the selection of godparents just as often solidified patron-client relations as it did relations among social equals.[24]

The cantors and politics

How did the cantors interact with city councilors, and how did they navigate the political scene? A common image holds that Bach was an embattled and unappreciated genius who worked with too few resources, notably in Leipzig, and whose colleagues and authorities stifled his creativity. Bach's petitions and letters, especially those of 1730, certainly establish that his professional identity and musical goals often put him at odds with the authorities. Ongoing reprimands everywhere Bach worked, and even a brief detention in Weimar, show that the authorities were often not appreciative of Bach, and also that they had significant control over his activities. However, when his complaints are studied against the fuller background of contemporary conventions and conflicts, Bach emerges as an occasionally frustrated genius who was adept at working with the political conventions of his day. In this, he very much resembled other musicians.

One major point of interaction between cantors and councilors was the appointment process. The selection process for cantors followed the same procedure as that for clerics, teachers, and other educated council appointees. Candidates wrote letters of application to the council when a position became free. The council discussed the

---

21 For an overview, see Wolff (2000), 319 ff.

22 See Hans-Joachim Schulze (1997), 'Anna Magdalena Bachs "Herzens Freündin:" Neues über die Beziehungen zwischen den Familien Bach und Bose,' *BJ*, 83, 151–153; Szeskus (2003), 63.

23 See Wolff (2000), 396–398 for a list of children and godparents.

24 Hartmut Zwahr (1978), *Zur Konstituierung des Proletariats als Klasse. Strukturuntersuchung über das Leipziger Proletariat während der industriellen Revolution* (Berlin: Akademie, R [1981] Munich: Beck), 175 & passim.

merits, including personality and reputation as well as teaching ability and musical acumen, of each candidate, invited several to audition, and then voted for one. The replacement of Kuhnau's predecessor Johann Schelle in 1677 was relatively uncomplicated.[25] In electing Kuhnau, councilors selected a local candidate who was well known to them and who was already installed as an organist in Leipzig.[26] The search for Kuhnau's replacement was more long-drawn out and perhaps more contentious than most. It was an experiment for councilors: some of them placed increased emphasis on appointing a 'famous musician,' a Capellmeister who would bring renown to Leipzig as a center of modern music, both secular and sacred.[27] However, the process followed the standard procedure: there were twelve initial candidates; councilors discussed the merits of each; and several candidates were invited to audition by presenting trials of their work. Bach actually did not apply during this first stage of the process; the leading candidate was Telemann, and Bach applied only in a second round, after Telemann rejected the council's offer.

Most councilors seem to have had little expertise in musical matters. Whereas they discussed the rhetorical structure and the public speaking skills of clerical candidates in detail, the specifics of the trial performances by Bach and his fellow candidates, and of candidates in other searches, were not discussed in the council minutes. Rather, availability, the ability and willingness to teach at the St. Thomas's school, and general cultural politics, were the focus of discussion. On the other hand, Bach's trial date and his starting date in his new position, along with the pieces he performed, were reported in the Hamburg and Leipzig newspapers, adding a public dimension that was lacking in searches for clerics and teachers.

The Pietist-Orthodox conflict had a major impact on the search for Kuhnau's successor, as it did in searches for clerics at this time. Councilors had different ideas of what kind of cantor they wanted – traditional or modern – and this difference in their goals was structured at least in part by their positions in the conflict. In his landmark articles on the political dimensions of Bach's appointment, Ulrich Siegele discerned competing factions among the councilors who eventually elected Bach cantor at St. Thomas's.[28] A so-called 'cantor's party' wanted sober, traditional church music and a cantor who could teach Latin to students at St. Thomas's. By contrast, a 'concert master's party' wanted a well-known musician who would deliver modern,

---

25 Protocols of council meetings: Arnold Schering, ed. (1918), *Sebastian Knüpfer, Johann Schelle, Johann Kuhnau. Ausgewählte Kirchenkantaten*, = *Denkmäler deutscher Tonkunst*, 1. Folge, vol. 58/59 (Leipzig: Breitkopf & Härtel, R [1957] Wiesbaden: Breitkopf & Härtel), xxiv–xxv.

26 Protocols of council meetings: Andreas Glöckner (1990), *Die Musikpflege an der Leipziger Neukirche zur Zeit Johann Sebastian Bachs*, = *BzBf*, 8, 144–145.

27 Protocols of council meetings: *NBR*, 100–101; 102–103.

28 Siegele (1983, 1984 & 1986), 'Bachs Stellung in der Leipziger Kulturpolitik seiner Zeit,' *BJ*, 1983, 7–50; 1984, 7–43; 1986, 33–67. Summarized and with further interpretation in Siegele (1997), 'Bach and the domestic politics of Electoral Saxony,' in John Butt, ed., *The Cambridge Companion to Bach* (New York: Cambridge University Press), 17–34.

operatic church music.[29] Several candidates of the 'concert master's party,' including Telemann and Johann Friedrich Fasch, who were known primarily for their musical virtuosity and not for their pedagogy, had indicated that they would not teach, possibly in consultation with councilors.

Siegele correctly surmised that city councilors Abraham Christoph Platz and Johann Job, members of the 'cantor's party,' had Pietist sympathies. Siegele's hypothesis is confirmed by Job's letters to Francke. On the other side, supporters of Orthodoxy and Baroque culture were also active in the city council, and were members of the 'concert master's party.' They included at least two powerful jurist councilors, J.F. Born and Bach's especial supporter Gottfried Lange.[30] Caspar Bose, a leading Leipzig merchant whose family became friends of the Bach family, also voted for Bach, and had earlier supported Baroque music in the city.[31] Judging from the council minutes, the pro-Baroque councilors were better informed about their favored candidates than the Pietists, but the Pietists also had a clear idea of the type of music they wanted. Members of both parties would have been in direct or indirect contact with their favorite candidates, and councilors clearly consulted with people who were musically informed.

The outcome of the cantoral search process was the election of Bach in a compromise between the factions. The concert master's party initially emerged victorious by securing the election of Georg Philipp Telemann, who was working in Hamburg. However, it seems that Telemann had applied mainly in order to obtain a raise in Hamburg, which he did. Bach submitted an application in December 1722, although it seems that he had entered informal negotiations by September. It is possible that Telemann himself encouraged Bach to apply.[32] Bach was also a candidate of the 'concert master's party,' but the definition of his teaching duties represented a compromise between the two parties.

* * *

Kuhnau's transition to the position of cantor would have been relatively simple. For Bach, then thirty-eight years old, for his second wife Anna Magdalena, and their five children, the job change involved a move from Cöthen to Leipzig; the family moved in May 1723. As the authorities did for other new appointees, the council had the Bachs' apartment renovated in advance.[33] The cantors' installment ceremony was like that of other council appointees, although music does not seem to have been

---

29 Siegele (1983). On the city councilors, see especially 9, 49; (1984) 35–36, 40–41; (1986) 48 ff.

30 Siegele (1983), 54 ff.

31 Stephen Rose (2005), 'Daniel Vetter and the Domestic Keyboard Chorale in Bach's Leipzig,' *Early Music*, 33, 39–53.

32 Wolff (2000), 219–220.

33 Hamburg *Staats- und Gelehrte Zeitung*, 29 May 1723, reprinted in *NBR*, 106.

performed for non-musical officials, as it was for Bach and, in all likelihood, other new cantors.[34]

Once they were installed, the Leipzig cantors had a variety of neutral and even positive interactions with councilors. One was the composition and performance of cantatas for the annual worship services for the installation of a new governing council. Here the cantors appear as representatives and even enhancers of the council's power. The cantatas convey the image of a council that securely grasped its divinely-willed authority. Bach composed at least three of these for Mühlhausen, including two after he left, and at least eight in Leipzig. Instrumentation was festive, including several trumpets and trombones. The texts are similar: drawing much of their language from psalms, they compare Leipzig to Jerusalem, praise God for sending just, worthy, and fatherly authorities to rule the city, and refer to basic principles of council governance. Concluding chorales, and some choruses, represent the perspective of the people (*das Volk*). Some solo arias and recitatives also admonish the *Volk* to value and obey the authorities.[35]

The cantors also directed music to honor the authorities, a tradition that dated to at least the Renaissance. By the Baroque era, they were leading large student groups which played, sang, and acted in elaborate productions that celebrated investitures of new clerical superintendents or University rectors, as well as political occasions such as peace treaties or Electoral visits. Most performances took place in front of the city hall, located on the city's main market square, which allowed for large audiences of town inhabitants. Many performances were preceded by a procession, and some even involved two singing choirs converging on the square. Bach composed music for a total of fifteen festive occasions to honor members of the Saxon Electoral house.[36] One, for example, was an 'evening serenade' for the visiting Elector August the Strong in 1727. Bach composed and directed an elaborate secular cantata. Before the main performance, students processed to the market square singing, playing trumpets and drums, and carrying torches to light the way.[37]

But the cantors also had a range of conflicts with the authorities. Bach's disputes with individual teachers and clerics, the Leipzig Consistory, the city council, and a feud from 1736 onward with the St. Thomas's rector, have often been characterized as being specific to his situation. But they were typical of battles that were endemic to the early modern era. Resources were one major issue. For example, in his *Entwurff*, or 'Short but most necessary draft for a well-appointed church music' of Summer 1730 Bach depicted the musical skills of St. Thomas's students, who sang during church services, in dire terms and indicated that stipends from the

34 Excerpt from city council proceedings, 1 June 1723, reprinted in *NBR*, 106–108.

35 Some texts are reprinted in Melvin P. Unger, ed. (1996), *Handbook to Bach's Sacred Cantatas* (Lanham, MD: Scarecrow), 243 ff., 415 ff., 672 ff., 420 ff., 100 ff., & 233 ff. See also Wolfgang Osthoff (1982), 'Bachs Ratswahlkantaten,' in Christian Kabitz, ed., *Bach und die Barockkunst* (Würzburg: Stürtz), 114–118; Wolff (2000), 286–288.

36 Wolff (2000), 362.

37 From Christoph Ernst Sicul (1727), *Das frohlockende Leipzig*, reprinted and translated *NBR*, 133–134.

council to some University students would improve the level of music performed in the churches.[38] On one level, these complaints can be read at face value: there certainly were gaps between the prescribed and actual resources available to Bach, and between Bach's high standards and those resources. At the same time, though, Bach was following typical conventions among individuals requesting anything of the authorities. People routinely portrayed their present circumstances in dire terms. Other musicians, including Johann Kuhnau, musicians at the New Church, and Telemann while he was in Frankfurt and Hamburg, all presented petitions which stressed the heavy demands on them and the problems with their pay and/or the instruments and musicians available to them. They, like Bach, went on to praise their respective councils as good and generous patrons and argued that with a bit more support, their goals would come closer to being realized.[39] Non-musicians followed the same strategy. For example, when people requested a pew, they described their lack of one in strongly negative terms and expressed in advance their gratitude if the church Director were to allot them one.[40] When city appointees such as substitute clerics and workers at St. George's requested temporary or permanent augmentations to their incomes, they lamented high prices and promised their devout gratitude if their wish were to be granted.[41]

Another form of conflict in which both Kuhnau and Bach engaged was the turf battle. For example, Bach argued with one cleric about the right to select hymns. Both Kuhnau and Bach fought with the University for the right to conduct the weekly public services in the University Church that were initiated in 1710. Kuhnau was given the right after the University's first appointee, Johann Friedrich Fasch left Leipzig in 1711. Bach, on the other hand, was unsuccessful despite a prolonged effort. Kuhnau had tried in vain to gain the right to direct music at the New Church; Bach did not try. Similar battles were fought constantly by non-musicians. During Bach's installation ceremony in Leipzig, for example, city councilor Lehmann and consistory representative Weiss sparred about which institution had the right to install the new cantor.[42] And from December 1720 to March 1721 the Privy Chancery and Upper Consistory delayed the confirmation of Salomon Deyling as Superintendent, complaining that the council claimed to have 'vocated and appointed' Deyling,

---

38 *NBR*, 145–151.

39 Memos from New Church music director Carl Gotthelf Gerlach to council, 1729 ff., Glöckner (1990), 153 ff.; Telemann to Frankfurt city council, 5 October 1717 and to Hamburg city council between 1725 and 1730, Telemann (1972), *Briefwechsel*, ed. Hans Grosse & Hans Rudolf Jung (Leipzig: VEB Deutscher Verlag für Musik), 26–27 & 31–32.

40 See AdN, Abt. III.160., *Schriftwechsel Kirchenstühle betr. v. 1701*, ff.

41 SAL, Stift III.A.16., *Acta, Das Hospital St. Georgen und Das demselben incorporierte Zucht und Waysen Hauss alhier betr.*, vol. I, 1717 ff., 100–101, 228–229^{v}, 263–264, 296–296^{v}.

42 Excerpt from city council proceedings, 1 June 1723, reprinted in *NBR*, 106–108.

although it only had the authority to appoint the St. Nicholas's pastor and to 'present' him as its choice for Superintendent.[43]

Councilors pursued an especially ambitious program of musical patronage between 1700 and 1750, part of their generally active patronage of public culture. This generated conflict for Kuhnau, but worked to Bach's advantage. Mayors Francis Conrad Romanus and Gottfried Lange, both of whom had close connections to the Dresden court and had been forced on the council by August the Strong, took the lead. In 1701, Romanus awarded the young Telemann, a law student at the University from 1699 to 1704, a commission to compose cantatas on alternating Sundays in St. Thomas's. In 1704, Romanus helped him to become music director of the newly renovated New Church. These councilors circumvented cantor Kuhnau because they felt he was not dynamic enough. They regarded Telemann, who was primarily involved with the Opera, as a more modern and exciting composer. They were spurred on by an order from the Elector in September 1701 to 'bring the music in the churches into good shape … since, especially during the fairs, prominent men (*fremde Herrschafften*) come to Leipzig.'[44] Lange, Bach's supporter on the council, also served as a link between the Dresden court and Bach, encouraging the production of music to glorify the Electors: he was the governing mayor when Bach composed four pieces honoring members of the electoral house.[45]

Kuhnau's ill health throughout his tenure contributed to his difficulties; councilors were reluctant to give him more responsibilities. His relatively traditional musical style was another factor. He regarded the Opera, which operated from 1693 to 1720, as well as concerts by the collegia and services at the New Church as competition for the attention of his audience and his student musicians. In 1720, he presented a detailed memorial to the council complaining that university students who had previously been eager to play in his churches were now more interested in playing the 'wild operatic' music of the New Church.[46]

Bach, by contrast, entered into a more stable musical scene. He arrived after the opera closed. His abilities, his interest in secular as well as sacred music, and the support of key councilors allowed him to consolidate and build on earlier developments. Many of his conflicts with the council arose because his activities as Capellmeister conflicted with the school duties of the cantor. Tensions between the school and the compositional and performing dimensions of Bach's position reflected the difficulties of juggling a growing workload, and were not unique to Leipzig: in 1717 and 1753, two different music writers commented that an active

---

43 SHStADD, Loc. 4573, *Die Wieder Ersezung der Superintendentur zu Leipzig mit Dr. Salomon Deylingen …*

44 Cited in Glöckner (1990), 17.

45 Siegele (2002), 'Wandlungen der Politik – Wandlungen Bachs,' in Ulrich Leisinger, ed., *Bach in Leipzig – Bach und Leipzig. Konferenzbericht Leipzig 2000* (Hildesheim: Olms), 465–477.

46 Kuhnau, *Project, welcher Gestalt die Kirchen Music zu Leipzig könne verbessert werden*, 29 May 1720. Reprinted in Philipp Spitta (1930), *Johann Sebastian Bach* (Leipzig: Breitkopf & Härtel, R [1979] Wiesbaden: Breitkopf & Härtel), 866 ff.

composing and performing schedule was incompatible with the school duties and ideal personality of a cantor.[47]

Councilors soon came to consider Bach's appointment as a Capellmeister a failed experiment. Over the years, numerous councilors went on record during meetings to complain that Bach was not fulfilling his duties as cantor. They included not only school director Christian Ludwig Stieglitz and Pietists such as Johann Job and Adrian Steger, who might have been expected to complain, but also Jacob Born, an active supporter of Baroque culture who among other things funded the enlargement of musicians' balconies in St. Thomas's in 1739,[48] and even Bach's supporter Gottfried Lange. This shows that councilors' interest in seeing school affairs regulated, and in subordinating the cantors, overrode their cultural politics. Stieglitz, director of St. Thomas's school, complained at the elections of new rectors in 1730 and 1734. He noted in 1734 that the rector's job was made difficult because the cantor 'did not do at the school what he was obliged to do.'[49] This included not participating in his inspection duty one week a month, which Bach apparently refused outright to do by 1730; the rector joined him in this refusal by 1734.[50] The councilors' frustration thus arose from their responsibilities as overseers of the school; they feared students sneaking out at night and causing trouble in the town, which would reflect poorly upon them. In 1730, councilors also wanted Bach to teach Latin, a request Bach could rightly consider unreasonable, since councilors had agreed in 1723 that another teacher would take over those classes. During the search for Bach's successor, Stieglitz left no doubt about his preferences: 'The School needed a Cantor and not a Capellmeister … Mr. Bach had been a great musician, it is true, but not a school teacher,' and the school needed someone 'who would be skillful in both capacities.' He also noted that successor Gottlob Harrer had 'promised to accept willingly his subordinate place:'[51] an implicit comparison to Bach, who had clearly not seen himself as a subordinate.

Among other things, while councilors surely appreciated Bach's stature outside the town walls, they must have wished that he did not travel as much. Bach traveled frequently to inspect organs and perform at courts. During his time in Leipzig he went on twenty-one documented trips, including two to Berlin, four to Cöthen, three

---

[47] The authors were Martin Heinrich Fuhrmann and Caspar Ruez. Brit Reipsch (1997), 'Über die Aufgaben und Bedeutung eines Kantors im Spiegel einiger musiktheoretischer Schriften vom Ende des 17. bis zum Ausgang des 18. Jahrhunderts,' in Wolf Hobohm et al., eds, *Struktur, Funktion und Bedeutung des deutschen protestantischen Kantorats im 16. bis 18. Jahrhundert* (Oschersleben: Ziethen), 21–28; 24–25.

[48] Herbert Stiehl (1984), 'Das Innere der Thomaskirche zur Amtszeit Johann Sebastian Bachs,' *BzBf*, 3, 16.

[49] Werner Neumann & Hans-Joachim Schulze, eds (1969), *Bach-Dokumente*, vol. II: *Fremdschriftliche und gedruckte Dokumente zur Lebensgeschichte Johann Sebastian Bachs 1685–1750* (Kassel: Bärenreiter), no. 278 and no. 355; Wolff (2000), 342 and 349.

[50] *NBR*, 172; Wolff (2000), 346, 350.

[51] Minutes of inner council (*Enge*) meetings of 29 July & 8 August 1750, in *NBR*, 245–247.

to Weissenfels, and six to Dresden. It is certain that he made many more trips to Dresden in particular.[52] These absences were in part what led to pronouncements such as mayor Jacob Born's during the August 1730 council meeting that Bach had 'little inclination to work.' Born was apparently referring to Bach's unwillingness to teach Latin, along with his missing of some music classes.

Bach would have been astonished to hear Born's pronouncement. Scholars have determined that he pursued the most demanding and productive composition schedule of his life between 1723 and 1729, completing several yearly cycles of cantatas for performance in the churches, as well as composing many secular pieces. He had thus energetically overhauled and modernized both the city's sacred and secular music scenes[53] – exactly what councilors had wanted when they elected him. Further, in 1729 Bach had taken over leadership of the New Church collegium musicum, an amateur group of mostly University students that also performed at the New Church. This ensemble performed the most recent secular music from Germany and Italy in concerts in Zimmermann's coffee house and coffee garden, once a week most of the year and twice-weekly during the fairs[54] – again enhancing the city's reputation as a center of modern culture. He had also diligently fulfilled most of his musical teaching duties at the school, and he gave private lessons to University students. He had composed and directed two well-received pieces to honor the visiting August the Strong. The councilors' lack of appreciation explains many of Bach emphases in his famous *Entwurff*. Here, Bach stressed the high demands that modern musical style made on German musicians, and referred to his high workload compared to that of court musicians, who had no school responsibilities. He also mentioned tense working conditions and authorities who were 'odd and little interested in music' in his October 1730 letter to Georg Erdmann.[55]

Ongoing competition between Pietist and non-Pietist councilors was also an issue. It was the Pietist Johann Job who said at the August 1730 council meeting that Bach was 'incorrigible.' Ulrich Siegele has pointed out that Bach's conflict with the council in 1730 came just a year after Bach became director of the New Church collegium musicum, which left him with even less time for his St. Thomas's school activities.[56] It is possible, as Siegele argues, that Bach's patron Gottfried Lange engineered his takeover of the collegium, that the 'cantor's party' was trying to get back at Lange's faction by disciplining Bach and reining him in, and that Bach's disputes of 1730 reflect these tensions.[57] There is no direct evidence to support Siegele's supposition, but given what we know about Job and Lange from other occasions, the scenario is plausible.

52 Wolff (2000), 208; J.N. Forkel, biography of Bach, reprinted in *NBR*, 419–482; 461.

53 Wolff (2000), 253 ff.

54 Ibid., 351 ff.

55 *NBR*, 151–152.

56 Siegele (1986), esp. 44–46.

57 Siegele (1997), 28–30.

The fact that Lange and Romanus were creatures of the Dresden court leads to the question of whether advocacy of Baroque style generally should be associated with the court. Thus, Siegele argues that the 'cantor's' party was actually a 'city' party, that Lange's cultural politics represented absolutist interests, and that Bach carried out an 'absolutist mission' in Leipzig.[58] However, the controversy seems to have been a politicized battle about culture in and of itself rather than a form of competition between city and court. It would be a stretch to see Bach as a representative of absolutism. Further, some Pietist councilors had ties to the court that were as extensive as Lange's. Platz, for example, held the high position of Saxon appellate councilor and was a jurist on the highest Saxon court, the Supreme Electoral Court. And while the absolutist Romanus was a protégé of August the Strong, he came from an established Leipzig family. Furthermore, many Leipzig merchants with ties to the council enthusiastically supported Baroque music by purchasing instruments and sheet music,[59] commissioning wedding cantatas from Bach and other composers, and by visiting the Leipzig Opera.

The adiaphora

The adiaphora of the Baroque era, including music, are best known through a debate between Pietist and Orthodox writers.[60] This debate provides a good point of entry to the topic. Pietists stressed the ease and frequence with which the adiaphora were 'misused,' corrupting participants, consumers, and observers. The debate had many generic features. The term and even the specific forms of culture discussed in the Baroque era were similar to those discussed around Europe during the Reformation. Debates on the proper and improper pursuit of culture went back to antiquity. Both Pietist and Orthodox writers defended their views primarily by citing Scripture, older theologians, and even ancient philosophers. However, in the debate that erupted in the 1690s, writers were often specific about the types of music, dance, and other entertainment they were addressing, and about the social contexts in which these were taking place. They were reacting to the flourishing of opera in Hamburg, Leipzig, other towns, and at courts, to the emergence of coffee houses and pleasure gardens, and to the impact of Italian operatic style and recitativ/aria structure on the cantata. They also condemned traditional village culture; but it is the urban scene which is of interest here.

An early debate on opera had been conducted in 1681 in Hamburg.[61] Also early on, in 1687, Spener had written in a theological opinion from Dresden that it would be

---

58 Ibid., 22, 25 ff.; quote: 26.

59 Rose (2005).

60 See Bunners (2004) 'Musik' & idem, 'Gesangbuch,' also in *GdP*, vol. IV, 121–142; Irwin (1993).

61 John Lindberg (1973), 'Der Pietismus und die deutsche Barockoper: Zusammenpall zweier Welten,' in Gerhard Hoffmeister, ed., *Europäische Tradition und deutscher Literaturbarock* (Munich/Bern: Francke), 251–257.

best to keep church music influenced by Italian style out of the service. At the most, it might be inserted at the end of the service, so that people who were not interested could leave. Hymns sung with devotion by the whole congregation were 'more pleasant to the ears of God.'[62] The debate began in earnest when Pietists including Gottfried Vockerodt, a disciple of Francke and rector of the Gotha gymnasium, and Christian Gerber went on the offensive. Many lived in Saxony, others in Brandenburg-Prussia, Hamburg, Lower Saxony and elsewhere. All condemned the moral corruption of youth obsessed by comedies, theatre, opera, other leisure pursuits, and fashion. In 1697 Vockerodt wrote, 'the misuse of music ... is a most dangerous reef, along which many a young soul, as if called by Sirens ... falls into dissoluteness and ungodliness.' Vockerodt also stressed that the 'first Christians' knew only music which honored God.[63] Pietists in the 1690s and later additionally, as Spener had, devoted much effort to criticizing the influence of modern, secular style on church music. As had some earlier Lutheran writers, Pietists argued that the new style of music shut the congregation out; it made them passive recipients, whereas congregational hymns made them more active participants and furthered their devotion. Pietists also argued that many 'common' people did not understand enough of music to appreciate the cantatas and organ music.[64]

Orthodox writers' arguments were more diverse from the beginning than the Pietists'. Their backgrounds were also more diverse. While almost all of the Pietist writers were clerics or academics, Orthodox writers included Johann Kuhnau, Weissenfels court composer Johann Beer, Hamburg and Weissenfels minister and lyricist Erdmann Neumeister, and Hamburg composer, performer, music critic and lawyer Johann Mattheson. In the 1690s Beer made the radical argument that music itself was incorruptible, and that the moral quality of a musician or piece of music was independent of his or its musical quality. However, also in the 1690s Kuhnau argued more typically of Orthodox writers in holding up the competent, serious, pious musician as a model, and satirizing the charlatan whose only goal was to entertain.[65] Most Orthodox writers emphasized the important doxological functions of music: Old Testament psalms specifically called for people to praise God in song and with instruments. They also stressed that Luther and later Lutheran theologians had encouraged music-making, that its definition as an adiaphoron made it neutral, and that it had considerable persuasive appeal for many congregants and could therefore enhance devotion. Along these lines, the trained theologian and teacher Gottfried Ephraim Scheibel wrote of a passion performance that 'the people surely

---

62 Martin Geck (1961), 'Ph. J. Spener und die Kirchenmusik,' *Musik und Kirche*, 31, 97–106 & 172–184; 176.

63 Vockerodt (1997), *Missgebrauch der freyen Künste, insonderheit der Music ...* (Frankfurt: Zunner), 13 & 23.

64 See also Joseph Herl (2004), *Worship Wars in Early Lutheranism. Choir, Congregation, and Three Centuries of Conflict* (New York: Oxford University Press), passim.

65 Johann Kuhnau (1700), *Der Musicalische Quack-Salber ...* (Dresden: Miethen & Zimmermann, R [1968] Nendeln: Kraus); Beer (1697), *Ursus vulpinatur, List wider List, oder musicalische Fuchs-Jagdt* (Weissenfels, self-published).

did not arrive so promptly or in such large numbers because of the pastor, but rather because of the music. ... I was amazed at how attentively people listened and how devoutly they sang along. The moving music contributed the most to this. Although the service lasted over four hours, everyone stayed until it was finished.'[66]

Pietist arguments remained almost constant into the 1730s, but Orthodox writers became more assertive over time in defending the virtues of secular music. By 1728, in his journal *The Musical Patriot*, Mattheson was claiming that operas were the best schools for church musicians (with good church music, however, being the ultimate goal of the schooling), and that opera and church music had common origins in the religious festivals of the Greeks and Romans. Scheibel, in an argument that Mattheson opposed, went as far as to claim that opera arias could be highly effective if they were given sacred texts; he gave examples of two arias from a Telemann opera that had been performed in Leipzig in 1717.[67]

* * *

While Pietists were unusual in the vehemence of their opinions, they were not alone in having doubts about modern culture. Orthodox writers also had reservations. Both stressed the delicate balance between propriety and disorder or excess in musical performance. Even in the 1720s, Mattheson, Scheibel, and others remained defensive on key points. They agreed with Pietists that music could easily be misused. In church, the ultimate goals must be to praise God and encourage devotion, especially by felicitous settings of texts. Kuhnau criticized musicians who used their skill to impress women: students serenading women, and cantors looking down at women's pews.[68] Orthodox pastor Albrecht Christian Rothe supported Vockerodt in condemning student serenades; Rothe and fellow pastor Georg Motz also agreed with Pietist condemnations of operas with lascivious or purely entertaining plots.[69] Orthodox writers remained elitist, distinguishing legitimate, well-educated, virtuoso musicians from common 'beer-fiddlers' and charlatans. They praised tasteful music performed in proper, sedate, elite gatherings and condemned 'wild' music performed in conjunction with excessive eating, drinking, and dancing. Even Scheibel wrote that 'long sonatas and *Intraden*, along with much-too-long preludes, which should be sung instead – these I call music for the instrumentalists, since few people understand such artistry, and it always seems to me that people don't know what to do in this time ... people feel as if they are hearing a concert by a collegium

---

[66] Scheibel (1721), *Zufällige Gedancken von der Kirchen-Music, Wie Sie heutiges Tages beschaffen ist* (Frankfurt & Leipzig: self-published, R [2002] Stuttgart: Cornetto), 30.

[67] Scheibel (1721), 35–36; Herbert Lölkes, afterword in Scheibel (1721), 1–7; 4.

[68] Mattheson (1728), *Der Musicalische Patriot* (Hamburg: self-published, R [1975] Leipzig: Zentralantiquariat der DDR), 140, 129–136, passim. Kuhnau (1700), 528.

[69] Rothe (1699), *Höchstnöthiger Unterricht von so genannten Mittel-Dingen* ... (Leipzig: Lancke), passim; idem (1699), *Eilfertige und Kurtze Abfertigung des weitläufftigen und vergallten Geschmadderes Herrn M. Gottfried Vockerodts* ... (Leipzig: Lancke), 52, 44–45.

musicum.'[70] Scheibel did not argue that the music of itself was bad, but that since many congregants did not have musical training, such music did not lead to positive results, and could also provide ammunition for critics of music. Scheibel also wrote, 'I freely admit that minuets, gigues, passepieds, etc [French dance forms] do not belong in the church, because they promote vain thoughts in listeners.'[71]

Enlighteners were also ambivalent about the new secular culture. John Brewer has portrayed English Enlighteners' concern that the positive, edifying potential of the new 'high culture' be harnessed, while its materialistic and carnal pitfalls be avoided.[72] German Enlighteners, whose moral weeklies borrowed heavily from their English peers, were even more anxious. Enlighteners in Germany reframed the adiaphora debate, focusing primarily on secular music. Their concerns were less with the sinfulness of modern culture than with people wasting time and money. But modern secular culture remained dangerous. Good taste and sober, high-status gatherings were continually opposed to common revelry, and the potential that one could slip from one to the other was often stressed. Widely read and reprinted moral weeklies such as the Hamburg-based moral weekly *The Patriot* and Johann Christoph Gottsched's *The Reasonable Tattleresses*, based in Leipzig and Halle, condemned students' and young women's dissolute and wasteful pursuit of fashion, dance, and members of the opposite sex; among those frivolous activities were attending the opera, playing instruments, serenading, and dancing.[73] The moral weeklies' authors devoted much effort to reforming attitudes so that their ideal of decorous, edifying consumption of culture would be attained.

As Joyce Irwin has pointed out, even beyond specific groups, such as Enlighteners and Orthodox writers who specifically debated Pietists, a strong tradition in mainstream Lutheran political and religious culture deeply feared the potential for disorder in church as well as secular music.[74] Regarding church music, admonitions that could easily be confused with those of Pietists were heard throughout the Baroque era from city councilors, nobles, and jurists. For example, a decree issued in 1645 in the principality of Saxe-Gotha specified that in towns, people who were able to should read in their prayer books during the performance of figural singing or organ playing. The decree mentioned that this was already a custom in some towns. The decree also called for less figural and Latin singing, with more in German instead.[75] In 1723 jurist Julius Bernhard von Rohr, who identified himself as an anti-

---

[70] Scheibel (1721), 50–51.

[71] Scheibel (1721), 41.

[72] Brewer (1997), *The Pleasures of the Imagination. English Culture in the 18th Century* (New York: Farrar Strauss Giroux).

[73] Gottsched, ed. (1725–26), *Die vernünfftigen Tadlerinnen* (Halle, R [1993], Hildesheim: Olms) vol. I, no. 4, 25–26; no. 5, 33; no. 7, 51; no. 10, 73–80; no. 12, 95; no. 20, 59; no. 28, 217–224; no. 39, 314; *Der Patriot* (1724–26), (Hamburg, R [1969–70], Berlin: de Gruyter), vol. I, 120; vol. II, 12 & 292.

[74] Irwin (1993), 35 ff.

[75] Synodal-Schluss (1645), reprinted in *Fürstlich Sächsisch abermals verbesserte Landes-Ordnung des Durchläucht Hochgebohrenen Fürsten und Herrn Herrns Ernsten ...*

Pietist and specifically countered 'those who speak ill of church music,' wrote in his commentary on Saxon ecclesiastical law, 'All misuse is to be avoided as much as possible. No theatrical music should be introduced into the church, the greatest part of the service is not to be spent on music ...' He also specified that organists 'should not *praeludiren* all too long, or as sometimes happens *divertiren* a quarter or even half hour long while the congregation talks or has unrelated thoughts.'[76] Similarly, city councilors routinely inserted phrasing into cantors' contracts and during appointment meetings that the cantors should not perform music that was too long.[77]

In part, pedagogical goals stood behind these admonitions. Councilors' duty to ensure the proper transmission of the Word was at stake: the authorities and clerics wanted congregants to understand the words of hymns and other liturgical music, and for people to remain otherwise focused on the Word of God. Thus, Rohr wrote that 'the ignorant *Volk* screams [Latin chants] at the top of its lungs without understanding their meaning.'[78] Earlier, officials in Gotha had also been concerned that people did not understand Latin chants. In the same vein, the Gotha decree anticipated later commentators in stressing that sermons should be easily accessible to congregants and not filled with unnecessary Latin phrases and obscure references.[79]

In part, though, a more basic tension stood behind the cautionary statements. Rulers, clerics, and intellectuals ultimately had limited ability to control church music, an important marker of status, authority, and devotion. Most musicians and many political figures wanted the music they composed and patronized to reinforce order and hierarchy, but many also wanted it to reflect current style. Most innovations emerged from secular music, especially from the opera, which was a problematic genre for many. Furthermore, as we saw in Chapter One, congregants made hymns their own in a variety of ways.

Secular music also came in for much critique. While music for political events and small elite gatherings, such as serenades honoring Electors on their visits to Leipzig, or music played at 'polite' assemblies, was pronounced acceptable, music performed for most secular occasions, including wedding dances, in taverns, in coffee houses, or outdoors at fairs was met with much more suspicion, and was extensively regulated in sumptuary law. The emphasis of the laws was on preventing consumption and display seen as inappropriate to the social status of the celebrants, and unseemly behavior on the dance floor.[80] Coffee houses, like taverns, were considered sites of

---

(Gotha: Schall, 1667), Lit A, 6.

76 Rohr (1723), *Vollständiges Ober-Sächsisches Kirchen-Recht* ... (Frankfurt & Leipzig: Martini), 803–804; 371.

77 For example, the appointment of Kuhnau as cantor and that of Melchior Hoffmann as New Church music director; Glöckner (1990), 145 & 10.

78 Rohr (1723), 784.

79 Synodal-Schluss (1645), 15–18.

80 Anon. (1667) *Fürstlich Sächsische abermals verbesserte Landes-Ordnung des durchläucht Hochgeb Fürsten u Herrn Hernns Ernsten, Hertzogen zu Sachsen, Jülich, Cleve u Bergk, Landgraffen in Thüringen* … (Gotha: Schall), 489–490; Johannes Schmidt, ed. (1800–

prostitution and inappropriate playing of card and other games as late as 1716.[81] Even the author of a 1725 guide to Leipzig, who provided a very positive description of the coffee houses, added a defensive note in writing that people played 'various witty and permissible chess, board, ladies' and billiard games.'[82]

* * *

What positions did the cantors take in these culture wars? Responses varied. Kuhnau was a complex figure. He was influenced by traditional theories which called for a strict separation of religious and secular musical styles. His support of new musical styles was also dampened because of his competition with the Opera and the New Church. In his church music, though, he was an innovator, early introducing the new operatic forms into his cantatas; he also composed two operas.[83] In Hamburg, as we have seen, Mattheson, cantor at one church for several years, took a leading role in debates on the adiaphora and Enlightenment. Telemann did not specifically engage the adiaphora debate, but he did on numerous occasions stress the power of music, including secular music played by collegia musica, to provide pleasure and calm.[84]

Bach famously wrote little about his ideas concerning music. Without the legal background of Mattheson, Telemann, Kuhnau and other musical colleagues, he may have been less inclined to enter the polemical fray. Perhaps he thought his music would speak for itself. Ultimately, no musical theory of the Baroque era fully accommodated Bach's church music, with its occasional long instrumental passages, dance rhythms, and parodying (arranging) of secular pieces for sacred use and vice versa. However, there is considerable evidence that Bach worked well with a range of Orthodox figures, beyond the figures explored above, while there is none that he worked closely with any Pietists. Bach knew the Orthodox cleric and librettist Erdmann Neumeister well, and set a number of his cantata texts. Many of the councilors and theologians whom Johann Sebastian and Anna Magdalena chose as godparents of their children in Leipzig can be identified as Orthodox or pro-

---

19) *Aeltere u neuere Gesetze, Ordnungen u Circular-Befehle für das Fürstenthum Weimar u. für die Jenaische Landes-Portion* ...(Jena: Göpfert), vol. II, 515–518, 547–548; Johann Christian Lünig, ed. (1724), *Codex Augusteus, oder Neuvermehrtes Corpus Juris Saxonici* ... (Leipzig: Gleditsch), 1466, 1470–1471.

81 See Chapter Eight, note 86.

82 Iccander (1725), *Das in gantz Europa berühmte, galante und sehens-würdige Königliche Leipzig in Sachsen* ... (Leipzig: Martini), 87–88.

83 George Buelow (1980), 'Kuhnau, Johann,' in *The New Grove Dictionary of Music and Musicians*, vol. X (New York: Macmillan), 793–803; Evangeline Rimbach (1966), *The Church Cantatas of Johann Kuhnau*, PhD thesis, University of Rochester (Ann Arbor: University Microfilms).

84 Telemann, dedication of oratorios to Frankfurt collegium musicum, ed. (1980), Werner Rackwitz and Eitelfriedrich Thom, *Singen ist das Fundament/Zur Musik in allen Dingen. Eine Dokumentensammlung* (Leipzig: Reclam), 82–84; poems in C.F. Weichmann, ed. (1721–38), *Poesie der Niedersachsen* (Hamburg, R [1980], Munich: Kraus), 284–288.

Baroque;[85] and none of them was Pietist. Johannes Wallmann argues persuasively that a well-known margin note by Bach in his Calov-edition Bible is actually a defense of instrumental music in church.[86]

Finally, early in his career Bach did articulate a clear pro-Baroque and anti-Pietist position. As Robin A. Leaver has noted, the pastor of the church to which he was appointed organist in the town of Mühlhausen was a Pietist. Bach and his first wife Maria Barbara chose the Orthodox pastor of another local church, who frequently clashed with his Pietist colleague, to be the godfather of two of their children.[87] In submitting a request for dismissal to the Mühlhausen town council in 1708, just a year after he had taken the position, he wrote:

> Even though I should always have liked to work toward the goal, namely, a well-regulated church music … and would, according to my small means, have helped out as much as possible with the church music that is growing up in almost every township, and often better than the harmony that is fashioned here, and therefore have acquired from far and wide, not without cost, a good store of the choicest church compositions … yet it has not been possible to accomplish all this without hindrance.[88]

This passage conveys musicians' sense of themselves as innovators and participants in a broad-based movement, one which some people opposed. Bach also added that his pay was too low and that he had been offered a position at the Weimar court; but his first and longest reference was to the apparent conflict.

* * *

In conclusion, what was specifically Baroque about the political structures, patronage system, religious practices, performance venues, and the interactions between musicians and political figures seen here? This system was not new; the confessional structures that were the foundation of appointment, payment, the liturgy, and much conflict had been established by the late 16th century. The system did, though, continue to evolve. The cantors' duties expanded to the point where their school duties became almost incompatible with their compositional and performance activities. Further, old tensions about the benefits and dangers of music continued to generate new forms of debate. The public, intense, and sustained nature of the Pietists' critique of 'theatrical' music was new, but the debate itself was not.

---

85 Martin Petzoldt (1982), 'Überlegungen zur theologischen und geistigen Integration Bachs in Leipzig 1723,' *BzBf*, 1, 46–52; 50–51.

86 The margin note: *Bey einer andächtigen Musique ist allezeit Gott mit seiner Gnaden-Gegenwart.* Wallmann (2003), review of Renate Steiger (2002), *Gnadengegenwart. Johann Sebastian Bach im Kontext lutherischer Orthodoxie und Frömmigkeit* (Stuttgart: Frommann Holzboog), *PuN*, 29, 327–332; 331–332.

87 Leaver (1991), 13–14.

88 Dated 25 June 1708. Reprinted in *NBR*, 56–57.

Historians have often noted that political figures in the Baroque era made active use of culture to further their absolutist agendas. Certainly both city councilors and the Electoral court harnessed the musical talents of Bach and other musicians. The Electors and some city councilors fit the profile of well-informed, hands-on planners of musical displays that projected an image of grandeur. The ongoing conflicts that surrounded cultural politics in the council, though, show that while pro-Baroque councilors could organize some impressive performances and even have a longer-lasting impact in some cases, the council as a whole had no unified cultural agenda. From Bach's perspective, the Pietist reaction among some members of the council to his compositional and performance style was surely annoying and possibly discouraging, but support from other councilors balanced out the opposition.

Finally, how did the urban Baroque patronage system contribute to the careers of Kuhnau, Bach, Telemann, and others? Despite Bach's aggravations with his patrons, the confessional system contributed to a vibrant musical culture in several ways. Positions as cantor, Capellmeister, and instrumentalist around central Europe provided a steady, if not munificent, income to thousands of professional musicians. As did people in other occupations, the musicians often intermarried and provided an early musical education to their children, a key to becoming proficient. Weekly services which were the main public forums in a given town, and frequent performances to honor rulers, provided abundant performance opportunities and large audiences. Not least, the urban patronage system existed in synergy with courts, with musicians as well as councilors moving easily between the worlds. Ongoing contacts with courts including Dresden, Berlin, and Weissenfels enriched Bach's musical life while he was in Leipzig. Councilors in large towns were also interested in promoting innovative music. Thus, it is no accident that Bach worked in Leipzig, and Telemann in Leipzig, Frankfurt, and Hamburg.

PART III
The Pietist alternative

Chapter Six

Sociability and religious protest: the collegia pietatis of 1689–1690

Leipzig's inhabitants had considerable leeway in their everyday religious activities. For example, during the worship service congregants arrived, departed, and socialized according to their interests. Families dealt with pews largely at their discretion. Hierarchies in and limits on religious practices were so well established by the 1650s that they were often unstated. This changed in 1689 and 1690, when a small group of University students and ordinary inhabitants who came to be called Pietists gathered in burghers' homes and students' rooms for prayer meetings called collegia pietatis. Orthodox clerics and the secular and ecclesiastical authorities in Leipzig and Dresden soon became suspicious of the meetings, and made them the subject of an extensive investigation. In Fall 1689 and from March to August 1690 the city council and University interrogated participants; further meetings were forbidden; and the leading students left Leipzig.

The collegia and the investigation into them were a pivotal moment in German Baroque religious life. They sparked what Ryoko Mori has aptly called the 'second wave' of Pietism: when Pietist students dispersed from Leipzig to towns around central Germany such as Jena, Erfurt, and Gotha they formed collegia and engaged in conflict with the authorities, making Pietism a 'social movement.'[1] Collegia and conflict also emerged in other large trading centers such as Hamburg, Frankfurt, and Breslau, and in other towns across Germany. Along with ordinary people and young students, some members of the elites were also eager to challenge the status quo. Spener's close work with Francke in planning and defending the collegia, and the involvement of figures such as Adam Rechenberg, reflect this readiness. The Leipzig collegia, and the investigation into them, were the most famous of those in any town. Numerous leading Pietists, including August Hermann Francke, Paul Anton, and Johann Caspar Schade were involved. Leipzig's status as a prominent university, trade, and print center, and home of an influential theological establishment, also

[1] Mori (2004), *Begeisterung und Ernüchterung in christlicher Vollkommenheit. Pietistische Selbst- und Weltwahrnehmungen im ausgehenden 17. Jahrhundert* (Tübingen: Niemeyer), 25 ff. & passim; quote, 55.

helped give lasting definition to both Pietist and Orthodox stances.[2] Indeed, the term 'Pietist' became widely known during the Leipzig investigation.[3]

There are two detailed studies of the collegia, and numerous shorter discussions.[4] What can a further examination add? Key here are the original transcriptions of the interrogations of participants in the collegia.[5] These protocols were buried in larger files in the territorial archive in Dresden; other scholars have known only excerpts made in the 18th century. The protocols allow for a fuller reconstruction of the collegia, and of the urban contexts in which they were embedded, than has been the case. Thirty-six people in all were interrogated. Students and burghers described how they became acquainted; how, when, and where they met; what they talked about; and their general opinions. The protocols provide unusually detailed insight into the religious thought and activities of ordinary people (including some who strongly disliked the Pietists). The protocols also provide essential perspective on the authorities' response, since official reports distorted the collegia in several ways.

---

2 See Christian Peters (1997), '"Daraus der Lärm des Pietismi entstanden." Die Leipziger Unruhen von 1689/1690 und ihre Deutung durch Spener und die hallischen Pietisten,' *PuN*, 23, 103–151.

3 Mori (2004), 24.

4 See Mori (2004); the 1921 Leipzig dissertation of Hans Leube, 'Die Geschichte der pietistischen Bewegung in Leipzig. Ein Beitrag zur Geschichte und Charakteristik des deutschen Pietismus,' R [1975] in idem, *Orthodoxie und Pietismus. Gesammelte Studien*, ed. D. Blaufuß (Bielefeld: Luther-Verlag), 153–257. The account in *Geschichte des Pietismus*, Martin Brecht (1993), 'Philipp Jakob Spener, sein Programm und dessen Auswirkungen,' (*GdP*, vol. I, 281–389; 333–338) is based on Leube and on later accounts by Francke. See also Peters (1997); James Van Horn Melton (2001), 'Pietism, Politics, and the Public Sphere in Germany,' in James Bradley & Dale van Kley, eds, *Religion and Politics in Enlightenment Europe* (Notre Dame: University of Notre Dame Press), 294–333, esp. 299–301; Günther Wartenberg (1987), 'Der Pietismus in Sachsen: Ein Literaturbericht,' *PuN*, 13, 103–114.

5 Halle professor Callenberg made excerpts in 1727. Mori, Leube, and others have also used a variety of printed sources. Mori additionally uses files generated in 1692 in the Stadtarchiv Leipzig. Of the six central files two, *Acta, die sog.* Pietisten *betr., ergangen 1690* (the council's interrogations, hereafter *Acta ... 1690*) and *Acta, Johann Andreas Schillingen und M. Andreas Friedeln betr. Ergangen vor E. Löbl. Universität Leipzig 1690* (the University's interrogations, hereafter *Acta ... Schilling & Friedel*), are bound out of context in another file, SHStADD, Loc. 10329, *Pietistica, oder Des Pietismi Halber von Dr. Spenern, Dr. Löschern, Dr. Wernsdorffen, und Dr. Marpergern gewechselte Schrifften ao. 1691–1714* ... Another file, containing interrogations of students and burghers in Fall 1689, was published in 1692 by Thomasius and Francke as *Gerichtliches Leipziger Protocoll Ein Sachen die Pietisten betreffend* (no place, no publisher), R [1981] in Erhard Peschke, ed., *August Hermann Francke. Schriften und Predigten* (Berlin: de Gruyter) (hereafter: *Gerichtliches Leipziger Protocoll*; original pages cited). It is not clear where the remaining three files are and what they contained. See Leube (1921), preface to the reissue.

Consistory correspondence on the investigation provides further insight into the perspective and workings of the authorities.[6]

The collegia emerged from a range of long-established forms of urban religious and political association and conflict; this background is discussed first. Common patterns of sociability among students, burghers, and sub-burghers, which led more directly to the formation of the collegia, are examined second, along with sociability during the collegia. It is important to examine the perspective of the townspeople. A picture is gradually emerging of inhabitants of Erfurt, Frankfurt, Lübeck, and other towns who had an appetite for more religious activity than the public worship service and family devotions offered.[7] Working closely with students or recent graduates, they met in small groups which drew the ire of the authorities. In Erfurt, Lübeck, and apparently in Hamburg they did so even before Spener inaugurated his Frankfurt collegium in 1670. However, their motivations are poorly understood, especially compared with those of clerics and nobles, the other main social groups represented among Pietists. (Although some peasants were drawn to Pietism, most were repelled by the emphasis on discipline and renouncing worldly pleasures. A number of Pietist village pastors in Saxony, Brandenburg-Prussia, and Southwest Germany were actually dismissed because their congregations rebelled against them.)[8] Further, the protocols provide the opportunity to examine the various roles of gender in the collegia. Women played relatively prominent roles in the collegia, as they did generally in Pietism, but these are also just beginning to be investigated in depth.[9] Women's activity was greatly exaggerated by the authorities, who saw the

---

6 SHStADD, Loc. 10330, *Den so gen.* Pietismum *betr. 1690 sqq.*, 68–104^{v}, (hereafter: *Den so gen.* Pietismum *betr.*). Some of this correspondence was previously known through copies.

7 Johannes Wallmann (1992), 'Erfurt und der Pietismus im 17. Jahrhundert,' in Ulman Weiss, ed., *Erfurt 742–1992. Stadtgeschichte, Universitätsgeschichte* (Weimar: Böhlau), 403–422; Jonathan Strom (2001), 'Early Conventicles in Lübeck,' *PuN*, 27, 19–52; Andreas Deppermann (2002), *Johann Jakob Schütz und die Anfänge des Pietismus* (Tübingen: Mohr), 94 and passim.

8 They include Justinus Töllner just outside Leipzig. See Jens Bulisch (1997/1998), 'Justinus Töllners Weggang aus Panitzsch. Ein Beitrag zur Frühgeschichte des Pietismus in Sachsen,' *Herbergen der Christenheit*, 21/22, 69–86; Tanya Kevorkian (1997), 'The Material of Faith: Religion and Society in Leipzig,' 1685–1725 (PhD thesis, Johns Hopkins University), 311 ff.; Mori (2004), 60 ff. See also David Sabean (1984), *Power in the Blood. Popular Culture and Village Discourse in Early Modern Germany* (New York: Cambridge University Press), Chapter Four; anon. (1703), *Vollständige Acten, welche zuförderst zu Tit. Herrn D. Hienrich Mattäi von Broke ...und M. Johanne Crasselio ...* (Halle: Grunert) on Johann Crasselius of Sara and Muckern outside Altenburg; Mori (2004), 27–28 & 39. Popularity of Pietism in the countryside: Wallmann (1992), 415.

9 See Melton (2001), 301–302; Mori (2004), passim; Ulrike Witt (1996), *Bekehrung, Bildung und Biographie: Frauen im Umkreis des Halleschen Pietismus* (Tübingen: Niemeyer); Lucinda Martin (2003), 'Möglichkeiten und Grenzen geistlicher Rede von Frauen in Halle und Herrnhut,' *PuN*, 29, 80–90; Ruth Albrecht (2004), 'Frauen,' in *GdP*, vol. IV, 522–555.

crossing of normative gender boundaries as a far more serious threat than that of status boundaries.

Thirdly, the investigation is examined. The amount of attention the collegia generated seems out of proportion to their scope. No more than perhaps sixty to eighty people were actively involved (although more were sympathetic), and individual gatherings generally included only as many people as could fit into a room in a burgher or student room. But the collegia were depicted as a major form of protest, a disruption of proper status and gender relations, and a threat to social and political order generally. The gathering of students, burghers, and sub-burghers, men and women to discuss Scripture presented a challenge to the parallel religious, social, and political structures that reinforced each other in Leipzig and other Protestant towns.[10]

Finally, participants' interactions with the authorities are discussed. As Ryoko Mori has also noted,[11] participants were surprisingly assertive in challenging ecclesiastical and social norms and even the legitimacy of the authorities. Their assertiveness highlights the appeal to the powerful as well as the poor, to male as well as female, as a basic feature of Pietism. This would seem to contradict the Pietists' reputation for working with the powerful. Spener, Francke and other Pietist leaders did indeed gain the patronage of influential nobles, especially noblewomen, in Saxony and elsewhere. Pietists played an important role in the centralization of the Brandenburg-Prussian state. Still, especially in the early years of the movement, religious fervor partially overrode identification with a particular social group. In the area of spirituality, all were active subjects. Pietists argued that true, 'inner' spirituality was independent of gender and social status and of formal theological study, and might actually be undermined by such study.

Contexts: urban association and unrest

It is difficult to classify the collegia. The authorities may well have reacted as vehemently as they did because they feared a political protest. The collegia came at the tail end of decades of conflict around urban Europe, and coincided with political unrest in other towns.[12] The memory of Leipzig burghers' partial seizure of power toward the end of the Thirty Years' War was also still alive for councilors. But the collegia were not a typical early modern political protest: burghers did not present petitions to the city council, and they did not formally call for any changes in religion or other matters. The collegia also differed from late medieval and early modern student protests. Often violent, these pitted students against councilors, town guards, artisans, and university officials on issues of curfews, clothing, hazing, and night-

10 On these structures, see especially Lyndal Roper (1989), *The Holy Household. Women and Morals in Reformation Augsburg* (Oxford: Clarendon).

11 Mori (2004), 1 & passim.

12 Christopher Friedrichs (2000), *Urban Politics in Early Modern Europe* (New York: Routledge), 62–64.

time street activities. By contrast, Pietist students and burghers developed close relations before, during, and after the collegia.

In several ways, the collegia and the debate surrounding them resembled the urban conflict of the early Reformation: some clerics and theology students became advocates of a style of worship and association modelled closely on the early Christian communities of the New Testament Epistles. Clerics and assertive burghers sought to reform a well-established religious system that they saw as corrupt and hierarchical. Women played a more active role than usual. And pamphlet wars, rich in personal invective, brought the conflict to a wide audience. Indeed, Leipzig city councilors may have been reminded of the townspeople and peasants of the early Reformation, who had on occasion risen up against the secular authorities.[13]

The collegia did emerge from various forms of early modern religious association and conflict that took place outside the space of the church. Most directly, they were rooted in traditional forms of sociability among students and burghers, especially student conversations with and counselling of burghers and their servants in the homes where they roomed and boarded. The collegia were also loosely related to household devotions led by 'house fathers,' widely practiced around Europe, which the authorities saw as an important complement to public services. There were other forms of religious association as well. As one burgher noted during his interrogation, one of his relatives thought that the collegia had originated in 'circles (*Kränzgen*) which they had held as good friends since the time of the epidemic (*Contagionszeit*),' presumably the 1680 plague epidemic.[14] Collegia had also been held in some other towns, especially in the 1660s and 1670s.

Further, the specific issues raised by Pietists were not new. Throughout the 17th century, Lutheran proponents of 'reform Orthodoxy' (for some, 'early Pietism') called for a restrained lifestyle much like that advocated by Pietists.[15] In England and North America, Puritans and Quakers likewise rejected feasting, dancing, music-making, and gambling. Others had also advocated such a lifestyle. For example, cleric Adam Bernd wrote that his mother 'was a true Pietist in her lifestyle, although this term was not yet known at the time' (in the 1670s and early 1680s).[16] The Pietists' purposeful conflict with the authorities was also not new. In Germany, as around Europe, intense religious beliefs brought individuals, usually men, into conflict with authorities in their villages and towns. Carlo Ginzburg's miller Menocchio and David Sabean's prophet Hans Keil are just two examples.[17]

---

13 Thanks to Lucinda Martin for this comment.

14 Interrogation of shoemaker Friedrich Siegmund Hanisch, 9 April 1690. *Acta ... 1690*, 63–67; 65v.

15 Hans Leube (1924), *Die Reformideen in der deutschen lutherischen Kirche zur Zeit der Orthodoxie* (Leipzig: Dörffling & Franke).

16 Adam Bernd (1738), *Eigene Lebens-Beschreibung* (Leipzig: Heinsius, R, [1973] Munich: Winkler), 19.

17 Ginzburg (1980), *The Cheese and the Worms: The Cosmos of a Sixteenth-Century Miller* (Baltimore: Johns Hopkins University Press; trans. John & Ann Tedeschi); Sabean (1984), Chapters One, Two, and passim.

One final tradition from which the collegia grew was the academic collegium given by masters (*Magistri*) of theology, philosophy, law, and medicine for younger students.[18] The theology *Magister* August Hermann Francke held his first collegium in 1687, three years after he first arrived in Leipzig. The subject material was traditional: scholarly exegesis of Scriptural passages, conducted in Latin and Greek. After Francke's 'rebirth,' or conversion to Pietism during a stay in North Germany in 1688, his goal became to communicate spirituality rather than academic learning: to 'convert' his fellow students.[19] During two visits in late 1688 and Spring 1689 to Philipp Jacob Spener, then Senior Court Chaplain in Dresden, Spener extensively advised Francke on the two collegia that he was scheduled to hold during Lent and Summer 1689. In these, Francke emphasized the devotional aspects of the scriptural passages he taught. His pedagogical method reinforced his new approach: at the end of each lecture, he opened the discussion to the audience. He took no money, so that poor students would be able to attend. The collegia were very popular, with over three hundred students crowding the lecture hall. Francke's friends Paul Anton and Johann Caspar Schade held similar collegia at the same time. Some burghers began to attend these collegia in Spring 1689.

Sociability: the formation and conduct of the collegia

The leaders of the collegia were a closely-knit group of young men. Most were in their late twenties, and almost all had come from outside Leipzig. Some were *Magistri* and some pre-*Magister*; they were referred to interchangeably as students by the authorities and by burghers. Some had known each other before coming to Leipzig: two were north Germans who came to Leipzig at Francke's request, and two were cousins. Most remained close friends until their deaths although they scattered throughout Germany.

The students attracted people from a wide range of occupations to the collegia. The majority of those who were interrogated, including the most outspoken figures, were property-owning burghers and their families. The largest number were artisans: a baker and his wife, a shoemaker and his wife, a roper and his son, a goldsmith, a book dealer, and a journeyman haberdasher (who was the brother of a Pietist student). Two were shopkeepers (they were also referred to as merchants). A few were members of the urban *Schreiber* class: the town grain registrar, and town mortuary registrar and his daughter. They held formal city offices, but were considered employees of the council rather than authorities themselves. Two men were identified simply as 'burghers.' The occupations of two women and two men were not given. Some sub-artisans, including a lace washer, a gardener and a guard, also came to the meetings.

A psychological profile of the collegia participants is more difficult to establish, and must remain partial and speculative. A majority of Pietists described a sense of

---

18 See Leube (1921), esp. 170 ff.

19 See Leube (1921), 170 ff. and passim; Brecht (1993), 333 ff.

alienation from mainstream society that probably encouraged them to join the Pietist movement. The collegia also attracted some people who were facing considerable mental and physical challenges. The lace washer Catharina Mey's husband suffered from melancholia. Three active Pietists died during or not long after the investigation (which of course caused considerable stress itself). Dorothea Elisabeth Henrich, daughter of the head mortuary registrar, died of unrecorded causes in July 1690.[20] The professor Joachim Feller committed suicide by jumping from a courtyard window.[21] And in 1693 the book dealer Johann Heinich died, among 'evil rumors,' after a period of insanity apparently brought on by another ailment.[22]

* * *

Before they formed collegia, students and inhabitants became acquainted through a range of routine interactions. Rooming and boarding arrangements were the most important form of contact. While August Hermann Francke lived in the University-owned Pauline Collegium, after an initial spell in Adam Rechenberg's house as a tutor for another student, he ate in burghers' homes. Francke got to know the most active burghers in the movement, those who were already active in Fall 1689, in this way. In his 10 October 1689 interrogation he stated that he sometimes ate at the baker Martin Meinig's, 'on which occasion he spoke good words with him, and was glad that a burgher also spoke of God and His word at meals.'[23] Meinig, interrogated on the same day, added that he had met Francke through a student who had roomed with him for a long time. Meinig 'often asked Herr M. Francke to eat with him, and he did as often as he could.' Francke also ate and pursued edifying conversation with shopkeepers Augustin Frentzel and Samuel Knauer.[24] Francke had become close to Spener himself as a house guest. From Christmas 1688 to the beginning of Lent 1689, Francke had been 'taken into [Spener's] house and to his table' in Dresden. In that period

> I enjoyed much love from him: I sat at his side twice a day, at noon and in the evening [at meals] and spoke with him, and was at his morning and evening hours of prayer. I considered it a great kindness to have a room across from his, and to sometimes be admitted into his room. I also wished to hear his sermons.[25]

Francke visited Spener again for a week and a half after Easter.

---

20 SAL, *Ratsleichenbuch* 1690–1698, 14.

21 Leube (1921), 211.

22 Caspar Würdig to Francke, 24 December 1693. AFS, C 275: 4.

23 Interrogation of Francke, 10 October 1689. *Gerichtliches Leipziger Protocoll*, 37–38.

24 Ibid.

25 Francke, *Bericht über sein Leben, 1687–89*, no date (after 1705), copy (of a published work?). AFS, D 84, 4–5^{v}.

The Pietists, like other students of medicine and theology, also visited inhabitants when they were sick. Francke became acquainted with the lace washer Catharina Mey, the most prominent woman among the Leipzig Pietists, when she called him to visit her husband Hans, a journeyman carpenter who had been *melancholisch* and unable to work for years. While he was there, Francke 'admonished her how to be pious and live a Christian life, and told her of the lives of other pious people.'[26] A medical student named Christian Gaulicke was first in the house of another active woman, Dorothea Elisabeth Henrich, to cure her mother of a fever.[27] Gaulicke and another student, Blebel, also visited the shoemaker Friedrich Siegmund Hanisch on different occasions when he was sick. Blebel mentioned the collegia and Hanisch asked to be taken along. Once he had gone and spoken with Francke, Hanisch realized that 'until then he had not lived as a Christian, and forthwith separated himself from the immoral company he had kept.'[28]

Students and burghers also met in bookstores, places where information was commonly exchanged and overheard. During his interrogation Francke stated that he got to know the book dealer Johann Heinich, an early and ardent Pietist, in his bookstore, and mainly spoke with him there.[29] Heinich added that he became acquainted with Francke after being given letters to bring him from Hamburg; since book dealers travelled regularly, they often transported letters and packets for people. Francke had recommended books to Heinich, but had not given him any religious instruction.[30] Afterward Heinich had heard that several book dealers' clerks gathered at other students' rooms for a collegium led by Schade after church on Sundays, and went along.

* * *

At the table, at the sickbed, and in bookstores students recruited their acquaintances to come to collegia. The baker Martin Meinig said that 'the students persuaded him during meals to go to the collegia ... even though at first he did not want to go, thinking that it was not suitable for him.'[31] The roper's son Christian Eckard said that he had gone to the collegia about four times 'on the suggestion of the students.'[32] Rosina Hanisch, wife of shoemaker Friedrich Siegmund Hanisch, stated that the student Blebel had urged her to go hear Francke preach in the University church, where sermons were normally open only to the University community, and to visit Catharina Mey because Mey was a 'Christian woman.'[33]

---

26 Interrogation of Catharina Mey, 1 March 1690. *Acta ... 1690*, 2–2^{v}.

27 Interrogation of Dorothea Elisabeth Henrich, 31 March 1690. Ibid., 38–39.

28 Interrogation of Hanisch, 9 April 1690. Ibid., 63–67.

29 Interrogation of Francke, 10 October 1689. *Gerichtliches Leipziger Protocoll*, 37–38.

30 Interrogation of Heinich, 1 or 10 October 1689. Ibid., 11–12.

31 Interrogation of 9 April 1690. *Acta ... 1690*, 67^{v}–69^{v}.

32 Interrogation of 9 April 1690. Ibid., 69^{v}–70.

33 Interrogation of 11 April 1690. Ibid., 71–74.

Once the Pietist network had begun to form, people attended meetings in the homes of like-minded burghers, which were also called collegia. These meetings, as well as the presence of an increasing number of inhabitants at University collegia, especially one held by Johann Caspar Schade, and impromptu gatherings held by students in their rooms in the Pauline Collegium, were a crucial break with tradition. In them, students, burghers, and their families left behind established patterns of interaction to discuss issues in an arena traditionally controlled by the clergy. Everyone, regardless of status, was ascribed the capability of interpreting Scripture. In a memorial he handed his interrogators, city grain registrar Samuel Voigt described one such meeting in his home. On a Sunday afternoon,

> Herr Müller, Heinich, Frentzel, Rückert, the window-maker Buchman, the shoemaker Friedrich Siegmund Hanisch, the baker from the Ritterstrasse [Martin Meinig], and Herr Ziel [a theology student] came to my house. Ziel read, explicated, and applied several verses of the First Epistle of John, admonished all to follow a Christian lifestyle and to flee the works of darkness for the works of light. Each of us contributed his sentiment on the subject and what he had understood of it. Then a copy of the Augsburg Confession came into my hand, and I read from Article 20 ... on true faith, and how good works reveal true faith externally, like the hands of an internally well adjusted clock ... Herr Ziel closed our gathering (*zusammenseyn*) as he had opened it, with one of his prayers.[34]

Other participants confirmed that burghers gave their opinions on scriptural passages. Christian Eckard, the roper's son, stated that 'young and simple people interpreted Scripture as they thought fit.'[35]

The Scriptural subjects of the collegia were the Epistles written by the Apostles to early Christian congregations: the Epistles of Paul to the Romans, Corinthians, Ephesians, Thessalonians, and Timothy; the First Epistle of Peter; the Epistles of John.[36] The early Christians and their leaders were literal models for the Pietists. Schade said during his interrogation that in the collegium he held in Spring 1690, he 'analyzed [the First Epistle of Peter] for its literal meaning and drew practical profits from it.'[37] This procedure was followed in other collegia as well. Among other things, the Pietists used texts that, like Peter's, emphasized equality among Christians, and emphasized the Mediterranean congregations' small number of faithful surrounded by sometimes hostile masses. This strengthened group identity among participants in the collegia.[38]

As several witnesses and informants testified, not everyone who came in contact with the Pietists welcomed them. Personal animosity among housemates seem to have influenced some people's responses to the Pietists. Elizabeth Karig, the widow

---

34 Voigt's memorial, ibid., 5^{v}.

35 Interrogation of Eckard, 9 April 1690. Ibid., 67^{v}.

36 Participants in the collegia mentioned these texts during their interrogations and in printed literature they published on the collegia.

37 20 March 1690. *Acta ... 1690*, 19–20.

38 1:17; passim.

of a day laborer who roomed in the house of mortuary registrar Christian Henrich, was troubled by the Pietists' critique of clerics and voluntarily complained to her confessor. Tailor Heinrich Schulze, the landlord of two students, was eager to denounce his tenants. Even some people who visited the collegia did not enjoy them. A man named Joachim Krumbholz stated that on the insistence of a friend, Zacharias Hezer, he had gone to one collegium held by Schade at the University. Krumbholz declared that nothing improper had been said at the collegium, but 'he had been glad when he left' and had never gone back. Since then, he had taken a negative position toward 'this undertaking' and as a result had fallen into 'enmity' with Hezer.[39] Karig, Schulze, Krumbholz and others stood at the beginning of a long line of people who had a negative reaction to the Pietists' intensity and lifestyle.

While the collegia were dangerously egalitarian by the standards of the day, they were still led by the students. Usually one student presided, and others were sometimes also present. In his memorial, Samuel Voigt wrote that at a meeting at Augustin Frentzel's house 'all gave their opinions in turn; the guard (*Lohnwächter*) added several words, and at the end Herr *Magister* Schade came and upon our request contributed his application.' There was a hierarchy even among the students. The baker Martin Meinig rented Francke a room in his house to use as a classroom and installed 'benches so that the students could sit. Herr Francke sat somewhat higher, on a chair that was on top of a couple of boards a quarter ell [about a foot] higher than the others.'[40] The students began to leave Leipzig in January 1690, but the collegia were well established by then, and most accounts of individual meetings mention students as leaders.

Still, the Leipzig inhabitants whom the Pietist students encountered brought an active interest in and curiosity about religion to the collegia. Shopkeeper Samuel Kanuer, very unusually for a burgher, had entered into a correspondence with Spener in 1680. He requested spiritual advice during the devastating 1680 plague epidemic and later asked whether having intercourse with his pregnant wife was acceptable. Spener responded to each inquiry with a lengthy missive.[41] He probably also put Francke in touch with Knauer. Baker Martin Meinig had sought Francke out by inviting him to his home for meals. The mortuary registrar's daughter Dorothea Elisabeth Henrich stated that she had become involved with the Pietists after going to the Leipzig jail, St. George's, to hear Francke preach. Francke's sermon on 'hot,' 'cold,' and 'lukewarm' faith had moved her to the realization that until then her faith and the whole conduct of her life had been merely 'lukewarm.' She resolved to seek a deeper spirituality.[42] While Francke, a charismatic preacher, influenced her, she had gone out of her way to hear him preach at an unusual venue.

---

39 Interrogation of Krumbholz, 11 April 1690. *Acta ... 1690*, 75^{v}.

40 Interrogation of Meinig. *Gerichtliches Leipziger Protocoll*, 10–11.

41 Spener's responses: Johannes Wallmann, ed. (2005), *Philipp Jakob Spener. Briefe aus der Frankfurter Zeit 1666–1686*, vol. IV, 1679–1680 (Tübingen: Mohr), 632–636 and 687–693. Knauer's letters are not preserved.

42 31 March 1690. *Acta ... 1690*, 38–39.

The investigation

The workings of the authorities were a mixture of the methodical, the scholarly, and the repressive. The early, University-based investigation was succeeded by a broader investigation. The consistories played a crucial role. The collegia were first investigated in Fall 1689, soon after a handful of burghers began attending Francke's University collegium. Initially the investigation remained an academic affair. The University theology faculty complained to the Upper Consistory that burghers were attending and that the students were criticizing the Leipzig Ministry. The Consistory ordered reports and an investigation.[43] The theology faculty interrogated fifteen students and five burghers in Fall 1689. Nothing seriously incriminating was found, and the conflict temporarily subsided. The Pietists were supported by philosophy professor Adam Rechenberg, who was serving as University rector during the 1689–90 academic year. Rechenberg slowed the investigation and warned Francke and others of edicts from Dresden before he made them public.

But the situation soon polarized. With Rechenberg's permission, Francke attained access to the files of the investigation in October 1689. He examined the files with his friend Christian Thomasius, who had gained the enmity of the theology faculty through his satirical journal *Monthly Conversations*, and in collegia of his own.[44] Thomasius continued his attack by writing a memorandum criticizing the method of the Fall interrogations as illegal. Using Thomasius's legal advice, Francke wrote to the Elector complaining of the theological faculty's attacks on him. Francke and Thomasius circulated copies of their complaints, which were later published along with the Fall 1689 interrogation protocols as the *Judicial Leipzig Protocol Concerning the Pietists*.[45]

Francke's move provoked a much larger investigation, which the Electoral authorities took out of the hands of the University. At this point, the dispute was no longer primarily an academic one. The theological faculty sent a report to the Upper Consistory in late February, in which individual faculty members defended themselves at length against what they construed as an attack on their honor. The fact that Francke had sought out Thomasius rankled deeply. The theologians also took issue with the collegia, which were expanding to a wider circle of students and Leipzig inhabitants. The Consistory, which apparently consulted the Privy Council, responded rapidly: on 10 March, it sent an order to the city council, the University,

---

43 Drafts of rescripts to the University: 12 & 23 August, 16 & 30 September, 28 October & 25 November 1689; SHStADD, Loc. 2126, *Rescripte, Universität Leipzig*, 1682–1700, 183–183^{v}, 184^{v}, 186–186^{v}, 188, 189^{v}, 191^{v}–192. The rescripts' increasingly shrill demands for a report, which was finally sent on 21 October 1689, indicate that Rechenberg was dragging his feet.

44 Rescripts from Dresden to the University of 10, 12 & 19 June 1689, ibid., 175^{v}, 176–176^{v}, 177^{v}. See also Georg Witkowski, *Geschichte des literarischen Lebens in Leipzig* (Leipzig: Teubner, R [1994] Munich: Saur), 203 ff.

45 *Gerichtliches Leipziger Protocoll* (see above, note 5).

and the director of the Leipzig *Kreis* (a representative of the Elector) forbidding the conventicles immediately on pain of imprisonment.[46]

The different authorities, each with jurisdiction over different inhabitants, acted in concert during the investigation. On 18 March, *Kreis* Director Johann Joachim Rothe and senior representatives of the University and city council met, discussed how to implement the order, and planned to meet regularly to exchange information.[47] Rothe declared that 'it is common knowledge throughout the city ... what has been going on; it seems that bad things could follow.' The authorities agreed to post twelve copies of the Upper Consistory's order around Leipzig, six each in German (for the city council and *Kreis* jurisdictions) and in Latin (for the University). Anyone who heard of further meetings was to report them. Interrogations of 'individuals who are found to be involved' were to be conducted in concert; burghers were mostly interrogated by the city council, and students by the University.

Eleven students and nineteen town inhabitants who had participated in the collegia, six women and thirteen men, were interrogated in Fall 1689 and between March and August 1690. Four other women and two men were interrogated as witnesses or informants. The authorities' goal seems to have been to collect information on the leading figures and the extent of the gatherings, not to interrogate everyone involved. Pietists whose positions were sufficiently powerful were protected from the interrogation process. But most of the leading students and burghers were interrogated.[48]

The authorities based their subsequent reports on the interrogations. Following common practice, they initially questioned witnesses, who were sometimes hostile to individual participants, or figures marginal to the movement. They were then able to attack the central figures more effectively during their interrogations. Many of the allegations made against the Pietists came from students and burghers who shared rooming and boarding arrangements with them. Paul Christian Häscher and Gotthard Fonne, two of seven students interrogated under oath as witnesses in September 1689, made several incriminating statements against Francke. The other students did not, although they supplied some details.[49] In the *Apologia oder Defensions-Schrifft*, written to the Elector in November 1689, Francke accused these two of lying under oath and claimed that his 'enemies' in the ecclesiastical establishment had based their attack on the 'unfounded gossip of students (*Tisch-Pursche*) and other people.'[50] In his October 1689 *Legal Reflection* on the proceedings, Christian Thomasius claimed

---

46 The Upper Consistory order, *Acta ... 1690*, 7–7^{v}, 23^{v}–24.

47 The protocol of the meeting and a copy of the German-language printed bill: ibid., 8–9.

48 Ibid. and *Acta ... Schilling & Friedel ...* Interrogations were recorded by city council and University registrars in the form of third-person paraphrased narratives of the participants' statements. The registrars seemingly wrote during the interrogations and tried to stay close to the statements of those being interrogated: the handwriting of the protocols is unpolished, and there are frequent insertions and changes of word or phrase.

49 *Gerichtliches Leipziger Protocoll*, 12–27.

50 Dated 7 November 1689. Printed in ibid., 4, 22.

that these two witnesses 'clearly reveal themselves as spies (*Spionen*) on the so-called Pietists.'[51]

Several burghers also made statements incriminating Pietists, including the tailor Heinrich Schulze. Schulze rented a room to student Johann Andreas Schilling. Summoned in July 1690, Schulze claimed that Schilling and his friends polemicized against the Leipzig Ministry, that Schilling had held a sermon in his room, that he had turned his younger brother Hans Georg, a journeyman haberdasher, into an *Unmensch*, and that he had demanded that a woman called Lehmann go into a room with him alone to receive religious instruction.[52] A few days later, Schilling and two other students were confronted with this evidence. They denied it, claiming that the criticism of the ministry that Schulze had overheard was contained in a book, Elias Praetorius's *Misuses of Clerical Office Today*, which Schilling had been reading aloud to his friends.[53] Schulze had more ammunition: when he was summoned a second time, in early August, testifying under oath this time, he stated that he had been standing at a window on the day in question and had seen exactly what Schilling had read from the book and what the students had said themselves.[54]

Nothing if not thorough, the city council called in Regina Lehmann, the woman Schulze had referred to. Frau Lehmann stated that the woman in question was actually a barmaid (*Bierschenckin*) who lived in her house. Hans Georg Schilling was 'her brother's journeyman,' and Johann Andreas Schilling often came to visit him. Once he had tried to talk about religion with the wife of 'her barman,' but the woman had not been interested. When the barmaid, Dorothea Lange, was interrogated, she said Schilling was a pious young man but had never bothered her.[55] The city councilor who reported to the University on her interrogation interpreted her statement skeptically: 'She did not want to know anything.'[56]

Elisabeth Karig, who roomed with the Henrichs, initially complained to her father confessor, Immanuel Horn, after a Sunday service in early March that Henrich's daughter Dorothea Elisabeth, the student Gaulicke, and other Pietist students had 'made her feel small of spirit and doubt the state of her soul.'[57] When she was interrogated, she added that the two taunted her about her traditional religiosity and slandered the Leipzig clergy.[58] The questions posed to Karig, attached to the protocol, indicate that the interrogators manipulated witnesses. Karig was asked

---

51 Ibid, 56.

52 Interrogation of Schulze, 23 July 1690. *Acta ...Schilling & Friedel*, 1–2.

53 Interrogations of Schilling, Schulze's children's tutor Johann Nicolaus Stall, who also lived in the house, and Martin Ebert, 26 & 29 July 1690. *Acta ... Schilling & Friedel*, 3–6. Hans Georg Schilling was interrogated on 25 July 1690; *Acta ... 1690*, 291^{v}.

54 2 August 1690. *Acta ... 1690*, 116.

55 Lehmann: 25 July 1690; Lange: 2 August 1690 (she was traveling outside Leipzig in July). Ibid., 106^{v}, 116.

56 30 July & 10 August 1690. Ibid., 6, 10.

57 Upper Consistory report of 31 March 1690.

58 Interrogations of Elisabeth Karig, 27 & 29 March 1690, with list of questions attached to the interrogation protocol. *Acta ... 1690*, 16–18^{v}.

leading questions such as 'Did not [Gaulicke and Dorothea Elisabeth Henrich] say that an enlightened person can and must be completely without sin?' Those who participated in the collegia were sophisticated enough to turn such questions on the interrogators, but Karig may not have been (and she does not seem to have wanted to).

Using information gathered in interrogations, reports were sent from Leipzig to Dresden, and orders were sent down from the Privy Council. Throughout, the Leipzig and Upper Consistories were the primary channels of communication. Consistory assessors and city councilors produced detailed reports in order to persuade political figures at court of their viewpoints. The consistories themselves were divided, and Elector Johann George III repeatedly ordered additional reports. Thus, the Upper Consistory sent an initial report to Johann George on 31 March, drawing on a Leipzig Consistory report of mid-March which emphasized the dangers of the collegia.[59] In mid-April Johann George demanded more information from the Upper Consistory's clerical councilors, Samuel Benedict Carpzov and Spener.[60] Each sent in a separate lengthy report. Carpzov, a brother of Leipzig theology professor Johann Benedict Carpzov, drew a stark picture of the disruptive implications of students' and burghers' mingling on terms of equality; of students criticizing their professors and, by extension, the secular authorities; and of the personal qualities of the ringleaders, Francke and Thomasius. Carpzov criticized the Pietists' religiosity as 'fanatical' and anti-intellectual.[61] Implying that the collegia contradicted basic Lutheran tenets, Carpzov also attached extracts of Luther's letters on prowlers and back-street preachers.[62]

Not surprisingly, Spener's report was far more favorable.[63] He emphasized that although there were widespread rumors about Pietism as a new sect, nobody could define the substance of any purported 'innovation,' or deviation from Lutheran dogma or ecclesiastical law. As Spener read the interrogation protocols, the scope of the collegia was being greatly exaggerated. The accusations being hurled by people with 'hostile intentions' were baseless. Spener noted that he was personally acquainted with Francke and Schade and was convinced of their orthodoxy. They were perhaps too eager, but were responding to a real lack of exegetical collegia at the University. Spener allowed that there may have been 'excesses' in the collegia conducted by burghers, but supported them in principle. He referred to collegia that he and others had held in Frankfurt and other cities, and offered a lengthy historical and theological justification of their merits.

In late July 1690, still not satisfied with the information he had received, Johann George ordered another report from two legal assessors, Jacob Born of the Leipzig

---

59 31 March 1690. *Den so gen.* Pietismum *betr.*, 1–9.

60 18 April 1690. Ibid., 17–19.

61 Carpzov to Johann George III, 15 May 1690. Ibid., 21–32^{v}.

62 Ibid., 33–35.

63 14 June 1690. Ibid., 36–63^{v}. Later published in *Letzte Theologische Bedencken* (1711) (Halle: Waisenhaus, R [1987], Hildesheim: Olms).

Consistory and Johann Georg Börner of the Upper Consistory.[64] While Born and Börner shared Carpzov's alarmist emphasis, they called for additional exegetical collegia at the University, as Spener had, and recommended that the investigation be taken completely out of the hands of the University, since there were no neutral professors there. Like Thomasius, they criticized the conduct of the interrogations. Many people had not been interrogated under oath, and some had been interrogated inappropriately as witnesses rather than as subjects of investigation.

The outcome of the investigation was determined by Fall 1690. By and large, the suggestions of the Orthodox assessors were implemented. Undermining Spener's effectiveness was the fact that he had fallen out of favor with Elector Johann George. There were hints that the investigation would never have begun otherwise.[65] Spener's position in turn weakened powerful Pietists in Leipzig such as Adam Rechenberg and his colleague Johann Olearius. The collegia were further forbidden, and the leading student Pietists, deprived of their stipends and forbidden to teach in the city, left if they had not already. Francke, Thomasius, Schade, Anton and others eventually found employment as pastors and professors in Berlin, Halle, and other towns in Brandenburg-Prussia. In Leipzig, the Pietist movement went underground or behind the scenes.

Participants and the authorities

As they investigated the collegia, the authorities were especially concerned by several sets of issues: the Pietists' meeting in private homes, criticism of clerics, burghers' alleged preaching, and women's active roles. In their reports, officials emphasized the importance of the public worship service, and argued that the collegia represented an illicit retreat from it and the clergy. The text of the order issued in March forbidding the collegia read,

> questionable conventicles and private meetings are being held, not only by students, but also by burghers and even women, especially Sundays ... in which Scripture is interpreted by participants as they see fit, and all kinds of novel things are undertaken that until now have been unusual in the Orthodox Protestant church.[66]

Upper Consistory assessor Samuel Benedict Carpzov wrote that among the Pietists,

> the preacher's office is regarded with contempt, and people are given the impression that on account of the spiritual Priesthood (*geistliches Priesterthum*, a central Pietist concept)

---

64 The order: 25 July 1690. *Den so gen.* Pietismum *betr.*, 67. The report: 10 November 1690. Ibid., 68–104.

65 Upper Consistory to Johann George III, 13 November 1691; Dresden to Saxon-Coburg, 21 November 1691, *Den so gen.* Pietismum *betr.*, 124–126, 129–130; 127–128, concerning a 1691 tract by Caspar Sagittarius, a Pietist professor in Jena. An extract of the tract, ibid., 130–131^{v}.

66 The Upper Consistory order, *Acta ... 1690*, 7–7^{v}, 23^{v}–24.

> everyone is capable of explaining Scripture to others; even that the thoughts expressed in private conventicles have more power and relevance than the sermon preached in a public church gathering.[67]

Participants were often asked whether there had been preaching at collegia.[68] The grain registrar Samuel Voigt was accused of preaching during a gathering in his home; he was told to restrain himself from the 'teaching office' and pursue his own, properly ascribed occupation.[69] Voigt argued that his talk to the friends gathered in his home did not constitute a sermon. Participants also argued that their meetings did not compete with public services since they were held after those services on Sunday afternoons. Several even claimed that they had never, until then, listened to sermons with greater attention or appreciation.

The Pietists did not convince the authorities. As legal assessors Jacob Born and Johann Georg Börner wrote to Johann George in November 1690, '[the Pietists] say that the pastors do not teach correctly, that they give the people the shell instead of the kernel.'[70] The assessors had a point. Francke himself had written to the Elector in November 1689, 'I would have done my conscience an injury if I had spoken the inestimable word of God and given my listeners nothing of it but mere husks and shells ... without concentrating on its main purpose, namely to make wise unto salvation [through faith which is in Jesus Christ],' a phrase drawn from the second book of Timothy.[71]

The Orthodox establishment linked its claim that the Pietists were withdrawing from the official, public religious arena to a claim that they were attacking law and order in Saxony generally and, by extension, the Elector himself. In his report to Johann George, Carpzov emphasized the close ties between ecclesiastical and secular elites in Saxony. He contrasted the gratitude that every Saxon subject should properly express for the privilege of being able to worship publicly to the 'shameful ingratitude' of the Pietists, who preferred to 'learn more privately, from unordained teachers or tatting maids and lace washers, than from those whom God has properly called through the authorities and congregations.' Carpzov also emphasized the potential for disorder on a larger scale that arose when men and women from different occupational groups mingled in such an unregulated setting.[72]

The issue of gender was central to the collegia and to the investigation. Pietists clearly challenged mainstream gender relations. As Lyndal Roper has shown, these

---

67 Report of 6 May 1690, 21–32v in *Den so genannten* Pietismum *betr.*, 21v & 27–27v. The same complaints were made in other reports, for example in Upper Consistory to Johann George III, 31 March 1690, ibid., 1–9; Born and Börner to Johann George III, ibid., 68–104v, as well as in printed tracts.

68 *Acta ... 1690*, passim.

69 Interrogation of Voigt, 7 March 1690, *Acta... 1690*, 2v, 5–6.

70 *Den so gen.* Pietismum *betr.*, 68–104v, 86.

71 King James Version of the Bible. *Apologia oder Defensions-Schrifft ...*, published in *Gerichtliches Leipziger Protocoll*, 7–8.

72 Report of 6 May 1690, 21–32v. *Den so genannten* Pietismum *betr.*, 27–27v.

relations structured the social, political and economic order of Protestant towns: at home, 'house fathers' ruled; 'city fathers' governed the city; and in church, clerics who served as 'father confessors' preached.[73] Both interrogators and Pietists treated the mixing of sexes as a more serious infraction than the mixing of status groups. The question whether women were present and spoke at collegia was put to all those who were interrogated. Pietists deliberately played down the role of women for fear of more serious official retaliation. Male participants excused the presence of women at the burgher collegia on grounds of convenience. Thus Samuel Voigt wrote of a meeting at his home,

> Because we knew each other, and were good friends, and disregarded those who had come uninvited, I had no reason to ask my wife and children, including my daughter who is only four years old, to leave the warm room, especially since they came and went from it.[74]

Other participants claimed that they had told women who had come uninvited to leave. When possible, they denied the presence of women altogether. Wives of Pietist burghers like Dorothea Meinig and Rosina Hanisch denied attending the burgher collegia; Dorothea Meinig admitted only to attending one University collegium and one sermon by a Pietist student, Ziel, in the University Church.[75] Several Pietists insisted that women did not participate in the collegia held in burghers' homes, even if they were present. Referring to one meeting, though, Samuel Voigt was more ambiguous about whether women spoke.

While women's roles in most of the collegia remain unclear, there were definite examples of female leadership. Johanna Eleonora Petersen, a leading early Pietist and wife of then Lüneburg Superintendent Johann Wilhelm Petersen, made at least one visit to Leipzig alone and led prayer meetings.[76] A longer-lasting circle formed around lace washer Catharina Mey. Francke seems to have selected Mey for her role when he visited her husband.[77] At the suggestion of Francke and other students, young women from several occupational backgrounds came to Mey for religious guidance: daughters of a country preacher, of an organist, and of Leipzig burghers, including the wife of a Pietist shoemaker. The women met about once a week throughout the winter of 1689–1690. Often Schade or another student came for part of the time to explain Scriptural passages and the sermons held in church. On one or two occasions a few of the men who were active in the other collegia attended those at Mey's house.[78] The authorities seized on the involvement of Mey and the women

---

73 Roper (1989).

74 Memorial, 7 March 1690. *Den so genannten* Pietismum *betr.*, 5^{v}.

75 Interrogations of Dorothea Meinig and Rosina Hanisch, 7 & 11 April 1690. *Acta ... 1690*, 53 & 70^{v}.

76 Leube (1928), 'Pietistisch-separatistische Bestrebungen in und um Leipzig,' *BSK*, 37, 49–70 and (1921), 206 ff.

77 Interrogation of Mey, 1 March 1690. *Acta ... 1690*, 2–2^{v}.

78 Christian Henrich to the city council, 4 March 1690; interrogation of D.E. Henrich, 31 March 1690; interrogation of Mey, 1 March 1690. Ibid., 3–4, 38–39, 2–2^{v}.

who came to meetings at her house to illustrate the disruptive nature of the collegia generally. In their reports, the gatherings came up again and again. If one had only these reports to go on, one would conclude that the extent of the women's activity was much greater than it actually was.[79]

Gender played still another role in the conflict. Pietist students and clerics in Leipzig and elsewhere, during and after the collegia, were repeatedly accused of sexual relations with women. These accusations are of interest regardless of whether they were true: they were intended to demonstrate that sexual disorder accompanied social and religious disorder. The student Johann Andreas Schilling's landlord Schulze accused him of demanding that a woman go into a room with him alone to receive religious instruction, something that the woman in question denied. And Elisabeth Karig, who roomed with the family of the mortuary registrar Henrich, accused Christian Gaulicke of telling her in the company of Dorothea Elisabeth Henrich that 'if she wanted to be enlightened, she should undress as if she were going to bed, and tried to explain this to her from the Bible.'[80] Karig hinted that Gaulicke and Henrich engaged in sexual activities, which Henrich denied. The issue followed Pietists afterwards as well. For example, in the late 1690s Johann Caspar Schade, then a pastor in Berlin, was accused of improper behavior with two girls aged thirteen and fourteen.[81]

* * *

The legal context of the investigation structured both questions and answers. University and city council interrogators aimed to determine whether participants in the collegia had broken certain laws. Pietists defended themselves against charges of heterodoxy and illegal gathering. At the same time, though, they deliberately challenged normative status, corporate, and gender relations, and even the legitimacy of the authorities in pursuing the investigation.

How accurate were individuals' statements? Statements concerning the numbers of gatherings, and the identities of those present, were probably accurate since they were usually corroborated by several people. Pietists were more likely to give vague or false answers to questions about what was said during the meetings, especially whether clerics and secular officials had been criticized. Statements made under oath were probably truthful, since swearing a solemn oath was considered a very serious step, and could change vague or untrue answers to an incriminating truth.[82]

---

79 S.B. Carpzov to Johann George III, 6 May 1690. *Den so gen.* Pietismum *betr.*, 23, passim. Born & Börner to Johann George, 10 November 1690. Ibid., 69v, 74v–75, 78v, passim.

80 Interrogation of Karig, 27 March 1690. *Acta ... 1690*, 17–18v.

81 Helmut Obst (1972), *Der Berliner Beichtstuhlstreit. Die Kritik des Pietismus an der Beichtpraxis der lutherischen Orthodoxie* (Witten: Luther-Verlag), 47 ff.

82 For example, Thomas Fritsch's shift from March to June 1690 in responding to questioning whether he published the tract *Christ-Vernünfftiges Gespräch* ... In *Acta ... 1690*, 9v & passim to 115.

However, while they were usually asked to confirm that they would make the same statement under oath, most Pietists were not asked to swear on their statements.

Participants tried to minimize the broader status and gender implications of the collegia. Recognizing that their gatherings broke with established rules, they emphasized that they were already 'good friends' with their fellow participants before the collegia, and that the meetings were nothing out of the ordinary. Samuel Voigt said of the meetings at his house, 'we were several good friends who came together and discussed.'[83] Dorothea Elisabeth Henrich said that 'Frau Mey did not teach or explain anything in particular to them, except when they asked and instructed each other as good friends.'[84] By contrast, but also in their best interests, most of the students who had organized the collegia insisted that they did not know the burghers who came very well, and that the burghers came without being invited.

However, the Pietists were surprisingly assertive in other ways. The basis of this assertiveness was a distinct code, which emerged rapidly in the course of the collegia and called on a literal reading of the Epistles and other New Testament books. While these readings had long been a staple of Orthodox Lutheranism, Pietists appropriated them to emphasize their minority, oppressed status, which they likened to that of the early Christians. Some Pietists defended their meetings as a simple expression of 'Christian love and friendship,' a common Pietist phrase drawn from the language of the Epistles. Further, Pietists' responses demonstrated knowledge of their rights under ecclesiastical law and the ability to dodge leading questions. Pietists thus subverted the framework that their interrogators tried to establish: they acted as religious subjects even in an official setting, not merely as objects. The grain registrar Samuel Voigt concluded a memorial on the collegia which he voluntarily sent to the city council thus: 'I hope my sirs and patrons will soon see the true truth of this matter. When the truth comes to light, all useless rumors and false appearances will have to creep away.'[85] When the shopkeeper Augustin Frentzel was asked whether he believed in the 'perfection of the reborn,' which Pietists were rumored to claim, a question put to all those who were interrogated, he pulled a copy of the New Testament from a satchel. Saying that 'he wanted to explain himself,' Frenzel read from a piece of paper he drew from it:

> Although it is God's truth that it is impossible to fully obey the Law in this life, it is also God's truth that the reborn do not resist, because God's seed remains in them ... He does them the honor of ... forgiving their trespasses ... I am pious through Christ, and I know and confess that there is nothing good in me if that [faith] should leave me. I must acknowledge this, because otherwise my sins will not be forgiven me.[86]

---

83 Interrogation of Voigt, 7 March 1690. *Acta ... 1690*, 2^{v}. See also Mack Walker (1992), *The Salzburg Transaction: Expulsion and Redemption in Eighteenth-Century Germany* (Ithaca: Cornell University Press), esp. 39–40.

84 Interrogation of D.E. Henrich, 31 March 1690. *Acta ... 1690*, 38–39.

85 Voigt to the city council, 7 March 1690. Ibid., 5–6.

86 Interrogation of Frenzel and the copy of his note, 8 May 1690. Ibid., 81^{v}–83.

The interrogators copied the note.

Even decades later, some individials influenced by Pietism acted with unusual assertiveness toward the authorities. In 1724 Maria Glafey, who had been committed to the old-age portion of St. George's, wrote several letters to a city councilor demanding better treatment and requesting to be freed.[87] Glafey wrote that she had grown up in Leipzig, mostly in the house of Pietist city councilor Abraham Christoph Platz. Around eighteen at the time of the collegia, she had been 'instructed' by Francke himself, whom she called her *Infamader* (*Informator*, or tutor), and had heard Francke's sermons. She wrote that she had made the message of Francke's last sermon in Leipzig, 'God sees, God hears, God punishes' the 'firm foundation of my heart,' and she used this message to threaten the councilor if her condition was not improved.

The interrogations also reveal a larger number of people who had independent ideas on religion and were willing to express them. In a town like Leipzig, with its well-travelled inhabitants and access to a variety of ideas through visitors and print, it is likely that the interrogations found only the tip of an iceberg. For example, goldsmith Christian Kreugemann stated that he attended Schade's collegium at the University four or five times, but that it had been unpleasant to listen to the goings-on. Nevertheless, Kreugemann continued that in addition to regularly attending church, he 'reads a variety of books by Papists, Arianists, and other adversaries and edifies himself from them because he sees how they err.'[88] The more cautious roper's son Christian Eckard stayed away from the collegia after going to several, he claimed, because 'it was easy to see that a heresy could arise once common artisans began to come.' Nevertheless, Eckard thought that Francke was 'a person highly enlightened by God.'[89]

* * *

The collegia and their investigation go to the heart of the relationship of ordinary inhabitants to the secular and religious authorities, and to how authority was exercised in early modern Leipzig. The collegia demonstrate that urban Protestantism could generate a powerful challenge to status and gender norms after the early days of the Reformation. Generally, the political and clerical elites successfully harnessed Lutheran doctrine after the fervor of the 1510s and 1520s. But the relationship between religion and official power was complex. Religious language often supported official authority and social hierarchy; but it could also serve to articulate protest and to encourage more egalitarian relations. Pietists were able to call on writings by Luther and other important Lutheran theologians, on ecclesiastical law, and on Scriptural

---

87 See Tanya Kevorkian (2000), 'The Rise of the Poor, Weak, and Wicked: Poor Care, Punishment, Religion, and Patriarchy in Leipzig, 1700–1730,' *Journal of Social History*, 34, 163–181, esp. 172–177.

88 Interrogation of Kreugemann, 11 April 1690. *Acta ... 1690*, 74ᵛ–75.

89 Interrogation of Eckard, 9 April 1690. Ibid., 67ᵛ.

passages to support forms of social and religious association that challenged the norm.

For its part, the investigation into the collegia shows how effective the secular and clerical authorities could be in suppressing dissent. What seems by present-day standards a small-scale set of gatherings was enough to call forth a major investigation. Councilors and university professors obtained thorough and detailed accounts of the extent and nature of the collegia by interrogating participants. Pietists in Leipzig were forced to go underground soon after the beginning of the main investigation in March 1690. This was so even though the institutions were far from monolithic, and the investigation was not effortless. Interrogators in Leipzig were somewhat hampered by the reticence of participants. Conflict between Orthodox and Pietist professors and consistory assessors, the different approaches of jurist and theological assessors, and local foot-dragging by Rechenberg in 1689 all slowed the investigation.

The investigation shows again that 'church' and 'state' were so intertwined that to question one was to question both. Indeed, it is artificial to separate the two. As institutions, the consistories best illustrate how clerics and secular officials worked together. Orthodox theologians and jurists both successfully argued to the Elector that in challenging and withdrawing from the public worship service, Pietists were attacking the secular authorities and imperiling the social order. The Pietists themselves linked the religious and legal, with Francke and Thomasius working together in Leipzig and, soon afterward, in Halle.

Finally, what factors drew people to the collegia? As we will see in the next chapter, this is a question that can be answered only partially with the sources on the collegia. However, the interrogations do provide some insights. Participants revealed a curiosity about religion and a desire to be more active and engaged than regular worship services or family devotions allowed. Burghers and sub-burghers hosted, attended, and participated in the collegia, and articulately defended their activities under interrogation, revealing a striking commitment to building their own religious lives. Some were ill or had ailing relatives, and were seeking intensive spiritual support. The leadership and persuasiveness of the students in sermons and in personal conversation were also important. The students' position was ideally suited to their activities and goals. On their way to being ordained clerics, they had the authority to lead burghers. At the same time, they still lived close to and even depended on burghers for food, housing, and work. Not least, their intermediary status probably helped make them eager to challenge standard ways of doing things.

Chapter Seven

The Pietist shadow network

The collegia pietatis of 1689–1690 were only the beginning of Pietist activity in Leipzig. Dozens of Pietists continued to meet and maintain an informal but tightly-knit network through the 1730s. This chapter shows how men and women from all walks of life worked with Pietist leaders to build a vital network that provided both material and spiritual support for its members. We will also see that interactions with ordinary people were an important part of the basic ideals, daily work, and broader goals of figures such as Francke and Canstein, and of local leaders such as city councilor Johann Job.

There were important continuities between the collegia and the network. Some participants in the collegia remained active: the Meinigs, Catharina Mey, Heinrich Julius Elers, Samuel Knauer, Samuel Voigt, and others. Pietists continued to transcend status boundaries, and women played a relatively prominent role. Like the collegia, the network was an alternative form of association, and its most important organizational and spiritual model was the early Christian church. Not least, August Hermann Francke continued to lead the Leipzig Pietists. In early 1692 he settled in Halle, only about twenty miles from Leipzig but in the territory of Brandenburg-Prussia.[1] He was appointed pastor in the community of Glaucha and professor of Near Eastern languages at the newly-founded University of Halle. Francke also established a system of schools and charitable organizations, the Franckesche Stiftungen. He remained a charismatic leader until his death in 1727. Whereas Francke and his high-profile projects were supported and encouraged by the Brandenburg-Prussian government, though, Pietists in Leipzig kept a much lower profile.

The Leipzig Pietists were part of an international community whose members travelled, formed local groups, and communicated by letter. Men and women from around central, northern and eastern Europe, North America and elsewhere wrote tens of thousands of letters to Francke. Because of its early links to Francke and other prominent Pietists, and its proximity to Halle, the Leipzig community may have been among the largest and most durable. Networks formed in other large German trading centers, including Hamburg, Frankfurt, Dresden, and Breslau, and there were movements in other towns around Protestant Germany. The scope, duration, and involvement of lay people in these movements remain unclear. However, emerging research and references by the Leipzig Pietists indicate similarities to other towns'

1 See Martin Brecht (1993a), 'August Hermann Francke und der Hallische Pietismus,' in *GdP*, vol. I, 440–539.

networks in composition, activity, a conflict-ridden relationship to non-Pietist clerics and secular authorities, and support by some elites.[2]

The first part of this chapter discusses the Pietists' epistolary models: contemporary letter-writing conventions, and the Epistles of the New Testament. As Hartmut Lehmann has pointed out, the extensive correspondence that Francke (and ordinary Pietists) conducted, following Spener's example, was a distinctive form of association through which individuals transcended local religious life.[3] Even non-Pietist contemporaries noted the Pietists' letter-writing: Johann Benedict Carpzov, the probable author of the famous *Unfug*, or *Thorough Description of the Pietists' Misconduct*, wrote of 'the letters that one sends the other, which must then be communicated to a third, fourth, and fifth, so that they all have the same news of one another.'[4]

The second part of the chapter examines the workings of the Leipzig network. While traditional patron-client relations structured many interactions, and the material and spiritual were often fused in ways typical of the time, many emphases and practices were specifically Pietist. Third, the Pietists' relationship to the world around them, to Orthodox clerics, public religious life, and the expansion of luxury consumption and secular culture is explored. The rejection of secular culture and luxury consumption was a basic element of Pietist religiosity in Leipzig and elsewhere. It gave an important impetus to separate from non-Pietists, and was a prominent identifying feature for Pietists. At the same time, though, many individuals continued to participate actively in public religious life, holding pews and building *Capellen*.

The topic of the Pietists' relationship to 'the world' raises the question of where the Leipzig Pietists stood on the Pietist spectrum. Like their peers in other towns during the 'second wave' of Pietism,[5] they hosted visits by 'radicals' such as Johanna Eleonora and Johann Wilhelm Petersen and the 'ecstatic maids.' Some individuals

---

[2] See Friedhelm Ackva (1995), 'Der Pietismus in Hessen, in der Pfalz, im Elsass und in Baden,' in *GdP*, vol. II, 198–224, esp. 198 ff. and 214 ff.; Martin Brecht (1995), 'Der württembergische Pietismus,' in ibid., 225–295, esp. 230 ff. and 238 ff.; Manfred Jakubowski-Tiessen (1995), 'Der Pietismus in Niedersachsen,' in ibid., 428–445, esp. 431–434 and 439–442; Claus Petzoldt (1971), 'Konventikelwesen in Dresden zwischen 1690 und 1750,' in *Studien zu einer Biographie Valentin Ernst Löschers* (PhD thesis, University of Leipzig, ms.), 65–164. On Breslau, see Adam Bernd (1738), *Eigene Lebens-Beschreibung* (Leipzig: Heinsius, R [1973] Munich: Winkler), 210 ff., 230 ff., 245; Ryoko Mori (2004), *Begeisterung und Ernüchterung in christlicher Vollkommenheit. Pietistische Selbst- und Weltwahrnehmungen im ausgehenden 17. Jahrhundert* (Tübingen: Niemeyer), 38 ff.

[3] Lehmann (2001), 'Grenzüberschreitungen und Grenzziehungen im Pietismus,' *PuN*, 27, 7–18; 12.

[4] Carpzov (?) (1693) is generally taken to be the author, although the tract was published anonymously. *Ausführliche Beschreibung des Unfugs, Welchen die Pietisten ... gestifftet* ... (no place: no publisher/Leipzig: Lancke), 56. On the publication history of this tract, see Martin Gierl (1997) *Pietismus und Aufklärung: Theologische Polemik und die Kommunikationsreform der Wissenschaft am Ende des 17. Jahrhunderts* (Göttingen: Vandenhoeck & Ruprecht), 359 ff.

[5] Mori (2004), 25 ff.

held apocalyptic beliefs from the 1680s until well after 1700, showing that 'Halle' and 'radical' Pietism cannot be neatly separated. In particular, such traditional labels do not adequately describe ordinary Pietists. Ideas and practices were fluid, and they changed over time. The same people who hosted visits by the radical couple, and held apocalyptic views well after the collegia, also held church pews. Even leaders shifted. From late 1692, Spener began to distance himself from 'radicals' to whom he had once been close, including the Petersens.[6] Francke did so later, as he gained increasing (although still embattled) political and institutional power.[7] Finally, by the 1720s there was a greater diversity of religious opinion in Saxony and beyond than there had been in the 1680s.

The last part of this chapter shows how a network of dedicated Pietists helped drive the dramatic expansion of the German print trade. It extends the argument of Martin Gierl that the Pietist movement prefigured and structured important aspects of the Enlightenment. Gierl has shown that the Pietist-Orthodox debate established German-wide communication patterns that Enlighteners adopted.[8] Here, we see how Pietist publishers, authors, and others who helped make Leipzig the center of German Enlightenment publishing were also active in the illicit publishing of the Pietist-Orthodox debate.

Hans Leube surmised the existence of an ongoing network in Leipzig on the basis of scattered references, but he wrote that after Spring 1690 'the historian can no longer grasp it.'[9] In recent discussions, one historian holds that Spring 1690 marked 'essentially the end of the Pietist movement in Leipzig;' Mori traces some activity to 1692.[10] However, rich and previously unused sources allow for a reconstruction of this network. From the 1690s onward, over 100 men and women in Leipzig wrote to Francke, and their letters have been preserved in Halle.[11] Their testimony is more subtle, layered, and individual than official records. About a third of the letter-writers were active in the Leipzig Pietist network. Roughly a third of the letters were from visitors. Twelve of the writers were women, and the majority, just over ninety, were

---

6 Veronika Albrecht-Birkner (2000), 'Zur Rezeption Johann Arndts in Sachsen-Gotha (1641/42) und in den Auseinandersetzungen um den Pietismus der 1690er Jahre,' *PuN*, 26, 29–49.

7 Ulrike Witt (1996), *Bekehrung, Bildung und Biographie: Frauen im Umkreis des Halleschen Pietismus* (Tübingen: Niemeyer), 157–158.

8 Gierl (1997).

9 Leube (1928), 'Pietistisch-separatistische Bestrebungen in und um Leipzig,' *BSK*, 37, 49–70, and idem (1921), 'Die Geschichte der pietistischen Bewegung in Leipzig. Ein Beitrag zur Geschichte und Charakteristik des deutschen Pietismus,' PhD thesis, University of Leipzig; printed in idem (1975), *Orthodoxie und Pietismus. Gesammelte Studien*, D. Blaufuss, ed. (Bielefeld: Luther-Verlag), 153–257; 206 ff.; quote: Leube (1921), 212.

10 Brecht (1993a), 448; Mori (2004), 31–32.

11 They are in the Archiv der Franckeschen Stiftungen (AFS). Cataloguing during the East German era made it easier to find letters from specific people and places. A few were written as early as 1691; Francke must have carried them with him to Halle.

men. While around half of the men wrote only short notes, most of the women wrote long letters or wrote several times.

The letters written to Francke tell us most about individuals' relations with Francke, and less about other facets of the Leipzig Pietists' religious lives. Other sources, such as pew records and investigation files, provide insight into the Pietists' participation in public religious life, and into their interactions with Pietists other than Francke. The letters themselves also include many indications about how Pietists socialized in Leipzig. Greetings forwarded to Francke, reports of literature delivered, and updates on various people's lives show that the Pietists regularly visited with one another and circulated information about their fellows. Because of restrictions on conventicles, the Leipzig Pietists likely gathered in very small groups, with one or two individuals or a couple visiting another home.

Epistolary models

The Pietists wrote in the context of an 18th-century flourishing of letter writing. Mail delivery was quick; a letter from Leipzig to Halle typically arrived in one day. An article on the 'Letter' in Zedler's encyclopedia, published in Leipzig in 1733, emphasized the everyday nature of letter-writing.[12] Far-flung affiliates of international merchant houses; musicians, painters, and clerics; emigrants from Germany to Pennsylvania and families within Germany; and Enlighteners also cultivated correspondence networks. Along with the Halle Pietists, Moravians, Puritans and Quakers also built extensive communication networks, with centers in Herrnhut, Bethlehem, London and elsewhere storing, distributing, copying, and publishing letters, reports and other materials.[13]

The precondition of any letter-writing is literacy. The Leipzig Pietists' letters reflected the generally high rate of literacy in Leipzig and in Saxony.[14] In Leipzig, many burghers engaged tutors for their children and servants, often, as we have seen, in exchange for room and board. In addition to the Latin schools of St.

[12] Johann Heinrich Zedler (1733), *Grosses vollständiges Universal-Lexicon aller Wissenschafften und Künste* (Halle & Leipzig: Zedler, R [1961–1964] Graz: Akademische Druck- u. Verlagsanstalt), 'Brief,' vol. IV, 1359.

[13] See Aaron Fogleman (1996), *Hopeful Journeys: German Immigration, Settlement, and Political Culture in Colonial America, 1717–1775* (Philadelphia: University of Pennsylvania Press), Chapter Three; Dena Goodman (1994), *The Republic of Letters: A Cultural History of the French Enlightenment* (Ithaca: Cornell University Press), Chapter Four; Frederick Tolles (1960), *Quakers and the Atlantic Culture* (New York: Macmillan); Francis Bremer (1994), *Congregational Communion: Clerical Friendship in the Anglo-American Puritan Community, 1610–1692* (Boston: Northeastern University Press); Marianne Wokeck (1999), *Trade in Strangers: The Beginnings of Mass Migration to North America* (State College, PA: Penn State Press), Chapter Three; Theodor Geissendoerfer, ed. (1939), *Briefe an August Hermann Francke. Mit Einleitung und Erläuterungen* (Urbana: University of Illinois Press), 21–79.

[14] Johann Kaspar Riesbeck (1783), *Briefe eines reisenden Franzosen über Deutschland* (Zurich, R [1976] Berlin: Rütten & Loening), 305.

Thomas's and St. Nicholas's, a well-developed network of one-teacher schools extended throughout the city.[15] Both girls and boys learned to read and write in order to keep business records and to correspond with trade partners and relatives. The letters written by women and artisans to Francke reflect this practical function of writing: the handwriting was practiced, if not polished; the writers were familiar with conventions of address, title, and opening and closing. Spelling and punctuation were often markedly oral, and some writers reproduced the Leipzig accent that is still heard today, spelling *Professor* as *Brafesser*, or *bewogen* as *bewochen*. Students and graduates of the University had more polished handwriting and orthography, used more Latin and French phrases, and sometimes wrote entirely in Latin. However, all individuals commanded not only basic skills, but also a colorful sense of metaphor and turn of phrase, sometimes derived from Scripture, at other times from everyday experience.

The Pietists' letters, like the Pietist network generally, were shaped by two distinct epistolary traditions. One was the complex of contemporary conventions of letter-writing. Numerous epistolary manuals published around and after 1700 instructed people in how to write a letter and properly address its recipient. Articles on 'Letter' and 'Epistola' in Zedler's encyclopedia mentioned that manuals were 'available in excess.'[16] One of the best known, Talander's (August Bohse's) *Always Prepared Letter Composer, or Detailed Guide to Writing to Nobles, Cavaliers, Patrons, Good Friends, Merchants and also Women*, was first published in Frankfurt and Leipzig in 1692, and was used as late as the 1730s.[17] Talander, like other authors of epistolary manuals, informed his readers of the rules governing letters of invitation, thanks, offering of services, admonition or punishment, farewell, and so on. The manuals were widely read. Baron Canstein referred to one letter he had received as 'dictated to [the author] by someone whose style is like Talander's, or he must have read Talander himself.' The author of the article 'Epistola' criticized people who imitated the manuals too closely.[18] Individual Leipzig letter-writers may have used one or more manuals, or consulted people who were familiar with them. In any case, they followed the rules prescribed in manuals and often used standardized phrases. For example, in letters of supplication they first excused themselves for writing, then

---

15 Otto Kaemmel (1909), *Geschichte des Leipziger Schulwesens* (Leipzig: Teubner), 301 ff.; SAL, Stift.III.A.16., *Acta, Das Hospital St. Georgen und Das demselben incorporirte Zucht und Waysen Hauss alhier betr.*, vol. I, 1717, ff., report of 16 October 1741, 259–259ᵛ.

16 Zedler (1733 & 1734), articles 'Brief' and 'Epistola,' vol. IV, 1359 & vol. VIII, 1427–1430.

17 August Bohse [Talander] (1692), *Der allzeitfertige Brieffsteller, Oder Ausfürhliche Anleitung, wie so wohl an hohe Standes-Personen, als an Cavalliere, Patronen, gute Freunde, Kauffleute und auch an Frauenzimmer, ein geschickter Brieff zu machen und zu beantworten ...* (Frankfurt & Leipzig: Boetius).

18 Canstein to Francke, 15 January 1715. Peter Schicketanz, ed. (1972), *Der Briefwechsel Carl Hildebrand von Cansteins mit August Hermann Francke* (Berlin: de Gruyter) 684; Zedler (1734), 'Epistola,' 1427.

praised Francke, explained the reasons for writing to him, and finally promised their deep gratitude in advance.

The Leipzig Pietists' other epistolary model, the New Testament Epistles ('letters'), was far removed from early modern conventions. Two themes in particular were common to the Epistles and the Pietists' letters. First were requests to pray for another and the assurance that distant communities or individuals were in the writers' prayers. One Dorothea Elisabeth Frentzel closed a letter to Francke thus:

> May the Lord accompany him [Francke] on his journey with his holy angels and tie our hearts closely in love and unity of spirit, and grant the grace that we may fight for each other in spirit. I hope my dear Herr Professor will pray *hertzlich* for me. I will also not neglect to pray for him, and hope that God will hear our prayers.[19]

The writers also relayed greetings from fellow Pietists to Francke, and asked Francke to forward their greetings to friends in Halle and elsewhere.

Second, Leipzig Pietists, like the authors of the Epistles, referred to one another as 'brethren in Christ,' and opened and closed with other phrases used by the Apostles. This was true especially for the Pietists who had been active in the collegia, and for others who wrote during the 1690s. Book dealer Johann Heinich opened one letter written in 1691: '*Jesum Crucifixum!* In the same dear friend of my heart.'[20] Grain registrar Samuel Voigt addressed Francke as 'Beloved Brother.'[21] One Anna Becker opened her letter written in 1695, 'Jesus be with us, from the heart much beloved and very dear Friend.'[22] A Dr. Freystein wrote on one occasion, 'My most esteemed brother' and on another, 'The Lord be with you, My Brother.'[23] Around 1700, as the University of Halle and Francke's institutions became established, writers turned to more formal salutations that mentioned Francke's status. For example, Johann Job addressed his letters, 'Highly esteemed and highly respected Herr Professor.' Some, like Samuel Knauer, combined the two.[24]

Earlier Lutherans had also used apostolic salutations. Martin Luther himself, who understood his relation to the Catholic Church much as the Pietists did theirs to Orthodoxy, adopted apostolic greetings in his letters in the early 1520s.[25] Later Lutheran theologians, including the Pietists' Orthodox adversaries, used similar formulas in their voluminous correspondence.[26] However, Orthodox clerics

19 To Francke, 4 September 1698. AFS, C 784: 10.

20 To Francke, Mf 29, 1691. AFS, C 195: 1.

21 14 September 1696. AFS, C 820: 3.

22 12 April 1695. AFS, F 11: 465.

23 2 April 1694 & 15 May 1693. AFS, C 257: 4 & 2.

24 25 March 1708. AFS, C 794: 43.

25 Timothy Wengert (1994), 'Martin Luther's Movement toward an Apostolic Self-Awareness as Reflected in his Early Letters,' *Luther-Jahrbuch*, 61, 71–92; Helmar Junghans (1985), *Der junge Luther und die Humanisten* (Göttingen: Vandenhoeck & Ruprecht).

26 See copies of Johann Benedict Carpzov's letters to Gottlieb Spizel: AFS, K 44a: 128–236.

addressed only each other, not lay people, as 'brother in Christ,' and the Orthodox authorities considered the Pietist practice itself improper. One accusation made against Francke during his October 1689 interrogation, for example, was that he had addressed a linen weaver from a town near Leipzig as a 'brother in Christ.' Francke denied this, but claimed that it would not have been a sin if he had.[27] Further, the Pietists' salutations, like their reading of the New Testament generally, held a literal meaning that they did not have for Orthodox theologians: like the early Christians, the Pietists perceived themselves as a small, threatened minority.

The shadow network

People on every rung of the social ladder were active in the Leipzig network: ordinary burghers, members of intermediary-status occupations and the elites. Sub-burghers were also active, but their presence is difficult to assess because they wrote few letters. For example, several people mentioned the lace washer Catherina Mey, but she does not seem to have written any letters, possibly because she was illiterate. A minimum of about two dozen active people can be identified for any one time, but references in the letters and other documents show that the actual number of Pietists was higher. Further, numerous people at the fringes of the movement were sympathetic but not necessarily active. For example, Maria Glafey, who wrote in 1724 regarding the impact Francke's sermons of 1688–90 had had on her, does not seem to be mentioned in other sources.[28]

Individuals' roles in the network reflected their occupational status. Leaders were members of the elites such as Johann Job, who maintained close contact with Francke by frequently writing and visiting Halle. Another leader closely tied to Leipzig was Heinrich Julius Elers, the head of Francke's printing operations in Halle and formerly a student participant in the collegia. Elers attended almost all of the Leipzig fairs, serving as Francke's agent; he stayed in rented rooms that functioned as an open house or salon, and reported almost daily to Francke in minutely detailed letters. Job and Elers were two of several leaders who served as communication hubs and kept Francke abreast of developments around Germany. In Dresden, Baroness Henrietta Katharina von Gersdorff, the wife of the Saxon privy council director and grandmother of Count Zinzendorf, was a supportive presence and corresponded extensively with Francke.[29] From Berlin, Baron Carl Hildebrand von Canstein, a highly placed Brandenburg-Prussian official, wrote Francke around a thousand letters between 1697 and his death in 1719.[30] These figures knew each other and

---

27 Anon. (Francke & Thomasius) (1692), *Gerichtliches Leipziger Protocoll in Sachen die Pietisten betreffend* (no place: no publisher, R [1981] in Erhard Peschke, ed., *August Hermann Francke. Schriften und Predigten* (Berlin: de Gruyter), 25.

28 See Chapter Six, note 87.

29 Her correspondence to Francke: AFS, C 18: 1–191. See also Witt (1996), 151–165.

30 Schicketanz, ed. (1972).

stayed in contact.[31] Because they served as correspondents, many other Pietists did not need to write.

A subject of many of the leading figures' letters, and an important, often-repeated negotiation that bound the Pietist network together, was patronage. By and large, the ways in which patronage was requested and granted reflected contemporary practices. However, a tie of piety was added, with petitioners as well as employees seeking Pietists. Johann Job often connected employers and employees, sometimes as an intermediary and sometimes as a patron in his own right. For example, in response to a request by Canstein to find an administrator for his estate, Job interviewed a young man from near Leipzig whose father he knew. Job recommended the clean handwriting of the son, who had begun studies at the University but had had to stop because of a lack of money. Job also wrote that his impression of the young man was that he was loyal and discreet; and he mentioned his 'fine, Christian father and siblings.'[32] Canstein himself concerned himself with individuals' employment in surprising detail.[33]

Less prominent Pietists were also patrons, employing maids from the Halle orphanage and recent graduates of the University of Halle. In 1711 a Leipzig widow, M.C. Besser, asked Francke to send her an 'honest girl' from the orphanage, promising to take good care of her. Francke wrote back two days later promising to send an 'honest and healthy girl,' and did. Ten days later Besser had decided to send her back and ask for another girl, since the girl was not happy in Leipzig and 'forced service does no good.' The girl was also 'already consort[ing] with people who have not learned the Ninth and Tenth Commandments.'[34] Another Leipzig woman, Johanna Bauer, a dedicated Pietist who wrote to Francke from 1703 to 1720, employed two Halle graduates in succession as tutors. Bauer hired the second tutor, a Herr Palenius who 'teaches the children very faithfully,' over the initial objections of her husband.[35]

The ultimate patron of the Pietist network was Francke himself. People constantly wrote to Francke asking him to find positions for them or their children, usually as academics or as servants for pious employers. Others wrote on behalf of friends, or wrote letters of introduction for friends or acquaintances to carry to Francke. Some had fallen upon hard times. Johann Mülmann, who signed himself as *trans. ling. Ital.*, wrote in 1702 and 1710 as a friendly correspondent. A few years later Mülmann, whose handwriting had deteriorated, wrote that at age seventy-two he was responsible for his ten-year-old grandson but could not earn much any more; he asked Francke to 'help the boy to his fortune.'[36] Another man asked Francke to find a

---

31 Job corresponded with Elers and saw him regularly at fair time, Job and Canstein met in 1703 and corresponded afterward, and von Gersdorff was in touch with Canstein and Elers.

32 Job to Canstein, 6 November 1703. AFS, C 232: 83.

33 See Canstein to Francke, 7 March 1702. Schicketanz, ed. (1972), 158–159.

34 To Francke, 3, 6, & 16 December, 1711. AFS, F 11: 335–345.

35 28 March 1703. AFS, F 14: 62–63.

36 To Francke, 22 July 1702, 14 March 1710, and n.d. AFS, C 799: a–c.

position for his sixteen-year-old daughter.[37] Recent university graduates from around Germany also wrote regularly, requesting either 'patronage' in general terms or more specific assistance. One was Dr. Johann Christoph Meinig, son of the baker Martin Meinig, who appealed to Francke as 'an always benevolent patron of our humble house, who honored my deceased father with constant love and friendship.'[38]

Both Pietists and non-Pietists made requests of various other types as well. Many appealed to Francke as a protector of the poor and weak. Joachim David Apell, a merchant who had been left by the death of his wife to care for two small children, requested a loan of 100 thaler. He wrote that 'it is unheard of that anyone who has needed comfort and help has left your most worthy orphanage without it.'[39] The goldsmith Hans Hansen from Hamburg, who was lodging in Leipzig with Pietist acquaintances, wrote in 1698 requesting that Francke help him study theology. He had long heard a call, but his parents had not had the money to let him study. The call had become so intense that 'my heart wants to break when I think that I will not become one who reveals God's will and makes souls blissful.' Hansen explained that he was writing 'because I have often heard of you as one who takes mercy on the poor and suffering.'[40] In 1716 a tailor who did not seem to be a Pietist requested Francke's help in collecting a loan of eight thaler, of which he had 'not yet seen a bat (*Flädermaus*) again.'[41]

The majority of letters concerning charity that reached Francke were requests for help; but many people also contributed money to Francke's projects. The 'good deed' of giving money to charitable causes was deeply imbued with spiritual meaning among Pietists, and was another link in the network. Francke's projects in Halle, especially the orphanage, were the most popular object of donations. Andreas Jäcklé, a graduate who had arrived in Leipzig unemployed, sent a ducat soon after he found a job.[42] In 1704 the widow of Leipzig professor Jacob Thomasius, and mother of Christian Thomasius, lent 300 thaler, with the interest to be used for the orphanage.'[43] The missionary activities of Halle theologians in India were another popular cause. Johanna Bauer sent four thaler which she had won in the Leipzig 'poor lottery' for this cause, writing that she hoped 'the Lord who fed 5000 men with five loaves of bread may direct His blessed power there [to India], that many thousands

37 To Francke, 12 May 1698. AFS, C 780: 3.

38 To Francke, 13 March 1726. AFS, C 799: 127.

39 To Francke, 30 January 1720. AFS, F 10: 247–249^{v}.

40 To Francke, n.d. (Spring 1698). AFS, C 77: 1. On 28 May 1698 Hansen wrote again, responding to a letter from Francke asking him to stay in Leipzig while he arranged something (C 77: 2).

41 Johann Georg Bilhardt to Francke, 4 August 1716. AFS, F 11: 151–154.

42 11 October 1708. AFS, C 66: 2.

43 Job to Elers, 14 June 1704. AFS, C 828: 65.

may eat and yet food be left over.'[44] Pietists from around Germany sent money to business or personal acquaintances in Leipzig for forwarding to Francke.[45]

Another practice linking Pietists was the occasional visit with Francke, to which people looked forward and then cherished as a memory. In 1698 Dorothea Elisabeth Frentzel expressed her desire to meet with Francke, writing, 'should it be God's will that I see and speak with you again and enjoy your admonition, this would be a heart-felt joy to me ... but should it not be His will, then may the Lord preserve us.'[46] Sigmund Abraham Wagner, a student in Leipzig, wrote in 1692,

> I do not know if you remember that we talked [last spring] in Erfurt ... but I remember well that you wished me the support of the Holy Spirit in my studies when I departed from the hall. If God wishes that I speak again soon with my dear Herr *Magister* to strengthen me in my weakness, I would be thankful to him.[47]

And Johann Job wrote in 1717, 'I hope it is God's will to give me the pleasure of seeing you once again in Halle and to enjoy a short edifying hour with you.'[48]

Francke strengthened his followers from a distance as well. For example, he sent glasses of *essentia dulci*, a medicine manufactured in Halle which was a major source of revenue for his enterprises, to people on request, usually for payment.[49] Johann Job requested it several times, and praised its 'good effect, through divine grace, on myself and my family.'[50] Francke also sent books, including printed versions of his sermons and reports of Halle missionaries in India. These were received eagerly. In 1724 a man named Johann Martin Bandau thanked Francke for a letter and the gift of a book of devotional prose, 'which is more precious to me than a box covered and filled with jewels.'[51] Francke sometimes sent one person material to pass on to friends. Heinrich Julius Elers also distributed literature when he was in Leipzig; he reported in 1721 that Johann Job had 'received several cleanly bound sermons on grace for himself, his wife, Mayor [Abraham Christoph] Platz, and other friends.'[52]

---

44 To Francke, 14 May 1708. AFS, C 827: 19.

45 Herr Riese to Francke, 2 September 1709. AFS, C 829: 22; Maria Elisabeth Crummer to Francke, 17 & 31 January, 1710. C 830: 5, 13.

46 To Francke, 4 September 1698. AFS, C 784: 10.

47 To Francke, 17 January 1692. AFS, C 821: 6.

48 To Francke, 3 July 1717. AFS, C 232: 49.

49 Renate Wilson (2000), *Pious Traders in Medicine. A German Pharmaceutical Network in 18th-Century North America* (University Park, PA: Pennsylvania State University Press), 72 and passim.

50 Job to Francke, 8 August 1702. AFS, C 232: 14.

51 19 February 1724. AFS, A 116: 345–347.

52 15 October 1721. AFS, A 175: 166.

Pietists and 'the world'

How did Pietists relate to the society around them and to public religious life? Their sociability in the early 1690s was particularly intense, and their relations to the surrounding world correspondingly hostile. Over time, hostilities abated somewhat, but continued into the 1740s. One constant from the time of the collegia onward was the Pietists' rejection of secular culture and luxury consumption. The Pietists had much to rail against in Leipzig, a city which in many ways embodied 'the world' that they wanted to flee. Despite all of this, though, they engaged actively in local religious life.

In the 1690s the Leipzig Pietists gathered with visitors and people living near Leipzig. The visitors would have shared details of meetings in other towns, helping to build a regional Pietist identity. They deliberately mingled with people from diverse social groups. Johanna Eleonora Petersen, born a noblewoman, and her husband Johann Wilhelm, who was later to be dismissed as Lüneburg Superintendent for his chiliastic views, visited Leipzig in May 1690, during the investigation into the collegia. Samuel Knauer put them up, and Knauer's fellow shopkeeper Augustin Frentzel invited them to dinner one evening. Johann Wilhelm held a sermon at Knauer's house and a *discurs* at Frentzel's; Johanna Eleonora visited Catharina Mey. During his interrogation, Frentzel stated that he had been exchanging letters with Frau Petersen during the previous six months.[53] Johanna Eleonora Petersen visited again in Summer 1691, holding a sermon at the house of a burgher.[54] Spener himself apparently set the tone for these interactions. According to the author of the *Thorough Description of the Pietists' Misconduct*, on a visit to Leipzig in 1687 during the Easter fair, Spener had stood in a balcony in St. Thomas's 'where honorable people but not such of his estate tended to stand at that time.' At a service in 1690 Johann Wilhelm Petersen stood 'in exactly the same place.' Furthermore, the author of the tract claimed that he and a student had seen Spener, dressed like a 'ruined shoemaker,' emerge from Shoemaker Street (*Schuster-Gässlein*) during his 1687 visit.[55]

Like other central German townspeople, Leipzig Pietists also supported the apocalyptic prophesying of charismatic lay Pietists in the early 1690s. In July 1691 several young women known as 'enchanted maids' from the towns of Halberstadt, Erfurt and Quedlinburg visited Leipzig and stayed with Martin and Dorothea Meinig.[56] The Meinigs hosted a prayer hour during which the 'maid' from Erfurt spoke in tongues. The visit drew crowds of over a hundred, and attracted the attention of the authorities.[57]

---

53 Interrogation of Frentzel, 8 May 1690, *Acta ... 1690*, 81^{v}–82^{v}.

54 Leube (1928); Leube (1921), 206 ff.

55 Carpzov (?) (1693), 14–15.

56 Leube (1928); Leube (1921), 206 ff.

57 Ibid.; Judd Stitziel (1995), 'God, the Devil, Medicine, and the Word: A Controversy over Ecstatic Women in Protestant Middle Germany 1691–1693,' *Central European History*, 29, 309–338.

Student and burgher Pietists also travelled to Böhlitz and Panitzsch, villages near Leipzig. Christian Töstlowe, a smith in Böhlitz who attended the Leipzig collegia, hosted at least one meeting in his home in 1691.[58] Justinus Töllner, pastor there, hosted a meeting during the collegia.[59] After the suppression of the collegia, the Leipzig Pietists visited him to attend services, meeting with him beforehand to sing hymns.[60] This would have helped them avoid charges of meeting as a conventicle. Töllner was the Leipzig Pietists' informal spiritual leader until 1697, when he was dismissed from his position (his peasant parishioners had complained of his harshness, and he had had several rounds of conflict with the consistories).[61] In their letters, several Leipzig Pietists referred to Töllner as 'the faithful shepherd of our souls.'[62] Book dealer Johann Heinich wrote to Francke in 1693: 'P.S. All dear friends send their heartfelt regards to [you], especially Herr Töllner of Panisch [*sic*] ...'[63] The Leipzig circle missed Töllner after his departure. Dorothea Elisabeth Frentzel wrote in 1698, 'God has created a gap among us and taken our faithful teacher and father of our souls, from whom we enjoyed many good things.'[64] Book dealer Johann Ludwig Gleditsch wrote around 1699, 'P.S. Please send my regards to H. Töllner, who was my very good friend while he was here.'[65]

Association with their fellows was accompanied by disdain for non-Pietists. One Dr. Freystein wrote in 1693, 'Many think they have left Babel and immediately attained the freedom to criticize and reject everything, but they still remain in their prideful Babel, and are less worthy and pious than those whom they regard in contempt as Godless children of the world.'[66] Mutual hostility continued after 1700. By around 1720 it was lessening. In 1719, leading Pietist and Orthodox theologians met and decided that Enlightenment skeptics and others posed a greater threat than did their old debate adversaries.[67] Some clerics overcame party affiliation. Leipzig Superintendent Salomon Deyling, for example, pleased Pietists after his arrival in 1720, although councilor Johann Job had unsuccessfully backed another candidate.[68] Heinrich Julius Elers declared one of Deyling's sermons 'very edifying and powerful

---

58 Mori (2004), 96–101.

59 Mori (2004), 60 ff.

60 Jens Bulisch (1997/1998), 'Justinus Töllners Weggang aus Panitzsch. Ein Beitrag zur Frühgeschichte des Pietismus in Sachsen,' *Herbergen der Christenheit*, 21/22, 69–86; 75.

61 Bulisch (1997–1998); Tanya Kevorkian (1997), 'The Material of Faith: Religion and Society in Leipzig, 1685–1725' (PhD thesis, Johns Hopkins University), 311 ff.; Mori (2004), 60 ff.

62 Knauer to Francke, 23 May 1708. AFS, C 794: 43.

63 10 March 1693. AFS, C 195: 6.

64 She does not refer to Töllner by name, but her description fits in with others' of him. 4 September 1698. AFS, C 784: 10.

65 Undated; written not long after a letter dated 16 February 1699. AFS, C 789: 8 & 9.

66 To Francke, 15 May 1693. AFS, C 257: 2.

67 Eduard Winter (1966), *Frühaufklärung. Der Kampf gegen den Konfessionalismus in Mittel- und Osteuropa und die deutsch-slawische Begegnung* (Berlin: Akademie), 82–86.

68 See Chapter Three, note 107.

... I and many others were much strengthened by it.'[69] And Job told Elers that Deyling 'is neutral, and doesn't want to spoil his relations with anyone.'[70]

Adam Bernd also did not belong to any one group. He resembled Pietists in his intensity and emphasis on accessible preaching. It was Pietist councilors such as Johann Job, Abraham Christoph Platz, and Adrian Steger (likely a Pietist), along with publisher Thomas Fritsch and professor Adam Rechenberg, whom Bernd most often described as giving him gifts, recommending him for clerical positions, and otherwise supporting him. However, noting with concern that some Orthodox figures considered him a Pietist, Bernd took pains to say that he was not one. Further, although Bernd visited Halle at least twice, he wrote of Justinus Töllner, whom he met there, 'I never met an odder man.' Töllner was irritated by Bernd's wig and his too-cheerful demeanor, and Bernd feared that Töllner would engage him in a dispute on the adiaphora.[71]

However, many intellectuals, and possibly non-intellectuals, remained hostile toward Pietists. Jurist Johann Bernhard von Rohr characterized them as potentially harmful 'sectarians' in 1723.[72] And Luise Adelgunde Gottsched was the author of *Pietists in Petticoats* of 1736, which lampooned the Pietists as gullible, greedy, and hypocritical.[73] For their part, Pietists in Leipzig and beyond retained a clear identity and cultivated an active network into the 1740s. In 1741, for example, Countess Christiane Charlotte Friederike zu Castell-Remlingen in southwest Germany, then aged nineteen, visited Leipzig for several months. She secretly wrote letters to her Moravian uncle, Count Ludwig Friedrich zu Castell-Rehweiler, asking him to address his letters 'to *Monsieur* Rehkopff, a well known master tailor of Leipzig ... a very Christian man ... who was greatly influenced by Francke's writings.'[74] Back in Rehweiler the Countess wrote, still secretly, that she had 'a true brotherly [*sic*] love toward all in whom I see something upright, and make no distinction among them ... my greatest *chagrin* is ... that I must still spend time with many people who love only the world.'[75] The Countess retained her Pietist sympathies later in life. Two of her sons, the Stolberg brothers, later became well-known *Sturm und Drang* poets.

---

69 Letter to Francke, 19 October 1721. AFS, A 175: 170.

70 Elers to Francke, 15 October 1721. AFS, A 175: 166.

71 Bernd (1738), 147, 207, 242–5, 287, 332.

72 Rohr, *Vollständiges Ober-Sächsisches Kirchen-Recht* ... (Frankfurt & Leipzig: Martini), 132.

73 *Die Pietisterey im Fischbeinrocke* (1736), (R [1993] in *Pietism in Petticoats and Other Comedies* [Columbia, SC: Camden House], trans. Thomas Keith and John Russell).

74 Fragment, 1741. Fürstlich Castell'sches Hausarchiv Ic5, 34. Thanks to Jesko Graf zu Dohna for telling me about these letters and for sharing his typewritten transcriptions of them. See August Sperl (1908), *Castell. Bilder aus der Vergangenheit eines deutschen Dynastengeschlechtes* (R [1993] Neustadt a.d. Aisch: Verlag für Kunstreproduktionen), 518–530; Horst Weigelt (1984), *Die Beziehungen zwischen Ludwig Friedrich zu Castell-Remlingen und Zinzendorf sowie ihr Briefwechsel. Ein Beitrag zur Geschichte des Herrnhuter Pietismus in Franken* (Neustadt a.d. Aisch: Degener) and Hans Walther Erbe (1928), *Zinzendorf und der fromme hohe Adel seiner Zeit* (Leipzig, R [1975] Hildesheim: Olms).

75 Ibid., 318; late 1741.

Perhaps surprisingly, many Pietists, including those who hosted the Petersens, remained engaged in Leipzig's changing religious life. Mayor Abraham Christoph Platz had *Capellen* built for himself and his family in the New Church, St. Nicholas's, and St. Thomas's. Platz's first and second wives and two of his daughters held pews as well. Johann Friedrich Gleditsch built a *Capelle* for his family in the New Church. In 1698, at the beginning of the drive to renovate the New Church, Samuel Knauer was among 102 Leipzigers who pledged money (sixty thaler) toward construction costs. In return, like many other donors, Knauer requested 'a comfortable man's and a woman's pew.'[76] His second wife Anna Martha and a son and daughter held additional pews there. Knauer, his first wife, and four other children also held pews in St. Nicholas's. Other Pietist families who held pews in St. Nicholas's and the New Church included the book dealers Fritsch, Gleditsch, and Weidmann; the shopkeeper Frentzel; the bakers Meinig and Wendel; town employees Voigt and Henrich; professors Rechenberg, Feller, and Kirch; and city councilors Job and Götze.[77] Perhaps they read in their hymnals or Bibles during the performance of organ music and the cantata, or timed their arrival and departure to avoid this music.

* * *

Their rejection of 'the world' around them helped drive the Pietists to seek each other out. Ordinary Pietists shared the sentiments of Pietist participants in the adiaphora debate. During the investigation into the collegia pietatis, for example, town employee Christian Henrich defended his daughter's activities by claiming that she and the other young women in Mey's circle 'have been much happier and had a calmer conscience than before, when they sought their pleasure in all kinds of worldly games and otherwise allowable distractions.'[78] Beginning with the collegia, an important part of the Pietists' stance was the citation of Scriptural passages condemning worldly living. Chapter Four of the First Epistle of Peter, for example, was the basis of one session of Johann Caspar Schade's 1690 University collegium.[79] The reading includes Peter's admonition that a Christian

> no longer should live the rest of his time in the flesh ... For the time past of our life may suffice us to have wrought the will of the Gentiles, when we walked in lasciviousness, lusts, excess of wine, revellings, banquetings, and abominable idolatries: Wherein they think it strange that ye run not with them to the same excess of riot, speaking evil of you ...

Note the passage's emphasis on tension with non-Christians.

---

[76] SAL, Stift. IX.C.15. *Original der Subscriptionsliste zur Renovation der Neukirche,* 1698.

[77] For specific pews and dates, see Kevorkian (1997), 307–311.

[78] Henrich to the city council, 4 March 1690. *Acta ... 1690*, 3–4.

[79] Interrogation of book dealer Johann Heinich. Cited here: 1 Peter 4:2–4. Bible, King James Version.

Sources on Samuel Knauer offer a rare opportunity to trace one lay person's thought over a period of almost thirty years. Knauer was head of the Leipzig shopkeepers' guild (*Kramerinnung*) and Francke's occasional dinner host in 1689; Francke referred to him as a 'Christian merchant.'[80] We saw in the previous chapter that Knauer had sought Spener's advice as early as 1680. His correspondence with Spener attests to the formative influence of 17th-century crises on Pietists. Knauer requested Spener's spiritual advice during the 1680 plague epidemic. He had shared Spener's response, a thoughtful if grim reflection on the plague as both vengeance and gift, with friends, and had it published.[81] Spener probably put Francke and Knauer in touch. Showing how Pietist networks could extend to intermarriage, one of Knauer's daughters married Paul Anton; another of Knauer's sons-in-law, a town leader (*Amtmann*) in Rochlitz, a small town near Leipzig, was also a Pietist. Knauer's second wife was raised in the house of Pietist-sympathizing cleric Johann Günther.[82]

Even in the prosperous times well after the plague, Knauer retained the apocalyptic mind-set of the early years of the Pietist movement, connecting luxury consumption with divine vengeance. He wrote in 1708, 'I have been in this city for 53 years, but the pride and arrogance of most souls and the excess in dress have never climbed as high as at present, so that I fear that God's vengeful punishment (*die Göttlichen Zorn Gerichte*) will break in heavily.' Knauer was thankful that his second wife was 'not given to the worldly vanities of this town' and he 'could not thank God enough for her.' Ever cautious, though, Knauer added that 'one has to be very careful to hold to the anchor of God's Word, so that one is not torn away by worldly currents.'[83]

Other Pietists in and around Leipzig resembled Knauer. Ryoko Mori has shown that Böhlitz smith Christian Töstlowe considered the plague epidemic a formative spiritual experience.[84] Jens Bulisch has shown that Töllner developed pronounced apocalyptic thought from the mid-1690s and retained it to at least 1708.[85] The large crowd that gathered to hear wandering separatist preacher Ernst Christoph Hochmann von Hochenau when he visited Leipzig in 1711 also attests to ongoing interest in apocalyptic Pietism. Hochenau preached the Wednesday after Easter on Luke 21:34 ff.: 'and take heed to yourselves, lest at any time your hearts be overcharged with surfeiting, and drunkenness, and cares of this life, and so that day come upon you unawares.' He was arrested by the authorities, as he was repeatedly around Germany between about 1700 and 1720.[86]

---

80 Interrogation of 10 October 1689. Anon. (1692), *Gerichtliches Leipziger Protocoll*, 38.

81 Johannes Wallmann, ed. (2005), *Philipp Jakob Spener. Briefe aus der Frankfurter Zeit 1666–1686*, vol. IV, 1679–1680 (Tübingen: Mohr), 632–636 and 687–693.

82 To Francke, 20 June 1694. AFS, C 794: 5.

83 To Francke, 23 May 1708. AFS, C 794: 43.

84 Mori (2004), 96–101.

85 Bulisch (1997/1998), 78.

86 Leube (1928); Leube (1921), 206 ff; Hans Schneider (1995), 'Der radikale Pietismus im 18. Jahrhundert,' in *GdP*, vol. II, 107–197; 124–128.

Some individuals added anti-clericalism to the mix. Christoph Mathäus Seidel, pastor in a village in the Leipzig Diocese, offered a stinging criticism of the 'luxury and waste' at the investiture dinner of Superintendent Thomas Ittig in 1699.[87] In 1695 *Magister* Johann Christian Lange wrote that he preferred the private worship he held in his room to the 'wrongheaded entity' and 'dishonoring of God's holy name' of public worship life in Leipzig. Lange was a Leipzig native who had studied in Leipzig, participated in the collegia, and then worked as a tutor for the Petersens' children in Lüneburg, returning in 1694.[88] And in 1708, Andreas Jäcklé, a recent university graduate who was looking for a job in Leipzig, wrote to Francke:

> I do not think that there is a preacher to be found here who is spiritually-minded and reborn in God, because they preach the opposite, and direct the poor people more toward Hell than toward Heaven in their sermons; they are all still unconverted heathens, dumb dogs (as the Prophet Isaiah says), who cannot punish.[89]

The reference to Isaiah is significant. The passage that Jäcklé cited continues, 'Yea, they are greedy dogs ... come ye, they say ... we will fill ourselves with strong drink; and to morrow shall be as this day, and much more abundant.' The book of Isaiah is in part a prophecy that God will lay waste to Jerusalem (which early modern Leipzigers often used as an Old Testament model for their city) should its inhabitants not turn away from their luxurious, wanton living and disregard for divine commandments. The book includes numerous references to material wealth and leisure pastimes: 'Their land also is full of silver and gold, neither is there any end of their treasures ... the harp, and the viol, the tabret, and pipe, and wine, are in their feasts: but they regard not the work of the LORD.'[90]

Along with the backgrounds of crisis, recent prosperity, and a literal reading of Scripture, other factors also help to explain the Pietists' attitude. Some articulated a broader sense of alienation from and dissatisfaction with mainstream society. This was especially true for the recent graduates, whose transitional social position was made more precarious by their Pietism. Andreas Jäcklé described his situation in Leipzig in Old Testament terms as that of an exile in Egypt, wandering in the desert, and crossing the Red Sea of troubles.[91] Lange portrayed his isolation from Orthodox religious culture as inseparable from isolation from the society as a whole. He called himself a 'stranger in the middle of [my] native city.' He agreed to his parents' request that he 'comport himself quietly and incognito' because of suspicions that still rested on him, did not visit his former acquaintances and 'patrons,' and even

---

87 Letter of 5 January 1700. AFS, D 83: 125–130; 129. Thanks to Terence McIntosh for this reference.

88 Lange was interrogated in October, 1689 and March, 1690. Anon. (1692),*Gerichtliches Leipziger Protocoll*, 30–31; *Acta ... 1690*, 28ᵛ. A long open letter 'to his father confessor,' 1 December 1695. AFS, D 57: 42–77; 55–56.

89 Letter of 11 October 170. AFS, C 266: 2.

90 Isaiah 56:11–12, 2:7, 5:12. Bible, King James Version.

91 To Francke. AFS, C 266: 1, 2.

'chose clothing in which I would not be too recognizable.'[92] In contrast, as head of the shopkeepers' guild Samuel Knauer was a respected burgher. Ironically, his profession was distributing new consumer goods to Leipzig's inhabitants. Still, Knauer felt insecure even about his own family, having 'many crosses to bear,' and he did not get along with several of his sons-in-law. City councilors Johann Job and Abraham Christoph Platz were even more prominent; but Job wrote frequently of his desire to move from Leipzig.

Printing and Pietism

One area of cultural innovation that Pietists embraced was the world of print. The Pietist-Orthodox debate, in the course of which at least 2000 tracts were published,[93] was part of the general expansion of the print trade at this time. Martin Gierl has delineated the learned background of the debate, authors' and publishers' strategies, and the publication history of a major Orthodox tract. He argues persuasively that authors on both sides of the debate helped pave the way for Enlightenment publishing by appealing to a broad public in German, among other strategies.[94] This study adds an important dimension to that picture. Leipzig Pietists who became central to Enlightenment publishing, including the Gleditsch brothers and Thomas Fritsch, formed a close-knit network with Elers, Francke, Leipzig councilors, and others. Their eagerness to engage in the debate reveals an intense religious commitment to their trade. The fact that such prominent figures often did so clandestinely also revises our understanding of publishing and distribution generally.[95]

Through their reception and distribution of this literature, ordinary Pietists were involved in the debate as well. There was a substantial audience for religious works in general, and Pietist-Orthodox debate tracts were devoured with particular eagerness. Three thousand copies of at least one Spener tract were printed,[96] and runs of 1500 to 3000 were common for other popular tracts.[97] Some saw a second edition, and especially in the 1690s tracts were a profitable genre.[98] Copies were generally distributed in at least two or three cities, so that the number of copies in Leipzig was fewer than the print run; but individual copies were often read by several people,

92 Lange, 1 December 1695, 42 ff.

93 Gierl (1997), 13.

94 Ibid., passim.

95 For more detail, see Kevorkian (1997), Chapter Six.

96 Spener's 1695 *Aufrichtige Übereinstimmung mit der Augspurgischen Confession*; Wittenberg theological faculty to August, 31 October 1695. SHStADD, Loc. 10330, *Den so gen.* Pietismum *betr. 1690 sqq.* (hereafter: *Den so genannten* Pietismum *betr*)., 288–290^{v}; 290^{v}.

97 August to Upper Consistory, 14 March 1711. SHStADD, Loc. 4600, *Die Confiscirung einiger Schrifften, Censur der Bücher und Vereydung der Buchdrücker betr.*, 1702–1714, 292–292^{v} (hereafter: *Confiscirung*). See also Gierl (1997), 359–362, 370.

98 Gierl (1997), 375 ff.

hand-copied, and pirated. One irate Orthodox theologian in Jena wrote in 1711, 'if there were no such greedy book dealers [such as Lancke's Heirs or Fritsch] the inner peace of the church and Christian harmony would be preserved.'[99] However, without demand dealers could not have made a profit.

Pietist and Orthodox debate tracts were published for each of the two main audiences identified by contemporaries in Leipzig, as elsewhere in Europe: male gymnasium and University graduates, and the 'common man.'[100] References to the latter as a reader and listener to sermons were frequent during the debate, and tracts were often addressed specifically to 'the common man' or 'the public.' Tracts published in Latin had a limited audience. Most, though, were published in German. They ranged from short pamphlets to lengthy polemics. Works such as the fourteen-page *Sensible Christian Conversation About the So-Called Pietists, Held in Passing by Two Good Friends in Magdeburg*, published during the investigation into the collegia pietatis, used simple language and the form of a conversation.[101] Johann Benedict Carpzov's nearly 200-page *Thorough Description of the Pietists' Misconduct*, surely interesting to many readers on account of its lurid descriptions of convulsionary Pietist 'maids,' had a run of 2000–3000 copies in its first edition, and 700 in its second.[102] The variety of venues through which tracts reached their readers also points to a diverse readership. Bookstalls near the University drew students and academics; dealers' and printers' bookstores had the largest selections and attracted burghers and visitors as well as students; and women and children carried religious and other works from door to door throughout the city.[103]

One context for a major debate like the Pietist-Orthodox controversy was that printers and dealers were among the most individualistic and confident, and the least humble toward the authorities of all occupational groups. They had long chafed against the confines of confessional strictures, and pursued their agenda with increasing determination in confrontations with the authorities.[104] Well before 1690, dealers published religious and erotic tracts that had not been censored, and were

---

[99] Dr. Phillip Müller to August, 25 March 1711. SHStADD, Loc. 10753, *Bücher-Sachen mit Register*, 1711–1723, 5.

[100] *Project wegen Anlegung eines Buchhandels bey dem Zucht-u. Waisenhause*, n.d. (between documents dated 1717 & 1718). In SAL, Stift III.A.16. *Acta, Das Hospital St. Georgen und Das demselben incorporirte Zucht und Waysen Hauß alhier betr.*, vol. I, 1717, 48–55; 53; Roger Chartier (1989), 'Texts, Printings, Readings,' in Lynn Hunt, ed., *The New Cultural History* (Berkeley: University of California Press), 154–175.

[101] 1690; no date or place.

[102] Carpzov (?) (1693). Gierl (1997), 369. See also below.

[103] SAL, Tit. XVII.152., *Büchercensur-Acten*, vol. II, 1691–1705, 61 ff.

[104] For example, in 1689 and 1690 several dealers led by J.F. Gleditsch rebelled against the custom of giving the theological faculty for copies of all books it censored. SHStADD, Loc. 1791, *Acta Die Bücher von der Censur bey der Theologischen Facultät zu Leipzig betr. 1689–91*. 1–15 and 4 unpag. fol. Printers: C*onfiscirung*; Josef Benzing (1963), *Die Buchdrucker des 16. und 17. Jahrhunderts im deutschen Sprachgebiet* (Wiesbaden: Harrassowitz), 264 ff.

investigated by the Upper Consistory and Book Commissars.[105] Another context was the dramatic growth of the book trade in the late 17th century.[106] The Leipzig book fair overtook Frankfurt's as the most important in the Holy Roman Empire around 1680.[107] Cooperating closely with local intellectuals, Leipzig printers and dealers established the city as a center for newly prominent, capital-intensive genres such as moral weeklies, dictionaries, and encyclopedias. Of the twenty-nine encyclopedias published in German from 1704 to 1737, seventeen, including Zedler's *Universal-Lexicon*, were published in Leipzig; eleven were published by the house of Gleditsch alone.[108]

While secular publications like encyclopedias helped drive print expansion, especially after about 1710, religious subject material and the fervent Pietism of leading book dealers were also important. Historians have long noted an association between Protestant religious movements and printing. Early Lutheran and Calvinist ideas were spread rapidly by the printing press; Protestant leaders thought of printing in spiritual terms; and the publication of religious works spurred the development of the 16th-century book trade.[109] Seventeenth-century Puritans published in England at the risk of imprisonment, torture, and death, becoming 'martyrs of the book,' or travelled to the Netherlands to publish in greater safety.[110] The connection between Pietism and printing has been well documented for Francke's enterprises in Halle, with an emphasis on the role of the absolutist state in promoting literacy.[111] The non-state sponsored Pietist involvement in production in Leipzig, though, was probably more important to overall German print and literary development.

Authors and dealers worked closely together in early modern publishing. This was particularly true during the Pietist-Orthodox debate. Leipzig publishers were the key figures in the network. The Gleditsch brothers, Johann Friedrich and Johann Ludwig, along with Thomas Fritsch, led religious as well as non-religious print

---

105 SAL, Tit. XVII.152., *Büchercensur-Acten*, vol. I, 1600–1690, 44 ff.

106 See Johann Goldfriedrich (1908), *Geschichte des deutschen Buchhandels vom Westfälischen Frieden bis zum Beginn der Klassischen Litteraturperiode (1648–1740)* (Leipzig: Verlag des Börsenvereins der deutschen Buchhändler, R [1970] Leipzig: Zentralantiquariat der DDR); Reinhard Wittmann (1991), *Geschichte des deutschen Buchhandels: Ein Überblick* (Munich: Beck).

107 Goldfriedrich (1908), 137 ff.

108 Ibid., 75.

109 See Elisabeth Eisenstein (1979), *The Printing Press as an Agent of Change. Communications and Cultural Transformations in Early-Modern Europe* (New York: Cambridge University Press).

110 See Keith Sprunger (1994), *Trumpets from the Tower. English Puritan Printing in the Netherlands 1600–1640* (Leiden: Brill).

111 See Richard Gawthrop and Gerald Strauss (1984), 'Protestantism and Literacy in Early Modern Europe,' *Past and Present*, 104, 31–55; James Van Horn Melton (1988), *Absolutism and the Eighteenth-Century Origins of Compulsory Schooling in Prussia and Austria* (New York: Cambridge University Press).

expansion around 1700.[112] Born near the Saxon town of Grimma, they learned their trade with the publishers Weidmann and Fritsch. Johann Ludwig married the widow of Moritz Georg Weidmann, and Johann Friedrich married the widow of Johann Fritsch. Each built up the business of his house, and each meanwhile trained his step-son to assume control of the paternal firm. Thomas Fritsch took over in 1693, and Moritz Georg Weidmann Jr. in 1714. While Johann Ludwig Gleditsch then withdrew from the book trade, Johann Friedrich opened his own business. All three houses flourished.[113] Other influential dealers were Johann Heinich and Heinrich Julius Elers. Heinich published and sold a wide variety of religious literature until his death in 1693; his widow, Magdalena, carried on the business until at least 1715. Elers's presence in Leipzig, and his contacts with Pietists there, helped him build up the Halle Orphanage Press. During his visits to the Leipzig fairs, he sold and traded many works as well as arranging for the publication of others.[114]

Another important part of the book network were clerics, academics, and religiously-minded city councilors. The most prominent figures in Leipzig were city councilors Friedrich Benedict Carpzov, a brother of the Orthodox Carpzovs, to whom Johann Ludwig Gleditsch referred as his 'great patron,'[115] and Johann Job. Carpzov and Job obtained, copied, translated, guided through censorship, promoted, and helped distribute literature. For example, in 1702 Francke sent Job an English tract on 'the interests of the common Christian church,' asking that Job have it translated and published. Job soon responded that he was having the work inserted into a periodical published by the dealer Groschuff, 'who knows only that I obtained it directly from England.'[116] Carpzov's letters to Francke were full of plans to publish a variety of works, including editions of standards like Luther and Arndt as well as more controversial items. Carpzov also used his network of contacts in the Netherlands and elsewhere to bring the latest ideas to Leipzig.

Often the roles of intellectuals, religious activists, political figures, and publishers blurred. Job and Thomas Fritsch themselves wrote treatises. Johann Heinich was a participant in the collegia and was among those interrogated. In 1694, Orthodox theologian Johann Benedict Carpzov wrote to Leipzig Superintendent Georg Lehmann that Elers was 'causing the Ministry great trouble.' He had recently been interrogated and warned to desist from unspecified activities, but 'stays with his

---

[112] Rudolf Schmidt (1902), *Deutsche Buchhändler, Deutsche Buchdrucker. Beiträge zu einer Firmengeschichte des deutschen Buchgewerbes* (Berlin: Weber, R [1979] Hildesheim: Olms), 322–324.

[113] Bernhard Fabian & Marie-Luise Spieckermann, 'The House of Weidmann in Leipzig and the Eighteenth-Century Importation of English Books into Germany,' in John Flood & W. Kelly, eds (1995), *The German Book 1450–1750* (London: British Library), 299–317.

[114] Schmidt (1902), 200–202.

[115] J.L. Gleditsch to Francke, 16 February 1699. AFS, C 789: 8.

[116] Job to Francke, 16 & 21 March, 1702. AFS, C 232: 4 & 5.

purpose and obstinate temper,' and had 'led many burghers in this city, especially women, astray.'[117]

Many religious works published by Pietist and Orthodox publishers alike appeared legally, with the approbation of censors and other authorities: the Bible, Luther, Arndt, Spener, and Francke. But many polemical tracts appeared illicitly despite repeated orders from Dresden starting in May 1690 that nothing be published or preached concerning Pietism.[118] (Note that not all territories issued such a *Verbot.*) Studies by Robert Darnton for the French Enlightenment, Hans-Jürgen Schrader for radical German Pietists, and others have uncovered the importance of clandestine publishing in early modern Europe.[119] The publication of Pietist and Orthodox tracts shared many features with the cases explored by Darnton and Schrader: it was difficult and dangerous, or at least stressful, to circumvent the authorities, ship, and sell. But in other ways, the publishing history of this debate differed markedly from that of other illicit works. In particular, as Gierl also emphasizes,[120] there was no sharp line between legal and illegal publishing: the largest publishers of tracts were prominent publishers, and many authors were well-known figures rather than obscure freelance writers.

In publishing illicitly, printers and dealers had to work around an impressive regulatory system. In Leipzig two Book Commissars, one the dean of the theological faculty and the other a city councilor, supervised the print process and reported to the Upper Consistory. Censorship rules were strict. With minor exceptions, everything that was printed had to be censored in advance by a University professor, a theologian for religious works, a jurist for legal works, etc. Religious works had to conform to Lutheran dogma and to Imperial civility rules toward the other confessions. Printers were required to take an oath to print only censored material, and to include on the title page their names, the author's name, the place of printing, and a full title.[121] Undermining the system, though, both Pietist and Orthodox officials used

117 J.B. Carpzov to Lehmann, 19 March 1694, copy. AFS, A 166: 11. See also S.B. Carpzov to Johann George IV, 2 March 1694, *Den so gen.* Pietismum *betr.*, 193–203, 199^{v}.

118 The original 12 May 1690 *Verbot*: SHStADD, Loc. 10329, *Pietistica oder Des Pietismi Halber von Dr. Spenern, Dr. Löschern, Dr. Wernsdorffen, u. Dr. Marpergern gewechselte Schrifften*, 1691–1714 ... *betr.* (hereafter: *Pietistica*), 266.

119 Robert Darnton (1995), *The Forbidden Bestsellers of Pre-Revolutionary France* (New York: Norton); idem (1976), 'Trade in the Taboo: The Life of a Clandestine Book Dealer in Prerevolutionary France,' in Paul Korshin, ed., *The Widening Circle. Essays on the Circulation of Literature in Eighteenth-Century Europe* (Philadelphia: University of Pennsylvania Press), 13–83; Hans-Jürgen Schrader (1989), *Literaturproduktion und Büchermarkt des radikalen Pietismus. Johann Henrich Reitz' 'Historie der Wiedergebohrenen' und ihr geschichtlicher Kontext* (Göttingen: Vandenhoeck & Ruprecht).

120 Gierl (1997), 352 ff.

121 See Agatha Kobuch (1987), *Zensur und Aufklärung in Kursachsen zur Zeit der sächsisch-pölnischen Union 1694–1763* (Weimar: Böhlau); Schrader (1989), esp. 108 ff.; Annabel Patterson (1984), *Censorship and Interpretation. The Conditions of Writing and Reading in Early Modern England* (Madison: University of Wisconsin Press); Daniel Roche

their power to control official publishing channels, allowing publications reflecting their views to pass and suppressing publications of the other side. In the 1690s the Orthodox Upper Consistory allowed the publication of anti-Pietist tracts in Saxony.[122] On other occasions, Pietists succeeded.[123] Both sides repeatedly complained to the authorities, especially to about 1720, with little impact on the production or sales of the other side. One major reason that many investigations failed was that the Book Commissars and other officials themselves were involved.

Investigations did not fail for lack of effort expended. In several cases dozens of people were summoned and interrogated, some more than once. At the Easter fair in May 1690, ninety-nine people, all sixty-three dealers and thirty-six printers present at the fair, who had come from as far afield as Copenhagen, Breslau, Amsterdam, and Königsberg, were forced to sign a statement agreeing not to sell any Pietist literature.[124] However, there were relatively few investigations; they were launched mostly to halt tracts that were deemed especially offensive. Dealers thus knew they were acting with impunity most of the time. This would explain why, during a large-scale investigation in December 1693, no fewer than fifty-four different tracts were seized from Johann Friedrich Gleditsch alone. Gleditsch had fifty copies of one Spener tract, and between one and fourteen copies of others. Seven other dealers (Lancke, Fleischer, Kloß, Groschhuff, Gross, Meyer, and Heinich) whose stocks were seized had between two and forty-two different tracts.[125]

Cooperation among authors, printers, and dealers facilitated the sale of illicit literature. Distribution was informal and anonymous, and controversial tracts sold quickly. Often students carried copies of a tract from one territory to another; they brought a bundle to a dealer and received one or more copies of the tract as payment. A fiction often employed to protect publishers was that an unknown person had left

(1994), 'Censorship and the Publishing Industry,' in Darnton & Roche, eds, *Revolution in Print. The Press in France 1775–1800* (Berkeley: University of California Press), 3–26; Gierl (1997), 352 ff.

[122] Pro-Pietists such as Consistory President Beichling and Elector Johann George IV were not able to track down authors and publishers. Beichling personally led an extensive but unsuccessful investigation into *Unfug*, even visiting Leipzig. The widely rumored author's, Johann Benedict Carpzov's, University theology chair carried with it the office of Book Commissar. SHStADD, Loc. 10330, *Den so genannten* Pietismum *betr.*, 147–148; 181–186; 210–225^{v}.

[123] Orthodox Superintendent Thomas Ittig proved that Johann Olearius, dean of the theology faculty, who determined which religious works appeared in the catalogue of the Leipzig book fair, had omitted several Orthodox tracts from one catalogue although he had received copies. Olearius apparently also allowed the works of Pietists. SHStADD, Loc. 1791, *Acta Die theologischen Streitigkeiten, wegen des Termini peremptorii betr. 1700*, vol. iiii, 1–29^{v}. See also SHStADD, Loc. 1792, *Theologische Streitigkeiten auf den Universitäten Leipzig und Wittenberg 1709 f.*

[124] The signatures: *Pietistica*, 268–269^{v}.

[125] SAL, Tit. XLVI.147. *Commissions Acta Die Pietistischen Enthusiastischen und Chiliastischen Schrifften betr.*, 1694–94, 34–41^{v}.

copies on a doorstep or inside a workshop, or had mailed copies, with a note that he would identify himself at the next fair and collect money for the copies sold.[126] The authorities usually failed even to find out the publisher of a tract, and were equally ineffective at stopping the sale of tracts. They were often informed when illicit material was being sold, but when the Book Commissars sent their deputies to bookstores to confiscate a tract they often found nothing. Even when dealers were caught, they were often able to talk themselves out of punishment. They might claim that they had not been able to tell the content of a tract from the title,[127] or that a printer had acted against a dealer's wishes by putting a falsified place, publisher, or other misleading or inadequate information on the title page. The identities of anonymous authors were never revealed under interrogation.[128]

* * *

The Pietists were intensely aware of the changes taking place around them. Their ideas and practices were a complex response to that change. They seized some new opportunities, while rejecting changes that they perceived as threatening. They had an intensely negative reaction to the secular culture and luxury consumption flowering around them. At the same time, they paralleled Enlighteners by establishing innovative forms of sociability and correspondence. They also took the lead in developing Leipzig into the center of the German-language book trade. They were thus part of the development of an increasingly multi-faceted urban culture, which some of their contemporaries cultivated in coffee houses, pleasure gardens, and at the Opera.

The Pietists combined the traditional and modern in their thought and activities. The ancient texts that they used as models pointed the way to new forms of sociability and a cosmopolitan identity. Pietists' geographic horizons were expanding to include the world, but they retained roots in local society as well, attending church, working, and associating with fellow Pietists within Leipzig's town walls. They partially abandoned their identification with a corporate group, but structured their network through patron-client relations that had many traditional elements. Perhaps most strikingly, men and women from a variety of social backgrounds worked as active partners with leaders such as Francke in building a long-lasting, vibrant network.

---

[126] Thomas Fritsch was one. Investigation into *Christ-Vernünfftiges Gespräch*, 1690: *Acta, die sogenannten* Pietisten *betr.*, 179ᵛ–300ᵛ.

[127] Leipzig Book Commissars to August, 1 January 1701. SHStADD, Loc. 10753, *Bücher-Sachen ab Ann. 1699–1711*, 25–25ᵛ, 29–29ᵛ.

[128] *Confiscirung*, 119–124; 122ᵛ–123ᵛ.

PART IV
The construction boom and beyond

Chapter Eight

Social change and religious life

The emergence of the Pietist network was only one form of change in Leipzig's religious life around the turn of the century. Public religion underwent many changes as well, notably through major construction projects that opened new churches to the public. These additions were a response to rapid social and economic change. The urban population grew steadily, crossing the 20,000 mark around 1690, reaching 23,000 in 1697, and growing to 28,500 by 1719. It would remain just under 30,000 for most of the 18th century.[1] Benefiting from their city's economic prosperity, many artisans, merchants, and professionals enjoyed increased buying power. At the same time, as in other European towns, poverty increased and the number of dislocated individuals in Leipzig and Saxony as a whole grew.[2]

The expansion of public life in the high Baroque era is usually discussed in terms of secular culture. Indeed, as we have seen, secular cultural offerings grew considerably at this time. However, the public religious arena remained at the center of urban communication, politics, and the negotiation and reproduction of social relations. Two churches abandoned during the Reformation were renovated and reopened: the 'New Church' (*Neue Kirche*) between 1698 and 1700, and St. Peter's in 1713. In addition, a new, large combination poor house, orphanage, insane asylum, and penitentiary named St. George's was built between 1700 and 1704. Its programs had considerable religious content, and the house included a chapel. Furthermore, the council introduced catechism services aimed at the poor in the renovated and the main churches. And in 1710 a group of professors initiated public weekly services in the University Church, St. Paul's (*Paulinerkirche*), also extensively renovating the church. There were similar developments in other trade centers: in Dresden, Hamburg, and Frankfurt, for example, the Frauenkirche, the Michaeliskirche, St. Catherine's, and smaller churches were built. Institutions such as St. George's were built in many German towns beginning in the later 17th century.[3]

---

1 F.G. Leonhardi (1799), *Geschichte und Beschreibung der Kreis- und Handelsstadt Leipzig* (Leipzig: Beygang), 253–255.

2 Helmut Bräuer (1994), 'Arme Leute in Sachsen im 18. Jahrhundert,' *Räume voll Leipzig. Arbeitsberichte des Stadtarchivs Leipzig*, 1, 72–87; idem, ed. and intro. (1996), *Der Leipziger Rat und die Bettler. Quellen und Analysen zu Bettlern und Bettelwesen in der Messestadt bis ins 18. Jahrhundert* (Leipzig: Reintzsch); Alexander Cowan (1998), *Urban Europe 1500–1700* (New York: Arnold), 162 ff.

3 Introduction, note 64; Cowan (1998), 162 ff.

Leipzig, views of eight buildings, engraving, 'Scenographiae Lipsiacae,' 1749 (Bach-Archiv Leipzig. Graph. Slg. 2/34, reproduced by permission).

Events in Leipzig were chronicled by contemporaries such as Christian Gerber and Anton Weiz. More recently, Günther Stiller described the liturgical expansion in the context of Bach's musical life in Leipzig.[4] Indeed, that expansion helped to set the stage for many of Bach's activities. Gerber's, Weiz's, and Stiller's accounts, though, neglect the dimensions of social interest and competition among institutions that drove the projects, and that emerge from rich and previously neglected archival

4 Christian Gerber (1717), *Die unerkannten Wohltaten Gottes in dem Chur-Fürstentum Sachsen, und desselben vornehmsten Städten ...*, vol. II (Dresden & Leipzig: Winckler); Anton Weiz (1728), *Verbessertes Leipzig, oder Die vornehmsten Dinge, so von Anno 1698 an bis hieher bey der Stadt Leipzig verbessert worden* (Leipzig: Lancke). Günther Stiller (1984), *Johann Sebastian Bach and Liturgical Life in Leipzig* (St. Louis: Concordia; German original, 1970), 39 ff. Stiller relies on printed sources.

material. This chapter, bringing together themes explored in the course of the book so far, discusses the roles of the main actors in the religious arena during this expansion, and the styles they cultivated in the new spaces. The chapter first examines the roles of the authorities and professors. City councilors and University professors took the initiative and increased their power. Clerics, consistory assessors, and the Dresden court resisted some of the changes, leading to prolonged power struggles. The chapter then explores the roles of burghers and sub-burghers. Burghers largely funded each project by paying for the construction of pews and making additional donations. They also actively sought out simple services at St. George's and St. Peter's. Sub-burghers, in contrast, were further marginalized by being forced to attend new catechism classes and being incarcerated in St. George's.

In developing new religious venues contemporaries turned to two styles, one parallel to and influenced by Pietism, the other high Baroque. The third part of the chapter addresses the often-posed question of how Pietist and non-Pietist ideas and practices related. As Udo Sträter has noted, it is often difficult to determine where those of one group left off and those of the other began.[5] In Leipzig, Pietist councilors and professors and materials from Halle did influence programs in St. George's, St. Peter's, and initially the University Church. Parallel developments rather than direct influence, though, account for most of the similarities: members of both groups responded to the same social changes, and they both continued to cultivate, albeit with shifts in emphasis, pre-existing Lutheran ideas and practices. Another important consideration is that around 1700, councilors had a new ability to legislate and build. Further, they were flexible and pragmatic in their approach, calling on varied styles to express different facets of their agenda.

Finally, economic expansion helped to stimulate musical culture: the renovation projects funded by burghers' and councilors' increased disposable income added musical spaces and liturgies that were autonomous from the established urban musical structures. A key role was played by collegia musica made up of student musicians. Like the collegia pietatis, the collegia musica were led by young people, broke new ground in the venues where they assembled, and engaged in conflict with established figures. Unlike the Pietist collegia, though, the collegia musica embraced new secular culture, playing not only in churches but also in coffee houses and at the Leipzig Opera. This cross-fertilization was to have a major impact on music generally in Leipzig. At the New Church, Georg Philipp Telemann was engaged to perform on holidays (and his successors also during the fairs). At the University Church, Johann Friedrich Fasch and his successors became well-known for performing high-quality music during the fairs. The students' accomplishments in the New Church in particular were considerable. In addition to Telemann, later luminaries such as Johann David Heinichen, Johann Georg Pisendel, and probably the young George Frederick Handel played there, making Leipzig an unparalleled center of student music-making. They not only introduced the concerted passion to Leipzig, but innovated in other ways as well.

---

5 Sträter (2004), 'Soziales,' in *GdP*, vol. IV, 617–645; 619–620 & ff.

The authorities

At a high point of their general economic and political power, Leipzig's city councilors greatly expanded their roles as patrons of religious life. They continued, though, to work with the traditional covenant-based language of governance, emphasizing their duty to ensure the spiritual welfare of Leipzig's inhabitants. Senior councilors who held positions as 'building directors' (*Baumeister*) served as directors of the new churches. They supervised the construction projects, were chief architects, and oversaw the allotment of pews. While the construction projects were expensive, they actually helped councilors realize their perennial goal of raising money: a portion of the burgher contributions was immediately put to use by being lent out, and the New Church, St. George's, and St. Peter's each became money-lending institutions. Interest from loans was used for maintenance and other expenditures.[6]

The council's goals and activities, and its interactions with other authorities, varied from one project to another. Providing additional seating for burghers was the main goal of the renovation of the New Church. Goals at St. Peter's and St. George's were more complex. At St. Peter's, the original mission was a social disciplinary one, but other pressing interests of the council such as self-display, financial gain through constructing *Capellen*, and accommodating burghers' wishes for more pews quickly moved to the forefront. By August 1710 councilors were discussing whether to install an organ and build balconies, where to place the council's special pew, how to arrange pews, and whether to leave free spaces for 'common' folk.[7] Soon after, plans were made to build two stories of *Capellen* around the edge of the church.[8] Councilors had nineteen *Capellen* built, which extended to the church doors and near the pulpit; they also squeezed in as many pews as possible.[9]

The city council also continued to pursue its original goal at St. Peter's, though. Different services addressed different social groups. Sunday morning services were attended mostly by pewholders, many of them wealthy.[10] Tuesday and Wednesday afternoon catechism services were held for alms recipients who were probably forced to attend; services on one day were for women, and those on the other day for men. St. Peter's pastor Adam Bernd also held a newly introduced catechism service in each of the main churches once a week.

The construction of the new St. George's was the council's most prominent public works project of this period. The new building replaced a much smaller house built

---

6 See SAL (no loc.), church *Rechnungen*. Values for the New Church converted from gulden.

7 *Memorial*, 30 August 1710. SAL, Tit.VII.B.110., *Acta Die Peterskirche betr.*, vol. 1, 1704 ff. (hereafter: *Peterskirche*), 60–60^{v}.

8 *Erinnerung bey Bau der Capellen*, n.d., between documents dated August 1710 & June 1711. *Peterskirche*, 61–62.

9 Burgher requests of 1711: *Peterskirche*, 66–69.

10 Adam Bernd (1738), *Eigene Lebens-Beschreibung* (Leipzig: Heinsius, R [1973], Munich: Winkler), 209.

between 1668 and 1671.[11] Religious motives were central to the project. Councilors stressed their obligation to provide for destitute inhabitants and discipline those who threatened the common weal, concepts that derived from the covenant theory of governance. Driving home this agenda, in 1725–26 a sculptor from Dresden was commissioned to make statues representing 'Love' and 'Punishment,' and a large stone sculpture of St. George himself in his classic pose on horseback slaying a dragon.[12] Shortly after the building was completed, it was filled with objects of charity (orphans, the elderly, and the mentally ill) and discipline (prisoners, including beggars and prostitutes). New buildings were added at substantial cost in 1725–26 and 1732–35. The council also spent a large amount of money on the construction of the house chapel: 1000 thaler of its 4000 thaler total contribution were earmarked specifically for the 'chapel, steeple, and bell.' Councilor and house director Johann Ernst Kregel contributed an additional 1637 thaler for the steeple.[13]

* * *

In planning services for the New Church, St. Peter's, and St. George's, the council encroached on the territory of the Leipzig clergy and Consistory. When it planned services in its first project, the New Church, the council proceeded with extreme caution.[14] As a result, and also because this renovation does seem to have stemmed mostly from burgher demand for pews, there were no immediate conflicts. Perhaps emboldened by its success, the council was less willing to consult with other authorities about St. George's and St. Peter's. Protracted struggles ensued. The clergy sought jurisdiction over liturgies and newly appointed clerics. The Dresden authorities wanted to be consulted about plans before they were implemented, criticizing the council's 'unauthorized' actions, its excess of confidence in its rights, and its arrogation of power that rightfully belonged to Electoral institutions. As usual, the consistories served as channels of communication, with assessors in Dresden and Leipzig supporting clerics.

The sharpest conflict concerned innovative services in St. George's, which competed with those at the main churches. In the old building, a cleric from another church had held simple services attended only by inmates. In the new building, though, councilors undertook a gradual expansion without consulting the Leipzig Consistory. Councilors clearly had plans for the chapel from an early date: their

11 For more detail, see Tanya Kevorkian (2000), 'The Rise of the Poor, Weak, and Wicked: Poor Care, Punishment, Religion, and Patriarchy in Leipzig, 1700–1730,' *Journal of Social History*, 34, 163–181.

12 SAL, St. George *Rechnungen* (no loc.), 1725 & 1726.

13 SAL, no loc., *Rechnung Über Den geführten Bau des von E. Edl. Hochw. Rathe Dem Hospital zu St. Georgen zu einem Zuchthause angewiesenen vormahligen Kornhauses im Brühl,* 1700–1704 (hereafter: *Rechnung Über Den geführten Bau*); later *Rechnungen.*

14 SAL, Tit. VIII.56, *Protocoll in die Enge*, 1694–1709. 4 April 1698, 85–88. See also C. Evers (1880), *Das Franziskaner Barfüßerkloster zu Leipzig. Geschichte der Matthäikirche zu Leipzig (frühere Neukirche)* (Leipzig: Böhme).

construction of pews and balconies led the Leipzig Consistory to complain by 1703 that they were attempting to recruit a broader audience of 'people from the city who want to attend services here.'[15] They appointed six students and then a regular cleric to preach and allowed townspeople to attend. The only major expenditures on luxury items in the house were for the chapel: an Italian *Stuccaturirer* was paid 425 thaler to finish the ceiling and altar; the confessional was upholstered in red leather and the pulpit covered with red satin; sculptors, metal workers, painters, and carpenters were hired to make and decorate Ionian capitals, pews, grates, and walls.[16] By mid-1705, the Consistory complained that the pastor was preaching to large crowds of 400 to 500 people and that councilors had also introduced new and unauthorized hymns, prayers, and the carrying around of a collection bag.[17] In an April 1706 meeting senior councilors debated 'whether and how' to follow an order for a report that had come down from Dresden. In the report they eventually sent, they defended their actions.[18] The Privy Council ultimately agreed to all of the council's innovations, despite the Leipzig Consistory's repeated complaints.[19]

Strife surrounding the introduction of new services at St. Peter's was more muted and quickly resolved. In November 1709, the council complained to Dresden of 'great ignorance among the common (*gemeine*) people ... of basic knowledge necessary to attain true Christianity,' mentioning that clerics felt similarly. In order to remedy this situation, it proposed to appoint a catechist who would conduct simple afternoon services in St. Thomas's, St. Nicholas's, and the New Church.[20] Catechism services in the main churches were intended for 'children and servants called (*convocirt*) from the houses of the city and *Vorstadt*.'[21] The main area of conflict related to jurisdiction over services. The council and Leipzig Consistory each wanted full jurisdiction; the Electoral authorities granted each partial jurisdiction.[22] Once this was settled, the council wrote to Dresden suggesting that the new appointment was a good opportunity to renovate St. Peter's. In this way, seating could be provided for

15 Leipzig Consistory to Upper Consistory, 8 June 1703. SHStADD, Loc. 9882, *Die von dem Rath zu Leipzig in dem neuangelegten sogenannten Armen- und Waysen-Hausse erbauete neue Capelle oder Kirch* ..., 1703–1706 (hereafter: *Neue Capelle oder Kirch*), 10–11^{v}. See also SAL, *Tit. VII.B.49, Acta, Anrichtung einer Kirche im neuen Armen- und Waisenhause betr. Ao. 1705*, (hereafter: *Anrichtung*), 7–34^{v}; *Neue Capelle oder Kirch*, 21–46. Elias Hoffmann was appointed the first pastor of St. George in 1705. He died in 1706. His brother was appointed next; after his death in 1713 Johann Adam Gehr took his place. E. H. Albrecht (1799), *Sächsische evangelisch-luther'sche Kirchen-und Predigergeschichte* (Leipzig: Self-published), vol. I, 618 ff.

16 *Rechnung Über den geführten Bau*, 76–98.

17 Leipzig Consistory to August, 5 July 1705 *Neue Capelle oder Kirch*, 49–49^{v}, 54–54^{v}.

18 *Protocoll in der Enge*, 1694–1709, meeting of 9 April 1706, 455–456.

19 *Neue Capelle oder Kirch*, 5 July 1705 to 5 March 1706; 54–75^{v}.

20 15 November 1709. *Peterskirche.*, 24–24^{v}.

21 Schedule of catechism services, December, 1711. *Peterskirche*, 74–76^{v}.

22 *Peterskirche*, 44–52^{v}.

people who did not hold pews at the other churches, especially residents of the poor areas (*Vorstädte*) just outside the city walls.[23]

Some councilors took a strong personal interest in planning the new catechism services. The council presented detailed outlines to the Electoral authorities, including suggestions for how to question people in catechism sessions, explicate Scriptural passages, and select hymns and liturgical chants, and for clerics' vestments.[24] Once the services had begun, councilors continued to take an active interest. For example, while hosting a dinner in November 1713, governing mayor Schacher suggested to Adam Bernd that catechists at St. Peter's switch from reading and explaining passages from the Old Testament and instead draw from the New Testament. Bernd submitted detailed theological and pastoral arguments for retaining the Old Testament passages, and his suggestions were followed.[25]

In appointing clerics, the council expanded its role as clerical patron; the clergy also benefited in that its size grew. The Superintendent and Consistory were consulted about, and in agreement with, the appointment of a deacon and sub-deacon at the New Church, and of a pastor and eight catechists at St. Peter's. They opposed the appointment of a regular cleric at St. George's, part of the larger conflict there. For each church, the Consistory obtained the council's guarantee that no baptisms, marriages, or funerals would be conducted: these would have cut into crucial income of clerics at the main churches. However, confession was heard at each new church, which contributed to the income of the clerics there. By the 1710s between 7000 and 9000 communion hosts were being distributed annually in the New Church.[26]

* * *

Strife at the University Church was the most lengthy and acrimonious of all. The professors' drive to gain a public pulpit threatened both the city council and the Consistory; and a church rich in tradition, located directly on the main market square and controlled by mighty theology professors, was a more potent forum than the small churches of St. George's and St. Peter's, located on the town walls, with their relatively humble pastors. St. Paul's had traditionally been used by university affiliates, and its services were classified as private. Ordinary Leipzig inhabitants, especially women, were actually forbidden to attend. Several professors first attempted to initiate regular, public services in early 1702. City councilors protested, and Privy Councilors denied the professors' request on the grounds that the city council had exclusive rights over public services in the city.[27]

---

23 City council to Privy Council, 29 June 1710. *Peterskirche*, 55–56.

24 See for example *Peterskirche*, 1704 ff., city council to Elector August, 15 November 1709, 24–24^{v}.

25 *Peterskirche*, Bernd to Schacher, November 1713, 124–127^{v}.

26 New Church, *Rechnungen*.

27 SHStADD, Loc. 6119, *Den Gottes Dienst in der Pauliner Kirche in Leipzig betr.*, 1702 ff. (hereafter: *Gottes Dienst in der Pauliner Kirche*); city council to Dresden, 3 April 1702,

The professors finally persuaded the court to allow a weekly Sunday service in 1710. No regular pastor would be hired; instead, professors would take turns preaching. The city council and Consistory, in a rare show of solidarity, protested strenuously. But the professors had apparently gained the backing of key figures at court, and the protests were to no avail, although they continued into the 1720s.[28] The University also entered the market in pews, constructing and allotting regular pews and *Capellen* to Leipzig inhabitants. At least 300, and probably many more, *Stühle* and *Bänklein* were allotted.[29] Twenty-four *Capellen* were built and allotted to professors and non-professors. The university pursued the market in *Capellen* with a vigor that shocked two Privy Councilors who inspected the construction while they attended the 1712 New Years' fair: as they reported to the Upper Consistory, the *Capellen* 'are being distributed for high sums in an auction-like style.'[30]

Burghers and sub-burghers

Demand by Leipzig burghers for pews was as important to the construction projects as was planning by councilors and professors. A burgher petition to the council that emphasized the shortage of pews actually initiated the renovation of the New Church.[31] After the initial renovation was completed, Director Winckler noted that 'many burghers would like to see a tower with a clock and bell.'[32] He also noted that 'some Leipzig burghers, especially those who live near the church, spoke often with the Director and beseeched him to add a service and prayer hour during the week.'[33] While the renovation of St. Peter's was begun for the purpose of coercing or encouraging the poor, servants and children into attending, this project became financially viable because hundreds of burghers paid for pews there. The university also allotted many pews to burghers. In all, at least 2000 *Stühle* and *Bänke*, and roughly 600 seats in *Capellen* were allotted in the New Church, St. Peter's, and

---

3–6ᵛ; University to August, 15 April 1702, 23–29ᵛ; Privy Councilors to Upper Consistory, 26 June 1702, 9–9ᵛ; 12.

28 *Gottes Dienst in der Pauliner Kirche*, University to August, 2 August 1710, 33–35; Privy Councilors to Upper Consistory, 16 August 1710, 31–31ᵛ; Leipzig Consistory to August, 18 October 1710, 40–41; city council to Dresden, 23 August 1710, 53–56; August to Upper Consistory, 20 December 1710, 57–57ᵛ, 64–64ᵛ; city council to Dresden, 22 November 1710, 73–79; further complaints also in this file.

29 Wilhelm Stieda (n.d.), *Der Neubau der Paulinerkirche in den Jahren 1710–1712. Aktenmäßige Forschungen über die Mitarbeit der Leipziger Gewerken* (Leipzig, no press), 76.

30 *Gottes Dienst in der Pauliner Kirche*. Zech and Adami to Upper Consistory, 1 February 1712, 125–127ᵛ, 141–142ᵛ; 125ᵛ–126.

31 SAL, 1703–04 New Church *Rechnung*.

32 SAL, no loc. *Hauptbuch der Neuen Kirche*, 1 January 1712 (hereafter: *Hauptbuch*), 9ᵛ–10.

33 SAL, Stift. IX.C.15. *Original der Subscriptionsliste zur Renovation der Neukirche*, 1698.

the University Church (pews built in St. George's were not initially allotted to individuals, although the account books include income from pew allotment from 1708 onward).

Burghers' roles varied from one church to another. For the New Church and St. Peter's, individuals contributed small set amounts for the allotment of their pews, and made a larger, 'voluntary' contribution to cover the construction of the pews. Regular pewholders contributed 29,800 thaler in this way to the New Church. Elites contributed another 8100 thaler for *Capellen* and burial places. Another 560 thaler was placed in collection boxes.[34] At St. George's, over 200 Leipzigers and over 70 visitors from other cities contributed over 9000 thaler, about two-thirds of the total cost of 14,757 thaler.[35] Most of the contributors from Leipzig whose occupations were listed were members of the local elites, but a number were tradesmen. A collection box set up at the construction site brought 400 more thaler. Burgher contributions toward seating in the University Church, including for *Capellen*, brought in nearly the full amount of construction costs, 9406 of 9918 thaler.[36] Ironically, with the exception of professors who built *Capellen*, the members of the academic community with whom burghers shared the church did not pay for their pews. Students occupied student balconies, and professors and their wives received *ex officio* pews. Also, many visitors to the Leipzig fairs who could not obtain seats in the other churches attended the University Church,[37] but did not have pews allotted to them.

It is worth looking more closely at the first pewholders in the New Church, the largest of the churches opened by the council, who formed the audience of the young Telemann and his successors. Just under 1200 people paid for pews to be built for them, with occupations listed for 88%.[38] Their social make-up was roughly similar to that in the main churches. Councilors actually specified that the New Church was to provide pews for people who had not been able to obtain them in St. Thomas's and St. Nicholas's, and pews were built on the same model as the most recent additions in the main churches.[39] By the 1710s, the New Church was actually being referred to as one of the three main churches. Contemporaries even complained that many New Church pews had been taken by people who had already held pews in St. Thomas's

---

34 New Church *Rechnung*, 1698–1700, 236–238.

35 *Rechnung Über Den geführten Bau*, 1–11.

36 Stieda (n.d.), 76.

37 *Gottes Dienst in der Pauliner Kirche*: Privy Councilors Zech and Adami to Upper Consistory, 1 February 1712, 125–127^{v}, 141–142^{v}; 141. Iccander (1725), *Das in gantz Europa berühmte, galante und sehens-würdige Königliche Leipzig in Sachsen* ... (Leipzig: Martini), 47–51.

38 Figures compiled from the *Rechnungen* of the New Church, 1698–1700 (SAL, no loc.).

39 Meetings in 1698 of the *Enge* and larger council; *Protocoll in die Enge*, 1694–1709, 85 ff. passim; *Protocoll in den Drey Räthen*, 1687–1709, 274–278; construction *Rechnungen* indicate instructions to craftspeople to build pews like the newest added in the main churches.

and/or St. Nicholas's.[40] As in St. Nicholas's, merchants made up by far the largest single occupational group, 23% of all pewholders. Most of the nineteen financers of *Capellen* were city councilors; a few were wealthy merchants. Members of intermediary-status occupations held 15% of all pews, similarly to St. Nicholas's.

But the religious experience in the New Church was somewhat democratized compared to that in the main churches. Artisans, their wives, children, and a handful of journeymen from over seventy trades made up 48% of all those who financed pews, a bit higher than the 43% in St. Nicholas's. And they held a much higher percentage of *Stühle*: over half of the female *Stühle* (53%) and almost half of the male *Stühle* (42%), as opposed to 13% for both sexes in St. Nicholas's. This was partly because *Bänklein* made up only 19% of seats allotted from 1698 to 1700, as opposed to 36% in St. Nicholas's. (In St. Peter's as well, *Bänklein* were only 17% of all pews allotted in 1712).[41] Members of the elites financed 35% of the pews in the New Church, lower than the 43% in St. Nicholas's. And several 'modern' occupations to which the exchange of information was of central importance were well represented: letter carriers, and tavern and hotel owners, who perhaps obtained pews for their guests to use.

There was an even more striking feminization of the religious experience in the New Church. Seventy percent of pews there were held by women, compared with 56% in St. Nicholas's. Councilors, who surely noticed that there was greater demand for pews among women than men in the main churches, probably ordered more women's pews built; early returns on contributions may also have influenced them. Even three years after the church opened, forty-eight men's *Stühle* and sixty *Bänklein* remained unallotted, as opposed to thirteen women's *Stühle* and no *Bänklein*.[42] This proportion was similar in St. Peter's, where 65% of the pews allotted in 1712 went to women, and more men's than women's pews remained unallotted.[43] In the New Church, the wives and daughters of men from sixty-nine different trades, as opposed to male representatives of forty-six trades, financed pews. Among the first holders of *Stühle* were Maria Regina Schmiedlein, the wife of a goldsmith, Johanna Sophia Lincke, daughter of a miller, and Magdalena Hahn, wife of a hatmaker. Holders of *Bänklein* included Maria Krause, wife of a shoemaker, Dorothea Rossmessler, wife of a harnessmaker, and Anna Knittel, wife of a tailor. Further, among the female holders of *Bänklein* were wives of a handful of very humble artisans and sub-artisans who were not seen in St. Nicholas's: the wives of a drover, a carriage driver and a laborer helped make up 2% of pewholders.

---

40 University to Dresden, 15 April 1702. *Gottes Dienst in der Pauliner Kirche*, 23–29; 27.

41 SAL (no loc.), 1712 St. Peter's *Rechnung*.

42 SAL, 1701–02 New Church *Rechnung*. 308 men's and 652 women's *Stühle*, and 30 men's and 188 women's *Bänklein* were allotted between 1698 and 1700.

43 SAL (no loc.), 1712 St. Peter's *Rechnung*.

Burghers also shared initiative with councilors at St. George's. They flocked to services there, and demanded admission when they were initially denied it. When he was questioned in 1705 by Superintendent Ittig, house pastor Hoffmann stated that the house guards allowed 'students, burghers, and other honorable men and women' in. 'The burghers,' he continued, 'complained that they had made large contributions to the poor house and it was not fair that they were not let in. They also threatened to stop contributing to the alms box if they were not allowed to attend services.'[44] The Consistory's complaint of 1703 had also mentioned townspeople's desire to attend services.

* * *

Sub-burghers' presence in the public religious arena also grew, but the diverse members of this group mostly appeared as objects of attempted discipline. In planning new catechism services, councilors compiled a list of streets from which people were apparently systematically gathered for traditional Lenten catechism exams, and debated whether to use the same method for the new catechism services. It is not clear whether they did or not.[45] The construction of allotted pews and *Capellen* in St. Peter's eliminated originally planned free spaces and unallotted pews, where the poor could have sat during Sunday morning services. A by-product of the council's goal of raising money,[46] this move called forth an impassioned if fruitless protest from councilor Abraham Christoph Kase, who noted that even as the number of poor in the city grew daily, their chance to hear the Word of God was diminishing.[47] In this memorial Kase additionally, as we saw in Chapter Two, lamented the loss of formerly free spaces in the main churches.

Disciplinary motives were also prominent at St. George's. Prisoners, mostly non-propertied individuals, many imprisoned for begging, were put to work rasping wood or spinning. Sunday services in the chapel and daily prayer hours were mandatory for inmates.[48] In 1703 director Kregel drew up a seating plan for Sunday services. It is not clear whether the plan was followed, but it is noteworthy for its ordering of social groups. Orphans were to sit on benches at the rear of the ground floor. Artisans employed to teach the orphans trades were to sit in the first balcony, and 'sinful women' in the second. Prisoners were to hear the service from a secure room in the basement beneath the chapel; a hole in the chapel floor would allow them to listen.

---

44 Ittig, report of questioning of Hoffmann on 25 June 1705. *Neue Capelle oder Kirch*, 49–49^{v}, 50–51^{v}.

45 Notes attached to a draft of 15 November 1709, unsigned, *Peterskirche*, 38–39^{v}; lists of streets from which people *gefordert* yearly, 53–54^{v}.

46 *Protocoll in die Enge*, 1694–1709. Meeting of 31 March 1702, 170–171.

47 Memorial of 20 December 1713. *Peterskirche*, 129–133.

48 Teachers' *Instruction*, *c.* 1706. SAL, Stift.III.A.14, *Das Zucht- Armen- und Waisen-Haus betr., Ergangen vor dem Rathe der Stadt Leipzig*, 1670–1717 (hereafter: *Zucht- Armen- und Waisen-Haus*), 81–84; 82.

The director himself was to sit in a *Capelle* at the rear of the church.[49] Udo Sträter and others have rightly criticized the over-emphasis on social discipline in recent work on institutions such as St. George's.[50] Indeed, overcrowding, underfunding, inmates' inability to work, and stealing and abuse by some employees undermined councilors' goals.[51] However, the new house did allow councilors to incarcerate or provide for the poor on a new scale.

Pietism and public religious practice

The theology professors who led the drive to hold public services at the University church, Gottfried Olearius and Adam Rechenberg, were Pietists. In 1700 and 1701 Rechenberg and Gottfried Olearius's father Johannes had conducted an extensive theological battle on whether individuals had a 'deadline' to repent of their sins, the *terminus peremptorius* debate, with Orthodox Superintendent Thomas Ittig.[52] Tensions had remained. Now the Pietists, who did not occupy clerical positions as some of their Orthodox colleagues did, gained a public pulpit of their own. Gottfried Olearius preached at the first public service on 31 August 1710. He made quick use of his pulpit by criticizing Orthodox services in scathing Pietist language, including veiled references to the Orthodox as Pharisees. The sermon was printed soon after by Thomas Fritsch, with a historic sermon that Luther had preached at the University church in 1545 attached.[53] In the same vein, in 1712 visiting privy councilors complained of 'innovative [i.e. Pietist] terms and doctrines' and 'unnecessary questions or futile and irritating debate issues' in sermons.[54] As we will soon see, though, the professors were able to reconcile fiery Pietist preaching with elaborate music.

City councilors' innovations in the area of poor care paralleled Pietist engagement with this issue. But should these be labelled 'Pietist'? The situation was more complex than with regard to the professors. Along with some direct Pietist influence, new liturgies and disciplinary programs reflected continuity with earlier Lutheran practice, and helped further councilors' pragmatic mindset and goals. There is also

---

49 Account of Daniel Petermann, Leipzig Consistory protonotary, 23 November 1703, 41–41^{v}, 44–44^{v}. *Neue Capelle oder Kirch.* 24 November 1703, ibid., 38–40^{v}; 38^{v}–39.

50 Sträter (2004), 624 ff.

51 Kevorkian (2000), 169 ff.

52 SHStADD, Loc. 1791, *Die theologischen Streitigkeiten, wegen des Termini peremptorii betr.*, 1700.

53 Gottfried Olearius (1710), *Die Wahre Herrligkeit Eines wohleingerichteten Gottesdienstes wurde am xi. Sonntage nach Trinit. A. 1710 aus Luc. xiix 9–14 in volckreicher Versammlung bey Eröffnung des ordentlichen Gottesdienstes in der Acad. Kirche zu St. Paul in Leipzig vorgestellet ... von D. Gottfried Oleario, der Heil. Schrifft P.P.* (Leipzig: Fritsch). Luther's sermon: on Luke 19: 41–48.

54 *Gottes Dienst in der Pauliner Kirche*. Zech and Adami to Upper Consistory, 1 February 1712, 125–127^{v}, 141–142^{v}; 126–126^{v}.

no evidence of strife within the council on these issues. Catechism was one area of change. It was part of long-established Sunday afternoon services in the main churches in Leipzig, which were attended mostly by servants and children, as well as of Lenten exams. Councilors updated and intensified the practice. Spener himself had expanded catechism services thoughout Saxony while he was Senior Court Chaplain, although the groundwork for this had been laid before his arrival.[55] Francke also considered catechism vital. As we saw in the previous chapter, Adam Bernd, who conducted new catechism services, did not fit neatly into any one group.

There were also parallels between St. George's and Pietist institutions. Both Pietists and Leipzig councilors placed new emphasis on the Reformation agenda of caring for, disciplining, and indoctrinating the poor, orphaned, and criminal.[56] Councilors took note of an institution similar to St. George's that Spener had established in the 1670s.[57] In Leipzig as in Pietist institutions, inmates became a newly prominent social and religious category; they were brought closer to the consciousness of the larger population even while they were cordoned off from it. Financing and construction in Leipzig took place in the public limelight, as they did in Halle, although Francke's institutions were unusual in that they were initially established outside typical noble or urban oversight, and funded by a far-flung network of supporters. The orphans in Leipzig, like those in Halle, became public figures, put on display for visitors (who could tour the institution) and expected to respond to charity with their 'poor' prayers.[58] Much like leaders in Halle, councilors placed great emphasis on educating the orphans, ensuring that they received thorough elementary training by employing three teachers who developed close relations with the children. Councilors carefully planned a teaching schedule and made regular outlays for teaching materials. Education in the old building had been less rigorous. Long-time St. George's pastor Johann Adam Gehr was a good friend of Adam Bernd;[59] but his religious style is unknown.

There were more direct connections between Halle and St. George's as well. In 1717 or 1718 an anonymous author who was almost certainly Johann Job proposed the establishment of a St. George's house press on the model of the Halle Orphanage Press.[60] While this suggestion did not reach fruition, another major project shaped by the quintessentially Pietist combination of edification, print, and profit did. In 1721,

---

55 Grünberg (1893), 224 ff.

56 See Sträter (2004).

57 SAL, Stift IV.28., *Armen-Anstalten zu Franckfurth am Mayn, Weimar, Berlin* (c. 1700).

58 SAL, St. George *Rechnungen,* 1704–1740 (no loc.) & SAL, Stift III.A.16., *Acta, Das Hospital St. Georgen und Das demselben incorporirte Zucht und Waysen Hauss alhier betr.*, vol. I, 1717 ff. (hereafter: *Hospital St. Georgen*), 16 July 1706, 23–32, 28^{v}–29; prayers: 1703 & 1712 *Rechnungen.*

59 Bernd (1738), 109, 125, 216.

60 *Project wegen Anlegung eines Buchhandels bey dem Zucht-u. Waisenhause*, n.d. (between documents dated 1717 & 1718); *Hospital St. Georgen*, 48–55. The handwriting is

4600 copies of a hymnal were ordered and, judging from the variety of types of paper and bindings used, sold to a diverse public. Postage expenses from Halle and a payment to a Halle bookbinder indicate that this may have been the famous Halle hymnal edited by Freylinghausen. Outlays for 'Halle hymnals' in 1714 and 1720, and for 'Halle Bibles' and 'Halle New Testaments' from 1723 onward demonstrate some support by the house for Halle style.[61] Or the house may have commissioned a Halle press to print the Dresden hymnal, the one most commonly used in Leipzig; Leipzig publishers often sent works to Halle to be printed. In any case, the project was a success, with the copies selling briskly over the next several years. In 1729 a run of 3000 copies of a 'new' hymnal was ordered, and it also sold well. This could have been the Leipzig hymnal published that year, or a new edition of Freylinghausen's. (Note that Johann Job was the author of nine hymn texts in the 1729 Leipzig hymnal, although this was not a 'Pietist' hymnal).[62]

Councilors also placed a new emphasis on the poor and weak in public services by introducing collection bags (*Klingelbeutel*). These had been used for much of the 17th century in some areas, but not in Leipzig. In introducing them between 1708 and 1716, councilors switched from the relatively unobtrusive practice of collecting alms in boxes placed at church doors to the highly visible, if not disruptive, one of 'bell men' (*Klingel Männer*) passing around collection bags with bells on them during the sermon.[63] Collection bags were first introduced in the main center of poverty, the St. George's chapel, in 1706, and in St. Peter's by 1712.[64] Not surprisingly, Johann Job co-authored a proposal in 1713 to introduce collection bags in the main churches.[65] Councilors had already received permission from Dresden in 1708 to do so, but they did only in 1716.[66]

There were broader contexts for councilors' engagement with poor care. One was traditional, pragmatic considerations. For example, councilors shifted to collection bags because they were concerned about a decline in revenues from the alms boxes. In 1708 they calculated how many 'souls' attended Sunday services, compiled the records of contributions to the alms boxes in all churches during the preceding ten years, and estimated how much congregants would contribute on average. The time

---

identical to that of another document in this file (156–159v) signed by Job, and to that of Job's letters to Francke.

61 St. George house *Rechnungen*, Rubric *Ausgaben in Gemein*, 1714, 1720, 1721, 1724, 1726, 1728, 1729, 1732–36, 1739, 1740.

62 Stiller (1984), 37–38; Christian Gottlieb Jöcher and Johann Christoph Adelung, eds (1787), *Allgemeines Gelehrten-Lexicon, Fortsetzung*, vol. II (Leipzig: Gleditsch), 2288–2289.

63 SAL, Stift. VII. B. 32, *Acta, Die Einführung des Klingelbeutels in hiesigen Stadt Kirchen ... betr.*, 1708 (hereafter: *Klingelbeutel*). Clerics supported the introduction. 'Bell men:' 1712–13 New Church *Rechnung*.

64 *Peterskirche*, 97.

65 *Klingelbeutel*, memorial of 2 November 1713, 26–29v.

66 Ibid., 26 ff., 38 ff.

of the sermon was chosen because the most people were present then.[67] Councilors also suggested that the collection bag be used in weeks when many people took communion, because 'the communicants tend to show their love toward the poor at that time.'[68]

Charitable efforts were even a feature of gatherings of a society known as *Die Vertraute* ('The Trusted'), founded in 1680 by leading merchants, most of whom were also councilors. The directors of St. George's while it was being expanded, Georg Bose and Johann Ernst Kregel, were members. A poor box was passed during festive meals, and beginning in 1695 the proceeds were invested yearly in letters of exchange. The society's first charitable donation was 200 thaler toward the construction of St. George's. Further occasional gifts were distributed to individual poor families and the city's alms office.[69]

Similarly, the association of poverty, literacy, and religion that we saw for orphans applied to other poor students as well, and dated to the 16th century. Students at the school of St. Thomas's had long been the recipients of extensive charity from Leipzig burghers, including meals and books. To earn their keep, they sang not only in the churches but also at funeral processions and for festivities in the homes of burghers. They were also put to work by burghers in various jobs, including scribes and fruit pickers.[70]

An even broader context, both for councilors and for Francke's institutions, was that poverty increased at the same time that the authorities had increased means with which to enclose the poor. In Leipzig, laborers at the fairs often found no regular work during the rest of the year. They swelled the ranks of marginal artisans and people from outside Leipzig who came to the city seeking work, alms, food, and lodging. Overtaxation and wars brought on by August the Strong's engagement in Poland contributed to social displacement.[71] From the 1720s onward, councilors and staff at St. George's repeatedly mentioned the rising tide of beggars.

Musicians and music patronage

The renovation projects led to an expansion of Leipzig's music hierarchy. As we have seen, the cantor, accompanied by an organist, instrumentalists, and the 'first' and best choir of the St. Thomas's school performed on alternating Sundays in St. Thomas's and St. Nicholas's.[72] The second choir performed less challenging motets and chorales in the other main church, along with an organist and, sometimes,

---

67 Ibid., 3–16.

68 Ibid., 4.

69 Herbert Helbig (1980), *Die Vertrauten 1680–1980. Eine Vereinigung Leipziger Kaufleute* (Stuttgart: Hiersemann), esp. 27–31.

70 Otto Kaemmel (1909), *Geschichte des Leipziger Schulwesens* (Leipzig: Teubner), 79 ff.

71 Bräuer (1994) and idem, ed. and intro. (1996).

72 Stiller (1984), 75 ff.

instrumentalists. The third choir performed in the New Church, where concerted music, including a cantata, was performed on holidays and during the fairs. The fourth and least able choir sang in St. Peter's, mostly chorales, and led congregants in the singing of hymns. J.S. Bach wrote somewhat uncharitably in his 1730 *Entwurff* that this choir was 'the residue, namely those who do not understand music and can only just barely sing a chorale.'[73] Music at St. George's, sung without the benefit of any student choir or organ, was even more plain. Burghers who attended services in St. George's and St. Peter's thus deliberately sought out a simple style. We will see that the original pewholders in the New Church, too, were not drawn by elaborate music. In fact, some may have been attracted by its simplicity. This may be why, as we saw in the previous chapter, at least six Leipzig Pietist families were among the first group of pewholders.

In contrast to the simple liturgies at St. Peter's and St. George's, music at the University Church and the New Church was festive and elaborate. Music at the University Church was partially incorporated into the urban hierarchy. Until 1710 the cantors directed music at quarterly academic services and some other occasions. From 1710 until he left in 1711, the University employed Johann Friedrich Fasch, later a well-known composer, and the collegium he had founded. Johann Kuhnau directed all services from 1711 until his death in 1722. Then, however, the University again appointed the collegium, now led by Johann Gottlieb Görner, to lead public services on holidays and during fairs, and this arrangement continued during Bach's entire tenure. Bach directed only the 'old,' academic services. The author of a 1725 Leipzig guide book wrote that the 'incomparable' music of the students 'under a great master's direction ... causes amazement on the part of great masters who come from far-away lands' on holidays and during fairs, while 'the famous Herr Bach' directed music for academic services.[74] Ironically given his unsuccessful attempts to gain control over public services, Bach had made his first visit to Leipzig in 1717, when he inspected the extensively restored and expanded organ, one of the finest in Germany.[75]

Music and musicans in the New Church had an even greater impact, despite their relatively low place in the urban hierarchy. They did not do so because of a planned approach by the council. Councilors provided an essential start for the music by building a fine organ, generously funding music on occasion, especially from the 1720s, and giving early support to Georg Philipp Telemann. However, in contrast to their hands-on approach to the construction project, they mostly were not vigorous proponents of music at the New Church. Rather, the deciding factors were cantor Johann Kuhnau's ill health, the presence of eager student musicians, and the brief support of a powerful mayor who favored modern church music. Leadership came from the music directors and musicians at the New Church, who had a shrewd sense

---

73 *NBR*, 145–161; 146.

74 Iccander (1725), 47–51; quote: 48.

75 Wolff (2000), 184, 187, 311 ff.; Iccander (1725), 50.

of what could be accomplished and what would appeal to the city's residents and visitors.

Music at the New Church was minimal in the first five years after it opened. Though we have few details on it, it probably consisted of no more than the basic liturgy, including hymns.[76] A teacher at the school of St. Nicholas's, Christian Augst [*sic*], played a harpsichord donated by Director Georg Winckler, and led a St. Thomas's student choir. In addition, Leipzig organ builder Christoph Donath lent the church a small positive (an organ without pedals) which was in use by the inaugural service in September 1699.[77] Performances on holidays were probably more festive.

Councilors showed real interest in promoting more elaborate music at the New Church at only one point, but the timing proved crucial for later developments. The completion of a large organ by Donath in 1704 provided the impetus for a major expansion of music. City councilors had begun discussing building an organ in early 1702, and signed a contract with Donath in Summer 1703.[78] Augst as well as Georg Philipp Telemann applied for the position of organist and music director. In council meetings, leading councilors expressed their support for Telemann as a good composer, and their interest in appointing a competent and well-known musician.[79] Mayor Francis Conrad Romanus was Telemann's main supporter. He may well have encouraged Telemann to apply, and may also have pushed along the construction of the organ. Romanus's earlier, 1701, commissioning of Telemann to compose and perform a cantata every two weeks in St. Thomas's had given him valuable experience as a church musician, which would have helped him as he applied to the New Church.[80] In contrast, Director Winckler would have actually initially preferred to retain Augst because he had already served for five years, but deferred to the majority, who argued that Augst was not a competent organist.

When the council deliberated in Summer 1705 about replacing Telemann after he left for an appointment in Sorau, we again find relatively little interest in music. Mayor Romanus had been imprisoned earlier that year, removing the council's major supporter of innovative music. Councilors concurred that ideally, cantor Johann Kuhnau would become director, but he was ill and was not able to control the students. Director Winckler went as far as to state that 'he would agree to anything, and has no interest' in the matter. Similarly lackadaisical discussions were held in 1715 and in 1720, when the office became vacant again.[81]

Still, on each occasion councilors voted to fill the position with another student leader of the New Church collegium, and in doing so they gradually expanded the

---

76 Glöckner (1990), 14 ff.

77 *Hauptbuch,* 6; Glöckner (1990), 16.

78 *Hauptbuch,* 9^{v}; Glöckner (1990), 18 ff.

79 Reprinted in Glöckner (1990), 146–148.

80 Ulrich Siegele (1997), 'Bach and the domestic politics of Electoral Saxony,' in John Butt, ed., *The Cambridge Companion to Bach* (New York: Cambridge University Press), 17–34; 32–33.

81 Glöckner (1990), 150–151.

music program. What motivated them to choose as they did? Positive reception of the music performed in the New Church, and the desire to continue to impress residents and visitors to the fairs, probably influenced some councilors, although they did not record this. Since spending as little money as possible was always among their prime considerations, it is most likely that councilors appreciated that the existing arrangement was convenient and relatively cheap. New Church music directors received fifty thaler a year, much less than a regular full-time appointment (Gerlach received a raise to one hundred thaler in 1730).[82] As Andreas Glöckner posits, the directors and other musicians probably gained most of their income from concerts with the collegium, from the Opera, and from other engagements in new musical venues.[83]

Even with those added sources of revenue, the student singers and instrumentalists probably earned only enough to supplement their budgets for room, board, clothing and entertainment. This would have been seen as acceptable at the time, when young men in junior, apprentice, or substitute positions routinely earned very little. What they gained was experience and connections. Additionally, one gets the clear sense that the students in the New Church collegium were driven by an excitement about the musical innovations that they were introducing, and encouraged by camraderie of the ensemble.

Collegia musica had existed at the University throughout the 17th century. Students had also long performed at occasions honoring visiting rulers and other dignitaries.[84] However, their music was also often associated with unruliness. For example, while coffee houses would eventually come to be seen as respectable places, in 1701 councilors characterized them, along with taverns, as prime sites for prostitutes to 'establish' themselves during fairs.[85] As late as 1716 the Elector, responding to councilors' suggestions, forbade the establishment of any new coffee houses, and again called for their regulation.[86] Councilor Adrian Steger called for Telemann to desist from his *agiren* at the Opera upon his appointment at the New Church.[87] And Cantor Kuhnau saw the students as a major threat to his ability to lead music in the city. In 1709 and 1720 he complained that students who performed with him at the main churches abandoned him to play at the New Church on holidays and during the fairs; he also complained of the 'operatic' nature of music at the New Church.[88] Still, councilors obviously valued the student contributions, as did residents and visitors. By 1717 the New Church collegium was performing twice a week at a chocolatier's; the collegium founded by Fasch also performed twice a week

82 Ibid., 154.

83 Ibid., passim.

84 Wolff (2000), 351.

85 To August, 12 November 1701. *Zucht- Armen- und Waisen-Haus*, 9–10v.

86 Johann Christian Lünig, ed. (1724), *Codex Augusteus, oder Neuvermehrtes Corpus Juris Saxonici* ... (Leipzig: Gleditsch), vol. I, 1857–1860.

87 Council meeting, 18 August 1704. Glöckner (1990), 146–148; 147–148.

88 Glöckner (1990), 72, 81–83.

by 1720. Over the years, both had engagements at a number of establishments.[89] And at the Opera, directed by the New Church collegium leaders until its demise in 1720, most musicians were also students.

Let us now examine the musicians themselves more closely. The leaders of the collegium resembled other musical students. They arrived (like their non-musical peers) at the age of twenty or younger and stayed on for several years. Most were law students, and came from small towns and villages in Saxony and Thuringia. Many arrived at the University already able to sing, play an instrument and compose at a high level. They developed their talents further by playing music with fellow students, establishing personal and professional relationships that they maintained throughout their lives. Many went on to become prominent church and court musicians.

Following these patterns, Telemann arrived in Leipzig in 1701 to study law at the age of twenty. He masterfully rode the wave of opportunities presented by the opening of new venues in the city. His impact was immediate and extensive, especially considering his short stay of only four years in the city. He soon began performing at, and composing for, the Opera, and founded the collegium musicum which was soon to be associated with the New Church. Telemann's influence in Leipzig continued long after he left. He was the council's first choice to replace Kuhnau as cantor. Several book dealers in Leipzig sold his cantata cycles and other works.[90] Telemann's setting of Hamburg senator/poet Brockes's passion was performed in the New Church in either 1717 or 1718.[91] Other works by Telemann were also performed in the New Church under his successors,[92] and probably at the main churches under Bach's direction.[93] His operas were performed at the Leipzig Opera.[94]

Other musicians at the New Church resembled Telemann in many ways. Andreas Glöckner has reconstructed their identities and the network they formed. Mostly law students, they were either active in or led the Opera until it closed in 1720, as well as leading the collegium. Melchior Hoffmann, who replaced Telemann in 1705, probably at the age of twenty-six, and led the collegium until 1715, was a law student born near Dresden. He had become a member of the collegium after his arrival in 1702, assisting Telemann and serving as a copyist.[95] Later leaders included Johann Gottfried Vogler (director from 1716 to 1720), Georg Balthasar Schott (1720 to 1729), and Carl Gotthelf Gerlach (1729 to 1761). Among other collegium members, Johann David Heinichen and Johann Georg Pisendel stand out. Heinichen,

89 Ibid., 23, 79–80, 86.

90 Georg Philipp Telemann (1972), *Briefwechsel*, Hans Grosse & Hans Rudolf Jung, eds (Leipzig: VEB Deutscher Verlag für Musik), 307 ff.

91 Glöckner (1990), 79.

92 Ibid., 129–131.

93 Steffen Voss (2005), 'Did Bach Perform Sacred Music by Johann Mattheson in Leipzig?,' *Bach Notes*, 3, 1–5; 1.

94 Scheibel (1721), *Zufällige Gedancken von der Kirchen-Music, Wie Sie heutiges Tages beschaffen ist* (Frankfurt & Leipzig: self-published, R [2002] Stuttgart: Cornetto), 35–36.

95 Glöckner (1990), 39–40.

later a prominent violinist at the Brandenburg-Prussian court, became a student at St. Thomas's in 1696 and a law student at the University in 1702.[96] Pisendel, later also a well-regarded instrumentalist, arrived a few years later, in 1709, giving a polished performance of a violin concerto by Torelli the first time he played with the group.[97]

The New Church musicians stayed in touch even after they left Leipzig, forming an active and supportive network. Telemann, for example, corresponded into the 1750s with Pisendel, who referred to him affectionately as 'my dearly beloved Sir Brother.'[98] Telemann's cultivation of this network helps account for the fame of his music, and for its performance and the sale of printed versions in Leipzig and elsewhere. It is no exaggeration to speak of Leipzig in the early decades of the 18th century as an incubator of the galant style.

To the picture developed by Glöckner we can add with probability, as a guest, the young George Frederick Handel. Handel, born in nearby Halle in 1685, attended gymnasium there, and gained early musical experience before moving to Hamburg in 1703. Telemann was to write in an autobiography of the regular communication the two had, and to the 'frequent visits we made to each other,' most likely between 1701 and 1703, when Telemann had arrived in Leipzig and Handel had not yet left central Germany.[99] Music in Leipzig, notably the Opera, would have been attractive to Handel, and Telemann may well have invited the young Handel to play.

We have little specific information on how congregants in the New Church heard the music at the church; but there are some clues. Since concerted music was performed there less often than in the main churches, listeners were probably more attentive. Contemporaries noted the unusually large instrumental ensemble.[100] The fact that the audience was more female than in the main churches may have had an impact, although what type is unclear. If congregants sang cantata and passion chorales, the chorales would have been more dominated by female voices than in the main churches, as hymns certainly were. Some congregants would have known the students from their performances in coffee houses, at the Opera, pleasure gardens, and ceremonies to honor visitors. Some would also have known them as student roomers, boarders, and tutors.

The music performed in the New Church has been partially reconstructed by Glöckner, although the picture is far from complete. Surviving manuscripts and descriptions indicate that through the 1740s, New Church music was stylistically at the forefront of new music and that it appealed to listeners. Into the 1720s, this usually meant influence from Italian opera. It also seems that composers made the

---

96 Ibid., 38.

97 Ibid., 73.

98 Telemann (1972), 347 ff.

99 John Butt (1997), 'Germany – Education and Apprenticeship,' in Donald Burrows, ed., *The Cambridge Companion to Handel* (New York: Cambridge University Press), 11–23; 22.

100 Andreas Glöckner (1990), *Die Musikpflege an der Leipziger Neukirche zur Zeit Johann Sebastian Bachs*, = *BzBf*, 8, 16, 71–72.

cantatas as accessible as possible to congregants; this included using chorales in many. Of Hoffmann's nine cantatas for which texts survive, four include chorales. By the time of Gerlach, the majority did: twenty-four of the thirty-one cantatas in his music library for which texts survive include at least one chorale.[101] From around 1730, cantatas performed at the New Church tended to become simpler, and both individual arias and whole cantatas were noticably shorter than those of Bach.[102] They emphatically represented modern cantata style, and would not have been attacked for being out-of-date, over-complex, and inaccessible, as Bach's were by his former student Johann Adolph Scheibe in 1737.[103]

An important innovation of the New Church musicians was to introduce the concerted, figural passion into Leipzig's musical life. Passions were especially popular with congregants, in Hamburg and Frankfurt as well as in Leipzig. These were very unusual performances for contemporaries, and they made a strong impression. Performed at the end of Lent at Maundy Thursday or Good Friday vespers services, a time when organs were shuttered and cantatas not performed, they featured large instrumental ensembles and style strongly influenced by opera. They were also much longer than ordinary cantatas. Not surprisingly, contemporaries offered vivid descriptions of them. Scheibel, as we saw in Chapter Five, raved about congregants' engagement with the first passion performance in a town that was in all likelihood Leipzig. The Pietist Christian Gerber, in an often-quoted passage that probably described the same performance, claimed that many congregants were dismayed at the operatic music; but in doing so he, like Scheibel, documented the deep impression that the occasion made.[104] Similarly, in his 1740 autobiography, Telemann described the context of the first performance of his Brockes Passion in Frankfurt in more detail than all but two other performances of his works.[105]

In a striking combination of music, venue, and purpose, Frankfurt councilors and Hamburg senators organized performances of these tales of sin and suffering, often in small churches linked to poor care, to raise money for the poor. The first performance of Telemann's Brockes Passion in Frankfurt in 1716 was actually a benefit for the Frankfurt combined poor house, orphanage, and workhouse. Councilors required congregants to carry the libretto for the passion into the service; proceeds from libretto sales went to the house.[106] No similar performances are known for Leipzig.

Regardless of any differences in style, Bach's relations to music and musicians at the New Church were extensive, and they were positive. He carried the newly-

---

101 Glöckner (1990), 46 ff, 97 ff.; Melvin P. Unger, ed., (1996), *Handbook to Bach's Sacred Cantatas* (Lanham, MD: Scarecrow), 51–54; 250–254.

102 Glöckner (1990), 92; 131 ff.

103 *NBR*, 337 ff.

104 Scheibel (1721), 30; Gerber (1732), 283–284.

105 Carsten Lange (2000), 'Zur Aufführung von Telemanns Brockes-Passionsoratorium in Frankfurt am Main,' in Peter Cahn, ed., *Telemann in Frankfurt. Bericht über das Symposium Frankfurt am Main, 26./27. April 1996* (New York: Schott), 142–162; 146 ff.

106 Lange (2000), 147.

introduced custom of passion performances to a high point. It is possible that his development of the cantata format that featured concluding and/or introductory chorales was influenced by New Church custom. Bach wrote positively about New Church music director Schott, and allowed him to serve as a substitute when he travelled out of town.[107] He recommended Gerlach, with whom he performed many times, for the position of New Church music director in 1729.[108] Several of Bach's works were performed at the New Church.[109] Not least, Bach was the leader of the New Church collegium musicum in its secular performances from 1729 to around 1741, with a break from 1737 to 1739, and he probably also led it occasionally before 1729.[110] It is possible that having access to the collegium inspired Bach's shift to composing more secular music and fewer cantatas after 1729. Further, Bach and Telemann knew each other well. The two had met before 1714, when Telemann became C.P.E. Bach's godfather. They met numerous times afterward, and mutually influenced each other's musical style. Bach had visited Hamburg in 1720, and was thus familiar with Telemann's working environment. He probably performed cantatas by Telemann in Leipzig.[111]

* * *

As they moved through a time of dramatic social and economic change, Leipzig burghers, councilors, and musicians continued to work within traditional institutional and political frameworks, and to rely on well-established forms of financial support by burghers and the council. But they invested those frameworks with new meaning, and musicians in particular began to move outside them as well. In the process, some actors in the religious arena gained power, while others lost ground. The ways in which they did confirm Bourdieu's theses that on the whole, a group's status outside a field is reflected in its status within the field, and that relations are negotiated through specific practices. Councilors, backed by their growing economic and political clout, expanded their power in public religious life. Clerics lost power relative to councilors, but gained in that the size of their estate grew. Burghers built on the prosperity generated by the trade fairs, and on the traditional association between property holding and political voice. They expanded their presence in the religious arena by funding thousands of new pews. Among burghers, members of the elites gained most status by constructing *Capellen*, but artisans also gained through their strong presence in the new churches. Sub-burghers were further marginalized. The consistories continued to serve as conduits of information and regulation, but assessors' interest in preserving tradition lost out to councilors' drive to innovate. Even the court at Dresden ultimately accepted councilors' initiatives. Finally, in this

---

107 Glöckner (1990), 84.
108 Ibid., 84, 88–89.
109 Ibid., 106–107.
110 Ibid., 84–85, 89–90; Wolff (2000), 351–361.
111 Voss (2005), 1.

context of expanding public religious life, young musicians seized new opportunities. Effectively addressing the urban population in a variety of venues, they were able to remake musical life in the city.

In preceding chapters we saw Pietists and non-Pietists engaged in intense public and private conflict. However, when one examines the evolution of practices such as alms collection and poor care, it becomes clear that the two were often compatible. Both Halle Pietists and Leipzig councilors added further emphasis to issues and institutions relating to the poor. New projects were a response to new social realities as they intersected with the council's mandate, institutional interests, and financial power. On these issues, councilors' actions speak for their interest in their collective power relative to other authorities and the unpropertied, and to their goal of raising money, rather than to an interest in religious disputes.

Conclusion

Having traced the evolution of public religious culture in Leipzig in the last chapter, it is time to locate that change in a broader cultural context. Between roughly 1680 and 1750, the secular and sacred facets of Baroque style flourished in tandem: councilors and burghers invested in coffee houses, colonial goods, and the Opera as well as in churches. Secular style had a huge influence on religious music. The traditional financial security provided by the Leipzig cantorate, combined with newer performance opportunities in the New Church and University Church, allowed Bach and student musicians to innovate in secular venues. It is actually difficult to distinguish between 'tradition' and 'innovation': in renovating churches, city councilors continued in a long-standing mercantile and entrepreneurial approach to urban patronage; and well-established practices of outdoor and indoor student music-making served as the basis for performances in coffee houses and elsewhere.

Pietists meshed uneasily with this Baroque culture. However, they also helped develop a richer and more multi-faceted urban life after 1680, establishing collegia and then a shadowy network. There were even parallels between Pietists and advocates of high Baroque style. When they made their early impact between the 1680s and the 1710s, many of the leaders of both movements were young, in their late teens and early to mid-twenties. Their activities had a rebellious flavor and were met with resistance by more established figures such as the Leipzig clergy and Cantor Kuhnau. By the 1720s, both Halle Pietists and the representatives of high Baroque or galant style had themselves become part of a more sedate establishment. In another parallel, interactions between students and well-informed, engaged inhabitants were key to the emergence of both groups.

The Enlightenment is a topic beyond the scope of this book; but Leipzig was a major center of the Enlightenment, and its representatives have appeared on numerous occasions. As we have seen, religious issues were central to the early Enlightenment. Further, the everyday practices of the Baroque religious arena were an essential part of the Enlighteners' world. Individual figures took a variety of positions. Publishers Thomas Fritsch and the Gleditsch brothers were Pietists. Luise Adelgunde Gottsched, in contrast, lampooned Pietists. Christian Thomasius attacked the Orthodox ecclesiastical system, and worked closely with Francke for several years before distancing himself from him. Johann Christoph Gottsched criticized some of the social features of Baroque religious life, but did not launch a general campaign against them.

How did musicians interact with Enlighteners and Enlightenment thought? J.S. Bach and his family were part of the sociability of Enlightenment Leipzig, owning tea and coffee services, performing at the coffee houses, and cultivating friendships with members of the Bose family and others. The 'progressive' Bach also appears in some features of his published instrumental work of the 1720s and 1730s, such as his emphasis on the use of French and Italian style, and in his definition of pieces as *galanterien*.[1] In addition, Bach set texts of Johann Christoph Gottsched as well as of Mariane von Ziegler, a prominent Leipzig saloniere and writer (and daughter of onetime mayor Francis Conrad Romanus). However, there were limits to Bach's embrace of Enlightened style. For example, he worked much more extensively with figures whose style is best described as Baroque, including Erdmann Neumeister and Saxon postmaster Christian Friedrich Henrici (Picander), who lived in Leipzig. Picander did not share Gottsched's Enlightened literary goals, and even conducted a literary feud with Gottsched's circle.[2] Further, from 1741 Bach did not regularly lead the collegium. While he was still actively engaged in a variety of projects, his compositions increasingly emphasized traditional counterpoint, the form in which his mastery was most widely recognized.[3]

Telemann engaged the Enlightenment much more actively. His emphasis on the primacy and clarity of the melodic line and on accessibility, for example, which appeared in the prefaces of his works and elsewhere, corresponded to Enlightenment literary models.[4] Telemann even contributed to the important Enlightenment collection *Poesie der Niedersachsen*,[5] and set texts by Enlighteners such as Barthold Heinrich Brockes and Friedrich Gottlieb Klopstock. Mattheson's *Musical Patriot* of 1728 was titled with reference to the moral weekly *The Patriot*, and Mattheson took up issues of the Enlightenment in other writings as well.

How did Baroque style, structures and practices fare in the course of the 18th century? The style came in for increased criticism from the 1730s onward. Scheibe's famous critique of Bach's church music style was not shared by all contemporaries, but it was an opinion which increasingly gained ground. Traditional practices that were not specifically Baroque were also attacked. Adam Bernd, for example, lamented that the authorities were gradually phasing out the strewing of churches with flowers and grass at Pentecost, the firing of guns at midnight on holidays, and other customs.[6] However, in Leipzig, as in many other towns, numerous usages viewed with contempt by Enlighteners were altered only in the 1780s, or even later. A reform-minded Leipzig Superintendent, supported by an activist mayor, argued

1 *NBR*, 129–130, 154, 167–168.

2 Sabine Ehrmann (1991), 'Johann Sebastian Bachs Leipziger Textdichterin Christiane Mariane von Ziegler,' *BzBf*, 9/10, 261–268.

3 See Christoph Wolff (2000), *Johann Sebastian Bach: The Learned Musician* (New York: Norton), 417 ff.

4 See Werner Rackwitz and Eitelfriedrich Thom, ed. (1980), *Singen ist das Fundament/ Zur Musik in allen Dingen. Eine Dokumentensammlung* (Leipzig: Reclam).

5 C.F. Weichmann (1721–1738), ed, *Poesie der Niedersachsen* (Hamburg: Kissner, R [1980] Munich: Kraus), vol. III, 284–288.

6 Adam Bernd (1738), *Eigene Lebens-Beschreibung* (Leipzig: Heinsius; R [1973], Munich: Winkler), 35–37.

in the 1780s that passing the collection bag during the sermon was an unseemly disturbance, and the council agreed to change the time to after the sermon.[7] Concerned to eliminate any appearance of Catholic ritual, reformers also abolished a custom dating to before the Reformation, of ringing the so-called 'transsubstantiation bell' at the (Lutheran) intoning of the sacramental words of communion.[8] St. Nicholas's was completely remodeled in the 1780s in Neoclassical style, and much of its Baroque decor was removed.[9]

Was Bach's occasional dissatisfaction with his position a sign of decline in urban musical life? Not necessarily: prominent cantorates remained sought-after during and even after Bach's lifetime. Telemann, for example, had obviously enjoyed the opportunities offered him in a large mercantile center during his student days. He went on to work in Frankfurt from 1712 to 1721 and in Hamburg from 1721 to his death in 1764. Along the way, he turned down generous offers by the court at Dresden in 1711 and by Duke Ernst August of Saxe-Weimar in 1717.[10] He developed his talents to most effect in Hamburg, becoming the most commercially successful German composer of his time by marketing his secular and sacred printed works to a broad range of amateurs, small-town cantors, and others. J.S. Bach's son Carl Philipp Emmanuel, frustrated by his own position at the court of Frederick the Great, applied for the position of Leipzig cantor twice, in 1750 and 1756. Rejected both times, he then successfully applied to the Hamburg position vacated by Telemann's death.[11]

However, the cachet of urban positions and the vitality of their audiences faded in C.P.E. Bach's lifetime. Shortly after C.P.E. Bach died, for example, Hamburg senators essentially dismantled the church music system that had been established in the 17th century.[12] In Leipzig, J.S. Bach's successors, while distinguished in their own right, were no longer as prominent as Schelle, Kuhnau, and Bach had been in their day. The new directions developed by the New Church musicians were more promising. In 1743 a concert society known as the *Grosses Concert*, which included New Church

---

7 SAL, Stift VII.B.32, *Acta, Die Einführung des Klingelbeutels in hiesigen Stadt Kirchen und dessen Wiederabschaffung betr.*, 1708, 85 ff.

8 Herbert Stiehl (1984), 'Das Innere der Thomaskirche zur Amtszeit Johann Sebastian Bachs,' = *BzBf*, 3, 36–38.

9 Gerhart Pasch (1989), '"Ein schönes Schauspielhaus!" Die klassizistische Umgestaltung der Nikolaikirche,' in Ernst Ullmann, ed., *'Die ganze Welt im kleinen ... ' Kunst und Kunstgeschichte in Leipzig* (Leipzig: Seemann), 155–171.

10 Wolff (2000), 188–179.

11 Stephen Clark (1984), 'The Occasional Choral Works of C.P.E. Bach,' (PhD thesis, Princeton University), 1 ff.

12 Reginald Sanders (2001), 'Carl Philipp Emanuel Bach's Ensemble for Liturgical Performances at the Hamburg Principal Churches,' in Hans Joachim Marx, ed., *Beiträge zur Musikgeschichte Hamburgs vom Mittelalter bis in die Neuzeit* (Frankfurt: Europäischer Verlag der Wissenschaften), 367–403; 391 ff.

musicians, began performing in private homes.[13] The next year the society rented a hall in the Three Swans Tavern which held between 200 and 400 people. In 1746, New Church music director Gerlach became first violinist and concertmaster of the society. The patronage environment and musical offerings of this ensemble, which would eventually evolve into the famed Gewandhaus Orchestra, gradually evolved away from Baroque patterns. Still, echoes of earlier patronage, audience behavior, and repertoire remained throughout the 18th century. Concerts were offered weekly during the winter and biweekly during the summer, with at least one extra concert per week during two of the fairs. A 1771 account mentioned that during Lent and Advent, secular music was replaced by *Concerts Spirituels*, especially oratorios. Also in 1771, a visitor described the audience's talking and other noise-making during performances. Amidst the growing popularity of the concerts and complaints about the poor condition of the tavern's hall, in 1780 mayor Müller (who was also supporting changes in religious life) and the city council offered the society one story in the Gewandhaus, or 'textile hall,' the trading floor of textile merchants during the fairs. The council also paid for the renovation of this new hall, which cost nearly 3600 thaler and was completed in 1781. The motto by Seneca which was painted in the hall, *Res severa est verum gaudium*, or 'True pleasure is a serious matter' (still the orchestra's motto today), indicated a new seriousness which the organizers hoped to bring to the endeavor.

[13] On the *Grosses Concert* and the development of the Gewandhaus Orchestra, see Andreas Glöckner (1990), *Die Musikpflege an der Leipziger Neukirche zur Zeit Johann Sebastian Bachs*, = *BzBf*, 8, 90 ff.; Rudolf Skoda (1986), *Das Gewandhaus Leipzig: Geschichte und Gegenwart* (Berlin: Ernst), 10–11; and, especially, Fritz Hennenberg (1984), *Das Leipziger Gewandhausorchester* (Leipzig: VEB Bibliographisches Institut Leipzig), 6–16.

Bibliography*

Archival Sources

Archiv der Franckeschen Stiftungen, Halle

Letters from about one hundred people written from Leipzig to August Hermann Francke; a few additional letters to other people in Halle.

Archiv der Nikolaikirche, Leipzig

Einnahm-und Auszgaben bey der Kirchen zu St. Nicolai. 1686–1728. Abt. III.532.

Schriftwechsel Kirchenstühle betr., 1701 ff. Abt. III.160.

Stadtarchiv Leipzig

Grundrisse der Nikolaikirche, 1750. Ratsrissarchiv, 246–249.

J.S. Riemer, *Continuatio annalium Lipsiensium Vogelii*, ms., 1714–1771.

Consistorialia, vol. X, Varia, 1619–1767. Tit. VII.B.11.

Protocoll In Versamlung aller 3 Räthe, 1682–1704. Tit. VIII.52.

Protocoll in den Drey Räthen, 1687–1709. Tit. VIII.41.

Protocoll in die Enge, 1694–1709. Tit. VIII.56.

Kirchen zu St. Nicolas Rechnung alhier zu Leipzigk, 1670–1730. no loc.

Ein Convolut mit 43 Consistorialabschieden, die Kirchenstühle und Kirchenbänke u. das Parochianenrecht in der Thomaskirche betr., 17. und anfang 18. Jh. Stift. IX.A.21.

Akta, einige Bänke in der Thomaskirche, welche den Studenten gehören sollen, betr., 1697–1708. Stift. IX.A.1.a.

Kirchen-Stühle, Capellen und Begräbnis-Stellen betr., vol. I, 1665–1712; vol. II, 1713–1766. Stift. X. 39a. & b.

*Published works that are cited in only one footnote generally do not appear here.

Commissions Acta Die Pietistischen Enthusiastischen u. Chiliastischen Schrifften betreffende, 1693–1694. Tit. XLVI.147.

Büchercensur-Acten, vol. I, 1600–1690; vol. II, 1691–1705; vol. III, 1705–1710. Tit. XVII.152.

Die Einführung des Klingelbeutels in hiesigen Stadt Kirchen und dessen Wiederabschaffung betr., 1708 ff. Stift. VII.B.32.

Kirchenstühle (St. Peter's). Stift. IX.D.14.

Rechnung der Neuen Kirchen in Leipzigk, 1701–1725. no loc.

Original der Subscriptionsliste zur Renovation der Neukirche, 1698. Stift. IX.C.15.

Hauptbuch der Neuen Kirche. no loc.

Das Frühbeichten in hiesigen Kirchen betr., 1672–1766. Stift. VII.B.18.

Acta, Die Privat-Communion in denen Kirchen vor denen Thoren alhier betr., 1736. Tit.VII.B.35.

Visitirung derer Schulen, ingl. Ermahnung vor der Beichte und absolution an diejenige welche zu communiciren sich vorgenommen betr., 1713. Tit. VII.B.34.

Acta, Das in der Peterskirche gebrauchte Gesangbuch betr., 1717–1718. Tit. VII. B.34.a.

Acta Die Peterskirche betr., vol. I, 1704 ff. Tit. VII.B.110.

Die Privat-Communion in denen Kirchen vor denen Thoren alhier betr., 1736. Tit. VII.B.35.

Das Beichte sizen und Communiciren in der St. Johannis Kirchen alhier betreffend, 1670. Tit. VII.B.61.

Specificatio der hier wohnhaften Catholischen und Reformirten, 1732. Tit.VII. B.126.

Generalia in Kirchen-Stuhl-Sachen betr., 1741. Stift.X.41.

Generalia und Consistorial-Verordnungen wegen Administration derer Piarum causarum, 1712 ff. Tit. VII.B.33.

Anrichtung einer Kirche im neuen Armen-und Waisenhause betr., 1705. Tit. VII. B.49.

Kirche zu St. Nicolai Verordnungen und Nachrichtungen ... 1740–1783. Stift. IX.B.4.

Rechnung der Kirchen zu St. Petri, 1712. no loc.

Rechnung des Hospitals St. Georgen/Des St. Georgen-Hauses vor Leipzig, 1671–1740. no loc.

Rechnung Über Den geführten Bau des von E. Edl. Hochw. Rathe Dem Hospital zu St. Georgen Zu einem Zuchthause ..., 1700–1704. no loc.

Rechnung über die bey Einführung von Superintendenten abgehaltene Schmäuse 1662–1670. Stift.IX.A.39.

Acta, Ein Scriptum [Das Lustspiel der Frau Gottschedin]: Die Pietisterey im Fischbein-Rocke betr., 1736. Tit.XLVI.187.

Varia, die Beamten des Georgenhauses betr., 1671–1779. Stift. III.A.110.

Varia, die Nicolaikirche betr., 1668–1841. Stift. IX.B.27.

Acta, Die Verzeichnisse der in Bürger-Häusern wohnenden Herren Studiosorum betr., 1731 ff. Stift. VII.C.151.

Das Zucht-Armen-und Waisen-Haus betr., Ergangen vor dem Rathe der Stadt Leipzig, 1670–1717. Stift. III.A.14.

Acta, Das Hospital St. Georgen und Das demselben incorporirte Zucht und Waysen Hauss alhier betr., vol. I, 1717 ff. Stift. III.A.16.

Sächsisches Hauptstaatsarchiv Dresden

Bestellung des Churfürstl. Sächßisch. Ober-Consistorii belangend, 1587–1704 (also: *Ober-Consistorium, Bestallungen*). Loc. 7428.

Die Ersetzung Der ordinar u. extraordinar theol. u. polit. Raths-Stellen beym Oberconsistorio, 1625–1743. Loc. 1874.

Ersetzung derer Ober-und Hoff-Prediger-Stellen, 1659–1696. Loc. 1706–1737. Loc. 4687.

—, [vol. II], 1706–1737.

Allerhand Schreiben an den Herrn Geheimden Rath, Gottfried Herrmannen von Beichlingen, als Praesidenten des Ober Consistorii zu Dreßden. von M. Anton Simon, 1699. Loc. 8575.

Instructions et Ordres du Roy pour le Comte de Lagnasco, ses Relations et Lettres au Roi et a ses Ministres sur ses negociations a la Cour de Rome ... 1724–1726. Loc. 3305.

Bestellung derer Superintendenten-Stellen oder Inspectionen in denen Churf. Sächß. Landen, vol. II, 1681–1704; vol. III, 1705–1730. Loc. 7430.

Die Bestellung der Herren Assessoren des Consistorii zu Leipzig betr. (Ergang. vor d. Consistorio zu Leipzig), vol. I, 1590–1708; vol. II, 1708–1731. Loc. 10737.

Das Consistorium zu Leipzig betr., 1709 ff. *ingleichen Bestellung eines directoris bey selbigem*, 1746–1762. Loc. 554.

Die Wieder Ersezung der Superintendentur zu Leipzig mit Dr. Salomon Deylingen, u. v. dem Rathe daselbst angemasste extension ihres Juris vocandi auf das Superintendenten Amt betr. Item Die Bestellung eines besondern Informatoris derer Gefangenen betr., 1720, vol. I, 1720–1815. Loc. 4573.

Assessuren des Consistorii zu Leipzig betr., vol. I. *Ergangen im Ober-Consistorio*, 1618–1731. Loc. 1916.

Advocaturen beym Consistorio zu Leipzig, 1707–1765. Loc. 4709.

Convolut Bosischer Schrifften u. Nachrichten den Statum publicum Ecclesiasticum et politicum betr. Von No. LXXV biß u. mit No. LXXX. Loc. 10299.

Ober Consistorial-Sachen. 1680–1690. Loc. 4560.
—, 1692–1695, 1699, 1701, 1702. Loc. 4564.
—, 1703, 1704–1705. Loc. 4565.
—, 1709–1710. Loc. 4568.
—, 1706, 1707–1708, 1713–1714. Loc. 4567.

Ober-Consistorial Berichte, 1702–1703. Loc. 4563.

Rescripte, Consistorium zu Leipzig, 1682–1692, 1693–1702, 1703–1711. Loc. 2061.
—, 1719–1722. Loc. 2062.

Rescripte, Universität Leipzig, 1682–1700. Loc. 2126.

Confirmationes derer Fundationem, Recessuum, Vergleiche, Bestallungen u. dergl. (Oberkonsistorium), vol. I, 1688–1689; vol. II, 1690–1692. Loc. 2013.
—, 1702–1704. Loc. 2015.

Verordnungs-Concepte des Ober-Consistoriums, 1699. Loc. 1563.
—, 1701. Loc. 1564.

Concept-Rescripte des Ober-Consistoriums, 1686–1705. Loc. 2079.

Die auf denen Churfürstl. Sächsischen Land-u. Ausschuß-Tagen verabhandeten Religions-u. Kirchen-Sachen, u. dieserhalb ertheilte Landesherrl. Assecurationes, 1592–1746. Loc. 10301.

Die Ausschreibung der allgemeinen Buß-Bet-u. Fasttage, vol. I, 1603–1719; vol. II, 1720–1750. Loc. 1887.

Die von dem Obern Consistorio projectirte neue Kirchen-Stuhl Ordnung betr., 1721. Loc. 4571.

Die Untersuchung des Leipziger Pietismi betr., 1690. Loc. 10330.

Churfürstliche Sächßische Commisions-Acta, Wegen unterschiedener Puncte, den sogenanten Pietismum und was dem anhängig betr., 1694. Loc. 10330.

Pietistica, oder Des Pietismi Halber von Dr. Spenern, Dr. Löschern, Dr. Wernsdorffen, u. Dr. Marpergern gewechselte Schrifften ao. 1691–1714 ... betr., 1690. Loc. 10329.

Den so genannten Pietismum *betr. 1690 sqq.* Loc. 10330.

Dr. Phil. Jacob Spener betr. 1686 sqq. Loc. 10330.

Acta, Den auff der Universitaet Leipzig abgeschafften Pietismum betreffend, 1690. Loc. 10330.

Fasciculus Allerley Irrgläubige, wie auch Die Pietisten u. Juden betr, 1638–1778. Tit. VII.B.131.

Die theologischen Streitigkeiten, wegen des Termini peremptorii betr., 1700. Loc. 1791.

Die zwischen denen Professoribus Theologiae zu Leipzig Dr. Rechenbergen und Dr. Ittigen entstandene Streitigkeiten über dem Termino Salutis peremptorio, 1700–1701. *Item Pietismum betr.* Loc. 10319.

Dr. Olearii Bericht von Dr. Carpzovii Programmate, darinnen Er Dr. Spenern angegrieffen, 1695. Loc. 1792.

Theol. Streitigkeiten auf den Univ. Leipzig u. Wittenberg, 1709 ff. Loc. 1792.

Die zwischen Dr. Jo. Oleario prof. Theol. zu Leipzig u. Dr. Valentin Ernst Löschern auch Dr. Gottlieb Wernsdorffen, beyden PP. Theol. zu Wittenberg entstandene Irrungen, den Pietismum betr., 1710 ff. *It. Der Theologischen Facultät auf der Universität Leipzig über den Superint. zu DD D. Valentin Ernst Löschern u. Dr. Gottlieb Wernsdorffen Prof. Theol. in Wittenberg geführte Beschwerde dass man sie in öffentl. Schrifften diffamirt*, 1714. Loc. 10330.

Confiscation unterschiedener Schrifften und Bücher, 1623–1713. Loc. 4600.

Die Einsendung derer confiscirten Bücher zum Geheimen Consilio betr., Ober-Consistorium, 1737. Loc. 10743.

Die confiscirung einiger Schrifften, Censur der Bücher und Vereydung der Buchdrücker betr., 1702–1714. Loc. 4600.

Die Bücher von der Censur bey der Theol. Facult. zu Leipzigk betr., vol. I, 1689–1691. Loc. 1791.

Bücher-Sachen mit Register, vol. I, 1699–1710; vol. II, 1711–1723. Loc. 10753.

Die von dem Rath zu Leipzig in dem neuangelegten sogenannten Armen-und Waysen-Hausse erbauete neue Capelle oder Kirch und darinnen angerichteten Gottes-Dienst ... betr., 1703–1706. Loc. 9882.

Die angeordnete Wochen Communion in den Kirchen zu Leipzig betr., 1694. Loc. 9882.

Was wegen des Beichtesizens ergangen, betr., 1711–1799, 1809–1815. Loc. 4571.

Die Kirchenbuße betr., 1689–1812. Loc. 4561.

Den Gottes Dienst in der Pauliner Kirche in Leipzig betr., 1702 ff. Loc. 6119.

Published Titles

Albrecht, Erdmann Hannibal (1799), *Sächsische evangelisch-luther'sche Kirchen- und Predigergeschichte von ihrem Ursprunge an bis auf gegenwärtige Zeiten*, vol. I, Diöces Leipzig, Leipzig: self-published.

Anon. (1667), *Fürstlich Sächsische abermals verbesserte Landes-Ordnung des durchläucht Hochgeb Fürsten u Herrn Hernns Ernsten, Hertzogen zu Sachsen, Jülich, Cleve u Bergk, Landgraffen in Thüringen …*, Gotha: Schall.

Anon. (Francke, August Hermann & Thomasius, Christian) (1692), *Gerichtliches Leipziger Protocoll in Sachen die Pietisten betreffend* (no place: no publisher), R (1981) in Peschke, Erhard, ed., *August Hermann Francke. Schriften und Predigten*, Berlin: de Gruyter.

Anon. (Carpzov, Johann Benedict?) (1693), *Ausführliche Beschreibung des Unfugs, Welchen die Pietisten ... gestifftet ...*, no place: no publisher (Leipzig: Lancke).

Anon. (1710), *Leipziger Kirchen-Staat, das ist Deutlicher Unterricht vom Gottes-Dienst in Leipzig*, Leipzig: Groschuff.

Anon. (1777), *Vollständiges Verzeichniß der Prediger in Leipzig, welche seit der Reformation des sel. Lutheri, nämlich von dem 1539 bis zu dem jetzigen 1777 Jahre zum Predigtamte berufen worden*, 3rd ed., Leipzig: Dürr.

Beachy, Robert (2005), *The Soul of Commerce: Credit, Property, and Politics in Leipzig, 1750–1840*, Boston: Brill.

Beer, Johann (1697), *Ursus vulpinatur, List wider List, oder musicalische Fuchs-Jagdt*, Weissenfels: self-published.

Benedict, Philip (2002), *Christ's Churches Purely Reformed. A Social History of Calvinism*, New Haven: Yale University Press.

Berg, Maxine & Eger, Elizabeth (2003), 'The Rise and Fall of the Luxury Debates,' in Berg, Maxine & Eger, Elizabeth, eds, *Luxury in the Eighteenth Century: Debates, Desires and Delectable Goods*, Houndmills: Palgrave, 7–25.

Berman, Harold J. (2003), *Law and Revolution*, vol. II, Cambridge: Harvard University Press.

Bernd, Adam (1738), *Eigene Lebens-Beschreibung*, Leipzig: Heinsius, R (1973), Munich: Winkler.

Bienert, Walther (1934), *Der Ausbruch der christlichen deutschen Neuzeit, dargestellt an Wissen und Glauben des Christian Thomasius*, Halle: Akademie.

Blanckmeister, Franz (1899), *Sächsische Kirchengeschichte*, Dresden: Sturm.

Blaschke, Karlheinz (1967), *Bevölkerungsgeschichte von Sachsen bis zur industriellen Revolution*, Weimar: Böhlau.

Bohse, August [Talander] (1692), *Der allzeitfertige Brieffs eller, Oder Ausführliche Anleitung, wie so wohl an hohe Standes-Personen, als an Cavalliere, Patronen, gute Freunde, Kauffleute und auch an Frauenzimmer, ein geschickter Brieff zu machen und zu beantworten. Alles mit gnugsamen* Dispositionen *und mehr als vierhundert ausgearbeiteten Brieffen, wie auch einen kurtzen Frantzösisch-Teutsch- und Italienischen Titular-Buch*, Frankfurt & Leipzig: Boetius.

Bollmann, Klaus (1963), 'Die Stellung des Inquisiten bei Carpzov. Eine Untersuchung über den gemeinen deutschen Strafprozess des 17. Jahrhunderts,' PhD thesis, University of Marburg.

Bourdieu, Pierre (1991), *Language and Symbolic Power*, trans. G. Raymond & M. Adamson, Cambridge: Polity.

—. (1987), 'Legitimation and Structural Interests in Weber' s Sociology of Religion,' in Lash, S. & Whimster, S., eds, *Max Weber, Rationality and Modernity*, Boston: Allen & Unwin, 119–136.

Bräuer, Helmut (1997), *Der Leipziger Rat und die Bettler. Quellen und Analysen zu Bettlern und Bettelwesen in der Messestadt bis ins 18. Jahrhundert*, Leipzig: Universitätsverlag.

—. (1994), 'Arme Leute in Sachsen im 18. Jahrhundert,' *Räume voll Leipzig. Arbeitsberichte des Stadtarchivs Leipzig*, 1, 72–87.

Brecht, Martin et al., eds (1993 ff.), *Geschichte des Pietismus*, Göttingen: Vandenhoeck & Ruprecht: Brecht, Martin, ed. (1993), vol. I, *Der Pietismus vom siebzehnten Jahrhundert*; — & Depperman, Klaus, eds (1995), vol. II, *Der Pietismus im achtzehnten Jahrhundert*; Lehmann, Hartmut, ed. (2004), vol. IV, *Glaubenswelt und Lebenswelten*.

—. (1993), 'Philipp Jakop Spener, sein Programm und dessen Auswirkungen,' in *GdP*, vol. I, 281–389.

—. (1993a), 'August Hermann Francke und der Hallische Pietismus,' in *GdP*, vol. I, 440–539.

Breuer, Dieter, ed. (1995), *Religion und Religiosität im Zeitalter des Barock*, Wiesbaden: Harrassowitz.

Brewer, John (1997), *The Pleasures of the Imagination. English Culture in the 18th Century*, New York: Farrar Strauss Giroux.

Bulisch, Jens (1997/1998), 'Justinus Töllners Weggang aus Panitzsch. Ein Beitrag zur Frühgeschichte des Pietismus in Sachsen,' *Herbergen der Christenheit*, 21/22, 69–86.

Bunners, Christian (2004), 'Musik,' in *GdP*, vol. IV, 430–455.

—. (2004), 'Gesangbuch,' in *GdP*, vol. IV, 121–142.

Butt, John (1997), 'Germany – Education and Apprenticeship,' in Burrows, Donald, ed., *The Cambridge Companion to Handel*, New York: Cambridge University Press, 11–23.

—, ed. (1997), *The Cambridge Companion to Bach*, New York: Cambridge University Press.

Carpzov, Benedict (1645 ff.), *Jurisprudentia Ecclesiastica seu Consistorialis Rerum & Quaestionum in Serenissimi ac Potentissimi Principis Electoris Saxon. ... Libri III*, Leipzig: Starck.

Chartier, Roger, ed. (1989), *The Culture of Print. Power and the Uses of Print in Early Modern Europe*, Cambridge: Polity.

—. (1989) 'Texts, Printings, Readings,' in Hunt, Lynn, ed., *The New Cultural History*, Berkeley: University of California Press, 154–175.

Cowan, Alexander (1998), *Urban Europe 1500–1700*, New York: Arnold.

Czok, Karl (1992), *Die Nikolaikirche Leipzig*, Leipzig: Edition Leipzig.

—. (1990), 'Leipzig nach dem "grossen Krieg" und im augusteischen Zeitalter (1648–1763),' in Sohl, Klaus, ed., *Neues Leipzigisches Geschichts-Buch*, Leipzig: Fachbuchverlag Leipzig, 100–131.

—, ed. (1989), *Geschichte Sachsens*, Weimar: Böhlau.

—, ed. (1987), *Wissenschafts- und Universitätsgeschichte in Sachsen im 18. und 19. Jahrhundert. Nationale und internationale Wechselwirkung und Ausstrahlung*, Berlin: Akademie.

David, Hans and Mendel, Arthur, eds (1998), *The New Bach Reader: A Life of Johann Sebastian Bach in Letters and Documents*, rev. Christoph Wolff, New York: Norton.

Davis, Natalie Zemon (1975), *Society and Culture in Early Modern France*, Stanford: Stanford University Press.

de Certeau, Michel (1984), *The Practices of Everyday Life*, Berkeley: University of California Press.

Deppermann, Andreas (2002), *Johann Jakob Schütz und die Anfänge des Pietismus*, Tübingen: Mohr.

Döring, Detlef (1992), *Pufendorf-Studien. Beiträge zur Biographie Samuel von Pufendorfs und zu seiner Entwicklung als Historiker und theologischer Schriftsteller*, Berlin: Duncker & Humblot.

—. (1989), *Samuel Pufendorf und die Leipziger Gelehrtengesellschaften in der Mitte des 17. Jahrhunderts*, Berlin: Akademie.

—. (1984), 'Das Leben in Leipzig in der Zeit des Dreissigjährigen Krieges. Dargestellt anhand der Annalen des Zacharias Schneider,' *Leipzig: Aus Vergangenheit und Gegenwart. Beiträge zur Stadtgeschichte*, 3, 151–175.

Duclaud, Jutta & Rainer (1990), *Leipziger Zünfte*, Berlin: Verlag der Nation.

Edler, Arnfried, 'The Social Status of Organists in Lutheran Germany from the 16th through the 19th Century,' in Salmen, Walter, ed., *The Social Status of the Professional Musician from the Middle Ages to the 19th Century*, New York: Pendragon, 1983; German original Kassel, 1971, 63–93.

Eisenstein, Elisabeth (1979), *The Printing Press as an Agent of Change. Communications and Cultural Transformations in Early-Modern Europe*, New York: Cambridge University Press.

Eller, Rudolf et al. (1960), 'Leipzig,' *Musik in Geschichte und Gegenwart*, vol. VIII, Kassel: Bärenreiter, 540–573.

Ephraim Carlebach Stiftung, ed. (1994), *Judaica Lipsiensia. Zur Geschichte der Juden in Leipzig*, Leipzig: Edition Leipzig.

Evers, C. (1880), *Das Franziskaner Barfüßerkloster zu Leipzig. Geschichte der Matthäikirche zu Leipzig (frühere Neukirche)*, Leipzig: Böhme.

Fellmann, Walter & Metscher, Klaus (1990), *Lipsia und Merkur. Leipzig und seine Messen*, Leipzig: Brockhaus.

Fisher, Alexander (2004), *Music and Religious Identity in Counter-Reformation Augsburg, 1580–1630*, Aldershot: Ashgate.

Forster, Marc (2001), *Catholic Revival in the Age of the Baroque: Religious Identity in Southwest Germany, 1550–1750*, New York: Cambridge University Press.

Francke, August Hermann (1981), *Streitschriften*, ed. Peschke, Erhard, Berlin: de Gruyter.

Frey, Axel & Weinkauf, Bernd, eds (1995), *Leipzig als ein Pleißathen. Eine geistesgeschichtliche Ortsbestimmung*, Leipzig: Reclam.

Friedrichs, Christopher (2000), *Urban Politics in Early Modern Europe*, New York: Routledge.

Geck, Martin (1961), 'Ph. J. Spener und die Kirchenmusik,' *Musik und Kirche*, 31, 97–106 & 172–184.

Geffcken, H. & Tykocinski, H. (1905), *Stiftungsbuch der Stadt Leipzig, im Auftrage des Rates auf Grund der Urkunden und Akten des Ratsarchivs*, Leipzig: Bär & Hermann.

Gerber, Christian (1732), *Historie der Kirchen-Ceremonien in Sachsen*, Dresden & Leipzig: Saueressig.

—. (1717), *Die unerkannten Wohltaten Gottes in dem Chur-Fürstentum Sachsen, und desselben vornehmsten Städten*, vol. II, Dresden & Leipzig: Winckler.

Gierl, Martin (1997), *Pietismus und Aufklärung: Theologische Polemik und die Kommunikationsreform der Wissenschaft am Ende des 17. Jahrhunderts*, Göttingen: Vandenhoeck & Ruprecht.

Gigas, Emil, ed. (1897), *Briefe Samuel Pufendorfs an Christian Thomasius (1687–1693)*, Munich: Oldenbourg.

Glöckner, Andreas (1990), *Die Musikpflege an der Leipziger Neukirche zur Zeit Johann Sebastian Bachs*, = *BzBf*, 8.

Göbel, J.S. (1794), *Ursprung, Geschichte und Verfassung der Consistorien in den Chursächsischen Landen. Ein Beytrag zur Statistik von Chursachsen*, Freyberg: Crazische Buchhandlung.

Goldfriedrich, Johann (1908), *Geschichte des deutschen Buchhandels vom Westfälischen Frieden bis zum Beginn der Klassischen Litteraturperiode (1648–1740)*, Leipzig: Verlag des Börsenvereins der deutschen Buchhändler, R (1970), Leipzig: Zentralantiquariat der DDR.

Gottsched, Johann Christoph (1725–26), *Die vernünfftigen Tadlerinnen*, R (1993) Hildesheim: Olms.

Graff, Paul (1937 & 1939), *Geschichte der Auflösung der alten gottesdienstlichen Formen in der evangelischen Kirche Deutschlands*, vol. I & II, Göttingen: Vandenhoeck & Ruprecht.

Gramit, David (2002), *Cultivating Music: The Aspirations, Interests, and Limits of German Musical Culture, 1770–1848*, Berkeley: University of California Press.

Grünberg, Paul (1893), *Philipp Jakob Spener*, vol. I, Göttingen: Vandenhoeck & Ruprecht, R (1988) Hildesheim: Olms.

Haan, Wilhelm (1880), *Die Episkopal-, Consistorial-und Diöcesan-Verfassung im ehemaligen Kurfürstenthume und jetzigen Königreiche Sachsen vor und seit Einführung der Reformation bis ... 1878*, Dresden: Baensch.

Hagenmaier, Monika (1989), *Predigt und Policey. Der gesellschaftspolitische Diskurs zwischen Kirche und Obrigkeit in Ulm 1614–1639*, Baden-Baden: Nomos.

Heartz, Daniel (2003), *Music in European Capitals: The Galant Style 1720–1780*, New York: Norton.

Helbig, Herbert (1980), *Die Vertrauten 1680–1980. Eine Vereinigung Leipziger Kaufleute*, Stuttgart: Hiersemann.

Herl, Joseph (2004), *Worship Wars in Early Lutheranism. Choir, Congregation, and Three Centuries of Conflict*, New York: Oxford University Press.

Hinske, Norbert ed. (1989), *Halle: Aufklärung und Pietismus*, Heidelberg: Schneider.

Hobohm, Wolf (1997), 'Kantatentextsammlungen der ersten Hälfte des 18. Jahrhunderts-Texte zur Musik?,' *BJ*, 83, 185–192.

—. (1973), 'Neue "Texte zur Leipziger Kirchen-Music,"' *BJ*, 59, 5–32.

Hoffmann, Winfried (1982), 'Leipzigs Wirkungen auf den Delitzscher Kantor Christoph Gottlieb Fröber,' *BzBf*, 1, 54–73.

Holtz, Sabine (1993), *Theologie und Alltag. Lehre und Leben in den Predigten der Tübinger Theologen 1550–1750*, Tübingen: Mohr.

Honecker, Martin (1968), *Cura religionis Magistratus Christiani. Studien zum Kirchenrecht im Luthertum des 17. Jahrhunderts, insbesondere bei Johann Gerhard*, Munich: Claudius.

Hörner, Hans (1933), *Gg. Ph. Telemanns Passionsmusiken. Ein Beitrag zur Geschichte der Passionsmusik in Hamburg*, Leipzig: Noske.

Hull, Isabel (1996), *Sexuality, State, and Civil Society in Germany, 1700–1815*, Ithaca: Cornell University Press.

Iccander (J.C. Crell) (1725), *Das in gantz Europa berühmte, galante und sehenswürdige Königliche Leipzig in Sachsen ...*, Leipzig: Martini.

—. (1723), *Das gesammte itztlebende Geistl. Ministerium im ganzen Churfürstenthum Sachsen ...*, 2nd edition, Leipzig: Martini.

Irwin, Joyce (1993), *Neither Voice nor Heart Alone. German Lutheran Theology of Music in the Age of the Baroque*, New York: Lang.

Jöcher, Christian Gottlieb, ed. (1750 ff.), *Allgemeines Gelehrten-Lexicon*, Leipzig: Gleditsch.

Johnson, James (1995), *Listening in Paris: A Cultural History*, Berkeley: University of California Press.

Junghans, Helmar, ed. (1989), *Das Jahrhundert der Reformation in Sachsen*, Berlin: Evangelische Verlagsanstalt.

Kaemmel, Otto (1909), *Geschichte des Leipziger Schulwesens*, Leipzig: Teubner.

Kaufhold, Karl Heinrich (1996), 'Messen und Wirtschaftsausstellungen von 1650 bis 1914,' in Johanek, P. & Stoob, Heinz, eds, *Europäische Messen und Märktesysteme in Mittelalter und Neuzeit*, Cologne: Böhlau, 239–294.

Keller, Katrin, ed. (1994), *Sächsische Prinzen auf Reisen*, Leipzig: Universitätsverlag.

Kevorkian, Tanya (2004), 'Changing Times, Changing Music: "New Church" Music and Musicians in Leipzig, 1699–1750,' in Weber, ed. (2004), 61–80.

—. (2002), 'The Reception of the Cantata during Church Services in Leipzig, 1700–1750,' *Early Music*, 30, 26–45.

—. (2000), 'The Rise of the Poor, Weak, and Wicked: Poor Care, Punishment, Religion, and Patriarchy in Leipzig, 1700–1730,' *Journal of Social History*, 34, 163–181.

—. (1998), 'Piety Confronts Politics: Philipp Jacob Spener in Dresden, 1686–1691,' *German History*, 16, 145–164.

—. (1997), 'The Material of Faith: Religion and Society in Leipzig, 1685–1725,' PhD thesis, Johns Hopkins University.

Kirn, Otto (1909), *Die Leipziger Theologische Fakultät in fünf Jahrhunderten*, Leipzig: Hirzel.

Kobuch, Agatha (1987), *Zensur und Aufklärung in Kursachsen zur Zeit der sächsisch-pölnischen Union 1694–1763*, Weimar: Böhlau.

Köhler, Johann Christian (1790), *Abhandlung von Kirchenstühlen und deren Rechten in Chursächsischen Landen*, Dresden: Gerlach, rev. and ed. (1830), Schilling, Ernst Moritz, Leipzig: Taubert.

Krause, Konrad (2003), *Alma Mater Lipsiensis: Geschichte der Universität Leipzig von 1409 bis zur Gegenwart*, Leipzig: Universitätsverlag.

Krickeberg, Dieter (1965), *Das Protestantische Kantorat im 17. Jahrhundert: Studien zum Amt des deutschen Kantors*, Berlin: Merseburger.

Krumwiede, Hans-Walter (1967), *Zur Entstehung des landesherrlichen Kirchenregimentes in Kursachsen und Braunschweig-Wolfenbüttel*, Göttingen: Vandenhoeck & Ruprecht.

Kruse, Martin (1971), *Speners Kritik am landesherrlichen Kirchenregiment und ihre Vorgeschichte*, Witten: Luther-Verlag.

Kuhnau, Johann (1700), *Der Musicalische Quack-Salber* ..., Dresden: Miethen & Zimmermann, R (1968) Nendeln: Kraus.

Kuhne, Kurt (1967), *Der Einfluß des Leipziger Schöppen Benedict Carpzov auf die Prozesse gegen die Hexen um Delitzsch*, Delitzsch: Kreismuseum Delitzsch.

Lange, Carsten (2000), 'Zur Aufführung von Telemanns *Brockes-Passionsoratorium* in Frankfurt am Main,' in Cahn, Peter, ed., *Telemann in Frankfurt*, New York: Schott, 142–162.

Lash, S. & Whimster, S., eds (1987), 'Legitimation and Structural Interests in Weber's Sociology of Religion,' in *Max Weber, Rationality and Modernity*, Boston: Allen & Unwin.

La Vopa, Anthony (1988), *Grace, Talent, and Merit. Poor Students, Clerical*

Careers, and Professional Ideology in Eighteenth-Century Germany, New York: Cambridge University Press.

Leaver, Robin A. (1997), 'The Mature Vocal Works and Their Theological and Liturgical Context,' in Butt, John, ed. (1997), 86–122.

—. (1991), 'Bach and Pietism: Similarities Today,' *Concordia Theological Quarterly*, 55, 5–22.

—. (1982), *Music as Preaching: Bach, Passions and Music in Worship*, Oxford: Latimer House.

Lehmann, Hartmut (2004), introduction, *GdP*, vol. IV, 1–18.

—. (2003), 'Engerer, weiterer und erweiterter Pietismusbegriff,' *PuN*, 29, 18–36.

—. (2001), 'Grenzüberschreitungen und Grenzziehungen im Pietismus,' *PuN*, 27, 11–18.

—. (1995), 'Vorüberlegungen zu einer Sozialgeschichte des Pietismus im 17./18. Jahrhundert,' *PuN*, 21, 69–83.

Leisinger, Ulrich, ed. (2002), *Bach in Leipzig – Bach und Leipzig. Konferenzbericht Leipzig 2000*, Hildesheim: Olms.

Lemper, Ernst-Heinz (1954), *Die Thomaskirche zu Leipzig*, Leipzig: Koehler & Amelang.

Leonhardi, F.G. (1799), *Geschichte und Beschreibung der Kreis- und Handelsstadt Leipzig*, Leipzig: Beygang.

—. (1790), *Erdbeschreibung der Churfürstlich- und Herzoglich-Sächsischen Lande*, vol. II, Leipzig: Barth.

Leube, Hans (1928), 'Pietistisch-separatistische Bestrebungen in und um Leipzig,' *BSK*, 37, 49–70.

—. (1924), *Die Reformideen in der deutschen lutherischen Kirche zur Zeit der Orthodoxie*, Leipzig: Dörffling & Franke.

—. (1921), 'Die Geschichte der pietistischen Bewegung in Leipzig. Ein Beitrag zur Geschichte und Charakteristik des deutschen Pietismus,' PhD thesis, University of Leipzig; printed in idem (1975), *Orthodoxie und Pietismus. Gesammelte Studien*, Blaufuß, D., ed., Bielefeld: Luther-Verlag, 153–257.

Lindberg, John (1973), 'Der Pietismus und die deutsche Barockoper: Zusammenprall zweier Welten,' in Hoffmeister, Gerhard, ed., *Europäische Tradition und deutscher Literaturbarock*, Munich/Bern: Francke, 251–257.

Little, Meredith & Jenne, Natalie (2001), *Dance and the Music of J.S. Bach*, expanded edition, Bloomington: University of Indiana Press.

Lünig, Johann Christian, ed. (1724), *Codex Augusteus, oder Neuvermehrtes Corpus Juris Saxonici ...*, Leipzig: Gleditsch.

Martens, Wolfgang, ed. (1990), *Leipzig: Aufklärung und Bürgerlichkeit*, Heidelberg: Schneider.

Martin, Lucinda (2003), 'Female Reformers as the Gate Keepers of Pietism: The Example of Johanna Eleonora Merlau and William Penn,' *Monatshefte*, 95, 33–58.

—. (2003), 'Möglichkeiten und Grenzen geistlicher Rede von Frauen in Halle und Herrnhut,' *PuN*, 29, 80–90.

Masur, Gerhard (1933), 'Naturrecht und Kirche. Studien zur evangelischen Kirchenverfassung Deutschlands im 18. Jahrhundert,' *Historische Zeitschrift*, 148, 29–70.

Mattheson, Johann (1728), *Der Musicalische Patriot ...*, Hamburg: self-published, R (1975) Leipzig: Zentralantiquariat der DDR.

McIntosh, Terence (1997), *Urban Decline in Early Modern Germany: Schwäbisch Hall and its Region, 1650–1750*, Chapel Hill: University of North Carolina Press.

Medick, Hans (1996), *Weben und Überleben in Laichingen 1650–1900: Lokalgeschichte als allgemeine Geschichte*, Göttingen: Vandenhoeck & Ruprecht.

Melton, James Van Horn (2001), 'Pietism, Politics, and the Public Sphere in Germany,' in Bradley, James & Van Kley, Dale, eds, *Religion and Politics in Enlightenment Europe*, Notre Dame: University of Notre Dame Press, 294–333.

Moccia, Sergio (1988), *Carpzov e Grozio. Dalla concezione teocratica alla concezione laica del diritto penale*, Naples: Editoriale Scientifica.

Mori, Ryoko (2004), *Begeisterung und Ernüchterung in christlicher Vollkommenheit. Pietistische Selbst- und Weltwahrnehmungen im ausgehenden 17. Jahrhundert*, Tübingen: Niemeyer.

Münch, Paul (1978), *Zucht und Ordnung. Reformierte Kirchenverfassungen im 16. und 17. Jahrhundert (Nassau-Dillenburg, Kurpfalz, Hessen-Kassel)*, Stuttgart: Klett-Cotta.

Neumann, Werner & Schulze, Hans-Joachim, eds (1963 & 1969), *Bach-Dokumente*, vol. I: *Schriftstücke von der Hand Johann Sebastian Bachs*; vol. II: *Fremdschriftliche und Gedruckte Dokumente zur Lebensgeschichte Johann Sebastian Bachs 1685–1750*, Kassel: Bärenreiter.

Oestreich, Gerhard (1982), 'The religious covenant and the social contract,' in idem, *Neostoicism and the Early Modern State*, New York: Cambridge University Press, 135–154.

Ostarhild, Friedrich (1964), *Die Nikolaikirche Leipzig. Geschichte des Gotteshauses und der Gemeinde 1160–1960*, Berlin: Evangelische Verlagsanstalt.

Parish, Helen & Naphy, William G., eds (2002), *Religion and Superstition in Reformation Europe*, New York: Manchester University Press.

Pasch, Gerhart (1989), '"Ein schönes Schauspielhaus!" Die klassizistische Umgestaltung der Nikolaikirche,' in Ullmann, Ernst, ed., *'... die ganze Welt im kleinen ...,' Kunst und Kunstgeschichte in Leipzig*, Leipzig: Seemann, 155–171.

Palisca, Claude (2001), 'Baroque,' in Sadie, Stanley, ed., *The New Grove Dictionary of Music and Musicians*, 2nd edition, vol. II, New York: Macmillan, 749–756.

Peters, Christian (1997), '"Daraus der Lärm des Pietismi entstanden." Die Leipziger Unruhen von 1689/1690 und ihre Deutung durch Spener und die hallischen Pietisten,' *PuN*, 23, 103–151.

Peters, Jan (1985), 'Der Platz in der Kirche. Über soziales Rangdenken im Spätfeudalismus,' *Jahrbuch für Volkskunde und Kulturgeschichte*, 28, NF 13, 77–106.

Petzoldt, Claus (1971), 'Studien zu einer Biographie Valentin Ernst Löschers. Löschers Berufung nach Dresden 1709. Konventikelwesen in Dresden zwischen 1690 und 1750. Katalog der Manuskripte Löschers 1688–1749,' PhD thesis, University of Leipzig, ms.

Petzoldt, Martin (2000), ed. and intro., *Texthefte zur Kirchenmusik aus Bachs Leipzier Zeit. Die sieben erhaltenen Drucke der Jahre 1724–1749 in faksimilierter Wiedergabe*, Stuttgart: Carus.

—. (1993), *'Texte zur Leipziger Kirchen=Music': Zum Verständnis der Kantatentexte Johann Sebastian Bachs*, Wiesbaden: Breitkopf & Härtel.

—. (1982), 'Überlegungen zur theologischen und geistigen Integration Bachs in Leipzig 1723,' *BzBf*, 1, 46–52.

Pevsner, Nikolaus (1928), *Leipziger Barock. Die Baukunst der Barockzeit in Leipzig*, Leipzig: Jess, R (1990), Leipzig: Seemann.

Reeckmann, Kathrin (2000), *Anfänge der Barockarchitektur in Sachsen. Johann Georg Starcke und seine Zeit*, Cologne: Böhlau.

Reinhard, Wolfgang (1988), 'Kirche als Mobilitätskanal der frühneuzeitlichen Gesellschaft,' in Schulze, Winfried, ed., *Ständische Gesellschaft und soziale Mobilität*, Munich: Oldenbourg, 333–351.

Reipsch, Brit (1997), 'Über die Aufgaben und Bedeutung eines Kantors im Spiegel einiger musiktheoretischer Schriften vom Ende des 17. bis zum Ausgang des 18. Jahrhunderts,' in Hobohm, Wolf, et al., eds, *Struktur, Funktion und Bedeutung des deutschen protestantischen Kantorats im 16. bis 18. Jahrhundert,* Oschersleben: Ziethen, 21–28.

Reuter, Christian (1980), ed. Jäckel, Günter, *Christian Reuters Werke*, Berlin & Weimar: Aufbau.

Roper, Lyndal (1989), *The Holy Household. Women and Morals in Reformation Augsburg*, Oxford: Clarendon.

Rose, Stephen (2005), 'Daniel Vetter and the Domestic Keyboard Chorale in Bach's Leipzig,' *Early Music*, 33, 39–53.

Rublack, Hans-Christoph (1989), '"Der Wohlgeplagte Priester." Vom Selbstverständnis lutherischer Geistlichkeit im Zeitalter der Orthodoxie,' *Zeitschrift für historische Forschung*, 16, 1–30.

Sabean, David (1990), *Property, Production, and Family in Neckarhausen, 1700–1870*, New York: Cambridge University Press.

—. (1984), *Power in the Blood. Popular Culture and Village Discourse in Early Modern Germany*, New York: Cambridge University Press.

Schäfer, Rudolf (1915), 'Die Geltung des kanonischen Rechts in der evangelischen Kirche Deutschlands von Luther bis zur Gegenwart,' *Zeitschrift der Savigny-Stiftung für Rechtsforschung, Kanonisches Abteil*, 5, 165–413.

Scheibel (1721), *Zufällige Gedancken von der Kirchen-Music, Wie Sie heutiges Tages beschaffen ist*, Frankfurt & Leipzig: self-published, R (2002) Stuttgart: Cornetto.

Schenke, Friedrich (1925), 'Pufendorfs Kirchenbegriff,' *Zeitschrift der Savigny-Stiftung für Rechtsforschung, Kanonisches Abteil*, 14, 39–61.

Schering, Arnold (1941), *Johann Sebastian Bach und das Musikleben Leipzigs im 18. Jahrhundert*, Leipzig: Kistner & Siegel.

—. (1936), *J.S. Bachs Leipziger Kirchenmusik*, Leipzig: Breitkopf und Härtel, R (1968) Wiesbaden: Breitkopf und Härtel.

Schicketanz, Peter, ed. & intro. (1972), *Der Briefwechsel Carl Hildebrand von Cansteins mit August Hermann Francke*, Berlin: de Gruyter.

Schilling, Heinz (1993), *Die Stadt in der frühen Neuzeit*, Munich: Oldenbourg.

—, ed. (1986), *Die reformierte Konfessionalisierung in Deutschland – Das Problem der 'Zweiten Reformation'*, Gütersloh: Gütersloher Verlagshaus.

Schirmer, Uwe, ed. (1998), *Sachsen im 17. Jahrhundert. Krise, Krieg und Neubeginn*, Beucha: Sax.

Schivelbusch, Wolfgang (1992), *Tastes of Paradise: A Social History of Spices, Stimulants, and Intoxicants*, New York: Pantheon; German original, 1980.

Schneider, Hans-Peter (1967), *Justitia Universalis. Quellenstudien zur Geschichte des 'christlichen Naturrechts' bei Gottfried Wilhelm Leibniz*, Frankfurt: Klostermann.

Schorn-Schütte, Luise (2000), 'Priest, Preacher, Pastor: Research on Clerical Office in Early Modern Europe,' *Central European History*, 33, 1–37.

—. (1996) *Evangelische Geistlichkeit in der Frühneuzeit: Deren Anteil an der Entfaltung frühmoderner Staatlichkeit und Gesellschaft: Dargestellt am Beispiel des Fürstentums Braunschweig-Wolfenbüttel, der Landgrafschaft Hessen-Kassel und der Stadt Braunschweig*, Gütersloh: Gütersloher Verlagshaus.

Schrader, Hans-Jürgen (1989), *Literaturproduktion und Büchermarkt des radikalen Pietismus. Johann Henrich Reitz' 'Historie der Wiedergebohrenen' und ihr geschichtlicher Kontext*, Göttingen: Vandenhoeck & Ruprecht.

Schulze, Hans-Joachim (1998), 'Bachs Kantatentexte: Fragen nach theologischem Gehalt, sprachlicher Qualität und musikalischer Brauchbarkeit,' in Steiger, Renate, ed. (1998), 339–342.

—. (1997), 'Anna Magdalena Bachs "Herzens Freündin:" Neues über die Beziehungen zwischen den Familien Bach und Bose,' *BJ*, 83, 151–153.

Sehling, Emil, ed. (1902), *Die evangelischen Kirchenordnungen des 16. Jahrhunderts*, vol. I, Leipzig: Reisland.

Shagan, Ethan (2003), *Popular Politics and the English Reformation*, New York: Cambridge University Press.

Siegele, Ulrich (1997), 'Bach and the Domestic Politics of Electoral Saxony,' in Butt, ed. (1997), 17–34.

—. (1983, 1984, & 1986), 'Bachs Stellung in der Leipziger Kulturpolitik seiner Zeit,' *BJ*, 69, 7–50; 70, 7–43; 72, 33–67.

Sommer, Wolfgang (1988), *Gottesfurcht und Fürstenherrschaft. Studien zum Obrigkeitsverständnis Johann Arndts und lutherischer Hofprediger zur Zeit der altprotestantischen Orthodoxie*, Göttingen: Vandenhoeck & Ruprecht.

Spitta, Philipp (1930), *Johann Sebastian Bach*, Leipzig: Breitkopf & Härtel, R (1979),Wiesbaden: Breitkopf & Härtel.

Stauffer, George (1993), 'Leipzig: A Cosmopolitan Trade Centre,' in Buelow, George, ed., *The Late Baroque Era: From the 1680s to 1740*, Englewood Cliffs: Prentice Hall, 254–295.

Steiger, Renate, ed. (1998), *Die Quellen Johann Sebastian Bachs: Bachs Musik im Gottesdienst*, Heidelberg: Manutius.

Stieda, Wilhelm (n.d.), *Der Neubau der Paulinerkirche in den Jahren 1710–12. Aktenmäßige Forschungen über die Mitarbeit der Leipziger Gewerken*, Leipzig.

Stiehl, Herbert (1984), 'Das Innere der Thomaskirche zur Amtszeit Johann Sebastian Bachs,' = *BzBf*, 3.

Stiller, Günther (1984), *Johann Sebastian Bach and Liturgical Life in Leipzig*, St. Louis: Concordia; German original, 1970.

Sträter, Udo (2004) 'Soziales,' in *GdP*, vol. IV, 617–645.

Strauss, Gerald (1986), *Law, Resistance, and the State: The Opposition to Roman Law in Reformation Germany*, Princeton: Princeton University Press.

—. (1978), *Luther's House of Learning. Indoctrination of the Young in Reformation Germany*, Baltimore: Johns Hopkins Press.

Strom, Jonathan (2002), 'Problems and Promises of Pietism Research,' *Church History*, 71, 536–554.

—. (2001), 'Early Conventicles in Lübeck,' *PuN*, 27, 19–52.

—. (1999), *Orthodoxy and Reform: The Clergy in Seventeenth Century Rostock*, Tübingen: Mohr.

Stroup, John Michael (1984), *The Struggle for Identity in the Clerical Estate. Northwest German Protestant Opposition to Absolutist Policy in the 18th Century*, Leiden: Brill.

Swartz, David (1997), *Culture and Power: The Sociology of Pierre Bourdieu*, Chicago: University of Chicago Press.

Szeskus, Reinhard (2003), *Bach in Leipzig. Beiträge zu Leben und Werk von Johann Sebastian Bach*, Wilhelmshaven: Noetzel.

Telemann, Georg Philipp (2001), 'Seliges Erwägen: Passionsoratorium in Neun Betrachtungen,' ed. Poetzsch, Ute, *Musikalische Werke*, vol. 33, Kassel: Bärenreiter.

—. (1972), *Briefwechsel*, ed. Grosse, Hans & Jung, Hans Rudolf, Leipzig: VEB Deutscher Verlag für Musik.

Thomasius, Christian (1722), *Historia Contentionis inter Imperium et Sacerdotium breviter delineata usque ad seculum XVI ... In usum Auditorii Thomasiani*, Halle: Renger.

—. (1695), *De jure Principis circa Adiaphora*, Halle: Salfeld.

—. (1690), 'Churbrandenburgischer Unterthanen Doppelte Glückseligkeit, so sie wegen des durch Churfürstliche scharffe Edicta verbesserten Geistlichen und Weltlichen Standes zugeniessen haben,' in idem (1705), *Außerlesene und in Deutsch noch nie Gedruckte Schrifften*, vol. I, Halle: Renger.

—. (1688–1689), *Freimütige, lustige und ernsthafte, jedoch Vernunftmässige Gedancken oder Monatsgespräche über allerhand, fürnehmlich aber neue Bücher* [*Monatsgespräche*]. Halle: Salfeld, R (1972), Frankfurt: Athenäum.

— & Brenneysen, Enno Rudolph (1696), *Das Recht evangangelischer Fürsten in theologischen Streitigkeiten, gründlich ausgeführet, und wider die papistischen Lehr-Sätze eines Theologi zu Leipzig …*, Halle: Salfeld.

— & Francke, August Hermann (1692), *Gerichtliches Leipziger Protocoll in Sachen die Pietisten betreffend*, No place: no publisher, R (1981) in Peschke, Erhard, ed., *August Hermann Francke. Schriften und Predigten*, Berlin: de Gruyter.

Tilgner, Gottfried (1717), preface to Neumeister, Erdmann, *Fünff-Fache Kirchen-Andachten*, Leipzig: Gross.

Tlusty, B. Ann (2001), *Bacchus and Civic Order: The Culture of Drink in Early Modern Germany*, Charlottesville: University Press of Virginia.

Todd, Margo (2002), *The Culture of Protestantism in Early Modern Scotland*, New Haven: Yale University Press.

Ulbrich, Claudia (1997), 'Zankapfel "Weiber-Gestühl,"' in Lubinski, Axel et al., eds, *Historie und Eigensinn. Festschrift für Jan Peters zum 65. Geburtstag*, Weimar: Böhlau, 107–114.

Unger, Melvin P., ed. (1996), *Handbook to Bach's Sacred Cantatas*, Lanham, MD: Scarecrow.

Vann, James Allen (1984), *The Making of a State. Württemberg 1593–1793*, Ithaca: Cornell University Press.

Veit, Patrice (1998), '"Daheime seine Zeit mit Singen, mit Beten und Lesen zugebracht": Über den Umgang mit Kirchenliedern im aussergottesdienstlichen Kontext,' in Steiger, ed. (1998), 329–335.

Vockerodt, Gottfried (1797), *Missgebrauch der freyen Künste, insonderheit der Music ...*, Frankfurt: Zunner.

Vogel, Johann Jacob (1714 & 1756), *Leipzigisches Geschicht-Buch oder Annales, das ist, Jahr- und Tage-Bücher der weltberühmten königlichen und churfürstlichen sächsischen Kauff- und Handels-Stadt Leipzig ...*, Leipzig: Lancke.

Vogler, Bernard (1994), 'Rekrutierung, Ausbildung und soziale Verflechtung: Karrieremuster evangelischer Geistlichkeit,' *Archive for Reformation History*, 85, 225–23.

Voss, Steffen (2005), 'Did Bach Perform Sacred Music by Johann Mattheson in Leipzig?,' *Bach Notes*, 3, 1–5.

Walker, Mack (1971), *German Home Towns. Community, State, and General Estate 1648–1871*, Ithaca: Cornell University Press.

Wallmann, Johannes (1992), 'Erfurt und der Pietismus im 17. Jahrhundert,' in Weiss, Ulman, ed., *Erfurt 742–1992. Stadtgeschichte, Universitätsgeschichte*, Weimar: Böhlau, 403–422.

—, ed. (2005), *Philipp Jakob Spener. Briefe aus der Frankfurter Zeit 1666–1686*, vol. IV, 1679–1680, Tübingen: Mohr.

Wartenberg, Günther (1988), *Landesherrschaft und Reformation. Moritz von Sachsen und die albertinische Kirchenpolitik bis 1546*, Gütersloh: Mohn.

—. (1987), 'Der Pietismus in Sachsen – ein Literaturbericht,' *PuN*, 13, 103–114.

Watanabe-O'Kelly, Helen (2002), *Court Culture in Dresden from Renaissance to Baroque*, Houndmills: Palgrave.

Weber, Hellmuth von (1949), 'Benedict Carpzov. Ein Bild der deutschen Rechtspflege im Barockzeitalter,' in *Festschrift für Ernst Heinrich Rosenfeld*, Berlin: de Gruyter, 29–50.

Weber, William ed. (2004), *The Musician as Entrepreneur, 1700–1914: Managers, Charlatans, and Idealists*, Bloomington: Indiana University Press.

—. (1997), 'Did People Listen in the 18th Century?,' *Early Music*, 25, 678–691.

—. (1992), *The Rise of Musical Classics in Eighteenth Century England: A Study in Canon, Ritual, and Ideology*, New York: Oxford.

Weiz, Anton (1728), *Verbessertes Leipzig, oder Die vornehmsten Dinge, so von Anno 1698 an bis hiehern bey der Stadt Leipzig verbessert worden*, Leipzig: Lancke.

Wex, Reinhold (1984), *Ordnung und Unfriede. Raumprobleme des protestantischen Kirchenbaus im 17. und 18. Jahrhundert in Deutschland*, Marburg: Jonas.

Whaley, Joachim (1992), 'Obedient Servants? Lutheran Attitudes to Authority and Society in the First Half of the 17th Century: The Case of Johann Balthasar Schupp,' *Historical Journal*, 35, 27–42.

Wilde, Manfred (2003), *Die Zauberei- und Hexenprozesse in Kursachsen*, Weimar: Böhlau.

Winter, Eduard (1966), *Frühaufklärung. Der Kampf gegen den Konfessionalismus in Mittel- und Osteuropa und die deutsch-slawische Begegnung*, Berlin: Akademie.

Witkowski, Georg (1909), *Geschichte des literarischen Lebens in Leipzig*, Leipzig: Teubner, R (1994) Munich: Saur.

Witt, Ulrike (1996), *Bekehrung, Bildung und Biographie: Frauen im Umkreis des Halleschen Pietismus*, Tübingen: Niemeyer.

Witte, John (2002), *Law and Protestantism. The Legal Teachings of the Lutheran Reformation*, New York: Cambridge University Press.

Wittmann, Reinhard (1991), *Geschichte des deutschen Buchhandels: Ein Überblick*, Munich: Beck.

Wolff, Christoph (2000), *Johann Sebastian Bach: The Learned Musician*, New York: Norton.

Wustmann, Gustav, ed. (1895), *Quellen zur Geschichte Leipzigs. Veröffentlichungen aus dem Archiv und der Bibliothek der Stadt Leipzig*, vol. II, Leipzig: Duncker & Humblot.

Zedler, Johann Heinrich (1730 ff.), *Grosses vollständiges Universal-Lexicon aller Wissenschafften und Künste*, Leipzig: Zedler, R (1961–1964) Graz: Akademische Druck- u. Verlagsanstalt.

Index

adiaphora 8–9, 14, 24, 119, 124, 136–43, 181–2
Alberti, Valentin 119–20
Amsterdam 190
Anton, Paul 147, 152, 161, 183
apprentices 61, 65, 69, 83, 212
Augsburg 15, 18, 20, 65, 80
Augsburg Confession 112, 114, 155

Bach, Anna Magdalena 1, 127–8, 130, 141
Bach, Carl Philipp Emanuel 216, 221
Bach, Johann Sebastian 14–16, 18, 20, 24, 29, 38–40, 88–91, 96, 100, 102–3, 121, 123–4, 141–3, 196, 210–13, 215–16, 219–221
  audiences of 9, 29, 40–45
  and city councilors 1–2, 123, 128–36
  and collegia musica 23, 135, 216, 219–20
  complaints by 1, 100, 111, 128, 131–2
  compositions 7–9, 38–9, 42–5, 215
  duties 123, 125–6, 129–30, 210
  and Pietism 124, 141–2
  social status 14, 126–8
Baroque 1–2, 4–6, 11, 13–15, 20–25, 29, 51, 53, 67, 71, 123–5, 130–31, 134, 136, 139, 141–3, 195–7, 219–22
  definition of 13
  Enlightenment critique of 13, 220–21
  historiography 4, 13, 18
  music audiences 7–10, 41–6
  Pietist critique of 11, 170, 182–4; *see also* adiaphora
Beer, Johann 137
beggars and begging 37, 80, 199, 205, 209
Beichling, Gottfried Hermann von 190n121
Berlin 12, 15–16, 49, 65, 106, 121, 134, 143, 161, 164, 175
Bernd, Adam 31, 35, 47, 50, 84, 89–90, 92–3, 95, 151, 181, 198, 201, 207, 220
Bohse, August 173
Born, Jacob 96–7, 112, 160, 162
Born, Johann Franz 96, 130
Bose, Caspar 83, 130
Bose family 20, 128, 220
Bose, Georg Heinrich 127, 209
Bourdieu, Pierre 4–7, 216
Brandenburg-Prussia 12, 18, 21, 99, 101, 109, 116, 120–21, 127, 137, 149–50, 161, 169, 175, 213
Breslau 16, 20, 24, 65, 89–90, 147, 169, 170n2, 190
Brockes, Barthold Heinrich 39, 44, 213, 215, 220
burghers 5–6, 14–15, 21, 30, 32, 56, 71–2, 74, 77–84, 89–91, 93–4, 97, 126
  and city council 77–84
  and clerics 84–8
  and collegia pietatis 147–61, 163, 165, 167
  and pewholding 53–74, 197, 202–5
  and Pietist network 172, 175, 180, 185–6, 189
  and renovation/construction of new churches 197–9, 202–5, 209–10, 216, 219

Calvinists 31, 50, 53, 65–6, 100, 109, 187
Canstein, Carl Hildebrand von 169, 173, 175–6
cantatas 8, 23, 25, 30, 33, 35, 38–47, 51, 121, 131, 133, 135–7, 141, 182, 210–11; *see also* libretti
  chorales 8, 38, 41–5, 131, 210, 214–16
  in the New Church 213–16
cantors 2, 14, 16, 38–9, 42, 89, 110, 123–43, 210, 213, 221; *see also* Bach, Johann Sebastian; Kuhnau, Johann; Schelle, Johann
  appointment 94, 128–9
  duties 123–6, 210
  social status 126–8

Capellen 32, 34, 46, 54, 63, 70–74, 92, 170, 182, 198, 202–5, 216; *see also* pews
Capellmeister 124, 129, 133–4, 143; *see also* cantors
Carpzov, Benedict 115–18
Carpzov family 87–8, 93, 114
Carpzov, Friedrich Benedict 96, 188
Carpzov, Johann Benedict 160, 170, 174n26, 186, 188, 190n121
Carpzov, Samuel Benedict 106–7, 120, 160–62
Catholics and Catholicism 4, 14, 18, 21, 31, 50, 53, 65, 81, 99, 107, 109, 121, 174, 221
chorales, *see* cantatas
city councilors, Leipzig 1–3, 5–6, 8, 10, 14–16, 18–21, 23–4, 31–5, 43, 47, 52, 77–93, 111–13, 123, 139, 141–3, 189; *see also* elites
  appointment of cantors 128–30
  appointment of clerics 93–7
  duties 80–82
  and Electoral court 99–104
  and Leipzig inhabitants 77, 79–84
  as patrons of music 39–40, 123–4, 127, 131–6, 139–40, 209–12, 215–17
  and pewholding 60, 62–6, 68, 70–74
  and Pietism 96–7, 147, 150, 157–60, 164–6, 169, 181–2, 185, 188
  and renovation/construction of new churches 195, 197–209
  social status 79–80
clerics 3–6, 8, 10–11, 14, 16, 21, 55, 60, 64–6, 68, 70, 77–9, 82, 85–6, 93, 99–103, 105, 108, 110, 115, 117–21, 123, 125–9, 131–3, 138, 140–41, 197, 199–202, 205–7, 216
  appointment of 10, 79, 81, 93–7
  as consistory assessors 100, 109, 111–14
  education 78, 88–90; *see also* Leipzig, University of, students
  and Leipzig inhabitants 78–9, 83–5, 89–93, 97
  and Pietism 149–51, 124, 142, 161, 163–7, 170–72, 174, 180–85
  Senior Court Chaplains 12, 48n93, 50, 86, 100–108, 152, 207
  social backgrounds 86–9
  village pastors 31, 87, 96, 100, 110, 149, 184
  and worship services 29–33, 35, 37, 40, 45–52, 199–202
Cöthen 124, 127, 130, 134
coffee and coffee houses 23–5, 34, 39, 125, 135–6, 140–41, 191, 197, 212, 214, 219–20
collection bags 33–4, 41, 200, 203, 208–9, 217, 221
collegia musica 23, 133, 135, 138, 141, 197, 210–13, 216, 220
collegia pietatis 2, 10–12, 14, 47, 49, 79, 97, 101, 106, 119–20, 147–67, 171, 174–5, 179–80, 182, 184, 186, 188, 219
communion 33–4, 40, 64, 79, 91–2, 97, 118, 201, 209, 221
confession and confessionalism 3–5, 2, 14, 18, 65, 100, 105, 107, 113–15, 117, 123, 142–3
confession (of sins) 64, 85, 91, 97, 127
congregants and congregations 2, 8, 14, 56, 58, 62, 65–6, 74, 79, 85, 90–91, 93, 95, 119, 147, 149, 155, 162, 208; *see also* burghers; elites; pews; sub-burghers; worship services
  and music 35–46 137, 139–40, 210, 214–15
  and sermon 46–51
  and worship service 29–35, 51–2, 202–6, 214–15
consistories 5–6, 12, 14, 16, 47, 71, 99–101, 108–12, 149, 157, 199, 216
  Dresden (Upper) Consistory 46, 66, 68–9, 71–2, 101, 105–7, 110–14, 132, 157–8, 160–61, 187
  Leipzig Consistory 16, 66, 68, 71, 82, 90, 96, 100, 110–14, 120, 123, 131–2, 160–61, 199–202, 205
  Wittenberg Consistory 110
consistory assessors 71, 96, 101, 107, 111–15, 120, 124, 127, 160–62, 167, 197, 199, 216

Danzig 1, 20
Deyling, Salomon 86n40, 89, 92–3, 97, 127–8, 132, 180–81

Dresden 16, 21, 71–2, 113, 127, 169, 195
Electoral court at 12, 14, 16, 21, 23, 56, 88, 96, 99–108, 112–13, 119, 123, 133–6, 143, 147, 152–3, 157, 160, 175, 189, 197, 199–202, 208, 216, 211

Electors of Saxony 5, 16, 18–19, 21, 55, 68, 80, 86, 95, 99–110, 112–15, 121, 131, 133, 140, 143; *see also* Dresden, Electoral court at; Johann George II, III, and IV; Frederick August II and III
Elers, Heinrich Julius 169, 175, 176n31, 178, 180–81, 185, 188
elites 1, 3–5, 14, 16, 18, 23, 79–80, 121, 126, 128, 138, 140, 162, 166, 203–4, 216; *see also* city councilors; consistory assessors; merchants
and clerics 87–9, 91–3, 97
and Electoral court 99
elite clerics 86–8, 101
and pewholding 56, 59–65, 74
and Pietism 12, 147, 170, 175
and worship services 32, 34, 49–50, 74
encyclopedias 53, 112, 172–3, 187
Enlightenment and Enlighteners 23, 51, 100–101, 117–18, 121–2, 124, 139, 141, 171–2, 180, 185, 189, 191, 219–20; *see also* Brockes, Barthold Heinrich; Gottsched, Johann Christoph; Gottsched, Luise Adelgunde; Klopstock, Friedrich Gottlieb; Thomasius, Christian; Ziegler, Mariane von
epidemics 11, 19, 35, 50, 151, 156, 183
Epistles 34, 42, 15, 155, 165, 170, 174, 182
Erfurt 147, 149, 178–9
everyday practices 2–5, 9–14, 29–31; *see also* clerics, appointment of; collegia pietatis; congregants; pews; Pietist network; worship services

Feller family 163
Feller, Joachim 97n104, 153, 182
Feller, Rahel 97n104

Francke, August Hermann 16, 47, 101, 119–21, 130, 137, 150, 166, 187–9, 191, 207–9, 219
and Leipzig collegia 12, 14, 152–4, 156–8, 160–63, 166–7, 175, 183
and post-1690 Leipzig network 15, 96, 130, 169–78, 180–81, 184–5, 188, 191
and Spener, Philipp Jacob 101, 119, 121, 147, 153, 170, 183
Frankfurt 12, 16, 20–21, 24, 31, 41, 65, 71, 80, 105, 119, 132, 143, 149, 160, 169, 187, 195, 215, 221
Frederick August II, Saxon Elector 14, 23, 96, 99–103, 107–8, 113–14, 127, 131, 133, 135–6, 209, 212
Frederick August III, Saxon Elector 127
French style 9n27, 39, 107, 139, 220
Frentzel, Augustin 153, 155–6, 165, 179, 182
Frentzel, Dorothea Elisabeth 174, 178, 180
Freylinghausen, Johann Anastasius 208
Freystein, Dr. 174, 180
Fritsch, Johann 164, 187
Fritsch, (Johann) Thomas 63, 181–2, 185–6, 188, 191n125, 206, 219

galant style 13, 15, 214, 219
Gaulicke, Christian 154, 159–60, 164
Gehr, Johann Adam 89, 93, 200n15, 207
Gerber, Christian 31, 33, 34, 37–8, 40, 44, 137, 196, 215
Gewandhaus Orchestra 222
Gierl, Martin 171, 185, 189
Glafey, Maria 47, 83, 166, 175
Gleditsch, Johann Friedrich 182, 185, 186n103, 187–8, 190, 219
Gleditsch, Johann Ludwig 180, 182, 185, 187–8, 219
Glöckner, Andreas 212–14
Görner, Johann Gottlieb 23, 210
Goeze, Melchior 45
Gotha 137, 147; *see also* Saxe-Gotha
Gottsched, Johann Christoph 24, 58, 73, 128, 139, 219–20
Gottsched, Luise Adelgunde 181, 219
guilds 89, 183, 185
and city council 80–81

and pewholding 55, 58, 60–63, 66, 73

Halle 121, 139, 214
Pietism in 15, 43, 51, 96, 161, 167, 169, 171–2, 174–8, 207, 217
publishing in 175, 187–8, 197, 207–8; *see also* Elers, Heinrich Julius
University of 97n104, 148n5, 169, 176
Hamburg 11, 16, 18, 20–21, 24, 31, 33, 41–2, 44–5, 65, 84, 90, 127, 129–30, 132, 136–7, 139, 141, 143, 147, 149, 154, 169, 177, 195, 214–16, 211
Heinich, Johann 153–5, 174, 180, 188, 190
Heinichen, Johann David 9, 15, 197, 213–14
Henrich, Christian 156, 159, 164, 182
Henrich, Dorothea Elisabeth 153–4, 156, 159–60, 164–5
Henrici, Christian Friedrich 220
Holy Roman Empire 15–16, 55, 101–2, 104, 107, 109, 116, 127, 187
hymns 8, 11, 31, 33, 35, 37–8, 40, 42–5, 51, 117, 121, 124, 132, 137, 140, 180, 200–201, 208, 210–11, 214
hymnals 4, 16, 29, 37–8, 42, 44, 45n83, 51, 182, 208

Italian style 21, 102, 104–5, 135–7, 200, 214, 220
Italy 13, 18, 61, 107
Ittig, Thomas 49, 85–6, 184, 190n122, 205–6

Jena 16, 147; University of 161n65, 186
Jews 53, 65
Job, Johann 1–2, 96–7, 128, 130, 134–5, 169, 174–6, 178, 180–82, 185, 188, 207–8
Johann George II, Saxon Elector 104, 113
Johann George III, Saxon Elector 12, 14, 100–101, 104–7, 120–21, 157–8, 160–62, 167
Johann George IV, Saxon Elector 104, 107, 190n121
journeymen 60, 61, 64–5, 67, 69, 83, 152, 154, 159, 204
jurists 16, 23, 50, 62, 79, 101, 109, 115–19, 121, 136, 139, 189; *see also* consistory assessors
as city councilors 79–80, 89, 96, 130

Kirch family 63, 182
Kirch, Gottfried 182
Klopstock, Friedrich Gottlieb 45, 220
Knauer, Anna Martha 182
Knauer, Samuel 153, 156, 169, 174, 179, 182–3, 185
Kuhnau, Johann 14, 39–41, 123, 125–6, 129–30, 132–3, 140n77, 143, 210–13, 219, 221
on the adiaphora 137–8, 141
complaints 132, 212
compositions 23, 39, 44

Lange, Gottfried 96, 103, 128, 130, 133–6
Lange, Johann Christian 34, 184
LaVopa, Anthony 88
law 16, 46, 81–2, 96, 140, 152, 162
ecclesiastical 12, 14, 53, 55, 66, 70–71, 108–12, 114–22, 125, 140, 160, 164–6; *see also* consistories
criminal 116–17
Lehmann, Hartmut 4, 11, 170
Leibniz, Gottfried Wilhelm 115, 119
Leipzig, University of 16, 63, 78, 82, 88–90, 99–100, 117, 150, 153, 155
professors 15, 47, 128, 131, 167, 189, 190n121, 197
University Church 30, 34, 132, 154, 195, 197, 201–3, 206, 210, 212–13, 219
students and graduates 1, 23, 63, 88, 125–6, 132–3, 135, 173, 176–7, 184, 186, 212–14
and collegia pietatis 147, 155–6, 163, 166, 182
and Pietist-Orthodox debate 119–20, 147, 157–9, 161, 164, 206
letters 15, 47, 83, 94, 96–7, 105, 119, 128, 130, 135, 154, 160, 166, 169–85
Leube, Hans 11n37, 171
libretti 16, 40–42, 44–5, 47, 51, 215
Luther, Martin 37, 45, 101, 103–4, 109, 115, 118, 160, 166, 174, 206
Lutheran Confession and theology 2n2, 4, 12, 16, 33–8, 70, 101–4, 107, 114–15, 124–5, 137, 139, 151, 160, 165–6, 174, 187, 189, 197, 206; *see also* adiaphora

Lutheran Orthodoxy 2n2, 6–7, 9–10, 12, 48–50, 96–7, 101, 106–7, 119–20, 124, 130, 147–8, 151, 161–2, 165, 170, 174–5, 180–81, 184, 206, 219

Mattheson, Johann 33, 41n65, 137–8, 141, 220
Meinig, Dorothea 163, 169, 179
Meinig, Johann Christoph 177
Meinig, Martin 153–6, 169, 177, 179, 182
merchants 16, 18, 20–21, 23, 32, 50, 55, 59, 60, 62–3, 65, 70, 72, 79–81, 88, 92, 96, 127–8, 130, 136, 152, 172–3, 177, 183, 195, 204, 209, 222; *see also* trade
Mey, Catharina 153–4, 163, 165, 169, 175, 179, 182
Mori, Ryoko 12, 147, 150, 171, 183
Motz, Georg 138
The Musical Patriot 138, 220

Neumeister, Erdmann 38–40, 137, 141, 220
New Church 30, 39, 42, 58, 73, 82, 85, 132–3, 135, 141, 182, 195, 197–204, 210–16, 219, 221–2
New Testament models 11, 151, 165, 170, 174–5; *see also* Epistles
Nuremberg 3, 15, 20, 80

Old Testament models 11, 49, 81, 103, 137, 184
Olearius, Gottfried 206
Olearius, Johann 161, 190n122, 206
opera 8, 11, 32, 41, 59, 102, 104, 126, 136–7, 139
  influence on church music 38, 40, 130, 133, 138, 140–41, 215
  Leipzig Opera 23, 39, 102, 133, 136, 141, 191, 197, 212–14, 219
organs and organists 16, 21, 33, 36, 39–40, 45, 67, 85, 94, 110, 121, 124, 127, 129, 134, 137, 139–40, 142, 163, 182, 198, 209–11, 215

passions 8, 38–40, 42–5, 137–8, 198, 205, 213–15; *see also* cantatas; libretti
pastors, *see* clerics
Der Patriot 139, 220
peasants 4, 61, 149, 151, 180; *see also* villages
Petersen, Johann Wilhelm 163, 170–71, 179, 182, 184
Petersen, Johanna Eleonora 163, 170–71, 179, 182, 184
pews 5–6, 10, 14–15, 19n55, 21, 24, 30–35, 37–8, 46–7, 53–74, 78–9, 82–3, 100, 121, 132, 138, 147, 170–72, 182, 197–205, 210, 216; *see also* *Capellen*
  allotment of 66–9
  as property 70–72
Picander, *see* Henrici, Christian Friedrich
Pietism and Pietists 2–3, 5–7, 9–12, 14–15, 206–10, 217, 219; *see also* Bach, Johann Sebastian; Baroque; burghers; city councilors; clerics; collegia pietatis; elites; Francke, August Hermann; Halle; Leipzig, University of; Pietist-Orthodox debate; publishing; Saxony; Spener, Philipp Jacob; sermons
  historiography 10–12, 147–9, 169–73, 197
  networks 14–15; 169–91
Pietist-Orthodox debate 96, 110, 113, 129, 167, 171, 185–91; *see also* adiaphora; Lutheran Orthodoxy; Pietism and Pietists
Pisendel, Johann Georg 197, 231
Platz, Abraham Christoph 96–7, 130, 136, 166, 178, 181–2, 185
pleasure gardens 20, 23, 39, 126, 136, 191, 214
the poor and poverty 15, 30, 33, 49, 64–5, 82–3, 86, 89, 91, 150, 152, 177, 195, 201–2, 205–9, 215, 217
publishing 16, 31, 55; *see also* Elers, Heinrich Julius; hymnals; libretti; trade fairs
  music 38, 43, 125, 208, 220
  Pietism and 171, 183, 185–91, 219
Pufendorf, Samuel von 12, 101, 115, 119–21

Rambach, Johann Jacob 43
The Reasonable Tatleresses, see *Die vernünfftigen Tadlerinnen*

Rechenberg, Adam 147, 157n43, 182, 206
Reformation era 6, 35, 42, 58, 66, 77, 99–100, 107, 115, 125, 136, 151, 166, 195, 207, 221
  and formation of consistories 108–10
  historiography 2–4, 108–9
  and origins of pewholding 55
  and roles of city councilors 81
  and roles of Electors 103–4
religious intolerance 65–6
religious field 3–15
Reuter, Christian 84, 90, 94n86, 95
Rohr, Julius Bernhard von 117–18, 139–40, 181
Rostock 84, 88
Rothe, Albrecht Christian 138

Sabean, David 151
St. George's chapel 197, 199, 201, 203, 205, 208, 210
  constructions of 20, 195, 198–9
  house of 30, 64, 82–3, 85, 132, 156, 166, 198, 206–7, 209
St. John's Church 30, 64, 85, 91, 96
St. Nicholas's Church 19, 29–32, 34–6, 39, 54, 57–74, 82, 85–6, 127, 182, 200, 203–4, 209, 211, 221
  School 127, 173
St. Peter's Church 30–31, 72–3, 82, 85, 86n43, 92, 195, 197–205, 208, 210
St. Thomas's Church 21–3, 29–32, 38–9, 44, 47, 58–9, 62, 69–72, 86, 89, 102, 111, 127, 133–4, 179, 182, 200, 203–4, 211
  School 1, 88, 125–7, 129, 131, 135, 209, 211, 213
Saxe-Gotha 139–40
Saxon Electoral court, *see* Dresden
Saxony 5–6, 14–16, 21, 23, 31, 43, 46, 49–50, 55, 84, 86–7, 93–4, 99–108, 110–11, 113–22, 125, 171–2, 175, 190, 195, 207, 213
  and Pietism 2, 11–12, 101, 137, 149–50, 162
  and Thirty Years' War 18–19
Schade, Johann Caspar 49, 147, 152, 154–6, 160–61, 163–4, 166, 182
Scheibe, Johann Adolph 215, 220
Scheibel, Gottfried Ephraim 40, 43–4, 137–9, 215
Schelle, Johann 39, 125, 129, 221
Schilling, Johann Andreas 159, 164
Schilling, Heinz 3
Seckendorf, Veit Ludwig von 12, 115, 119–21
secular authorities, *see* city councilors; Electors
sermons 14, 16, 33–5, 40–41, 44, 85, 91–5, 104–5, 119, 140, 186, 208, 209, 221; *see also* clerics; worship services
  clerical appointment and 47–8, 50, 95
  Pietists and 47, 49, 105, 119, 153–4, 156, 159, 162–3, 166–7, 175, 178–80, 184, 206
  reception of 29–31, 46–51
Siegele, Ulrich 129–30, 135–6
Spener, Philipp Jacob 12, 14, 100–101, 105–7, 119–21, 136–7, 147, 149–50, 152–3, 156, 160–61, 170–71, 179, 183, 185, 189–90, 207
Stiller, Günther 196
students, *see* Leipzig, University of
Superintendents: Dresden 107, 111, 113
  Leipzig 35, 49, 84–7, 89, 93–4, 97, 100, 111, 113, 127–8, 131–3, 163, 180, 184, 188, 190n122, 201, 205–6, 220
  Lüneburg 179

Talander, *see* Bohse, August
teachers and teaching 81, 83, 85, 94, 110, 137, 172, 205, 211
  cantors and 1, 14, 123, 125–6, 128–31, 134–5
  Pietism and 120, 161–2, 165, 176, 180, 207
Telemann, Georg Philipp 9, 13, 15, 39–42, 45, 129–30, 132–3, 138, 141, 143, 197, 210–16, 220–21
Thirty Years' War 11, 18–19, 93, 104, 115, 150
Thomasius, Christian 12, 14, 87, 101, 115, 117–22, 148n5, 157–8, 160–61, 167, 219
Thomasius, Dorothea Sophia 87, 89
Töllner, Justinus 95, 149n8, 180–81, 183

trade 11, 16, 18, 20–21, 23, 31, 77, 79, 101, 147, 173, 195; *see also* merchants
book trade 63, 185, 187–8, 191
trade fairs 16, 19–20, 61, 64, 77, 99, 102, 175, 179, 202–3, 209, 216, 222
and music 23, 39, 102, 133, 135, 197, 210, 212, 222
and publishing 176n31, 187–8, 190–91

Die vernünfftigen Tadlerinnen 24, 58, 73, 139
villages 16, 21, 31, 38, 58, 85–6, 89, 95, 111, 136, 151, 180, 213; *see also* peasants
Vockerodt, Gottfried 137–8
Voigt, Samuel 155–6, 162–3, 165, 169, 174, 182

Walker, Mack 94
Weidmann, Moritz Georg 182, 188
Weimar 123–4, 128, 142, 221
Weissmantel family 66-7
Weissenfels 1, 113, 124, 134, 137, 143
Weiz, Anton 196
Winckler family 20
Winckler, Georg 73, 202, 211
witchcraft trials 116–17, 121
Wittenberg, University of 63, 88
Wolle, Christoph 88, 128
worship services 8–9, 29–52, 56–9, 64, 199–202, 206, 208, 210–12; *see also* cantatas; clerics; congregants; passions; sermons

Ziegler, Mariane von 128, 220